Lyzzy,

"HISTORY PORTENDS THE FUTURE" is a para-phrase of the Moniker on the steps of the National Archieves in Washington, D.C. As you embark on your US Army Military Intelligence career, remember to reflect on what has happened previously, in order to make your decisions on what course you will pursue! Be true to yourself!

Fair Winds & following Seas!
All the Best
Commander Ed Majewski Jr USN, Ret.
"MAJIC"

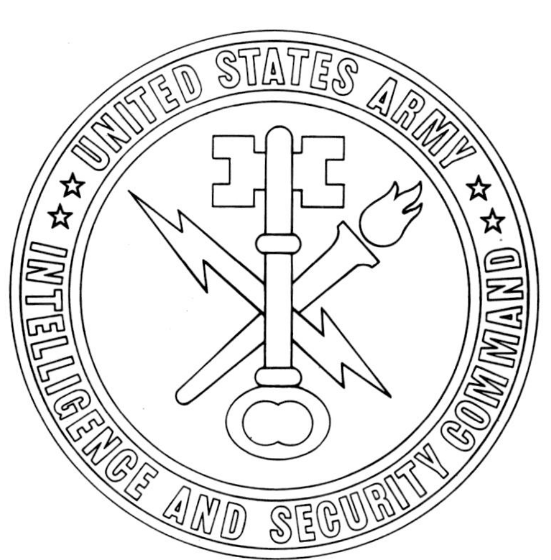
UNITED STATES ARMY
INTELLIGENCE AND SECURITY COMMAND

The Military I

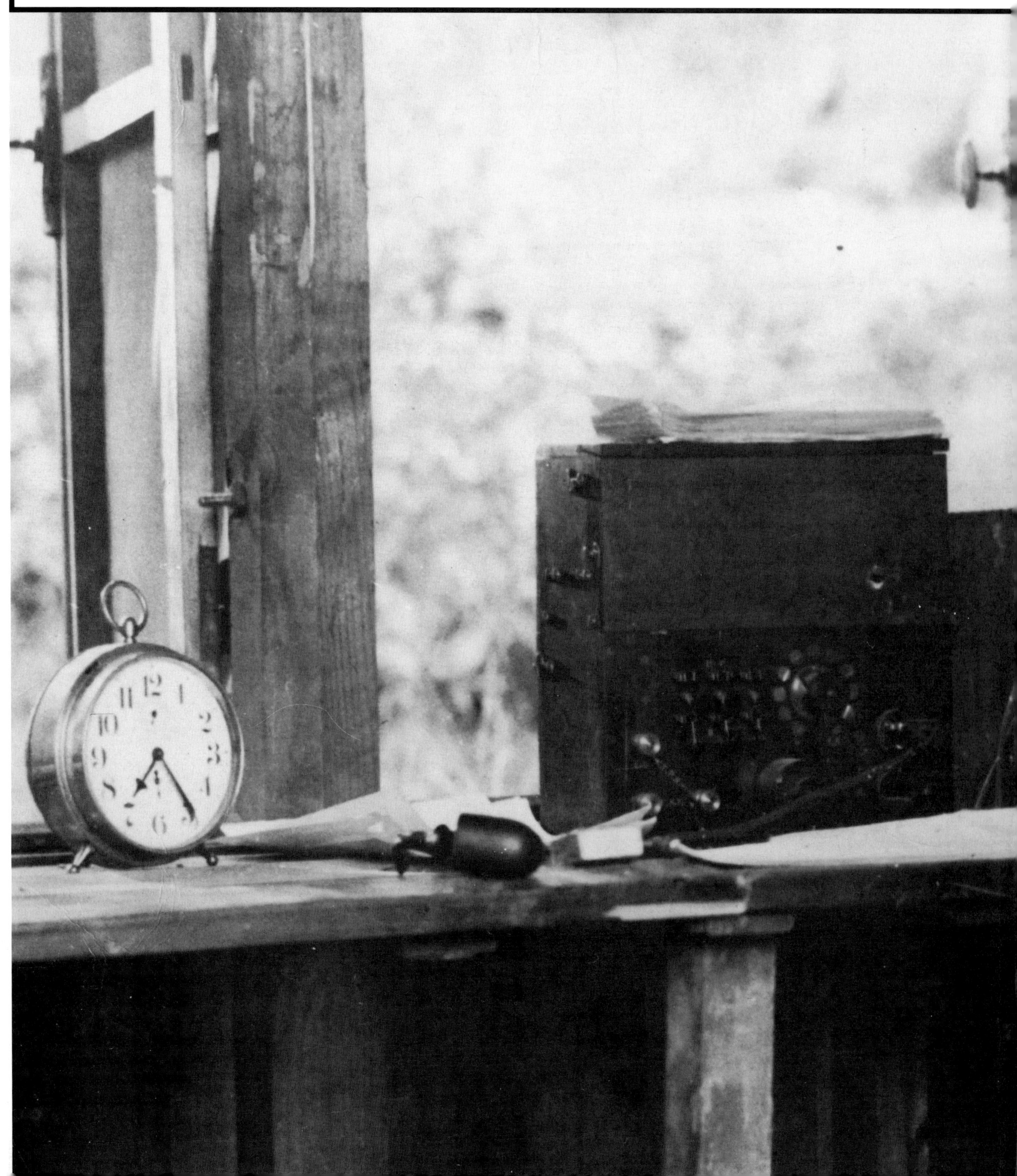

telligence Story

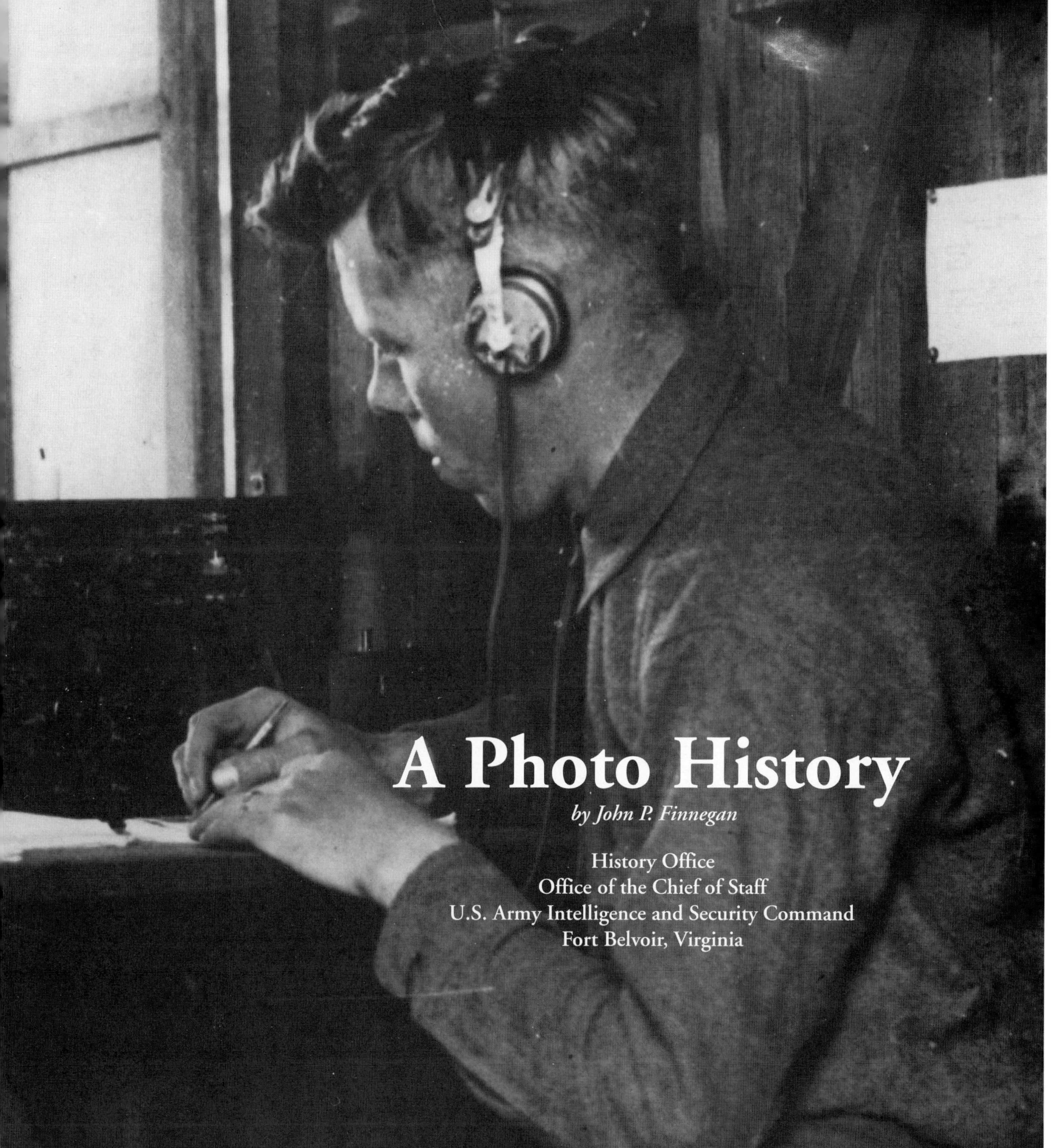

A Photo History

by John P. Finnegan

History Office
Office of the Chief of Staff
U.S. Army Intelligence and Security Command
Fort Belvoir, Virginia

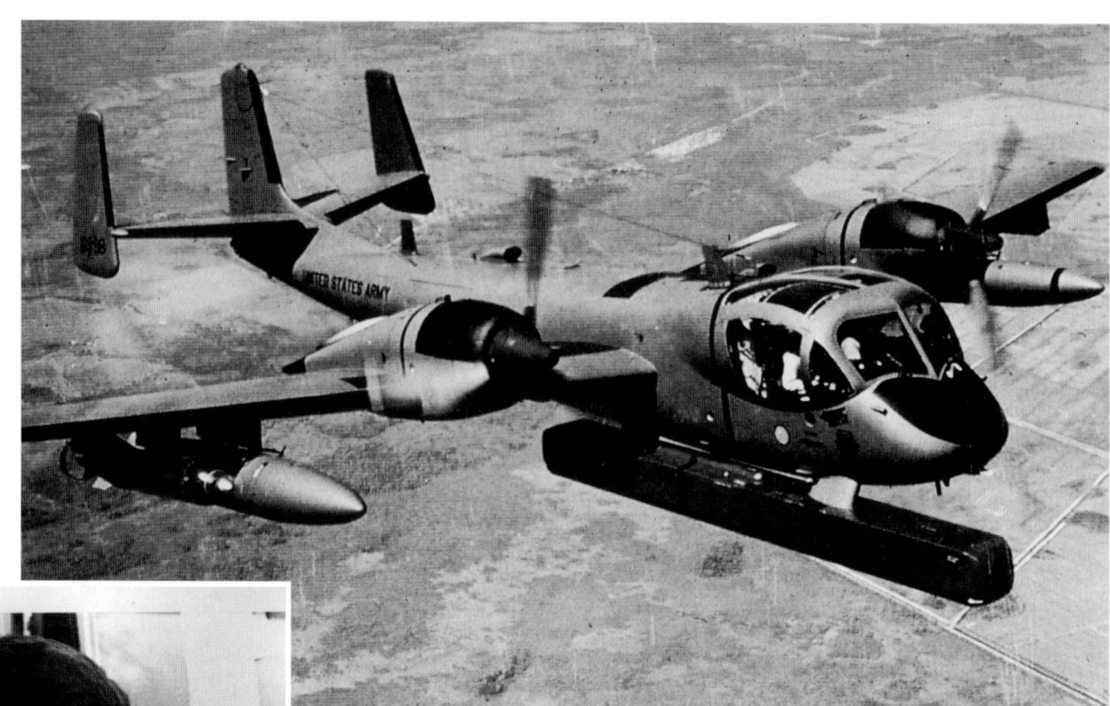

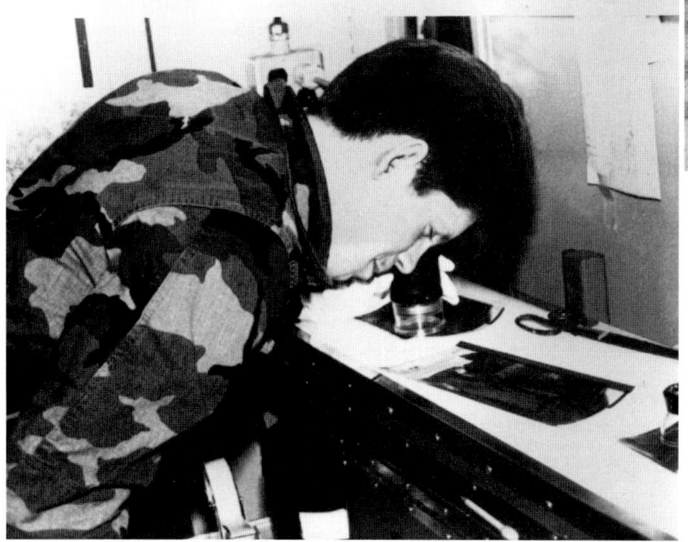

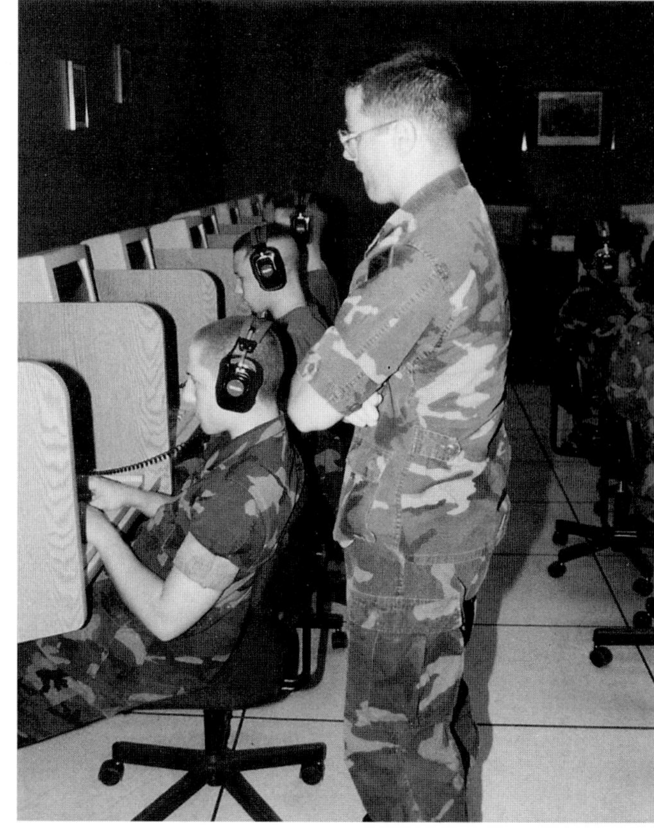

Library of Congress Cataloging-in-Publication Data

Finnegan, John Patrick.
The military intelligence story : a photo history / by John P. Finnegan. — 2nd ed.
p. cm.
1. Military intelligence—United States—History. 2. United States. Army—History. I. Title.
UB251.U5F564
355.3943290973—dc20 94–19170
CIP

For sale by the U.S. Government Printing Office
Superintendent of Documents, Mail Stop: SSOP, Washington, DC 20402-9328
ISBN 0-16-049335-8

Foreword

JAMES L. GILBERT

Command Historian, U.S. Army Intelligence and Security Command, Fort Belvoir, Virginia

THE NEED FOR MILITARY INTELLIGENCE—the collection of information on adversaries—is as old as war itself. However, the emergence of Military Intelligence as a distinct professional discipline within the Army is a comparatively recent development. For most of recorded history, intelligence was collected by cavalry, scouts, and spies, and each commander served as his own intelligence officer. It was not until the nineteenth century that the armies of the most advanced Great Powers in Europe developed intelligence staffs. The United States, pacific and isolationist, lagged well behind in this field. A permanent intelligence presence on the General Staff was not established until the United States entered World War I. By this time, however, technology had vastly expanded the range of collection mechanisms available to military intelligence. In many respects, then, World War I proved to be a major milestone in the development of Military Intelligence within the United States Army: rudimentary intelligence organizations were set up, and most of today's intelligence disciplines put in place.

Professionalization of military intelligence—MI—within the United States Army was a longer process, and took place against the backdrop of international conflicts. In response to the demands of World War II and the Cold War that succeeded it, the Army found it necessary to train specialized intelligence personnel, field large intelligence units, and finally create a Military Intelligence (MI) Branch within the Regular Army to manage its intelligence assets. The creation of an all-volunteer Army, the expansion of tactical intelligence units, and the integration of previously scattered intelligence disciplines into a cohesive whole further professionalized MI and brought it into the mainstream of the Army. These developments culminated in the formation of the MI Corps, an action that brought all MI soldiers into a single large regiment and firmly identified MI with the military traditions that went back to the Army's roots.

This book illustrates the multifaceted diversity of modern Military Intelligence. To as great an extent as is possible, it aims to portray both the continuities between the past and the present and the successes of the MI community today. The photographs selected, it is hoped, adequately represent the different intelligence disciplines and depict a representative sampling of the organizations within the MI community.

Like previous publications released by the History Office, U.S. Army Intelligence and Security Command, this book was prepared in partial fulfillment of the mission of helping military intelligence specialists prepare to meet today's challenges by providing a better understanding of the past. The book is designed to familiarize the individual soldier both with the rich heritage of military intelligence and its present day manifestations. It is hoped that it will be found useful at all levels of command and in various training programs.

The Author

JOHN PATRICK FINNEGAN GRADUATED *magna cum laude* from Boston College in 1957 with an A.B. in English Literature. After a period of civilian employment with the National Security Agency and military service in the U.S. Army Counter Intelligence Corps, he went on to receive a Ph.D. in American History from the University of Wisconsin-Madison. Between 1964 and 1979, Dr. Finnegan taught United States History at a number of institutions of higher education, including Ohio University, the overseas divisions of the University of Maryland, Chicago State University, and Texas Tech University. He also served as a Principal Education Officer with the Nigerian Federal Ministry of Education and as Senior Lecturer in History with the University of Ibadan, Nigeria. Joining the Federal Civil Service in 1979, the author worked as an archivist at the U.S. Army Cryptologic Records Center and as an historian with the U.S. Army Center of Military History before accepting his present position as an historian with the U.S. Army Intelligence and Security Command.

Dr. Finnegan is also the author of *Against the Specter of a Dragon: The Campaign for American Military Preparedness, 1914–1917,* and of *Military Intelligence: A Picture History.* Most recently, he co-edited *U.S. Army Signals Intelligence in World War II: A Documentary History* with James L. Gilbert.

Preface

JOHN PATRICK FINNEGAN
Fort Belvoir, Virginia

THE ORIGINAL IDEA FOR THIS BOOK CAME from Major General Charles F. Scanlon, U.S.A. (Ret.), former Commanding General, United States Army Intelligence and Security Command (INSCOM). During his tenure as INSCOM commander, General Scanlon realized the end of the Cold War and the subsequent relaxation of international tensions allowed a fuller portrayal of Military Intelligence activities than was previously thought possible. INSCOM's present commander, Major General John D. Thomas, Jr., suggested that the publication be updated to reflect the sweeping changes that have overtaken the Military Intelligence community since the book first appeared.

The key ingredient in any picture history is provided by the photographs themselves. This book would not have been possible without the efforts of the staffs of the National Archives and Records Administration, the Library of Congress, the National Security Agency, the U.S. Army Graphics Center, the U.S. Army Cryptologic Records Center, and the INSCOM Public Affairs Office. Special thanks are owed to Major General Joseph A. McChristian, U.S.A. (Ret.), Mr. James Finley of the Military Intelligence Museum, Fort Huachuca, the Public Affairs Office of the U.S. Army Intelligence Center and Fort Huachuca, and all the other Military Intelligence units who contributed to the effort.

Encouragement, oversight, and support for this project were provided by General Thomas and by INSCOM Chief of Staff Colonel Larry L. Miller. Mr. James L. Gilbert, INSCOM Command Historian, served as overall supervisor, editor, and critic, while Mrs. Karen Kovach, writer-editor of the INSCOM History Office, assisted in publication planning and coordination. Mr. James D. Currie, Jr., INSCOM Chief of Publications and Printing, expedited production.

The project benefited from the assistance of Mr. T. Gardner, Jr., head of the INSCOM Photo Lab, and of Mr. Robert J. Bills, staff photographer. Sergeant Linda Evans took many of the DESERT STORM photos while on assignment for the command in the Persian Gulf. Mr. John Grier of the Government Printing Office provided a handsome format for the final product. The author alone is responsible for any mistakes.

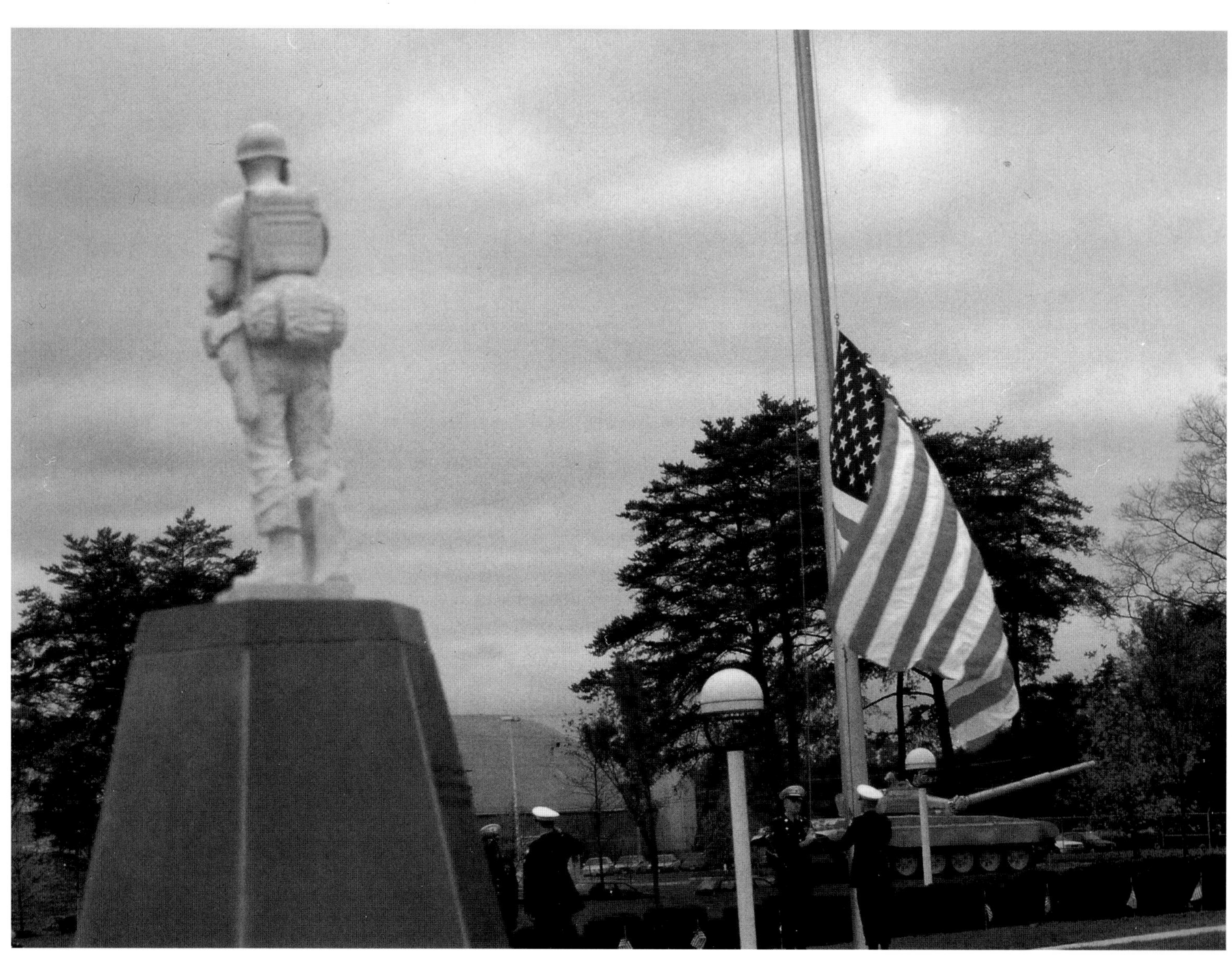

Contents

Foundations

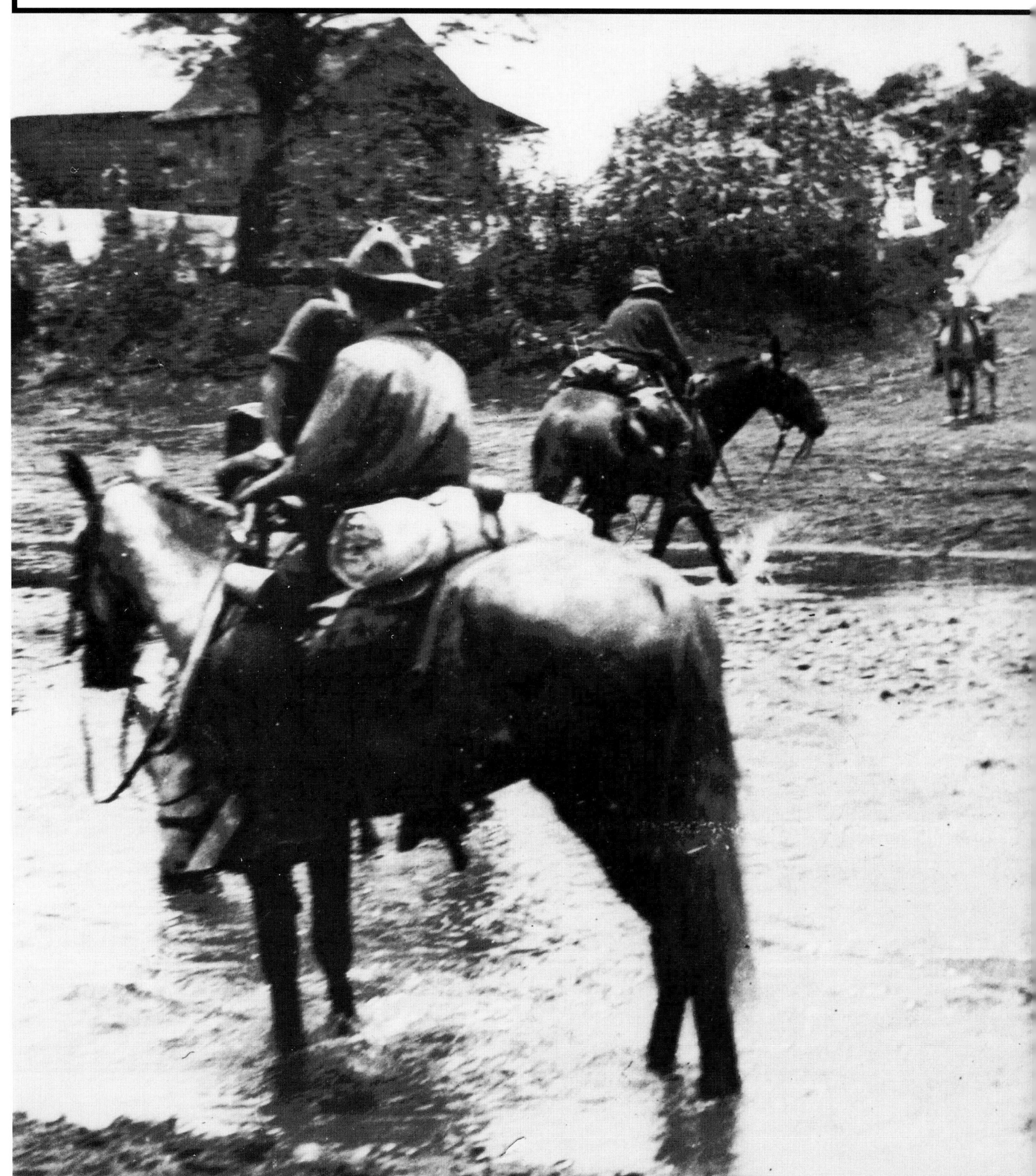

Part I

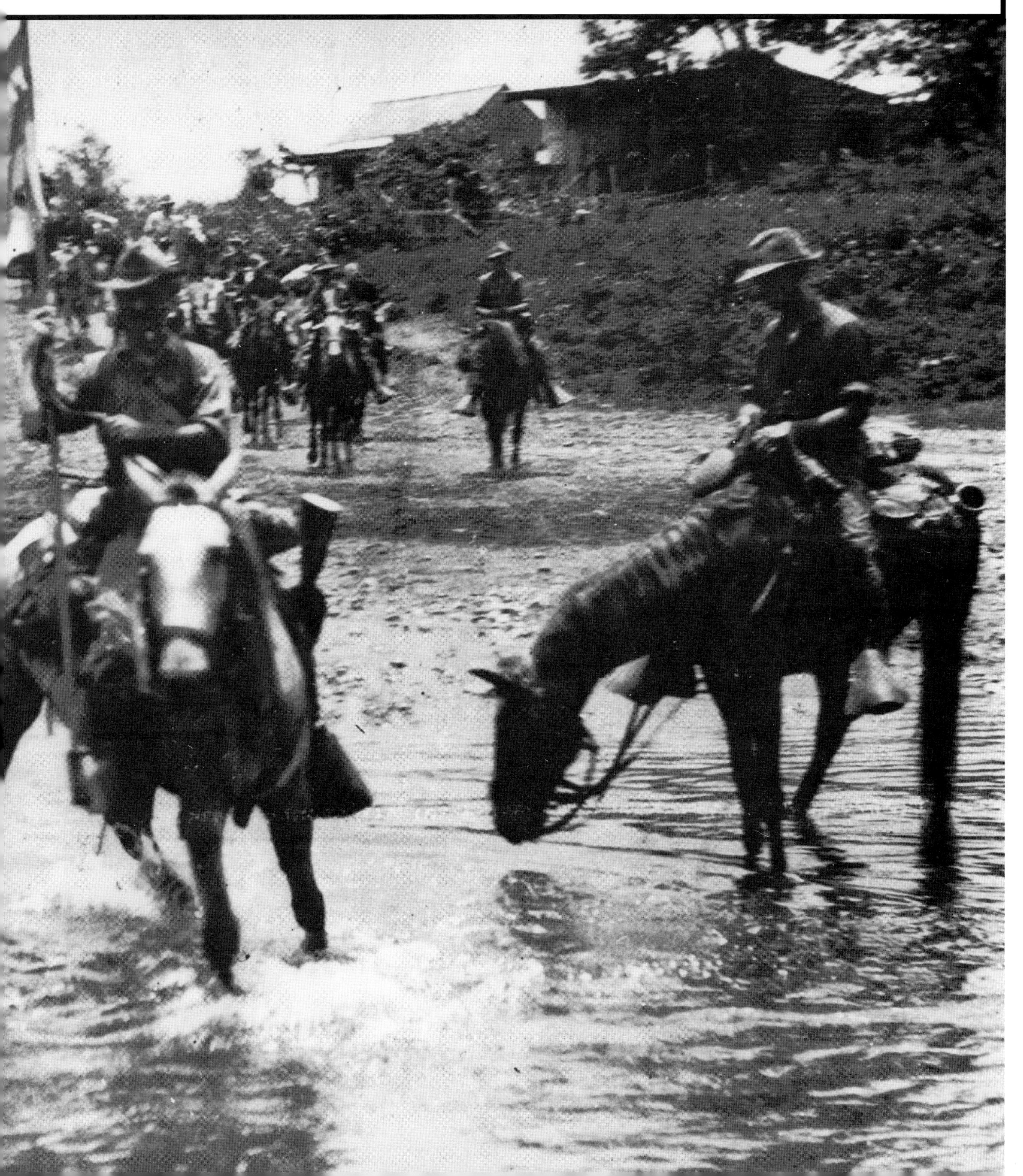

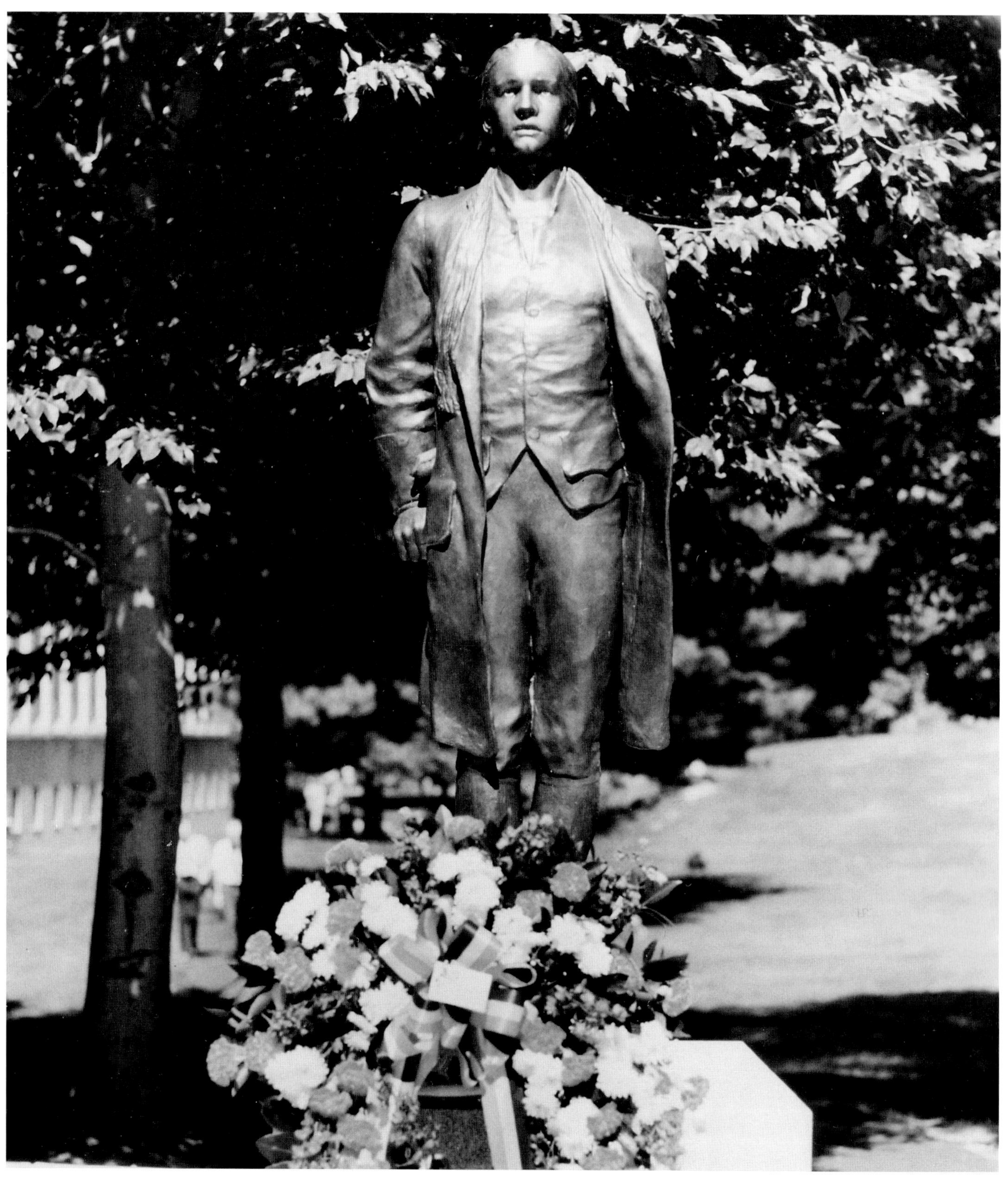

Nathan Hale

This idealized statue of the Revolutionary War's most famous spy stands in front of the headquarters of the Central Intelligence Agency.

Early Beginnings 1775–1917

THE HISTORY OF U.S. MILITARY INTELLIGENCE goes back to the very beginnings of the nation. During much of the American Revolution, George Washington personally directed the Continental Army's intelligence service, running a number of highly successful intelligence operations. Nathan Hale, the unfortunate amateur spy with but one life to give for his country, may have been the most publicized intelligence agent of the American Revolution, but he was not the best. One of Washington's spy networks penetrated the highest levels of the British headquarters in occupied New York City; the intelligence provided by this group led to the discovery of Benedict Arnold's treason. Nor was operational security neglected. The campaign that led up to the British defeat at Yorktown succeeded due to Washington's orchestration of a masterful deception operation that left the enemy baffled about American intentions until it was too late.

Despite its noteworthy successes during the American Revolution, military intelligence was largely neglected in the years that followed. Military institutions and intelligence practices did not fit in easily with American values. The American Revolution had been won by a professional regular force, the Continental Army, amply supported by an intelligence system as sophisticated as the 18th century would allow. However, this fact seemed too uncomfortable for Americans to accept. A national myth developed that the Revolution had been fought by patriotic amateurs. As a corollary, it was widely accepted that the country had scant need of permanent military institutions or a permanent military intelligence organization. In case any conflict developed, it was felt citizen armies would rise up and overwhelm the foe. Since Providence was on America's side, it was unnecessary to know anything about potential enemies in advance.

The circumstances of American life tended to enforce this myth. Although the young nation faced serious menaces on the North American Continent in its early years, the Pax Britannica that followed the War of 1812 allowed the United States to develop in an environment of unparalleled security, protected by wide oceans and facing only feeble resistance to its continental expansion. For most of the early 19th century, until the Civil War broke out, the United States was able to survive with a Regular Army of only 10,000 men. Under these conditions, the chances for the development of a professional military intelligence service were slight.

The picture during the first hundred years of American history was not completely bleak. President Thomas Jefferson's establishment of the United States Military Academy at West Point in 1802 not only ensured the Regular Army a supply of professional officers, but also encouraged topographic intelligence as an Army specialty, because of the strongly engineering-oriented nature of the Academy's curriculum. The transcontinental expedition of Lewis and Clark was a noteworthy example of topographic intelligence, as were the subsequent explorations undertaken by Captain Zebulon Pike in the Southwest. The Army formed an elite Corps of Topographic Engineers in 1838; this organization, which lasted until the Civil War, mapped the American West. One of the most famous members of the Corps was John C. Fremont, the "Pathfinder" who figured so prominently in the early history of California. Engineer-trained Academy graduates provided invaluable intelligence to the Army of General Winfield Scott during the Mexican War as it marched to Mexico City.

Nevertheless, the hard fact was that for most of the early period of U.S. history, the nation had neither an adequate military nor adequate military intelligence. Despite the existence of intelligence collection mechanisms such as cavalry, scouts, and topographic engineers, intelligence within the Army lacked permanent organization and a directing brain. When war came, intelligence organizations were mobilized on an ad hoc basis, in much the same fashion as the mass citizen armies that did the fighting. When peace was restored, everyone went home, and the vestigial Regular Army returned to its normal bureaucratic procedures. The inevitable result was that the Army was handicapped at the beginning of every conflict and sometimes suffered from intelligence shortfalls until well into the war.

The great national drama of the Civil War illustrates the point perfectly. The early efforts of both the Union and Confederate armies in the intelligence field were stumbling. The raw new Union Army was particularly handicapped. It lacked good cavalry for reconnaissance, and Alan Pinkerton, the private detective who served for a time as intelligence chief of the Army of the Potomac, provided mostly misinformation. Eighteen months after the fighting had begun, the chief of staff of the Army of the Potomac noted grimly that "we were as ignorant of the enemy in our immediate front as if they had been in China." Only in 1863 did the main Northern army develop an efficient intelligence organization. The Army of the Potomac's Bureau of Military Information was able to collate reports sent back by agents, scouts, and cavalry patrols with information gleaned from prisoners and deserters and produce an accurate estimate of the Confederate order of battle.

On the other hand, intelligence collectors were now able to exploit new technologies. Both Union and Confederate armies made use of observation balloons at the beginning of the war, although the lone Confederate balloon was lost in action, while the Union Army eventually lost interest in the project. Observers intercepted enemy semaphore messages, and attempts were made to obtain enemy message traffic by tapping telegraph lines. In self-defense, both sides resorted to the use of simple codes and ciphers.

After the Civil War, however, things went back to normal. The huge Union Army was demobilized, and the intelligence resources that had supported it were discarded. Once the military's role in the Reconstruction of the post-Civil War South had ended, the Regular Army was cut back to a force of 25,000. The late-19th century Army was a force designed for Indian-fighting, not for major conflict. Under these conditions, every commander served as his own intelligence officer, and the only specialized assets that seemed to be needed were the familiar collection mechanisms of cavalry and Indian scouts.

Surprisingly, under these unpromising conditions, military intelligence at last came into its own. Tides were sweeping over the country that would end American isolation and necessitate the formation of a permanent military intelligence organization for the first time in American history. By the 1880's, a rapidly industrializing America found itself moving into a new era. This was a period of profound change which witnessed the beginnings of bureaucratization and professionalization of American life, and an increasing tendency for the nation to edge into the international arena. These same currents also affected the nation's armed forces. In 1881, the Navy set up an Office of Naval Intelligence, and in 1885, the Army followed suit, creating its first permanent intelligence organization, the Military Information Division of the Adjutant General's Office. An alert and professional Army needed to keep itself informed about military developments in the rest of the world. In 1889, the Army instituted a military attaché system which, among other functions, submitted intelligence reports on events of military interest occurring overseas.

The 1890's witnessed a series of foreign policy crises which culminated in the Spanish-American War of 1898. The war proved to be a watershed for both the United States and its Army. America emerged from the conflict as a world power of the first rank with a foreign empire in the Philippines and the Caribbean. There were also some intelligence milestones. The Signal Corps deployed an observation balloon at the Battle of Santiago, and the necessity of confronting an insurrection in the Philippines involved the Army in counterintelligence work.

In the aftermath of war, America's new global responsibilities brought about a dramatic increase in the strength of the Regular Army, which was quadrupled in size. The Army also achieved a modern organization when a War Department General Staff was set up in 1903. The increasing importance of intelligence to the Army was recognized by the fact that the Military Information Division was made one of the three functional elements of the General Staff.

The Signal Corps went on to take pioneering steps in adapting technology to the purposes of intelligence. The Corps continued to experiment with observation balloons, and was quick to seize upon the new possibilities of heavier than air flight. The Army acquired its first airplane in 1909. By the time Brigadier General John J. Pershing led an American Punitive Expedition into Mexico in 1916 to stop Pancho Villa's depredations, the Army had a whole squadron. Pershing's forces even attempted aerial photography. Additionally, the invention of radio allowed the Army to explore the field of signals intelligence. Signal Corps personnel manning the "radio tractors" that accompanied Pershing's forces monitored the communications of the Mexican government.

However, the evolution of military intelligence in the early 20th century proved not to be a smooth one. Paradoxically, as the Army's technical capacities in this area grew, its intelligence organization was allowed to wither away. The Second Division of the General Staff, which performed intelligence functions, was merged into the Third, which conducted operational planning. Soon, intelligence work at the General Staff level ceased to be done at all. By 1916, the Army was less prepared in this area than it had been in 1898. When the storm finally broke upon America in 1917, the Army would once again have to improvise an intelligence organization.

Human Collection

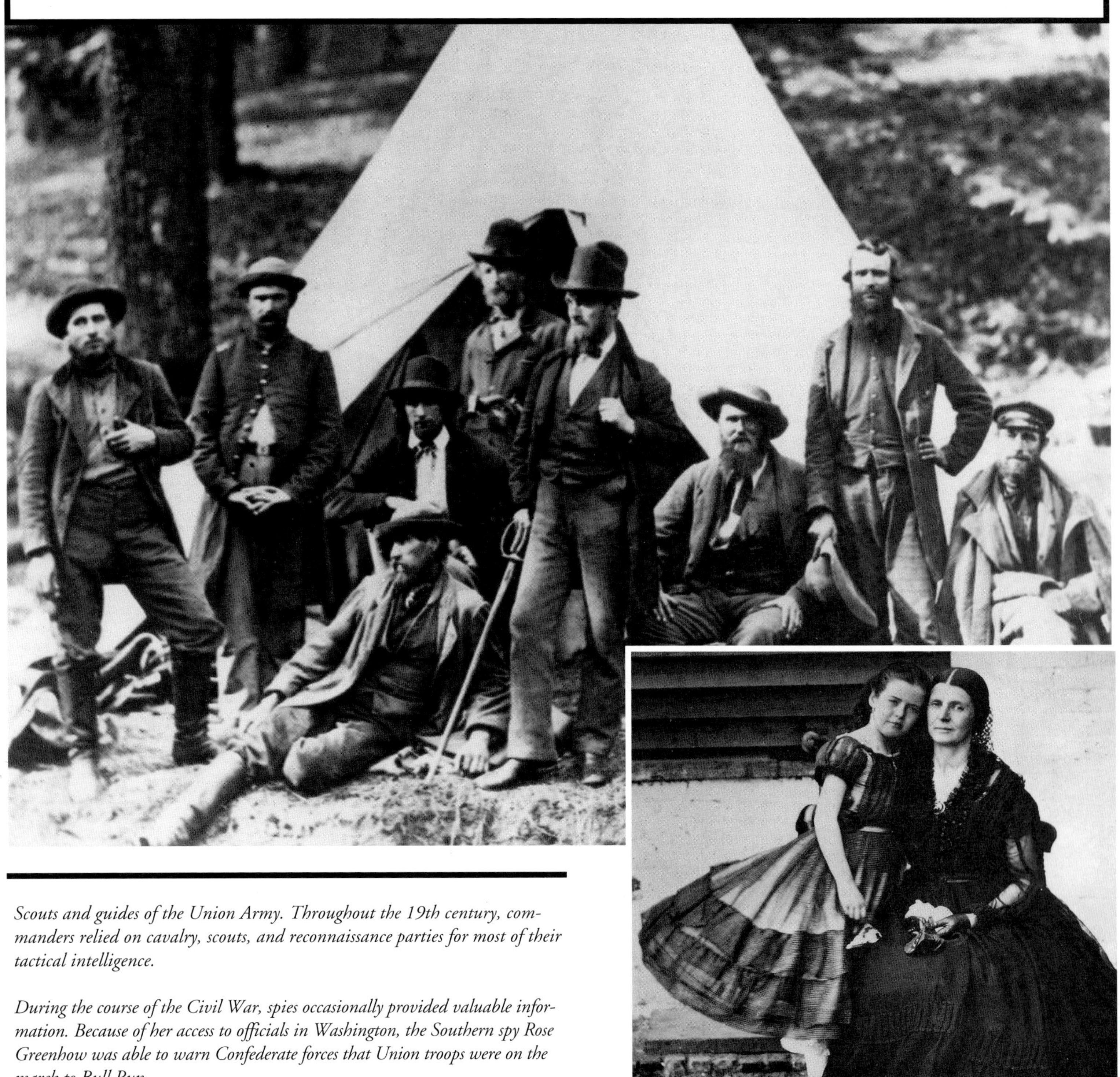

Scouts and guides of the Union Army. Throughout the 19th century, commanders relied on cavalry, scouts, and reconnaissance parties for most of their tactical intelligence.

During the course of the Civil War, spies occasionally provided valuable information. Because of her access to officials in Washington, the Southern spy Rose Greenhow was able to warn Confederate forces that Union troops were on the march to Bull Run.

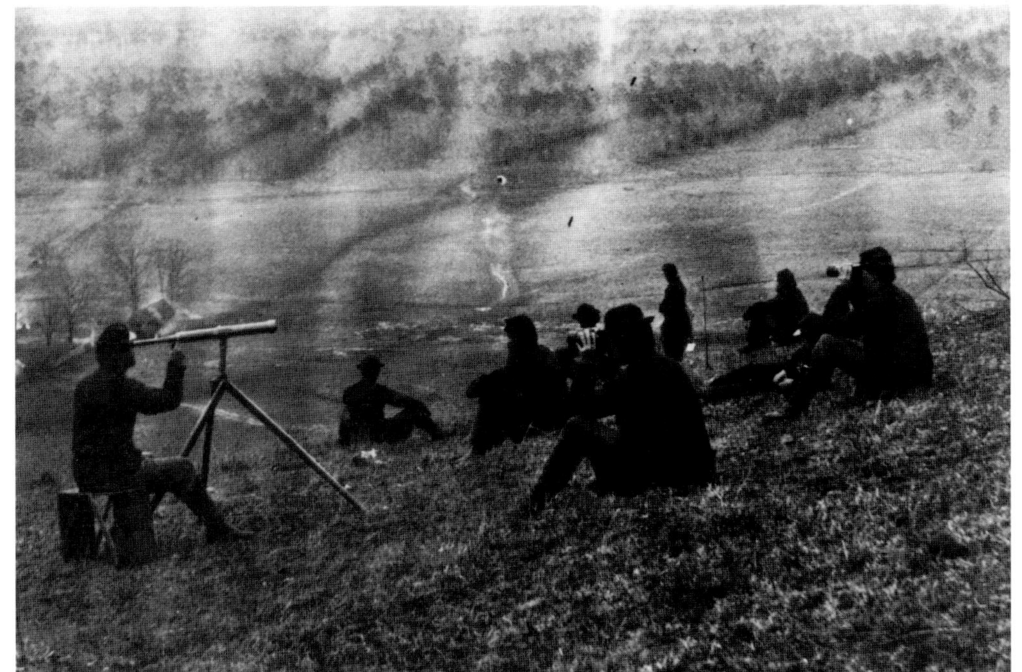

Civil War collection operations. Union soldiers man an observation post in Virginia in 1862.

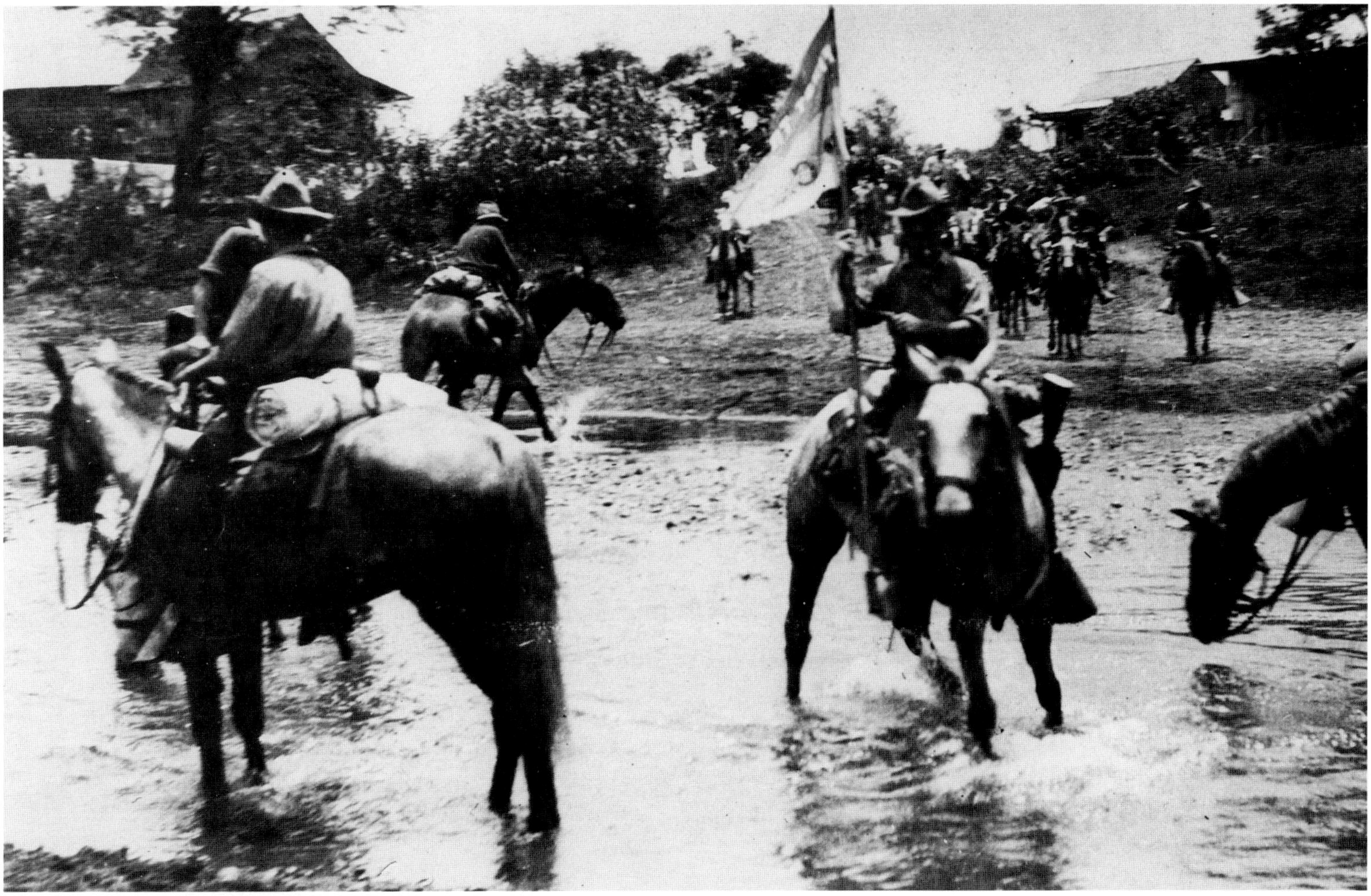

In addition to serving as a combat arm, horse cavalry acted as the "eyes of the army." A cavalry patrol in Puerto Rico during the Spanish American War.

The Impact of Technology

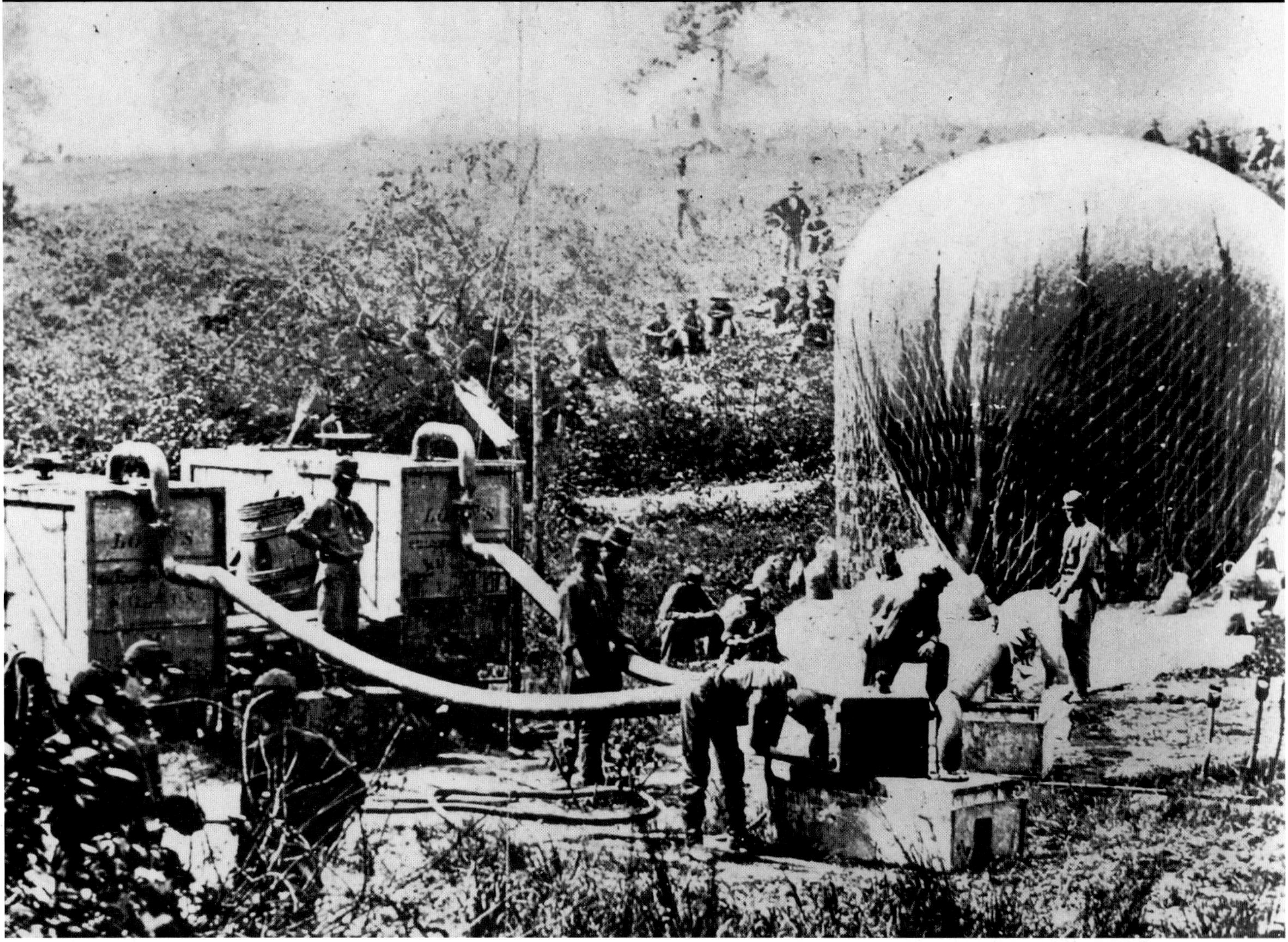

By the middle of the 19th century, advances in technology allowed breakthroughs in intelligence collection techniques. The balloon Intrepid *is inflated during the Battle of Fair Oaks in 1862.*

Communications intelligence became a factor during the Civil War. Armies intercepted signal flag and telegraph messages sent by their opponents, forcing both sides to make use of simple codes and ciphers. This cipher device was utilized by the Confederates.

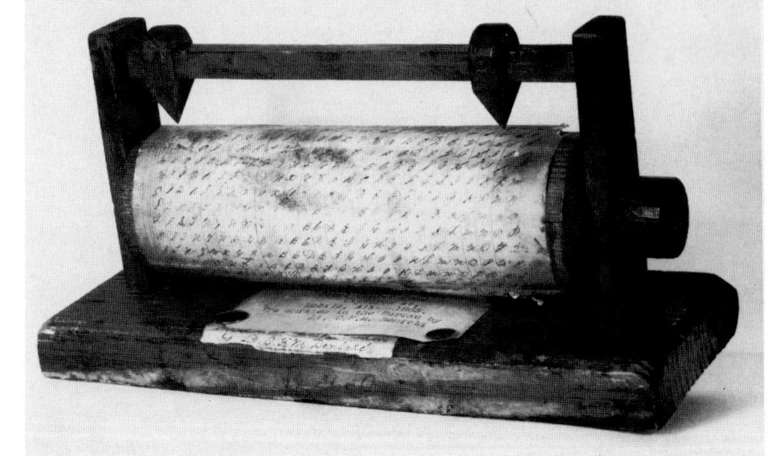

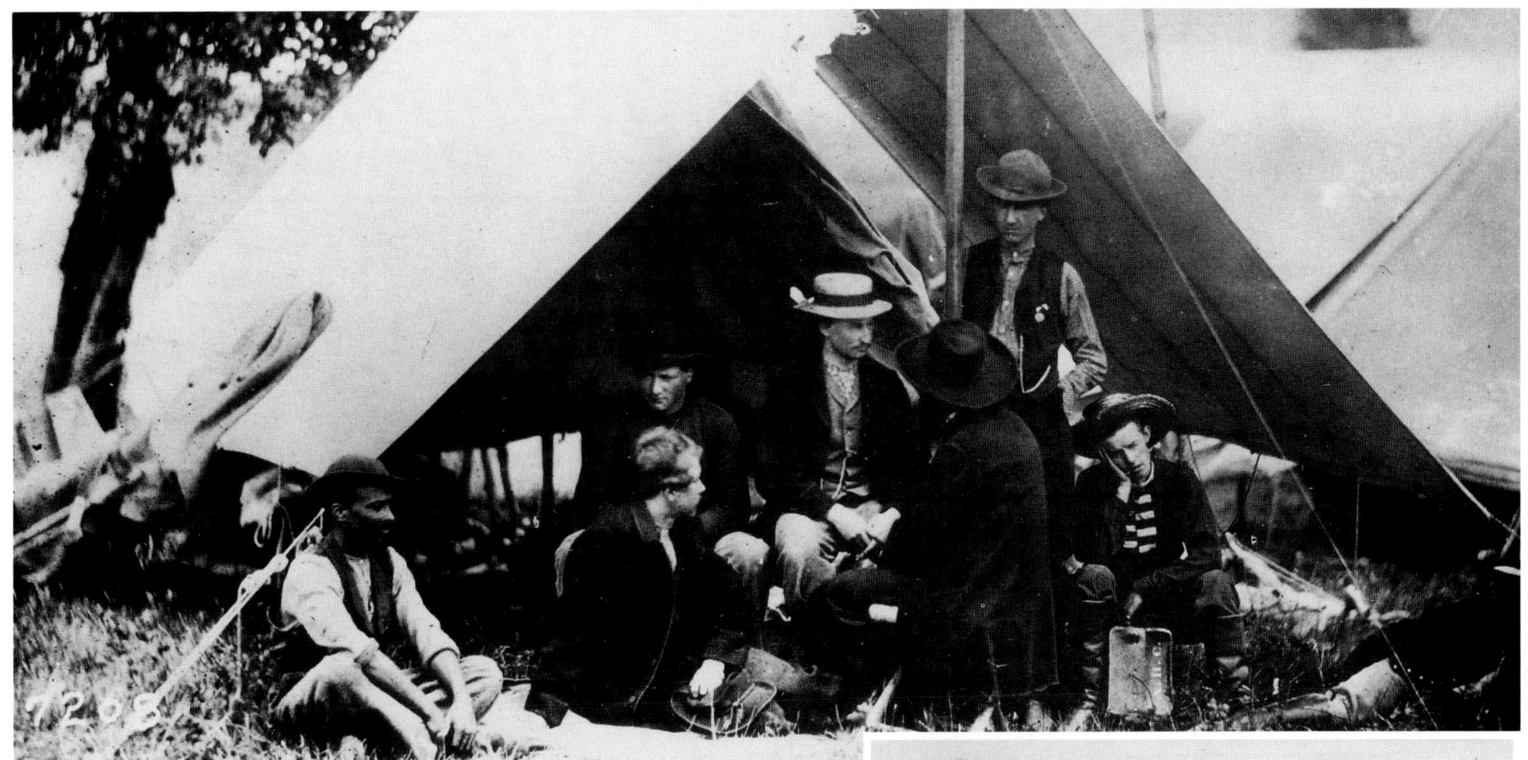

A party of Union telegraphers in the field.

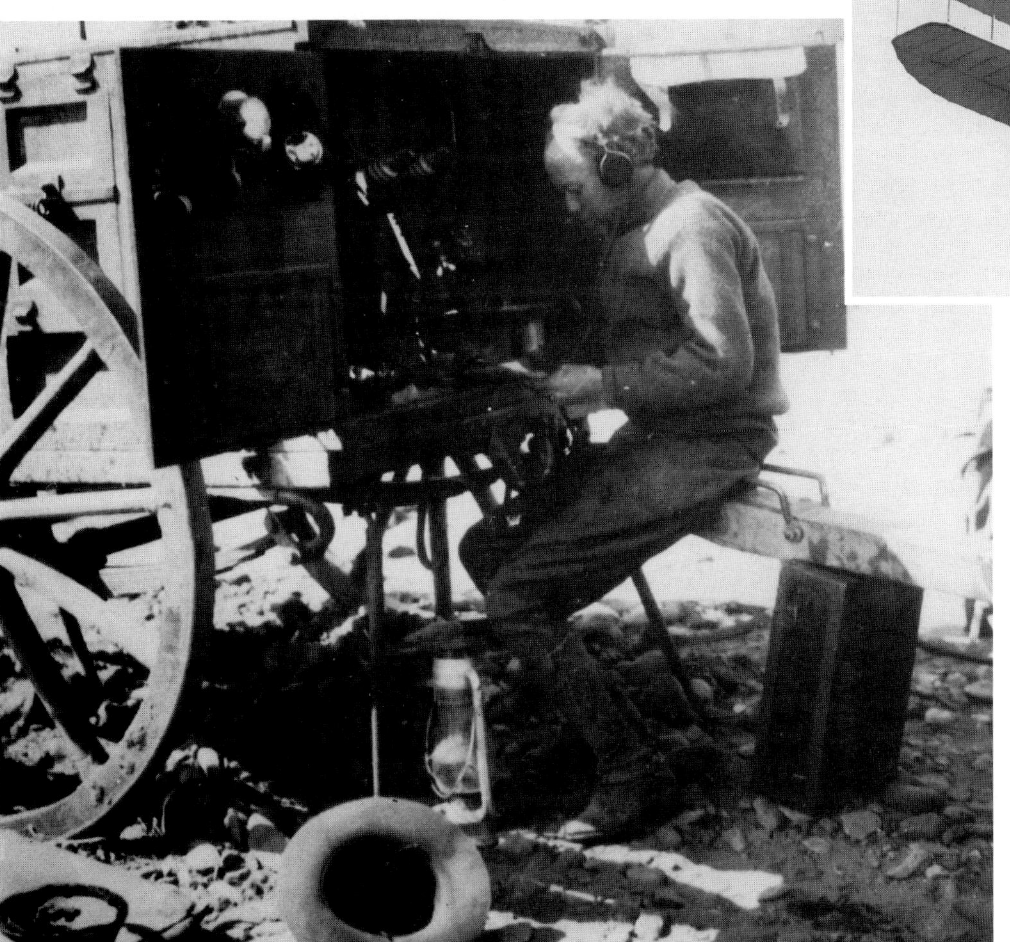

Beginning in the 1890's, the Signal Corps showed a renewed interest in developing aerial collection platforms, experimenting with balloons, dirigibles, and aircraft. An early Wright pusher biplane flies over the Fort Myer parade ground.

The widespread use of radios by major armies in the 20th century opened up new dimensions for intelligence. A radio operator with Pershing's Mexican Punitive Expedition.

Organizing Intelligence

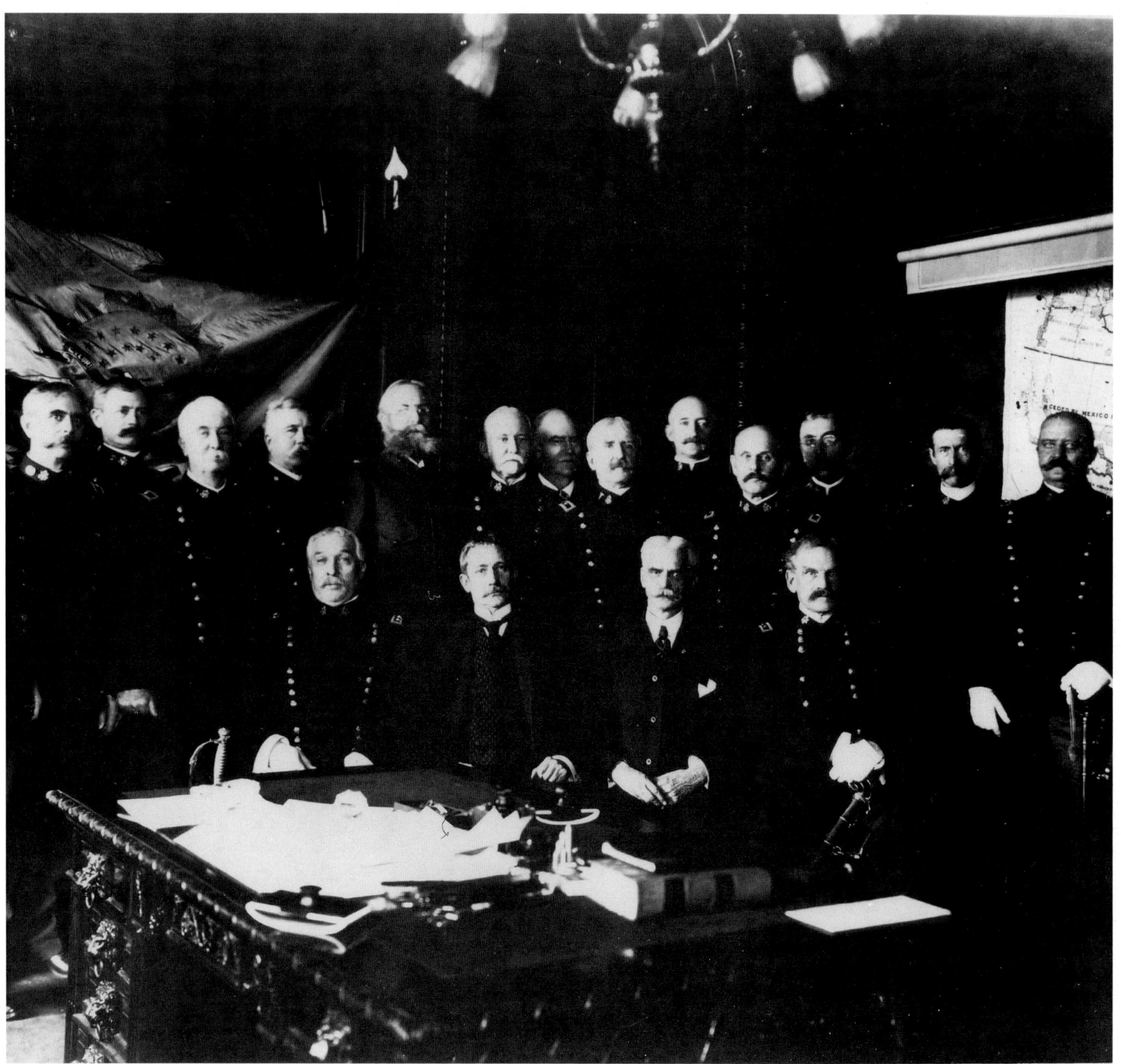

Secretary of War Elihu Root meets with members of the Army's brand-new General Staff in 1903. The Military Information Division was moved from the Adjutant General's Office to become the Second Division of the Staff.

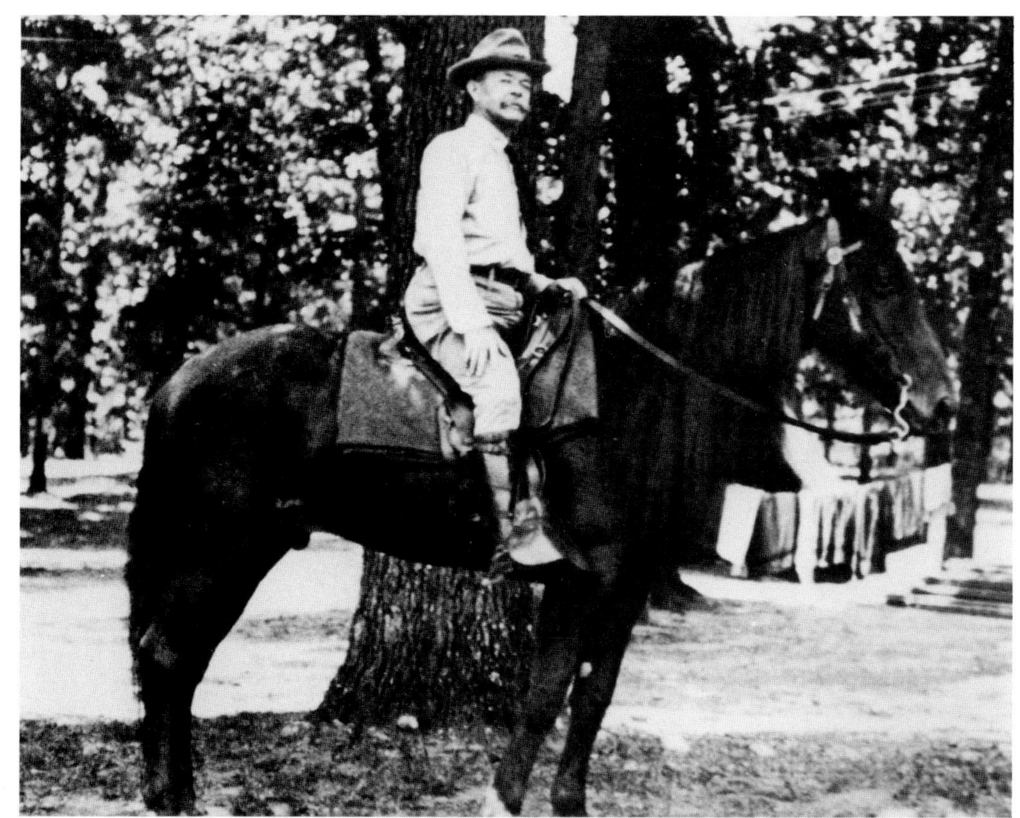

1LT Francis Vinton Greene was sent to Russia as a military attaché in 1877 to observe the Russo-Turkish War. However, the Army did not set up a permanent military attaché system until 1889.

Overseas powers also sent military attachés to the United States. A group of foreign military and naval attachés during the Spanish-American War.

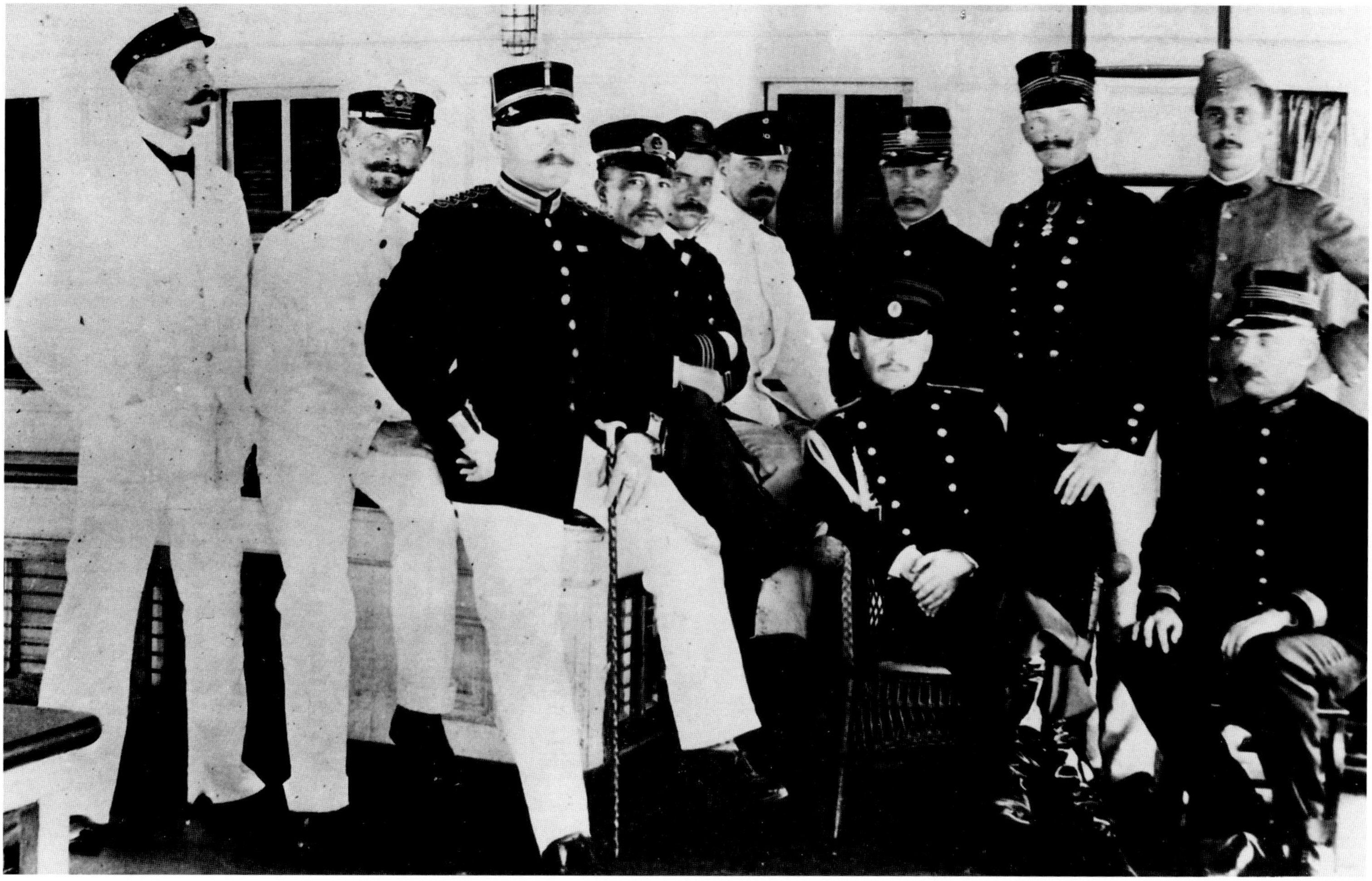

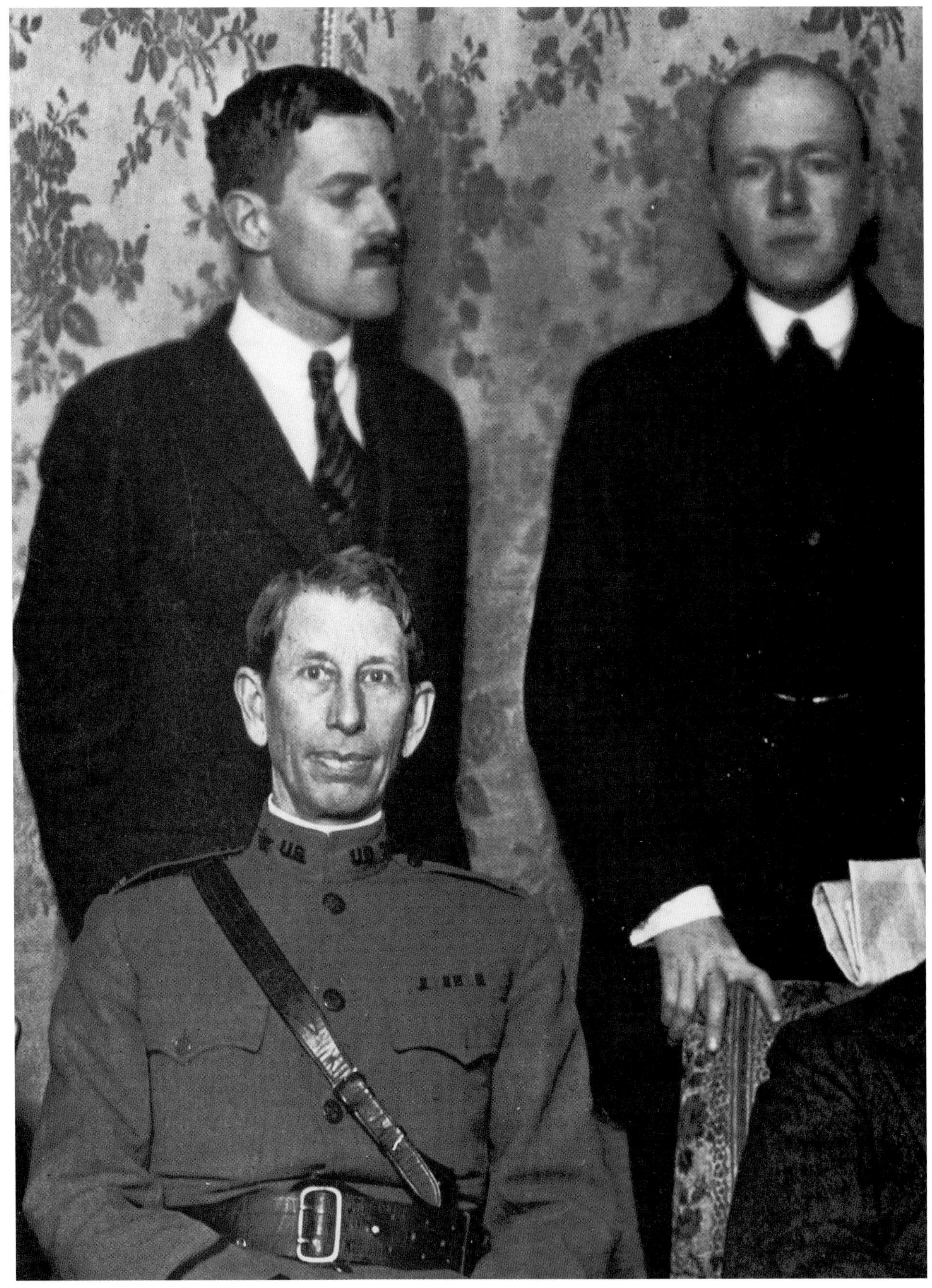

Intelligence continuity. Seated, COL Ralph M. Van Deman, first head of War Department intelligence in World War I. Above him stands Allen Dulles, OSS station chief in World War II and later legendary Director of the Central Intelligence Agency.

Military Intelligence in the World Wars, 1917–1945

American entry into World War I in April 1917 proved to be a major watershed in the development of the United States Army and of military intelligence. In the space of 17 months, the U.S Army was transformed from a constabulary into a draft-raised force of 4,000,000 men, half of it deployed overseas. At the same time, the Army's moribund intelligence organization was revivified. By the end of the war, the Military Intelligence Division had become one of four equal divisions on the War Department General Staff, and Army units down to the level of battalion had been provided with intelligence staffs. Since there were not enough Regular Army officers to go around, most intelligence slots were filled by reservists recruited through the familiar "old-boys" network. Additionally, most of today's modern intelligence disciplines had appeared.

When the war began in 1914, the Germans had managed to annihilate a complete Russian field army at Tannenberg with the aid of communications intelligence—COMINT. Once the United States entered the war, it was quick to develop a cryptologic element of its own. The War Department's Military Intelligence Section established MI–8, a subsection assigned the dual mission of making and breaking codes. By the end of the war, MI–8 had set up its own intercept service along the Mexican border. In a parallel development, the American Expeditionary Forces in France organized Signal Corps monitoring stations which furnished intercepted traffic to Radio Intelligence Sections at Pershing's General Headquarters and the two numbered field armies.

Army intelligence also took to the skies. In France, observation balloons were used to overwatch enemy lines and direct artillery fire, while scout aircraft provided both visual and photographic coverage of enemy dispositions. Interpreters used stereoscopic lenses to discern the details contained in aerial photographs. In this way the new intelligence discipline of photographic intelligence—PHOTINT—was born.

Moreover, the Army became heavily involved in counterintelligence (CI) work both in the Continental United States and overseas. At home, the Army was seriously concerned with a possible (but largely unrealized) threat that might be presented by German spies, saboteurs, and disaffected aliens. Overseas, the Army attempted to protect the integrity of its forces in an unfamiliar environment. As a result, the Army instituted a professional enlisted counterintelligence force, the Corps of Intelligence Police.

Finally, the Army collected human intelligence (HUMINT) through traditional and non-traditional means. Intelligence was collected by observers, scouts, reconnaissance patrols, and interrogation of prisoners of war. Additionally, Brigadier General Dennis E. Nolan, Pershing's intelligence officer, made use of agents operating behind enemy lines. The army fielded no Mata Hari's, but was able to build up nets that monitored the movement of German troop trains across the bridges that crossed the Rhine River.

The twenty years of peace that followed World War I were a fallow time for the Army. The National Defense Act of 1920 provided for a force of 280,000 Regulars, backed by National Guardsmen and reservists. But lack of adequate appropriations ensured that this remained a paper force. Military Intelligence suffered along with the rest of the Army. The Military Intelligence Division was cut back to a staff of 20 officers. For the most part, as George Marshall later reminisced, military intelligence was reduced to "little more than what a military attaché could learn over at a dinner, more or less, over the coffee cups."

Nevertheless, Army intelligence, though diminished, did not revert to its pre-World War I state. The intelligence staff organization put in place during World War I continued. The Corps of Intelligence Police maintained a tenuous existence. In 1921, the Army established a Military Intelligence Officers Reserve Corps, thus establishing a professional nucleus of intelligence officers that could be drawn upon in any future mobilization. Even in peacetime, dedicated officers of the Army Air Corps continued to expand the frontiers of aerial photography.

The intelligence discipline which showed most signs of prospering during the peace, however, was that of signals intelligence. Immediately following the armistice, the cryptanalytic section of the War Department's MI–8 moved to New York City and became a clandestine "Black Chamber" jointly funded by the War and State Departments. This was discontinued in 1929, but the work was continued by the Army Signal Corps through its Signal Intelligence Service, or SIS. During the 1930's, the SIS not only made significant advances in cryptology, but established its own intercept arm. To support tactical operations in the field, the Army's first intelligence unit was formed in 1938: the 1st Radio Intelligence Company.

American entry into World War II resulted in an expansion of the Army's intelligence apparatus by an order of several magnitudes. Changes affected every intelligence discipline. As a result of a major reorganization of the Army staff in 1942, a separate Military Intelligence Service (MIS) was created to act as the operating arm of the Military Intelligence Division. In turn, MIS organized a Military Intelligence Training Center at Fort Ritchie, Maryland, to train interpreters, interrogators, order-of-battle specialists, and photo interpreters. These intelligence personnel were then formed into specialized teams and dispatched to overseas theaters to support the intelligence staffs of the Army's combat formations. To meet the particular needs of the war in the Pacific, MIS also established the Military Intelligence Service Language School at Camp Savage, Minnesota. This school, which later was relocated to Fort Snelling, Minnesota, trained thousands of Niseis—second-generation Japanese-Americans—to act as language specialists.

On 1 January 1942, the Corps of Intelligence Police was redesignated more appropriately as the Army Counter Intelligence Corps, or CIC. CIC activities in the continental United States raised questions within and without the Army, and in 1944 most CIC personnel in CONUS were merged with investigators of the Provost Marshal's Office to form a new Security Intelligence Corps. However, by the end of the war, the CIC had expanded to 5,000 officers and men, and CIC units were deployed with Army tactical elements down to the level of division.

The most dramatic advances in Army intelligence in World War II took place in the field of communications intelligence. In 1940, the SIS had managed to decipher Japanese diplomatic messages enciphered by the so-called PURPLE electro-mechanical machine cipher. This made the United States government privy to many of the Japanese government's most closely guarded secrets, although it could not prevent the disaster at Pearl Harbor. Following the Japanese attack, the SIS relocated to new quarters at Arlington Hall Station, Virginia; was redesignated as the Signal Security Agency; and began a vast expansion. After a long struggle, SSA was able to decipher the major code systems used by the Japanese military. By the end of the war, 2,200 military personnel and 5,600 civilians were working at Arlington Hall, processing messages intercepted by the 2d Signal Service battalion, SSA's worldwide collection arm. It is estimated that the efforts of SSA may have shortened the war in the Pacific by two years.

Arlington Hall Station furnished the Army with the raw data in the form of decrypted Japanese communications. The job of transforming this into intelligence was provided by the Special Branch of the Military Intelligence Service. In 1943, the importance of the whole COMINT effort was vastly enhanced by the liaison established between MIS/SSA and the British code breaking center at Bletchley Park. The British shared with their American counterparts their degree of success against German communications. It was mutually agreed that each party would fully share intelligence derived from COMINT and that in the future the Americans would concentrate on the Japanese problem, the British on the German. It was also agreed that Special Branch would disseminate to American commanders COMINT derived both from British and American sources.

By the time World War II came to an end, COMINT had become the Army's single most important intelligence source. The Special Branch of MIS lost its monopoly over this intelligence source and was broken up on the eve of the Normandy invasion, on the grounds that it was no longer possible to produce valid intelligence without access to COMINT. A new Special Branch was established to supervise the tightly-controlled COMINT dissemination process. The logical culmination of the process came in December 1944, when the Signal Security Agency, previously controlled by the Army's Chief Signal Officer, was placed under the operational direction of the Military Intelligence service.

At the tactical level, as opposed to the strategic one, Army intelligence was decentralized. As previously indicated, the MIS furnished intelligence staffs with small teams of HUMINT and PHOTINT specialists. While almost all PHOTINT was provided by the high-performance reconnaissance aircraft of the Army Air Forces, divisions had their own aerial assets in the form of "Piper Cubs" used for artillery spotting, liaison, and general reconnaissance. Counterintelligence support for the troops in the field was provided by CIC detachments attached to the Army's fighting divisions and higher formations. A variety of Signal Corps units, variously designated as Signal Radio Intelligence Companies or Signal Service Companies, provided tactical COMINT, concentrating on the exploitation of enemy low- and medium-level encryption systems. Specialized HUMINT services were provided unit commanders by the Organization of Strategic Services (OSS), a militarized intelligence and special operations element operating under the control of the Joint Chiefs of Staff.

As we examine the history of Military Intelligence during this period that spanned two world wars, we can see substantial continuities running through the discrete intelligence disciplines of HUMINT, COMINT, PHOTINT, and CI. However, due to the communications revolution, the growing skill of cryptanalysts, and the development of automation as an adjunct of code breaking, the importance of COMINT as an intelligence source increased exponentially. The only new discipline that surfaced in World War II was that of electronic intelligence (ELINT), as radar emerged as both an intelligence tool and an intelligence target.

Nonetheless, while much remained unchanged in the intelligence business, there was a monumental change in the amount of resources the Army was now forced to invest in collecting, processing, and disseminating intelligence. One need only contrast the handful of people who worked in MI–8 in World War I with the almost 8,000 men and women who toiled at Arlington Hall Station.

MI in Two Wars: HUMINT

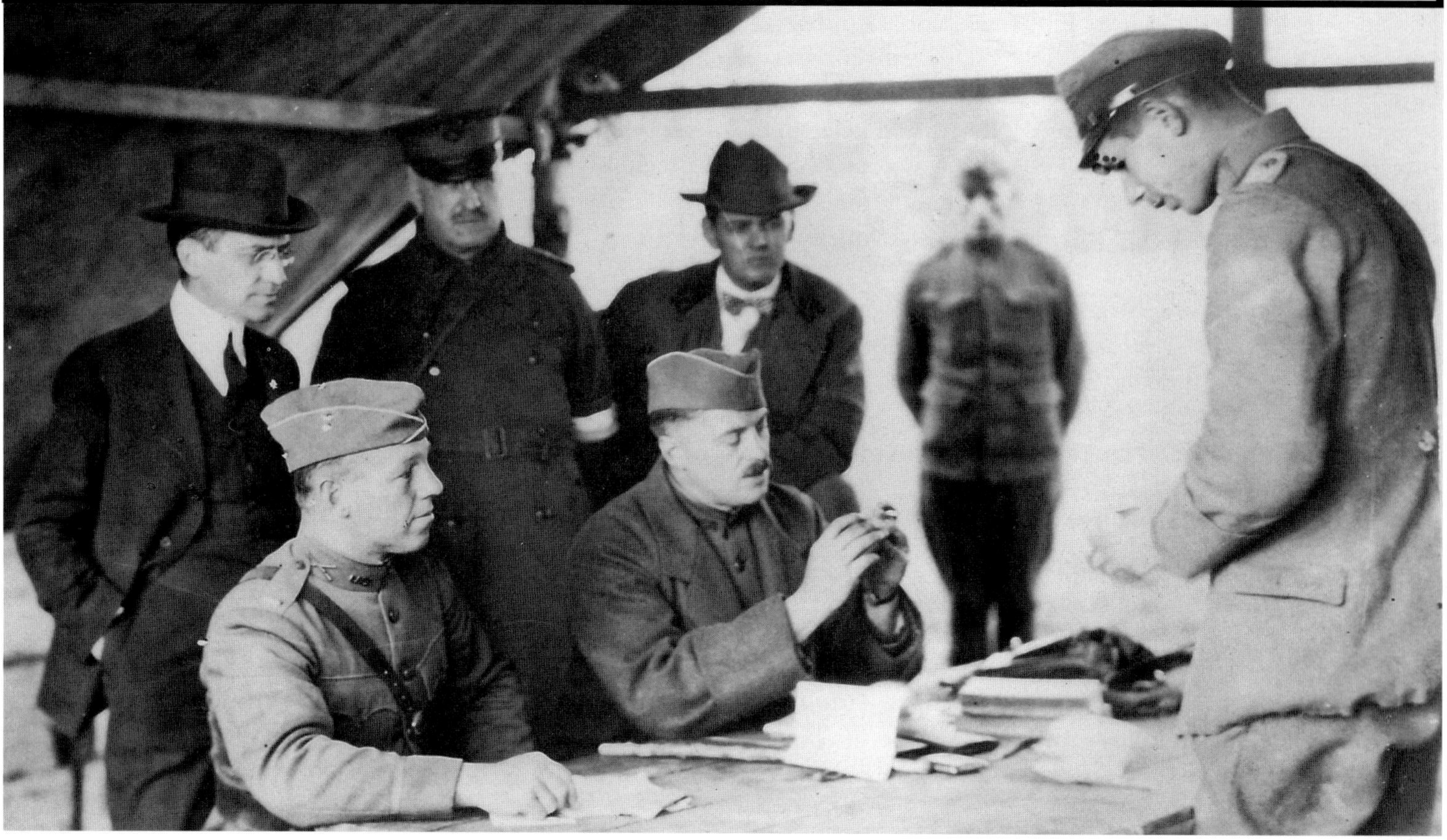

As Secretary of War Newton D. Baker looks on, AEF intelligence officers interrogate a German prisoner of war in 1918.

An American intelligence officer interrogates a French civilian during the liberation of France in 1944.

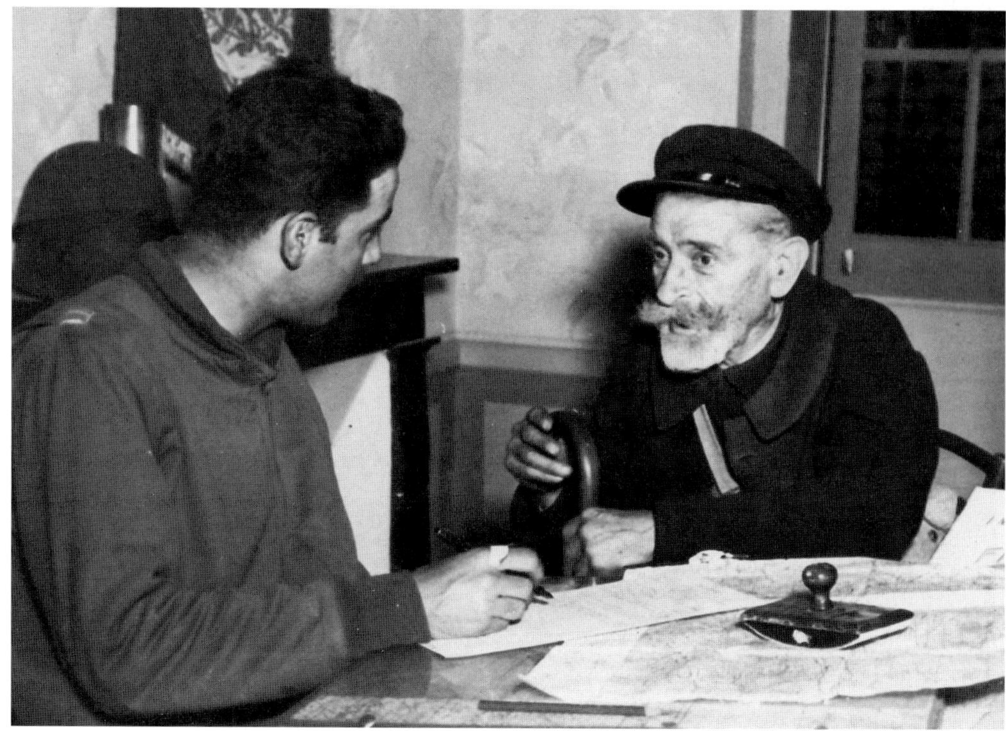

COMINT

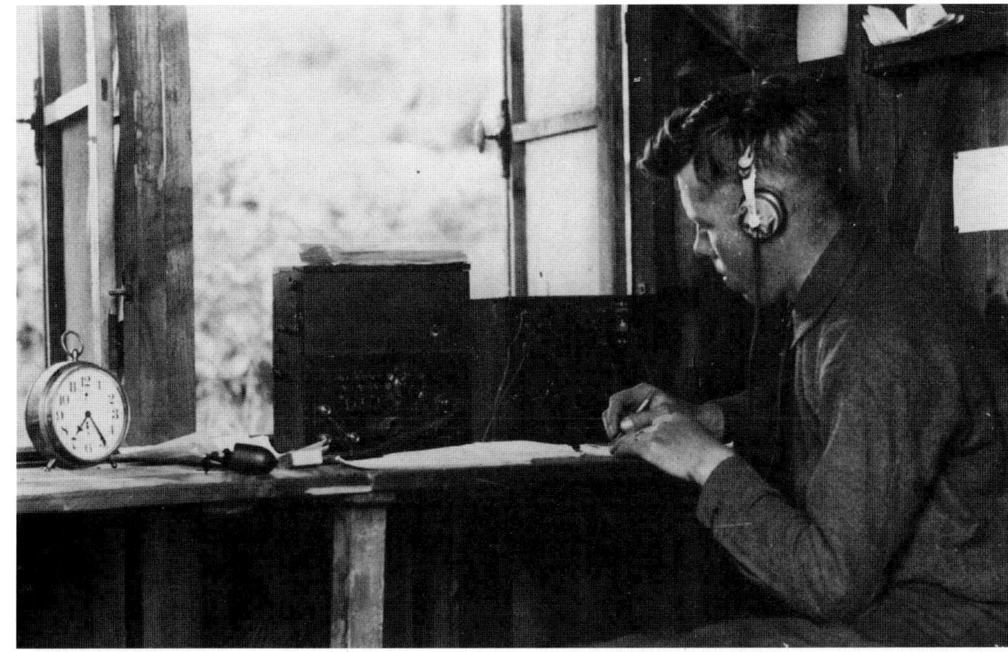

An intercept operator of the American Expeditionary Forces in France in World War I.

Cryptanalysts of the Signal Security Agency work under crowded conditions at Arlington Hall in World War II. The Signal Security Agency spearheaded the Army's massive communications intelligence effort.

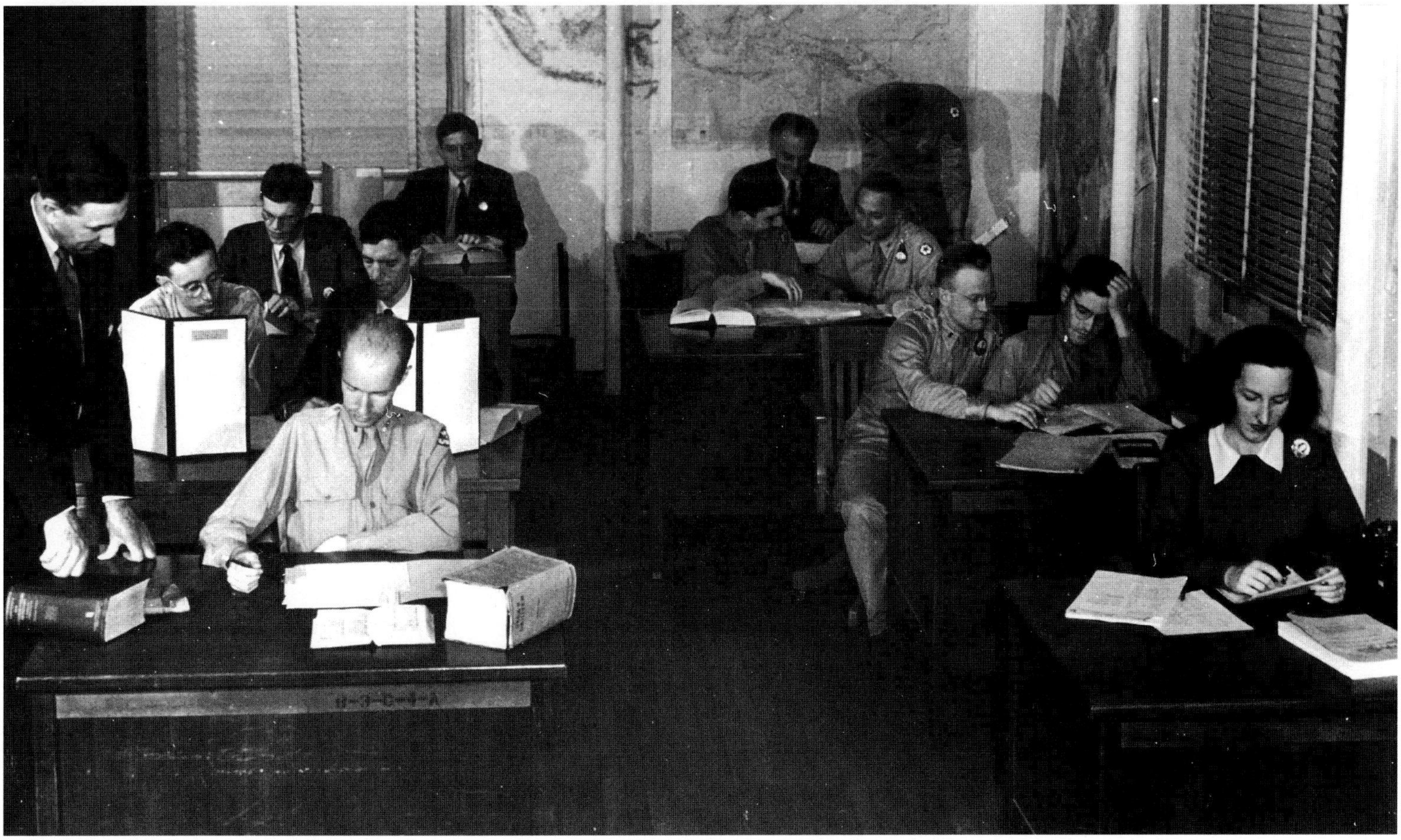

PHOTINT

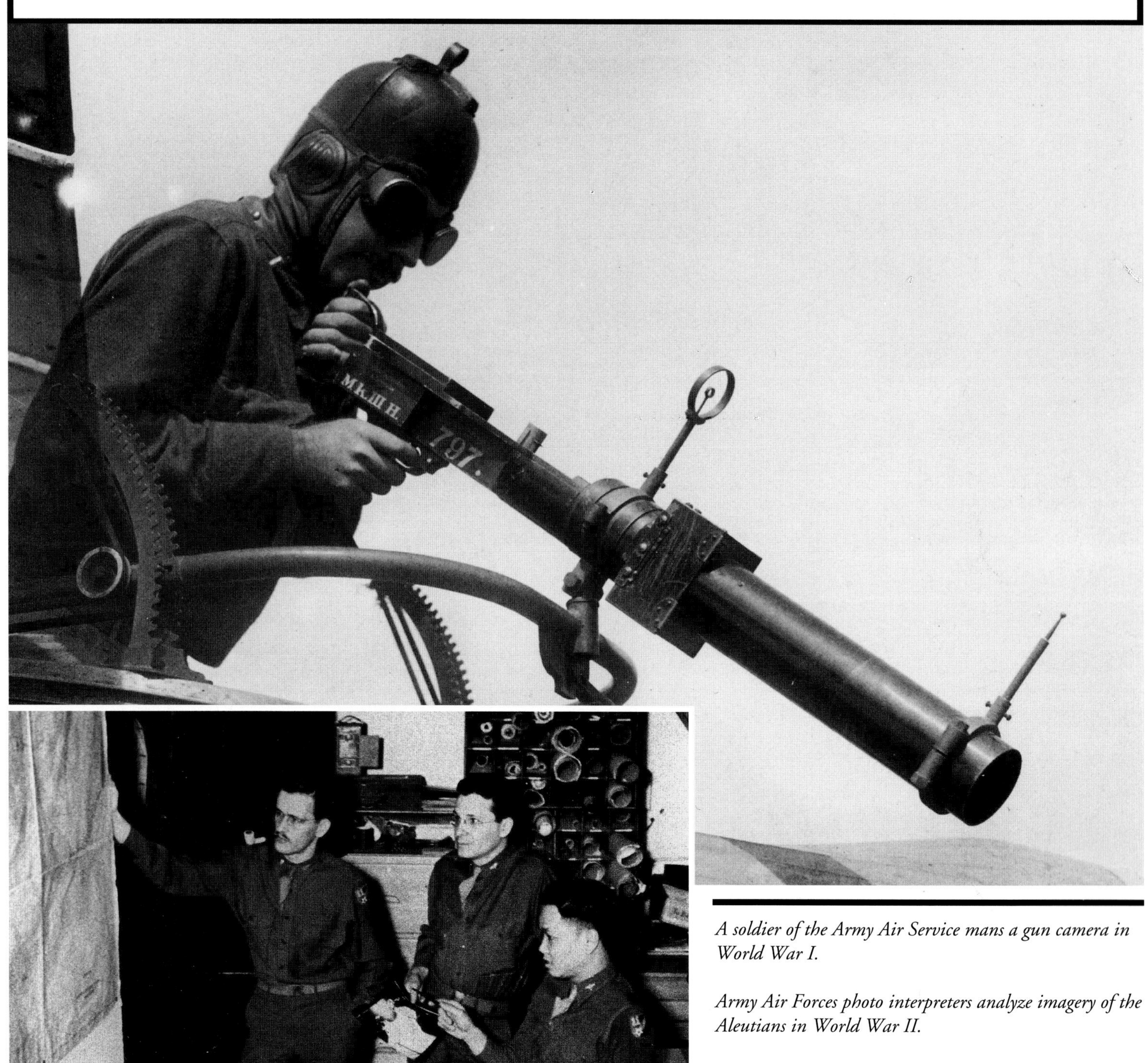

A soldier of the Army Air Service mans a gun camera in World War I.

Army Air Forces photo interpreters analyze imagery of the Aleutians in World War II.

Counterintelligence

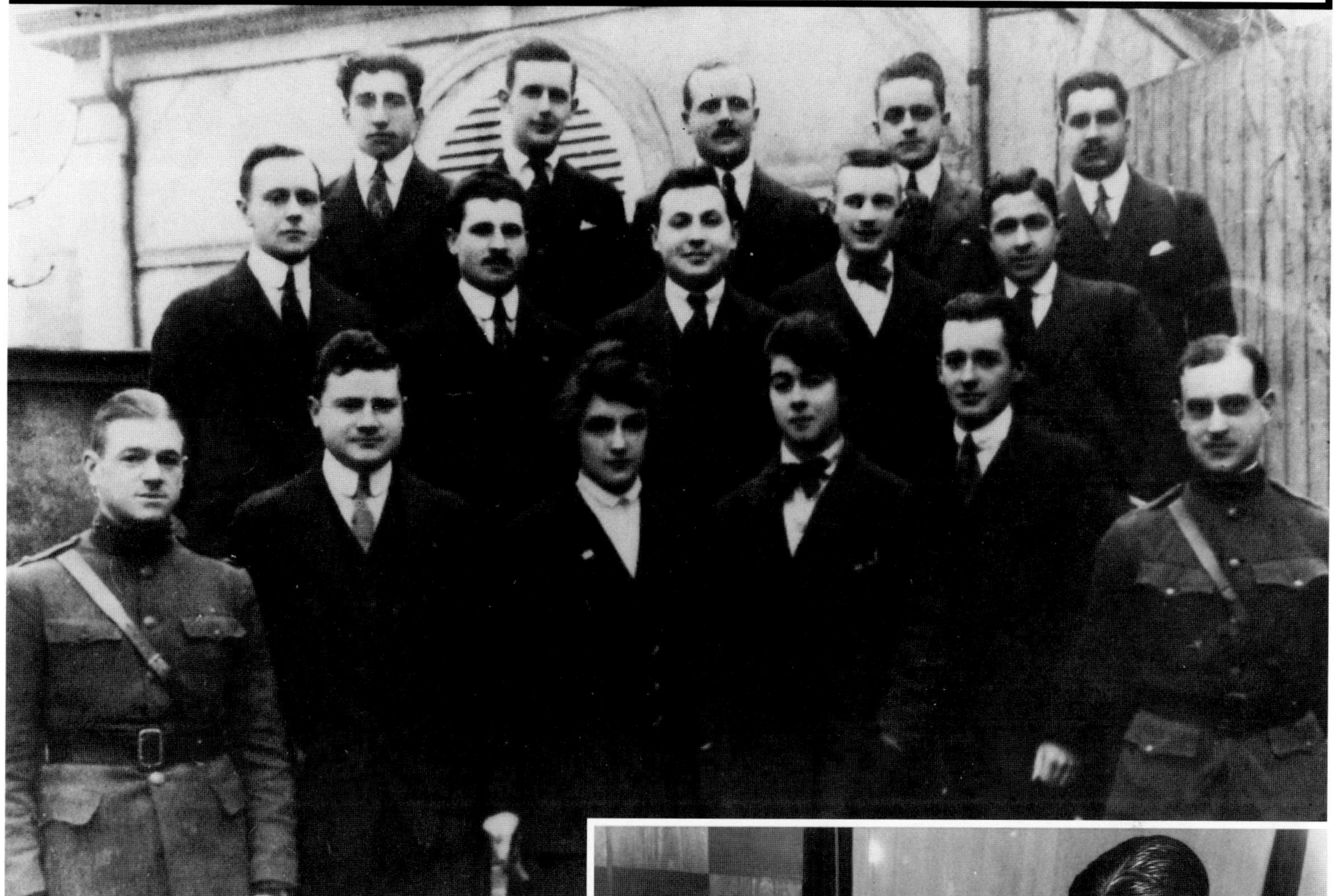

Plainclothes agents of the Corps of Intelligence Police pose for a group picture in France. Officers stand in front. The female personnel were civilian secretaries.

A Counter Intelligence Corps agent attached to the 94th Infantry Division interviews a Dutch engineer in 1945.

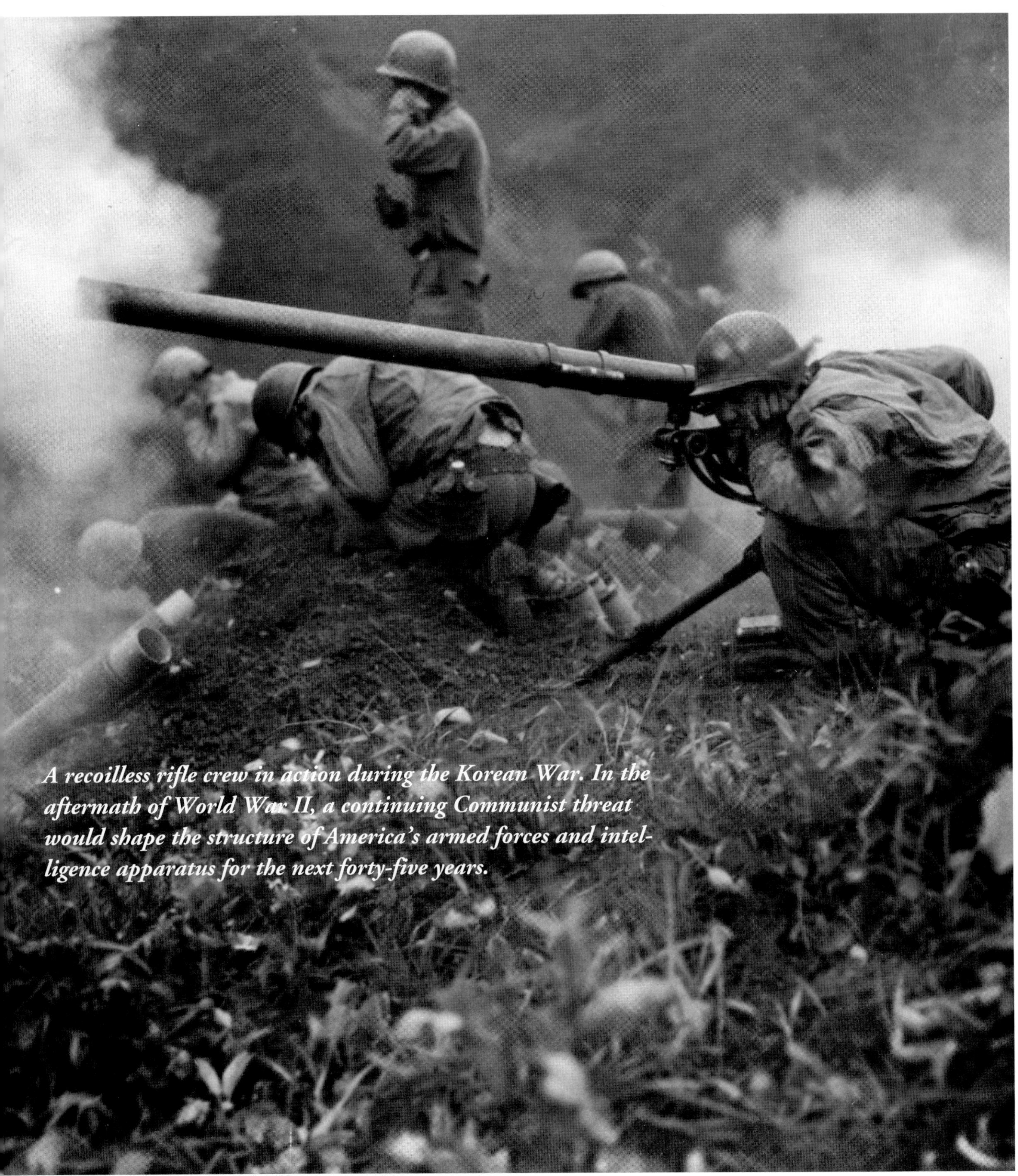

A recoilless rifle crew in action during the Korean War. In the aftermath of World War II, a continuing Communist threat would shape the structure of America's armed forces and intelligence apparatus for the next forty-five years.

Cold War and Shooting Wars, 1945–1973

American victory in World War II was followed by demobilization on a sweeping scale. The great armies that had liberated Europe and broken the power of Japan in the Pacific melted away. Despite its wartime successes, the Army seemed almost irrelevant to many Americans. Optimists trusted in the new international collective security organization, the United Nations, to preserve the peace. Pessimists placed their confidence in America's monopoly of the atomic bomb. Only the need to maintain occupation forces overseas prevented even greater retrenchments in American ground forces.

While Army intelligence was inevitably affected by the shift from war to peace, the transition impacted upon its various components in disparate ways. The Military Intelligence Service Training Center at Camp Ritchie was discontinued, and the Military Intelligence Service itself merged into the Army's intelligence staff. On the other hand, the fact that large counterintelligence elements were needed to support the occupation resulted in the strengthening of the Counter Intelligence Corps. Wartime experience in the signals intelligence field resulted in the formation of the Army Security Agency (ASA) in September 1945. Operating under direct control of the Army intelligence staff, ASA melded into a single organization all communications intelligence and communication security personnel, installations, and units.

In the aftermath of World War II, it quickly became apparent that peace was not, after all, at hand. The nation soon found itself locked in a global ideological and politico-military confrontation with an aggressive and expansionist Soviet Union. This Cold War would drag on for the next forty-five years. The United States once again looked to its defenses. The draft was revived in 1947, and Congress passed legislation to unify the armed services under a Secretary of Defense and to create a Central Intelligence Agency. In 1949, the United States set up the Armed Forces Security Agency (later National Security Agency) to exercise centralized direction over the nation's cryptologic effort. The new agency absorbed a good portion of ASA's personnel and functions.

In 1950, however, the onset of the Korean War and the subsequent Chinese military intervention exposed the weaknesses that remained both in the American military and in its intelligence structure. In the process of meeting these successive challenges, American forces were repeatedly bloodied: North Korean forces overran and almost annihilated Task Force Smith in the early stages of the conflict; the Chinese Peoples Liberation Army badly cut up the 2d Infantry Division five months later. Confronted by unexpected enemies in an unfamiliar countryside, Army intelligence was hard put to transition from peace to war. Well along into the conflict, Eighth Army Commander General James Van Fleet would complain that "it has become apparent that during the between-war interim we have lost through neglect, disinterest, and possible jealousy, much of the effectiveness in intelligence work that we acquired so painfully in World War II. Today, our intelligence operations in Korea have not yet approached the standards we reached in the final year of the last war."

Nonetheless, the shock of the Korean War did give a new impetus to the development of Army intelligence. There was a rapid growth both in personnel and in organizational structure.

At the Department of the Army level, the staff of the Assistant Chief of Staff, G–2, reached a strength of over 1,000 personnel.

For the first time in its history, the Army fielded large intelligence units: military intelligence service groups and battalions, organized on cellular lines. The Army Security Agency was revitalized by the Korean War. Previously, most ASA assets had been concentrated at fixed sites, performing a peacetime strategic mission. The agency now found a new role in providing support to tactical operations, activating communication reconnaissance groups, battalions, and companies to support commanders at every level.

In the aftermath of Korea, Army intelligence moved towards greater professionalism while attempting to exploit the potentialities of new technologies. The perceived need for a new emphasis on human intelligence led the Army to introduce a training course in this discipline in 1954. In the process, the mission of the existing Counter Intelligence Corps School at Fort Holabird, Maryland, was expanded and it became the Army Intelligence School. The following year, all combat intelligence training was centralized at Holabird. Army Security Agency personnel, however, continued to train at ASA's own facility at Fort Devens, Massachusetts.

Integration of intelligence disciplines in training was followed by attempts at greater integration in the field. In 1957, the Army developed new units organized under the "Military Intelligence Organization" concept that incorporated counterintelligence, human intelligence, and combat intelligence specialists in a single battalion. In 1961, CIC and human intelligence personnel were consolidated into a single Intelligence Corps. In 1965, the Chief, Intelligence Corps, was given an additional assignment as Commanding General of the U.S. Army Intelligence Command, a new Army major command which had the mission of conducting all counterintelligence operations in the United States. This presented span-of-control problems, however, and the Intelligence Corps was discontinued as part of the solution.

In 1955, the Army Security Agency redefined its own mission, absorbing responsibility for conducting electronic intelligence and communications-related electronic warfare operations from the Army Signal Corps. In turn, ASA surrendered its functions of cryptomateriel distribution and repair to the Signal Corps. The realignment was logical, since electronic intelligence was an aspect of what was now known as signals intelligence (SIGINT) and since electronic warfare closely impacted on signals intelligence and used the same types of equipment. Since ASA had become the proponent of a weapons system—electronic warfare—it was relieved of direct subordination to the Assistant Chief of Staff for Intelligence and placed under control of the Army Chief of Staff.

The Army also continued to make large strides in the areas of aerial reconnaissance and photo intelligence. Reconnaissance helicopters entered the Army inventory, replacing the "Piper Cub"-type aircraft on which the Army had relied since World War II. In 1959, the Army acquired a dedicated surveillance aircraft, the AO–1 Mohawk. The Mohawk could be variously equipped with aerial cameras, side-looking airborne radars, or infrared sensors. Additionally, the Army acquired access to national-level imagery products during the 1950's, and fielded its first military intelligence battalions, aerial reconnaissance support, to exploit photographs generated by Air Force platforms. Because of the growing importance of infra-red and radar, the discipline of PHOTINT was officially redesignated as imagery intelligence—IMINT—in 1964.

The evolution of the discrete disciplines within military intelligence in the 1950's and early 1960's was paralleled by two other developments. One was a move towards centralization. In 1958, a reorganization of the Department of Defense had eliminated the responsibilities of the individual armed services for warfighting. Under the new concept, each armed service would be responsible for procuring, training, and supplying its own troops to unified and specified military commands operating under the umbrella of the joint chiefs of Staff. The logic of this approach carried over into the intelligence field. In 1961, Secretary of Defense Robert S. McNamara created a unified Defense Intelligence Agency (DIA). DIA exercised responsibilities for most intelligence production and was responsible for administering a unified defense attaché system. It absorbed much of the staff of the Office of the Assistant Chief of Staff for Intelligence.

The second significant development that took place during this period was the Army's decision to place military intelligence on a professional footing. Ever since World War II, intelligence staff positions had been held by officers detailed from the combat arms, while the overwhelming majority of intelligence officers performing specialized assignments had been reservists who chose to remain on active duty. Although there were Military Intelligence and Army Security Branches in the Army Reserve, these were not open to active duty personnel. However, by 1962, most reservists performing intelligence duties were due to retire. Meanwhile, it became apparent that appropriate leadership for the large intelligence units now fielded by the Army could only be provided by professional intelligence officers, just as the existence of ordnance units implied the need for an Ordnance Branch. Responding to these demands, the Army created an Army Intelligence and Security Branch in 1962 to perform combat service support functions. In 1967, this was given the more appropriate designation of the Military Intelligence (MI) Branch, and its functions upgraded to those of combat support.

While these events were in train, the nation and its Army were becoming growingly involved in a new foreign policy crisis.

Ever since 1954, the United States had supported the government of South Vietnam with military advisors. As that government came under increasing pressure from a Communist-backed insurgency, more advisors were sent in, along with helicopters and aircraft. South Vietnam became a demonstration setting to prove that counterinsurgency techniques and "nation-building" could defeat a guerrilla threat. Unfortunately, the demonstration went awry; by 1965, the United States was involved in a full-scale land and air war on the mainland of Asia.

From the intelligence standpoint, South Vietnam presented difficult problems. The enemy was elusive, the terrain hidden by jungle canopy, and the loyalties of the local population uncertain. Nevertheless, what was now a highly professional intelligence organization helped to ensure that the United States Army never suffered a single major tactical defeat in the course of a war that would drag on some eight years. New technologies were brought into play to assist the intelligence effort: automation, the use of various night vision devices, unattended ground sensors; "people-sniffers" that detected human odors; and the widespread employment of Special Electronic Mission Activity aircraft by ASA elements. However, while intelligence could avert defeat, it could not by itself bring about victory. The United States had chosen to fight a limited war by incremental means and with no clear strategy beyond the hope that the opponent would one day call the whole thing off. This hope proved to be misguided.

Meanwhile, the social, political, economic, and psychic costs of maintaining a draft-raised army fighting a seemingly endless war in the jungles of Southeast Asia began to take their toll within the United States itself. The home front began to bubble over. Unfulfilled expectations of progress created by the Great Society programs of the mid-1960's led to a series of major riots in inner cities across America, while an antiwar (and anti draft) movement took over the nation's campuses, precipitating violent confrontations. The Army was repeatedly called upon to supplement civilian authorities in maintaining public order. Both national-level authorities and those Army commanders tasked with a civil disturbance mission soon discovered that the domestic intelligence provided by the FBI and state and local authorities was not adequate. As a result, the Army was directed to mount a domestic intelligence collection program, using counterintelligence assets. Army intelligence thus became engaged both on the battlefront and on the home front in a war whose political support was quickly beginning to erode.

The ending was not a happy one. The conflict in Vietnam was resolved by a phased withdrawal of American troops, coupled with a program of "Vietnamization" in which local forces were built up to carry on the fight. In 1973, a peace agreement was finally cobbled together, and the last American forces left the Republic of Vietnam. Peace, however, was not at hand. In 1975, North Vietnam overwhelmed the struggling republic in a massive conventional assault. At home, Army intelligence came under partisan attack, and the intelligence community soon found itself regarded with public suspicion and trammeled by unparalleled restrictions.

Korean War

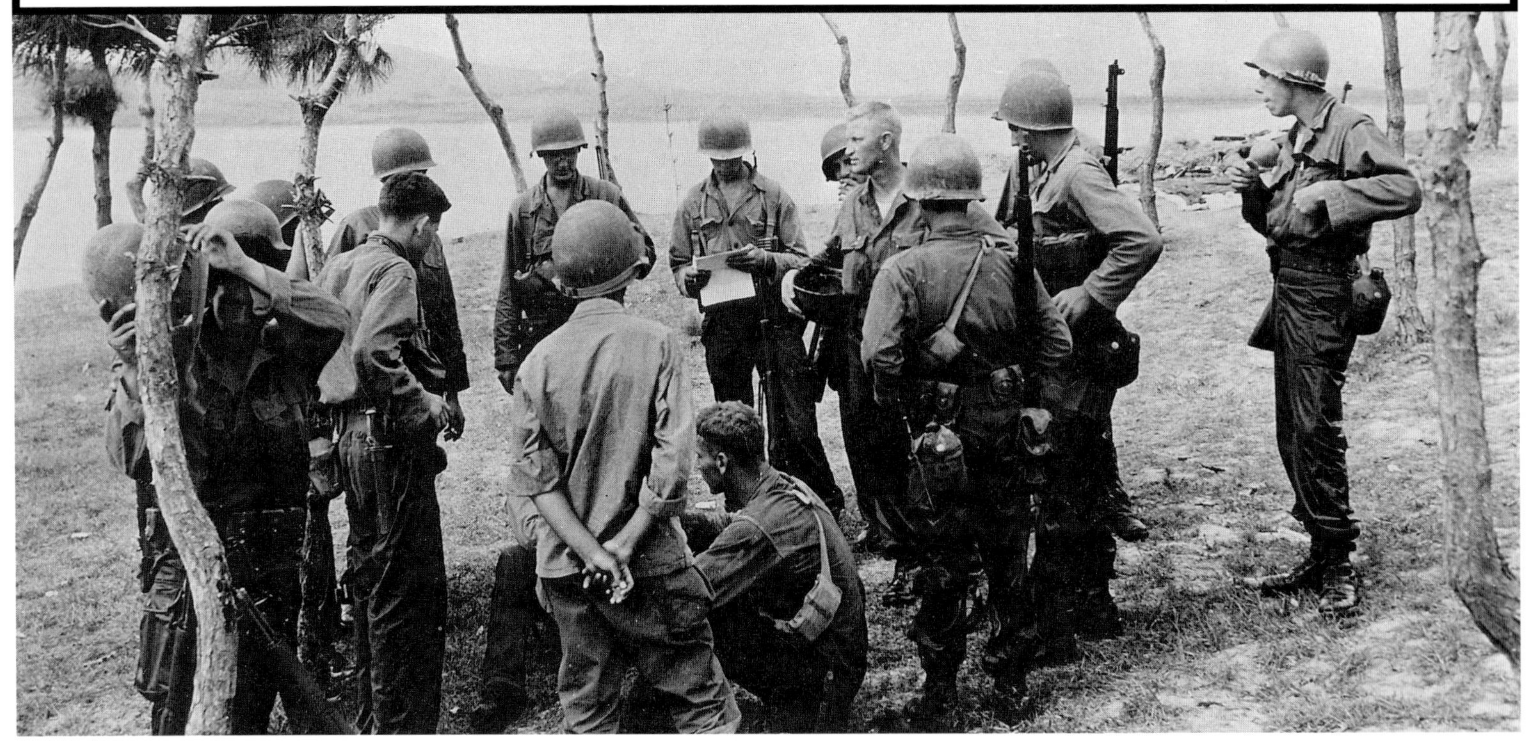

A ground patrol rests beside the Naktong River. As the noted military commentator S.L.A. Marshall put it, "Infantry is the antenna of combat intelligence."

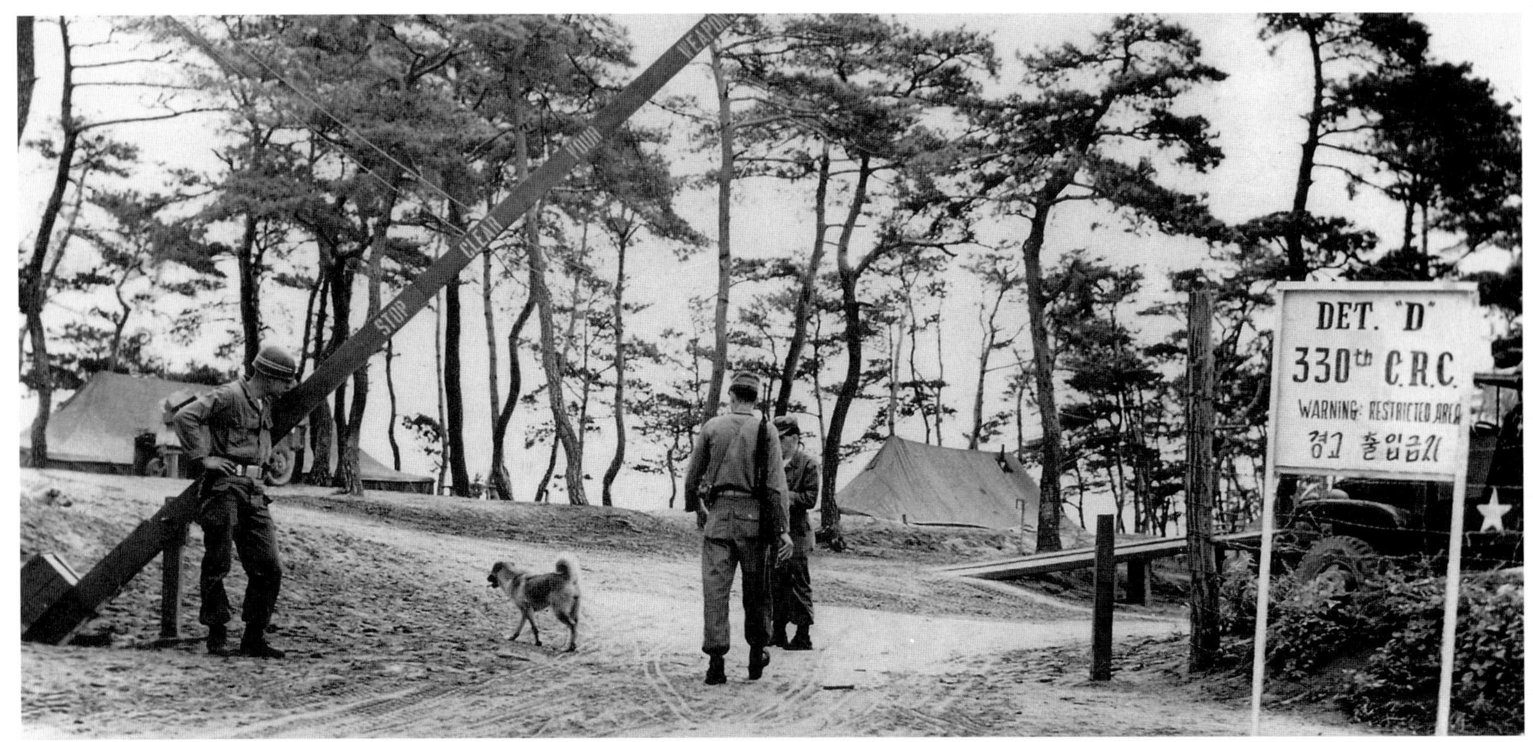

Compound of the Army Security Agency's 330th Communication Reconnaissance Company in Korea.

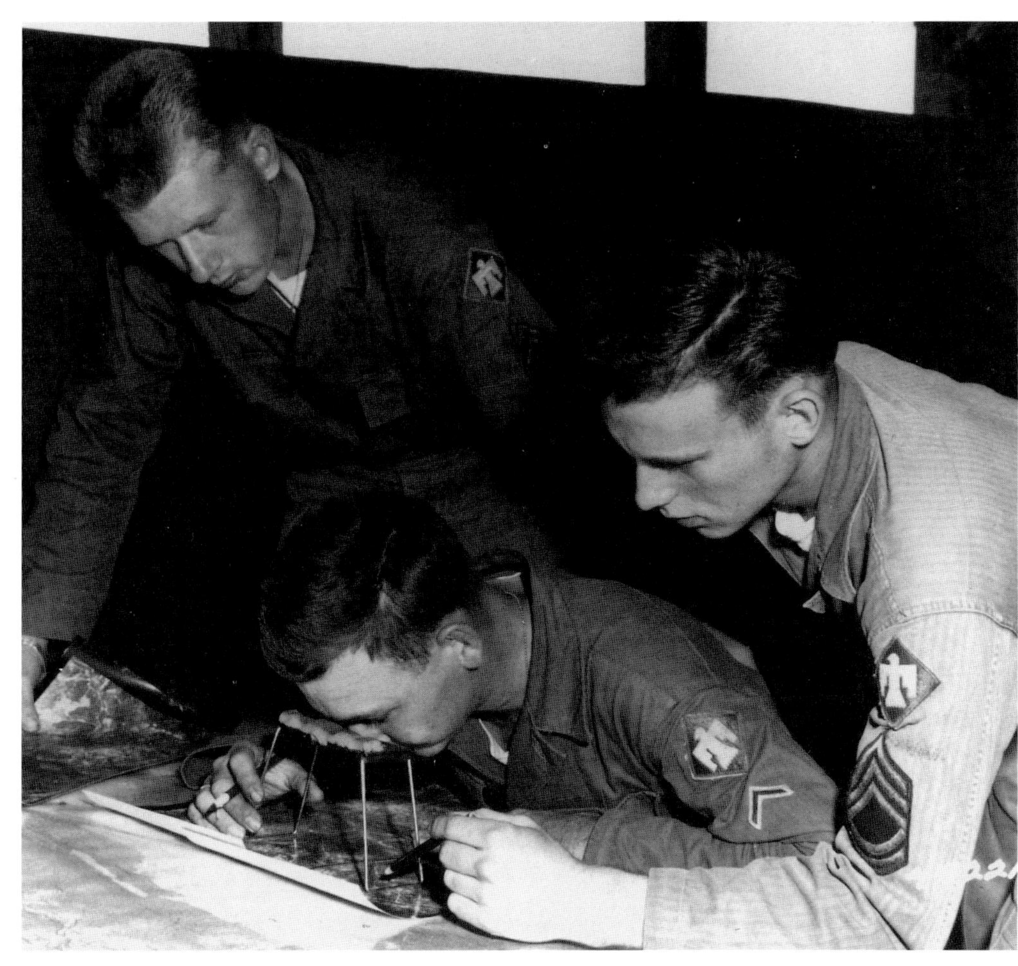

Photo interpreters of the 45th "Thunderbird" Division analyze imagery of the rugged Korean terrain.

Technical intelligence: a soldier examines a captured Soviet-made heavy machine gun.

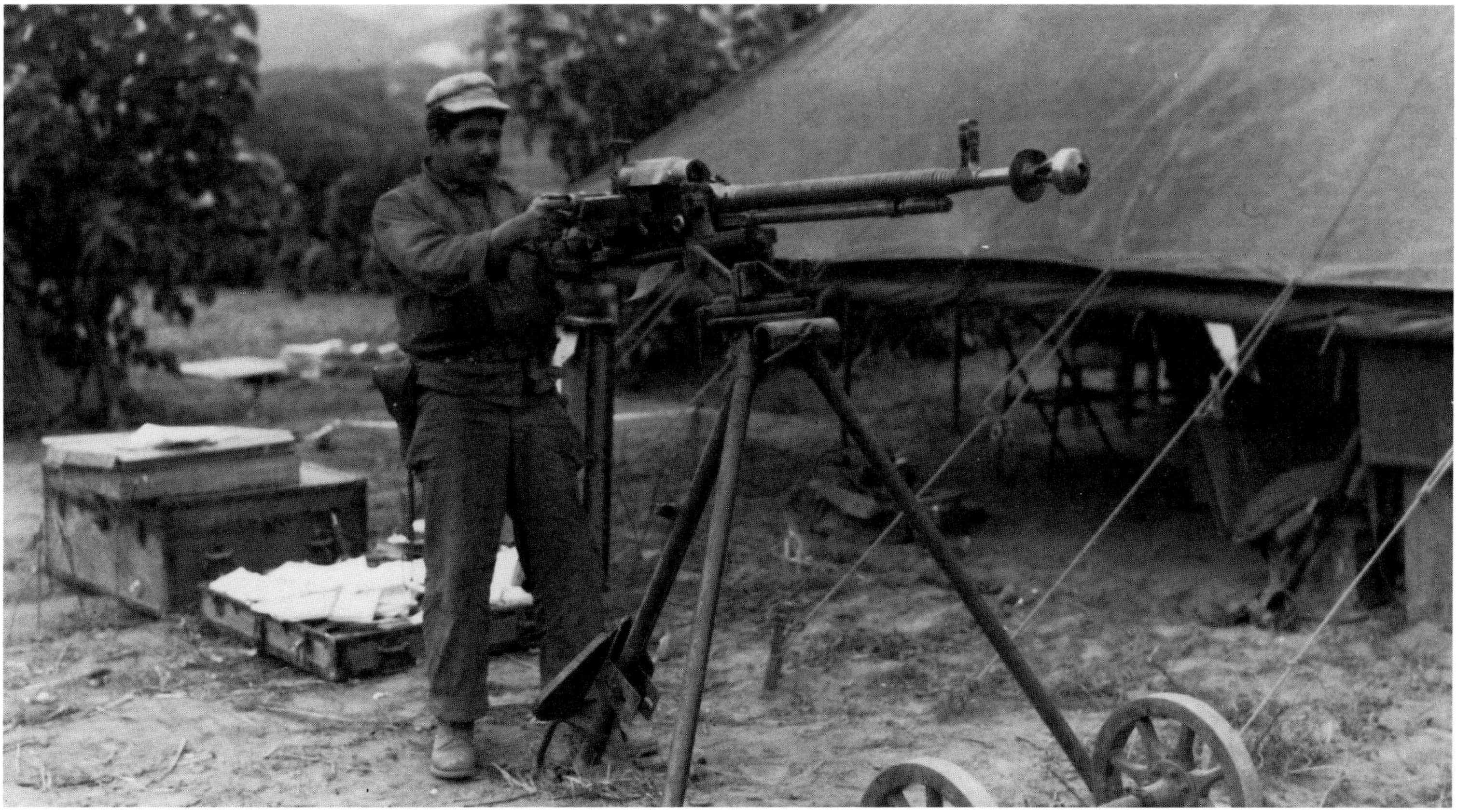

Professionalization

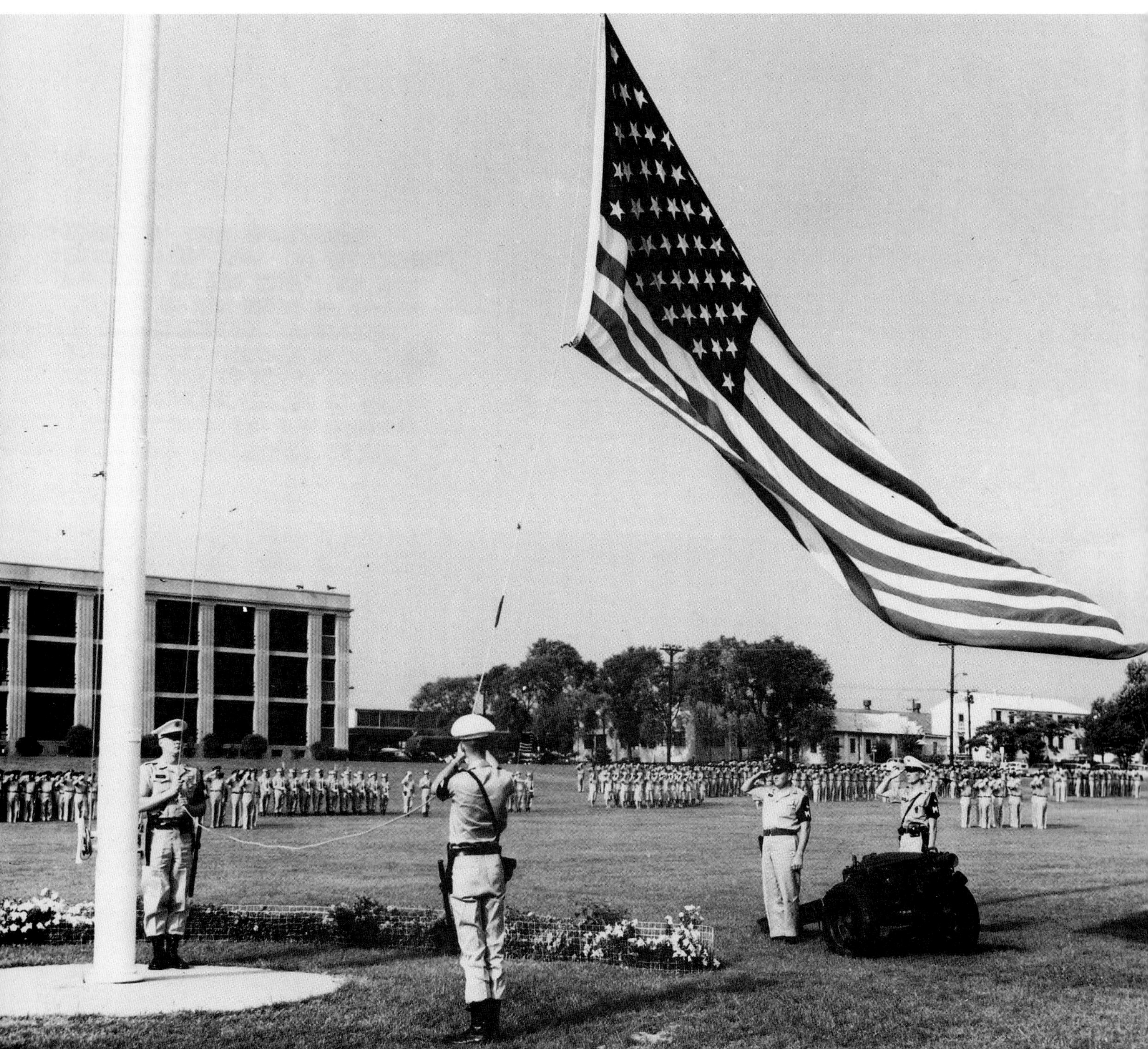

In 1955, the Army centralized most intelligence training at the Army Intelligence School at Fort Holabird. Here, the colors are lowered over Holabird's Furlow Field.

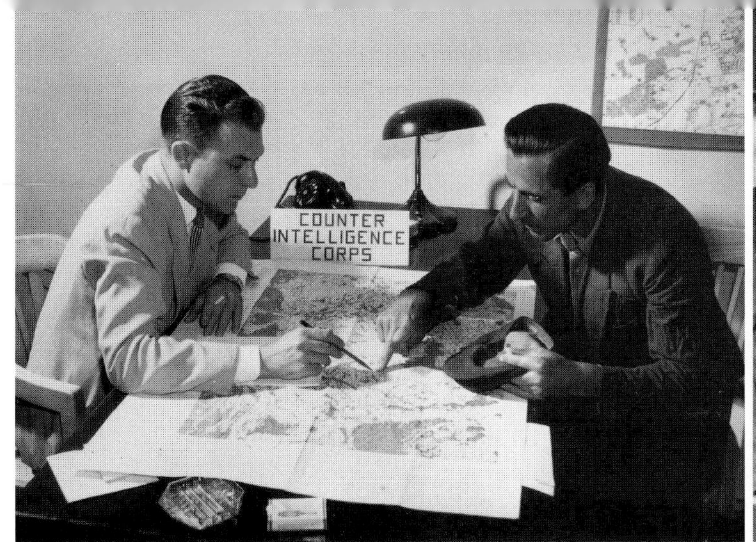

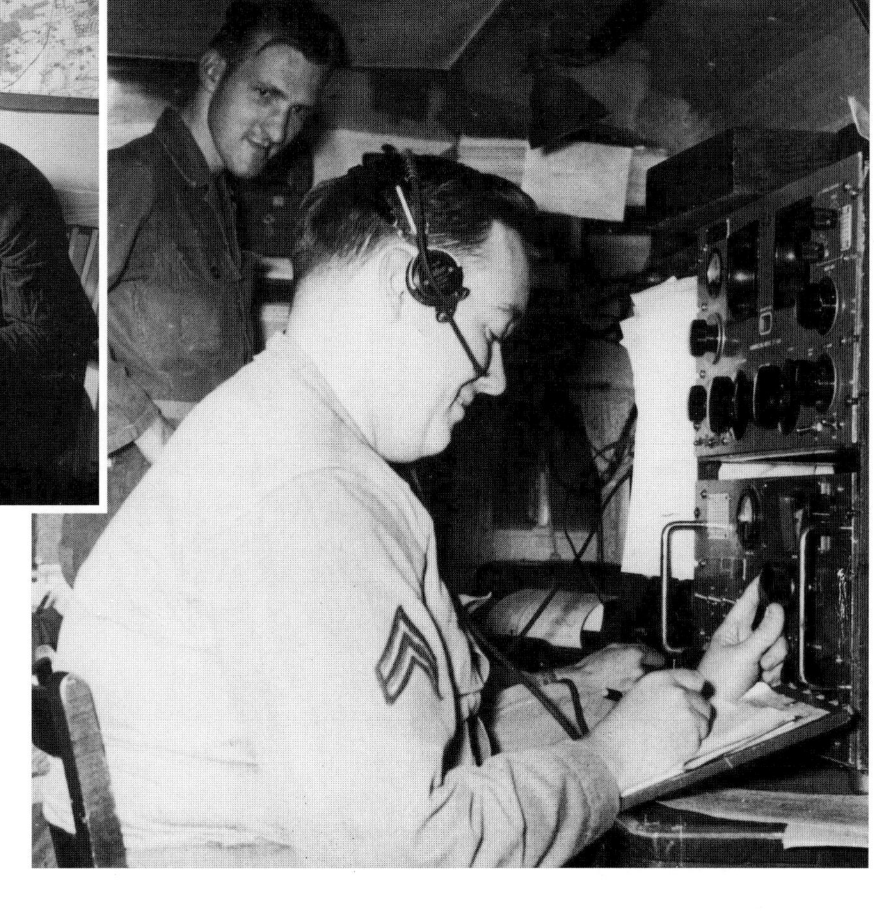

Counterintelligence training in Austria. In 1961, the Army merged the Counter Intelligence Corps with collection personnel to form a consolidated Intelligence Corps.

The Army Security Agency continued to carry out a vital national mission both in war and in peace. ASA personnel man positions in the 1950's.

Overseas operational site of the 276th Army Security Agency Company in 1962.

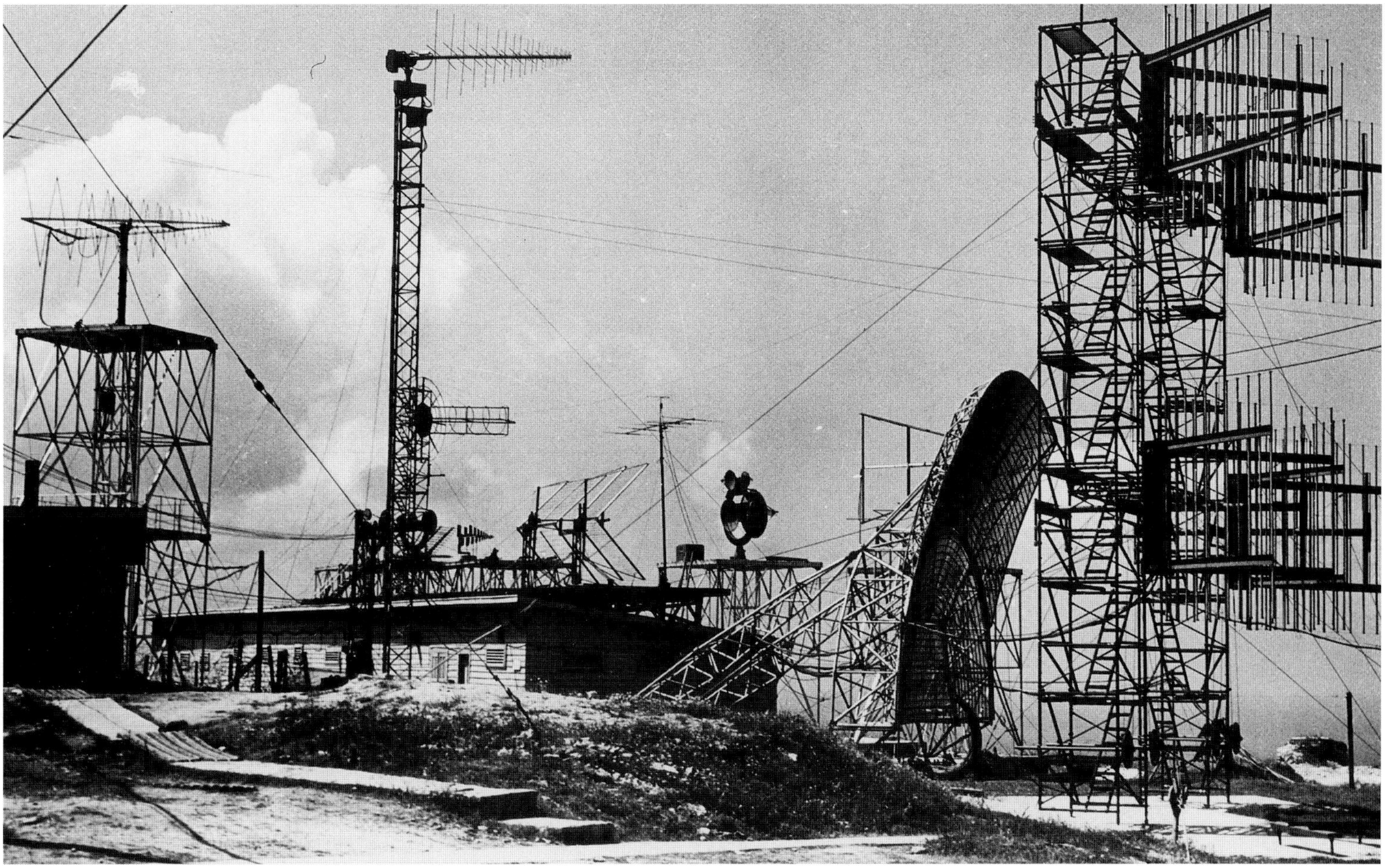

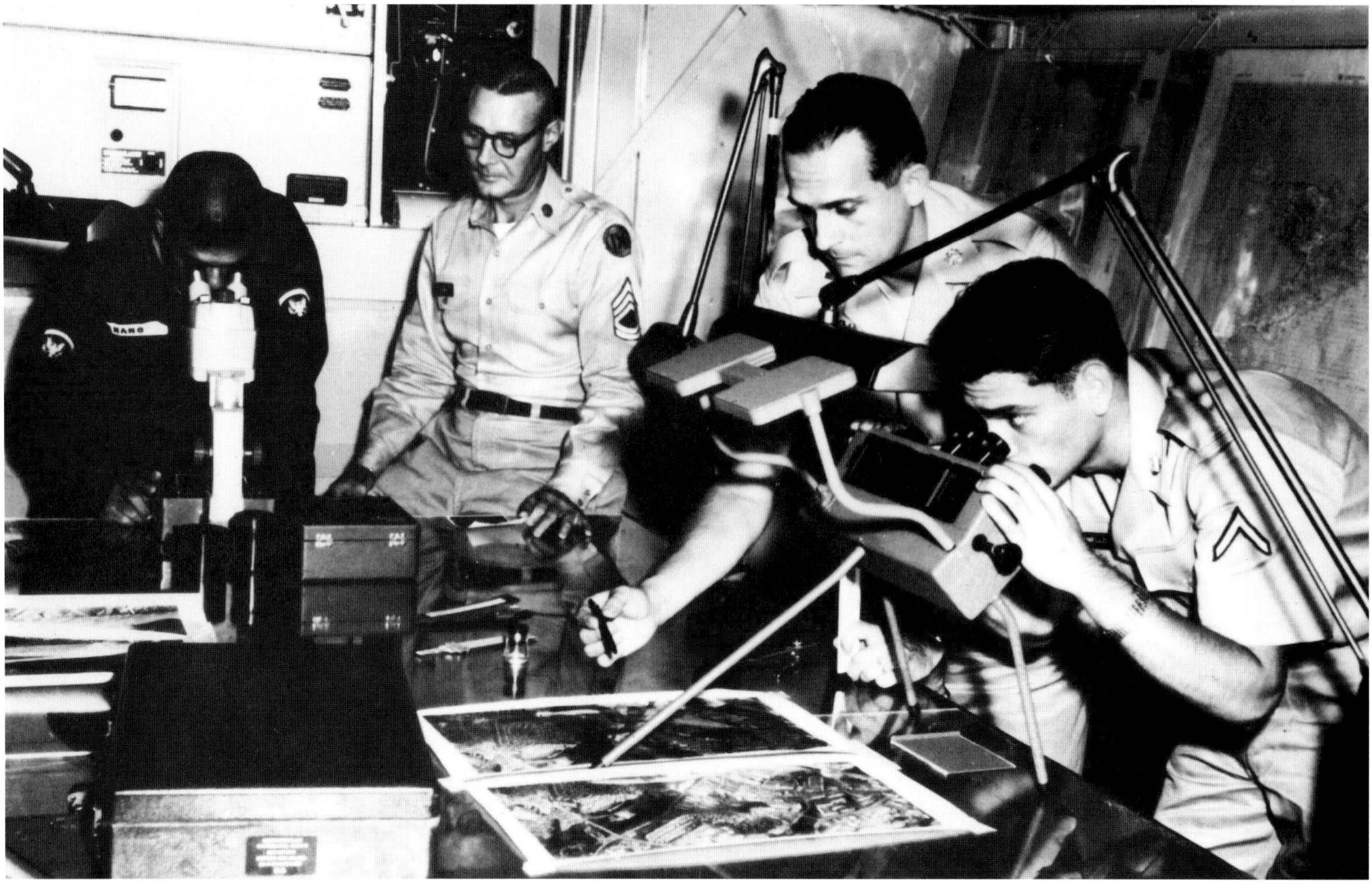

In 1964, the Army redesignated the discipline of photographic intelligence as imagery intelligence. Imagery interpreters on Okinawa in 1965.

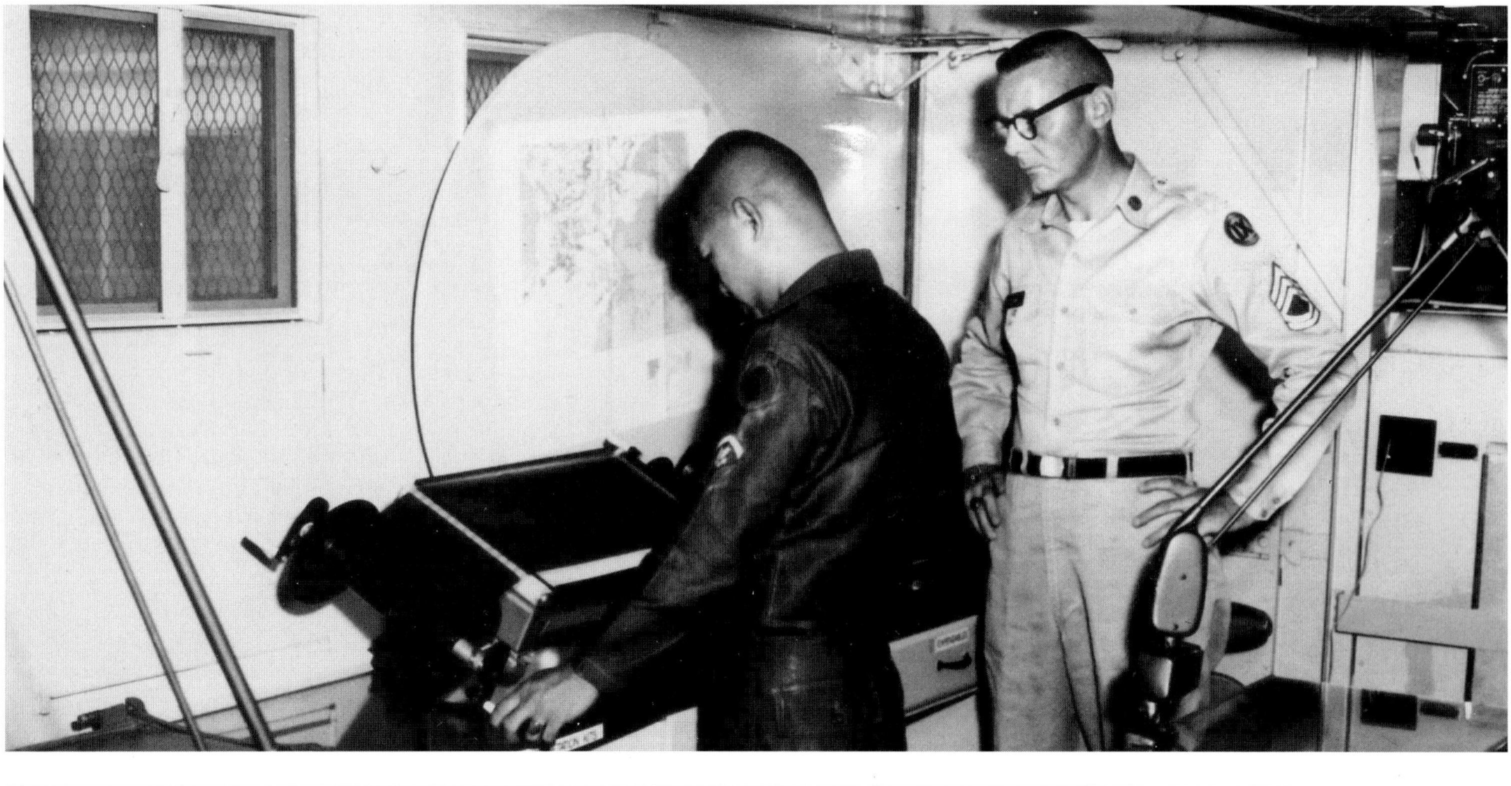

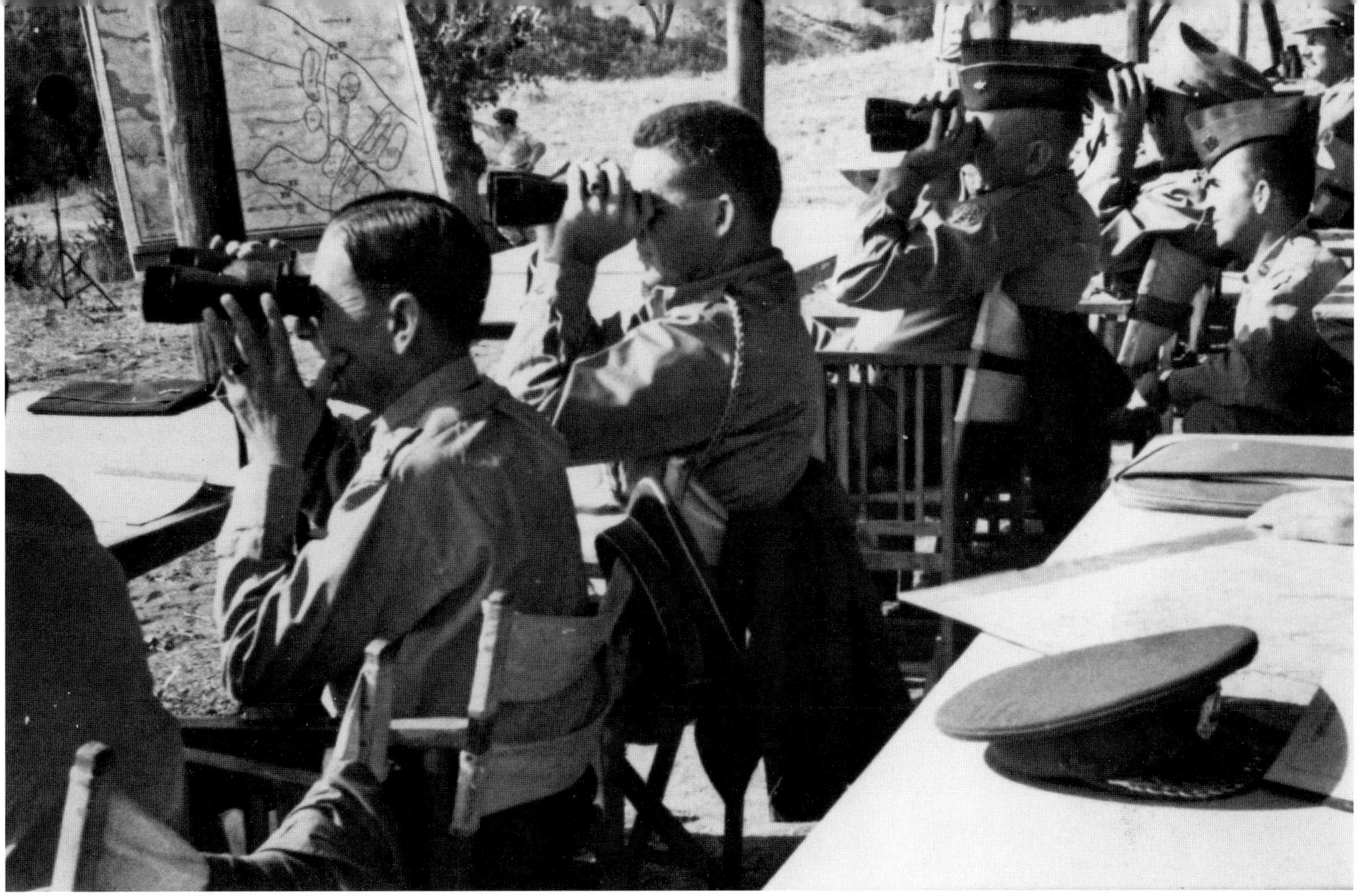

The military attaché system remained an important source of information for the Army. Here, attachés observe Greek Army maneuvers in 1959.

As Assistant Chief of Staff for Intelligence, MG Alva Fitch sought to fully professionalize military intelligence by making it a branch of the regular Army.

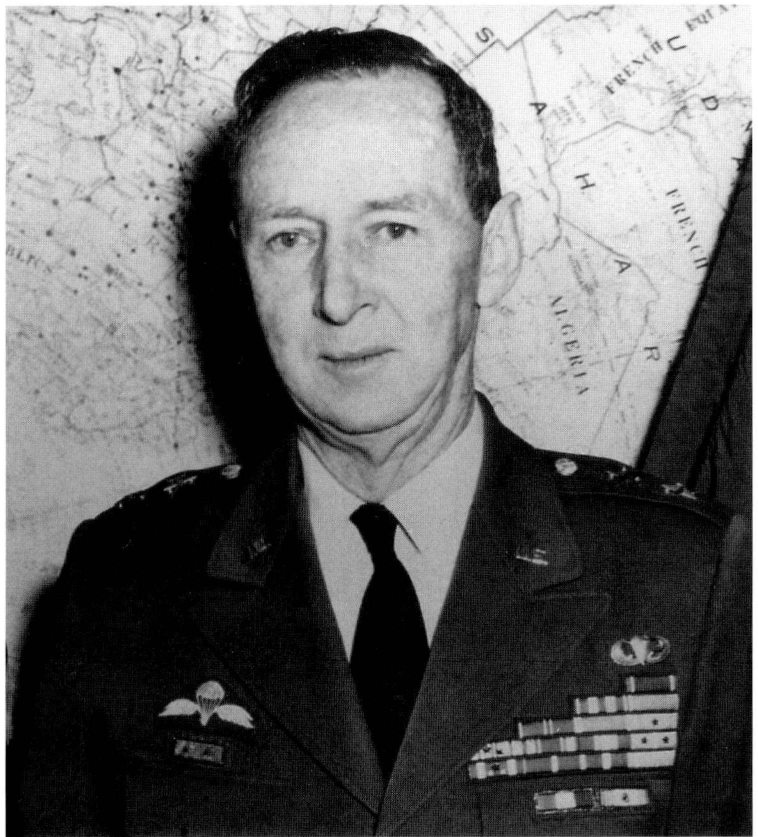

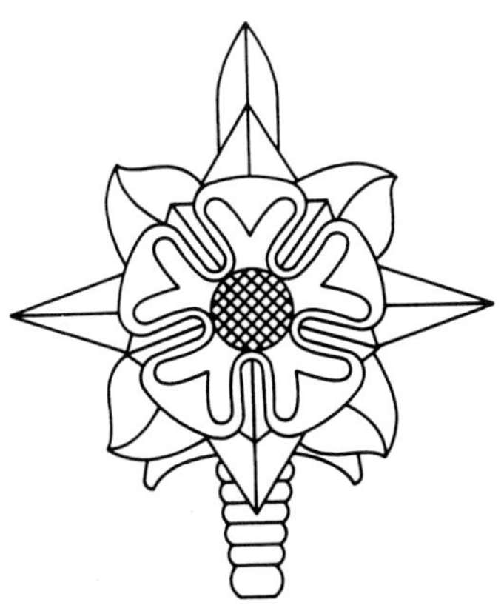

Military Intelligence Branch Insignia

Vietnam

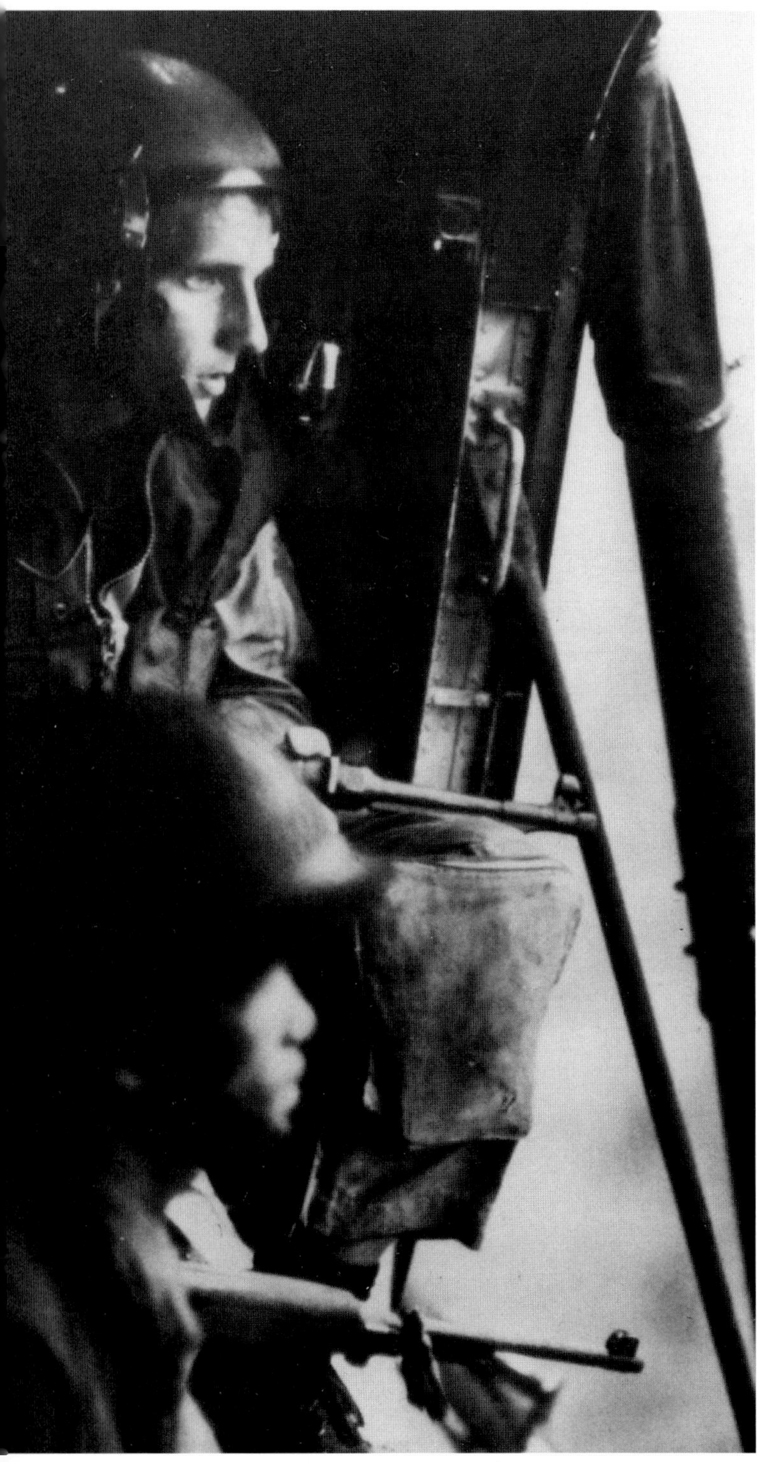

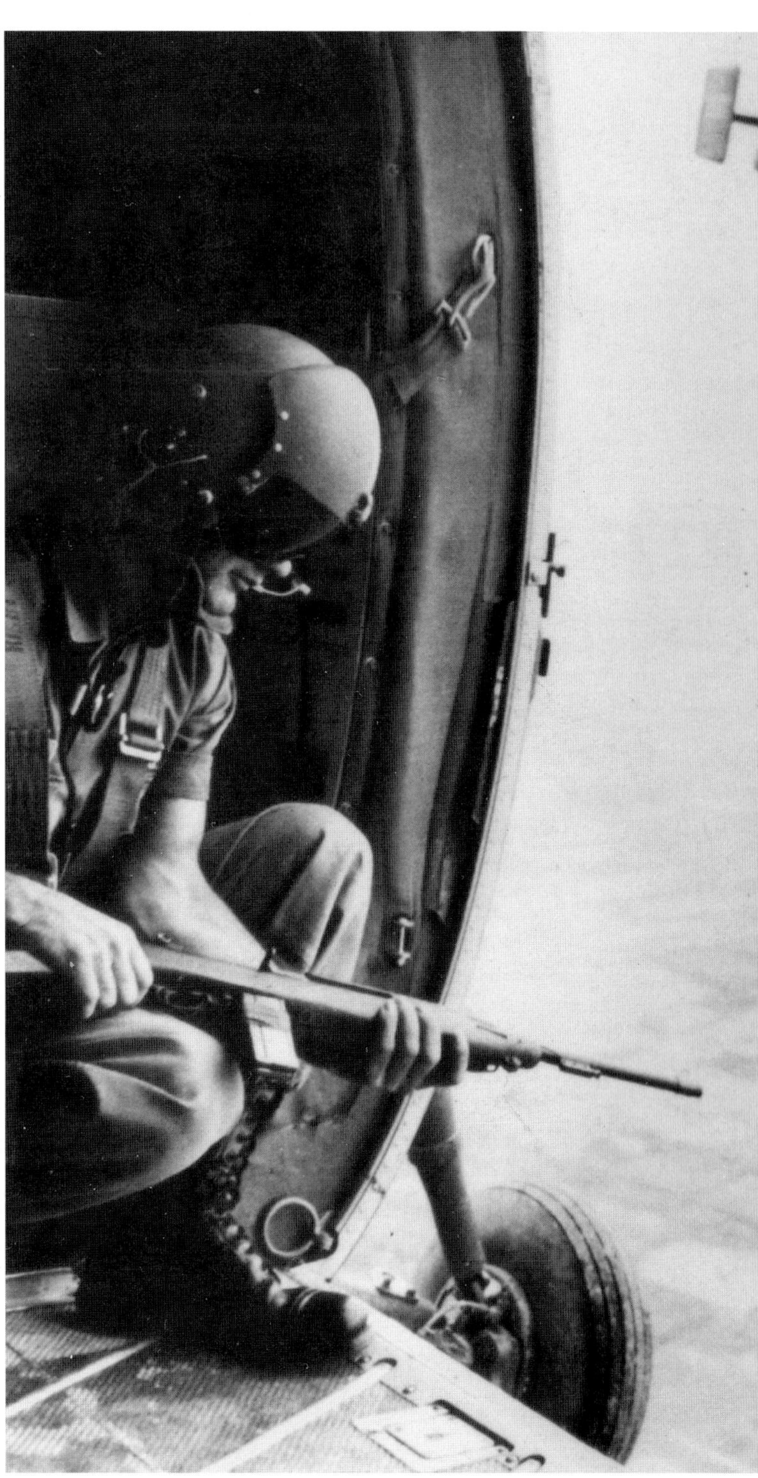

American helicopters ferry Army of the Republic of Vietnam (ARVN) troops and their U.S. advisors in an airborne assault on guerrilla positions. ARVN's lack of success soon drew America into a wider war.

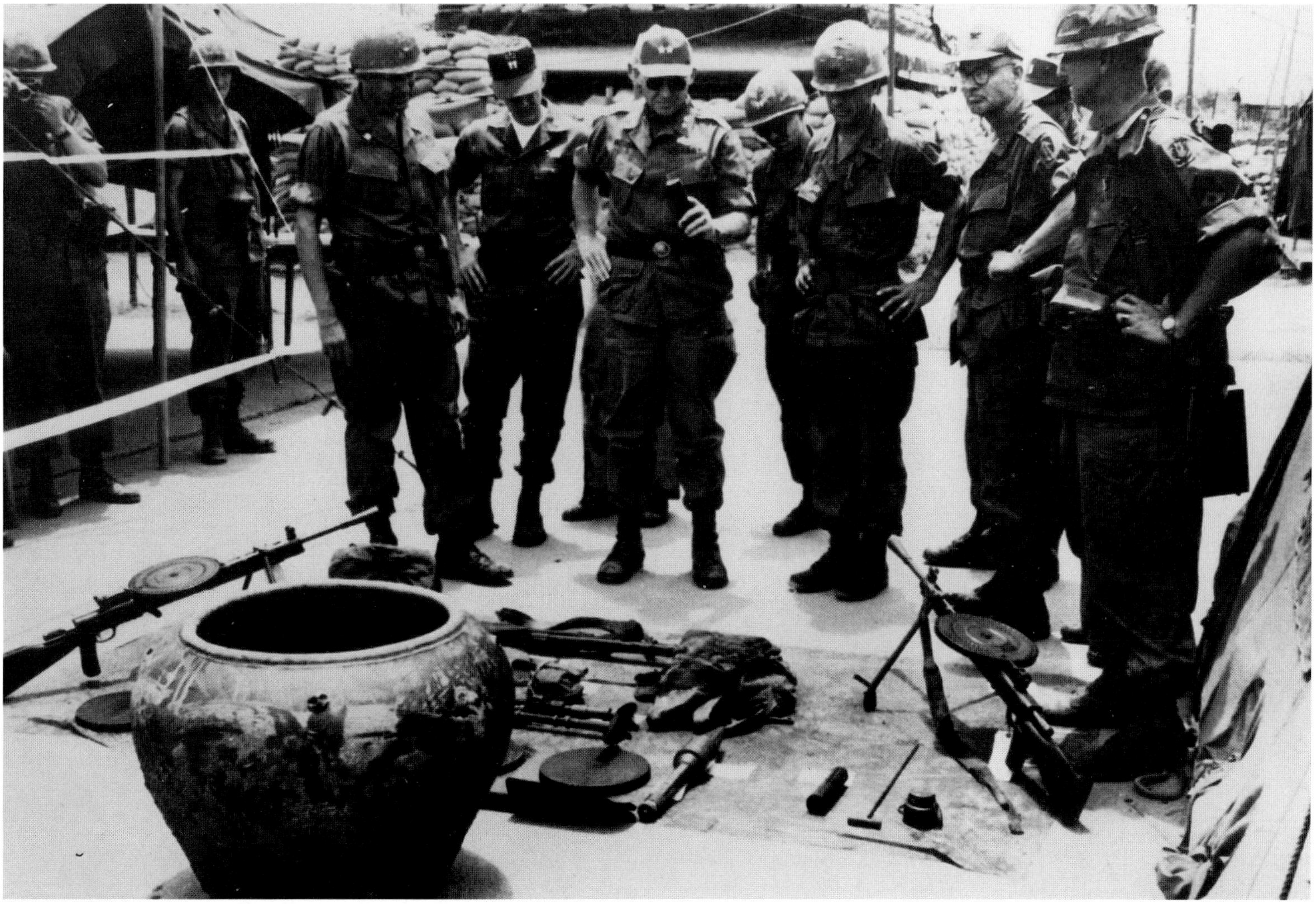

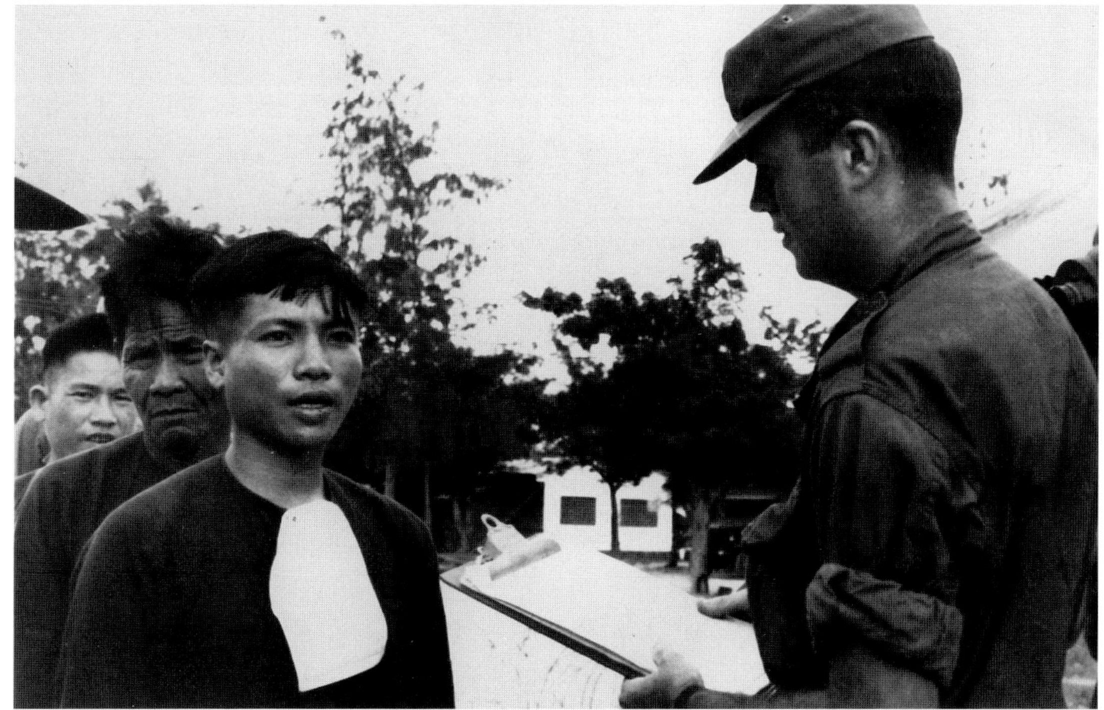

MG Joseph A. McChristian, J–2 of U.S. Military Assistance Command, Vietnam (MACV), inspects captured Viet Cong equipment.

An officer of the 191st Military Intelligence Detachment interrogates a captured Viet Cong.

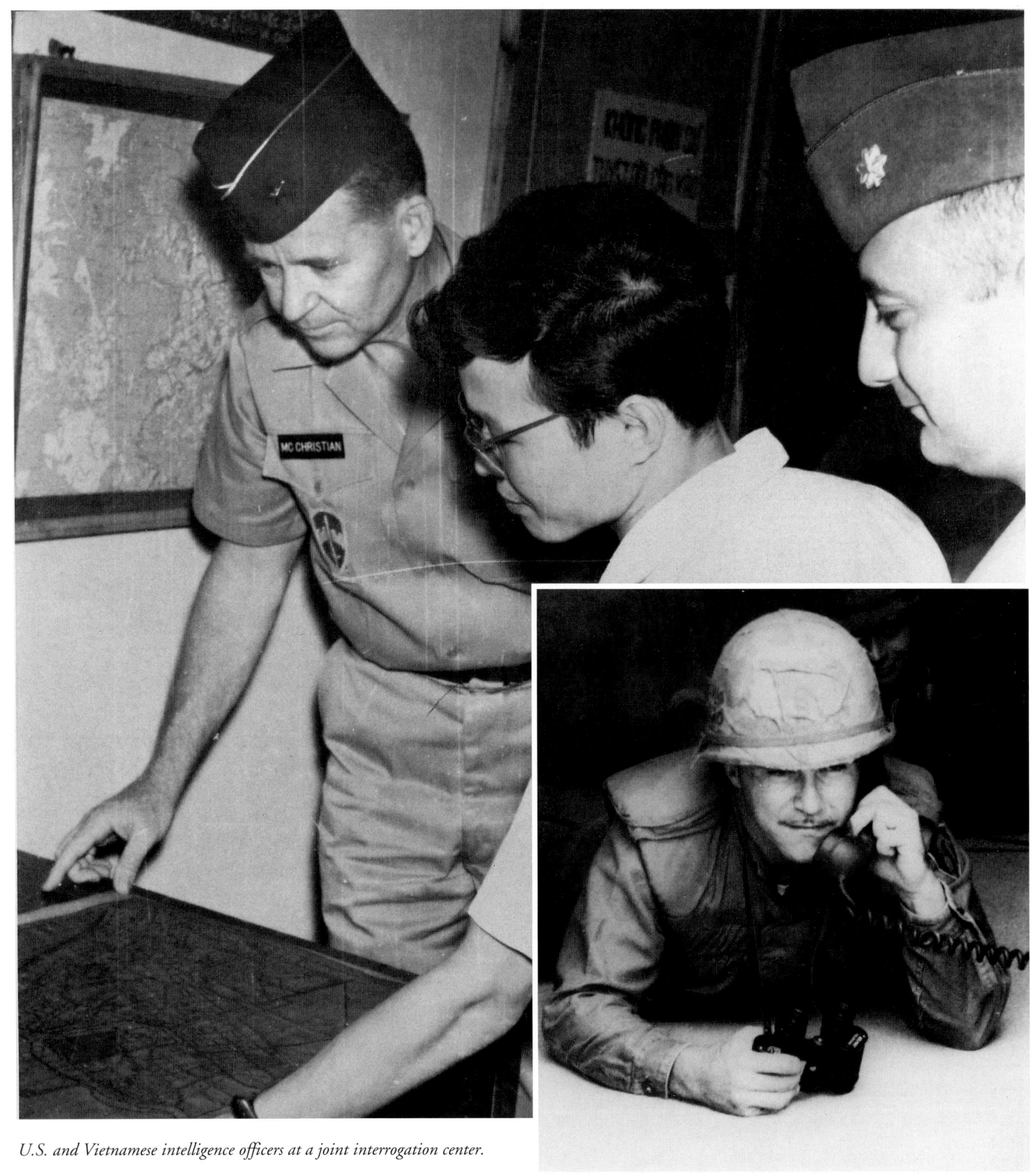

U.S. and Vietnamese intelligence officers at a joint interrogation center.

An officer of the 219th MI Company in Vietnam.

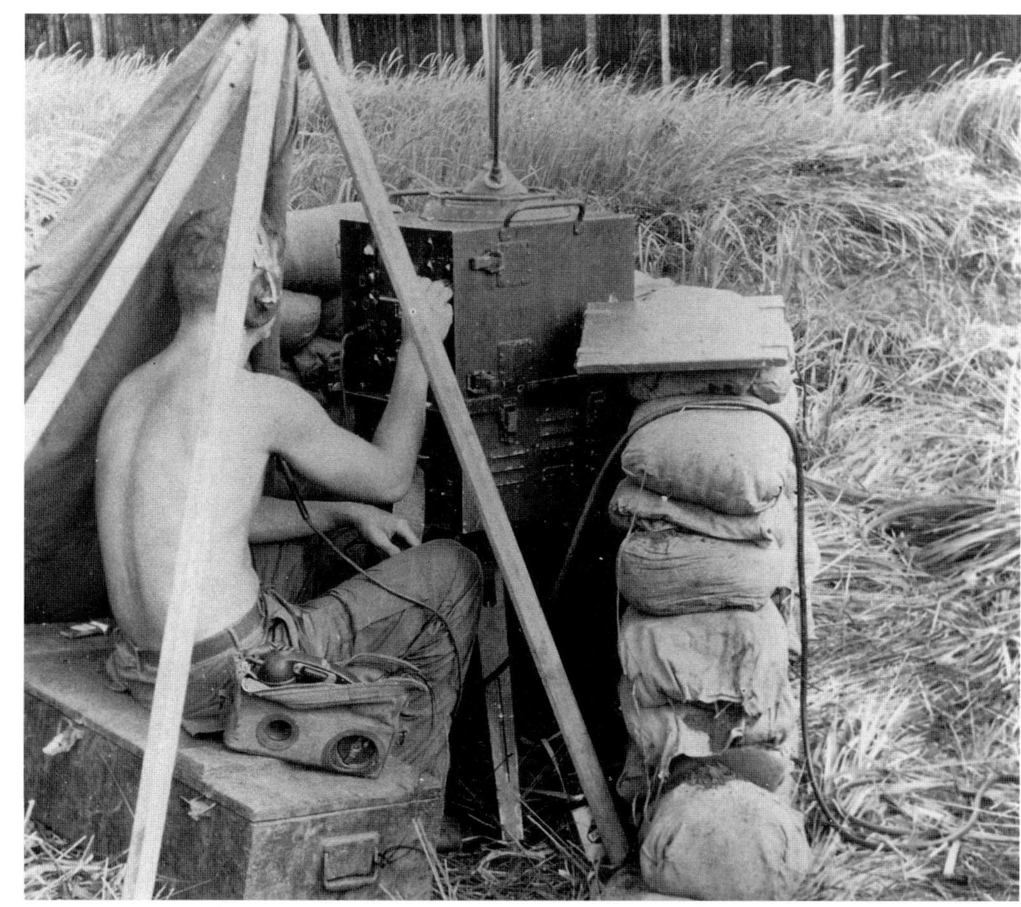

A direction-finding position of ASA's 407th Radio Research Detachment sets up in a field of elephant grass.

A helicopter equipped with the LEFT BANK collection system sits on the tarmac at Phuoc Vong.

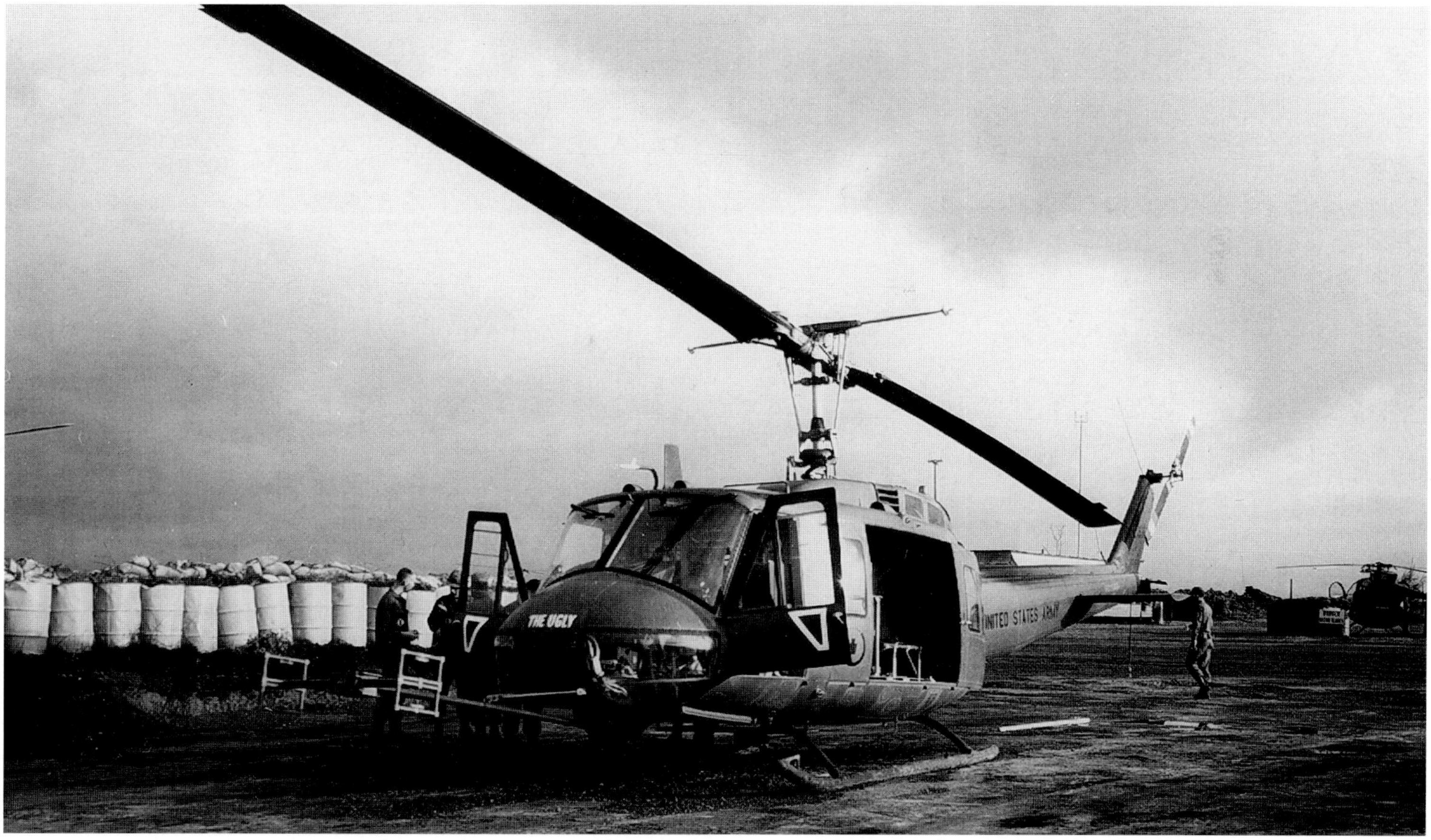

Transitions

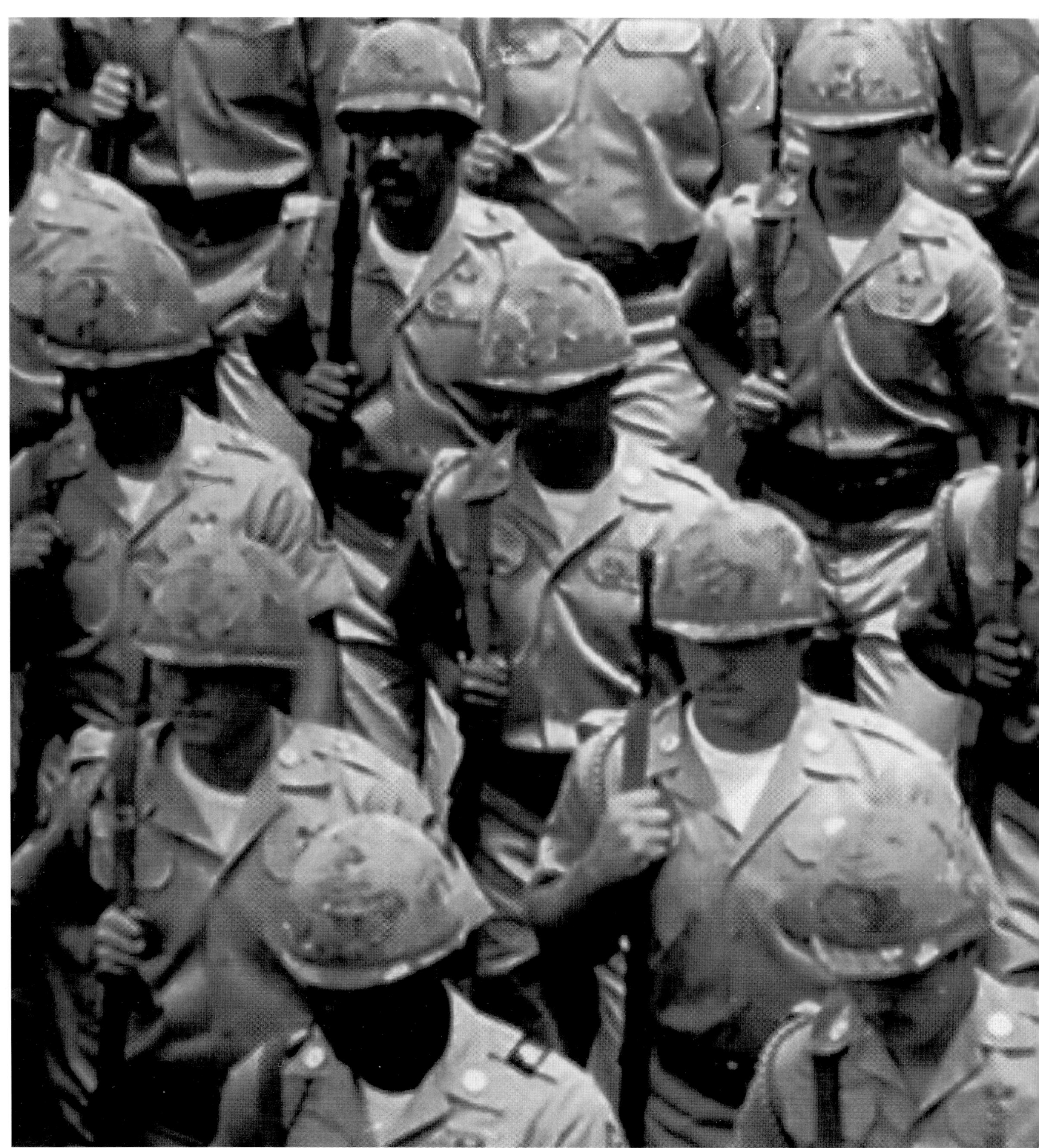

Part II

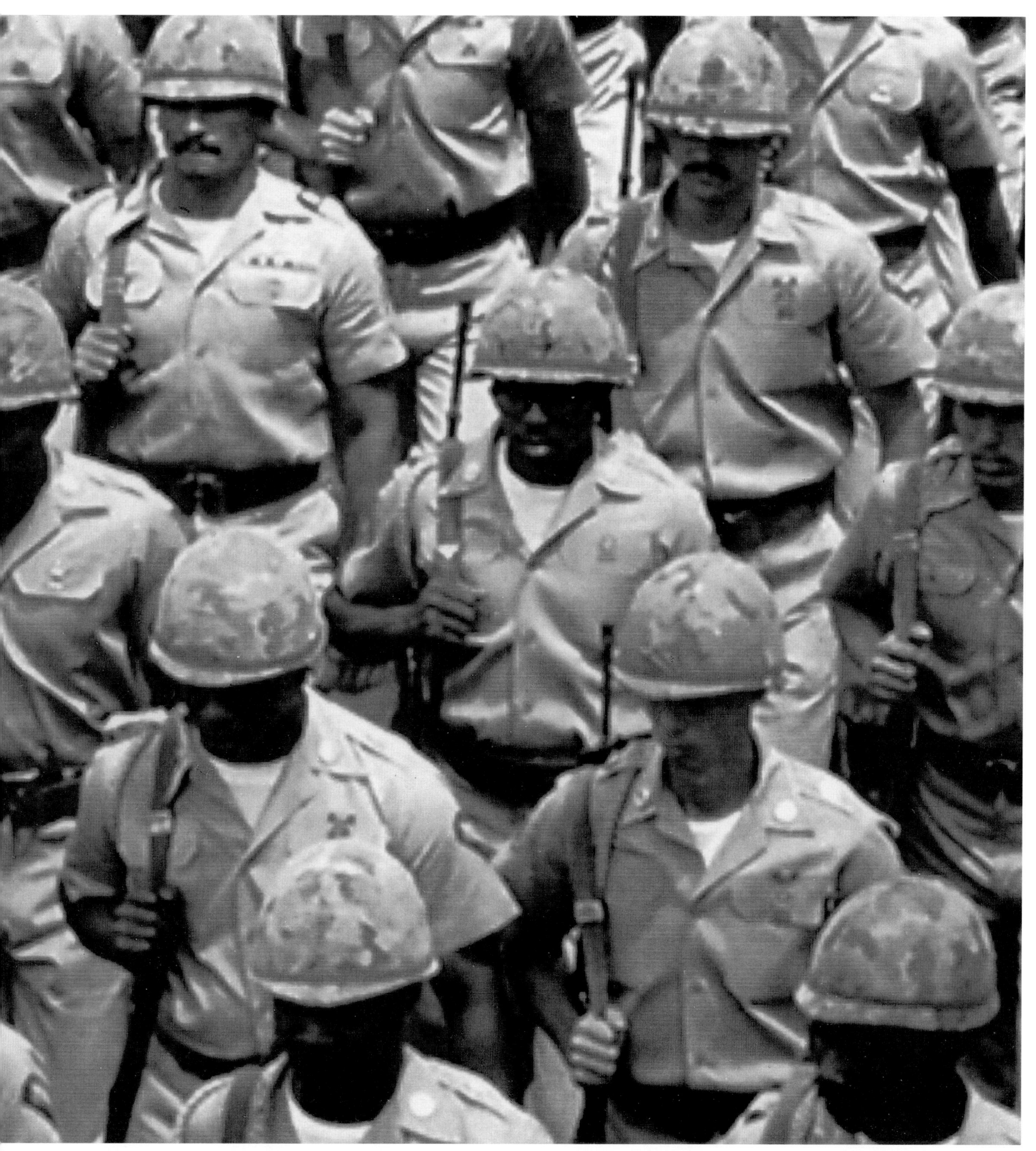

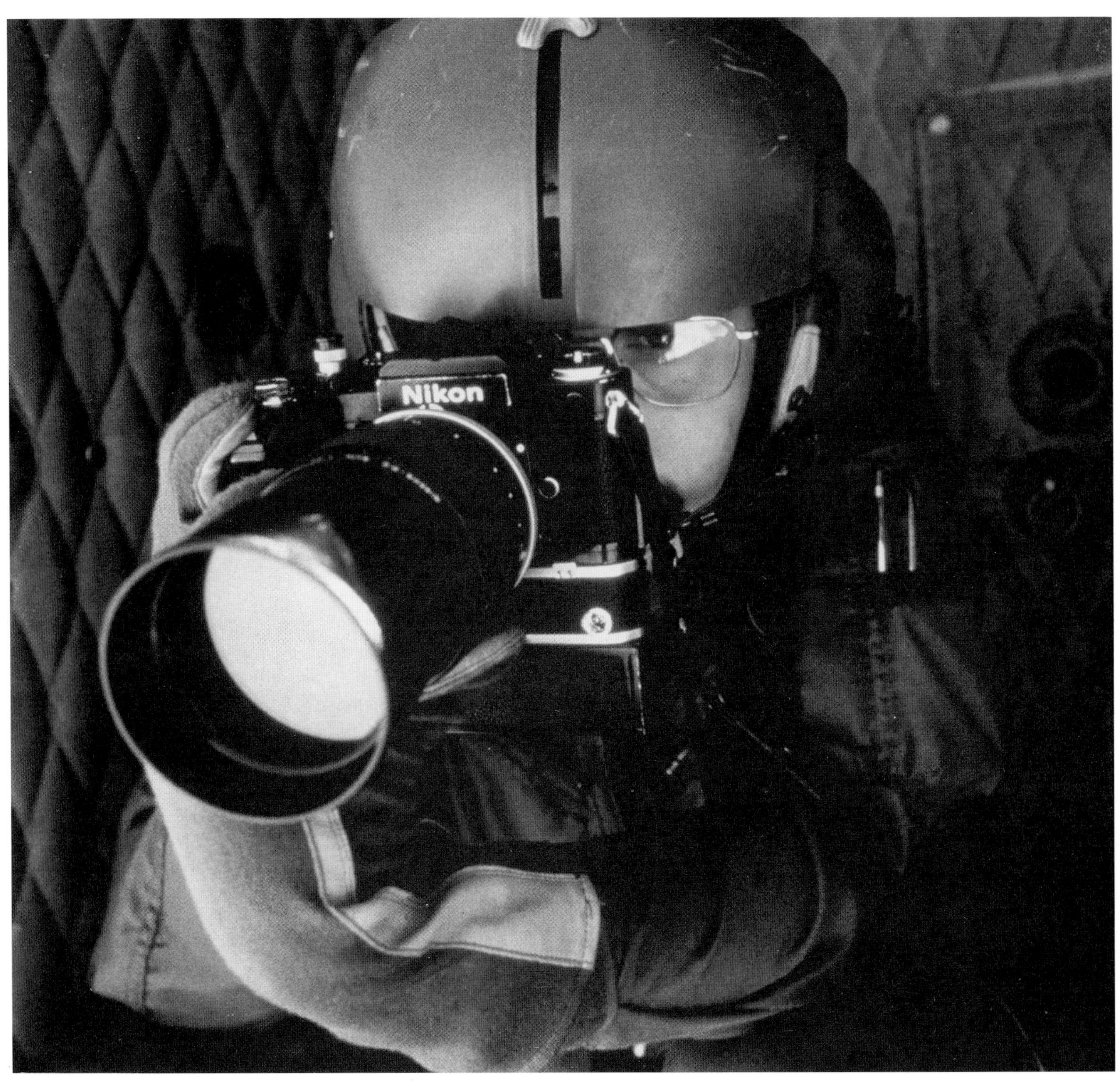

An Army aviator focuses a hand-held camera from his helicopter. The use of airborne platforms became increasingly important in carrying out the Military Intelligence mission.

Remaking An Army

The early 1970's was a time of troubles for the whole Army. The decision to stage a phased withdrawal from Vietnam led to a drastic decline in the force. In 1969, at the peak of the war, the Army had 1,500,000 men and women in its ranks. By 1973, this number had been reduced by almost half. There were serious morale problems, accompanied by incidents of drug abuse, racial unrest, and indiscipline. In 1972, Congress acceded to President Richard M. Nixon's recommendations and voted to terminate the draft, an action which eased tensions on the home front but which also effectively deprived the Army of access to much of the nation's pool of college-trained personnel and caused daunting problems of recruitment. Hostility to the military seemed to dominate the national mood.

Military intelligence was particularly hard hit. It was not only affected by the general drawdown of resources and the popular disillusionment with the military but by accusations that it had engaged in improper practices in the field of domestic intelligence. The termination of the draft was especially hurtful to military intelligence because of the special requirements of the intelligence sector for higher-caliber enlisted personnel. In response, the Army began to aggressively recruit women soldiers to fill intelligence positions.

This was a period of steady retrenchment. The U.S. Army Intelligence Command (USAINTC) was pared down in strength and mission until it lost its viability as a major Army command and then was replaced by the U.S. Army Intelligence Agency (USAINTA), a field operating agency of the Assistant Chief of Staff for Intelligence. The Army Security Agency gave up its traditional regional headquarters overseas and a number of stations it had manned for years were discontinued. The Army intelligence staff was also cut back.

At the same time, however, this was a period of redirection to meet new challenges. After the long distraction of Vietnam, military intelligence turned its attention once again to the need to satisfy requirements in the European Theater, America's most vital area of commitment. The Yom Kippur War of 1973 between Israel and her Arab neighbors clearly indicated that the Army would have to pay greater attention to electronic warfare (EW) in any future high-intensity conflict.

With so many elements of the intelligence situation in flux, the Chief of Staff decided that it was an opportune moment to initiate a study of the entire Army system for collecting intelligence and waging EW. The various elements in the system had been allowed to evolve in isolation. The Army Security Agency, the largest single intelligence element in the Army, traced its roots and operating style back to the Army Signal Corps. The U.S. Army Intelligence Agency carried on the traditions of the old Counter Intelligence Corps. Arrangements for training Military Intelligence personnel reflected this divided heritage. It was now time for a general reassessment, to make sure that the Army's needs in the intelligence arena were being met in the most efficient and cost-effective way. The Intelligence Organization and Stationing Study (IOSS), which the Chief of Staff directed at the end of 1974, led to the most sweeping reorganization of military intelligence in a generation.

Ending A Conflict

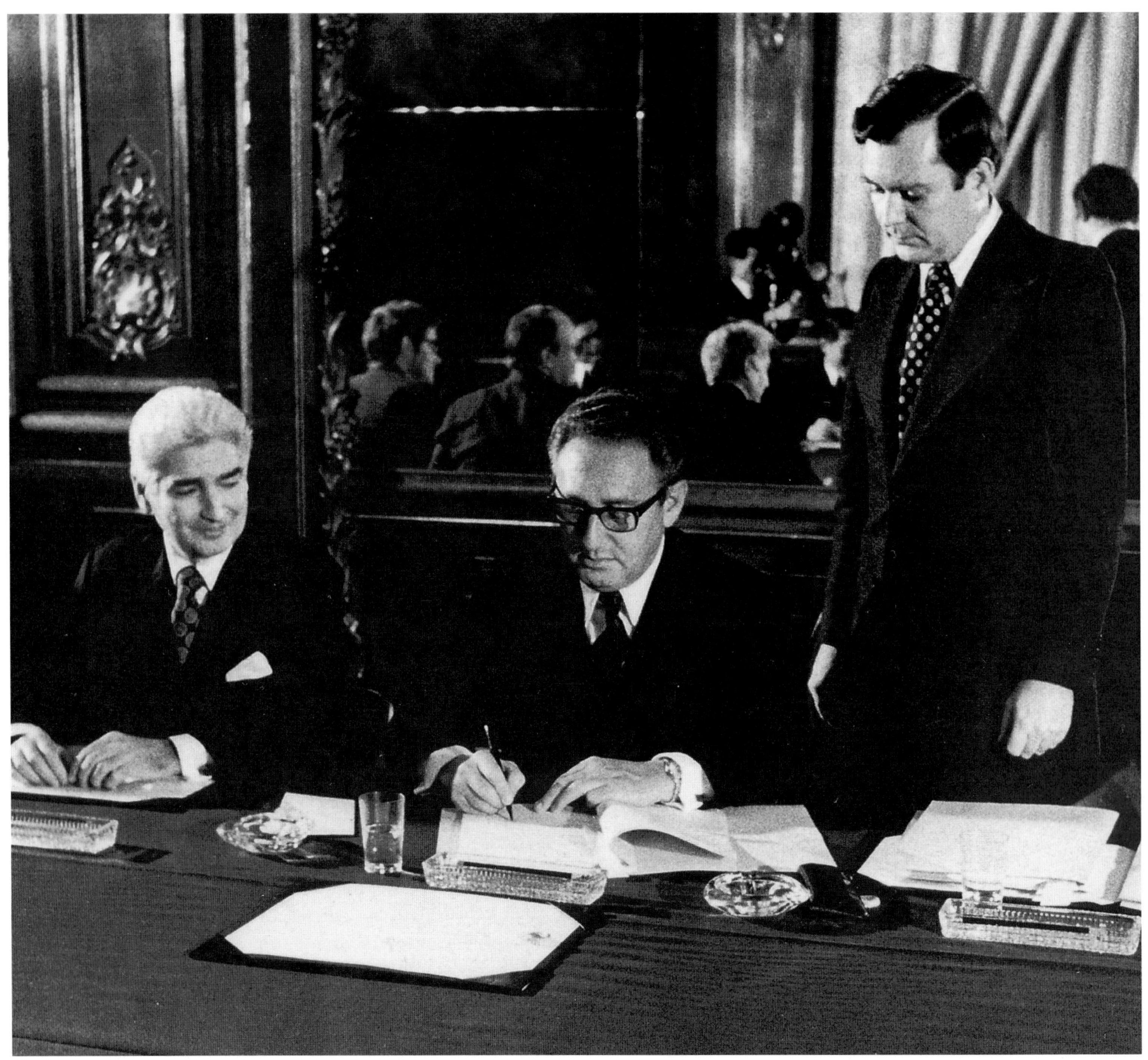

Protracted negotiations with North Vietnam eventually led to American diplomats signing a peace settlement in Paris in 1973. Meanwhile, overall Army strength contracted steadily as U.S. troop units were withdrawn from Vietnam.

Drawing Down

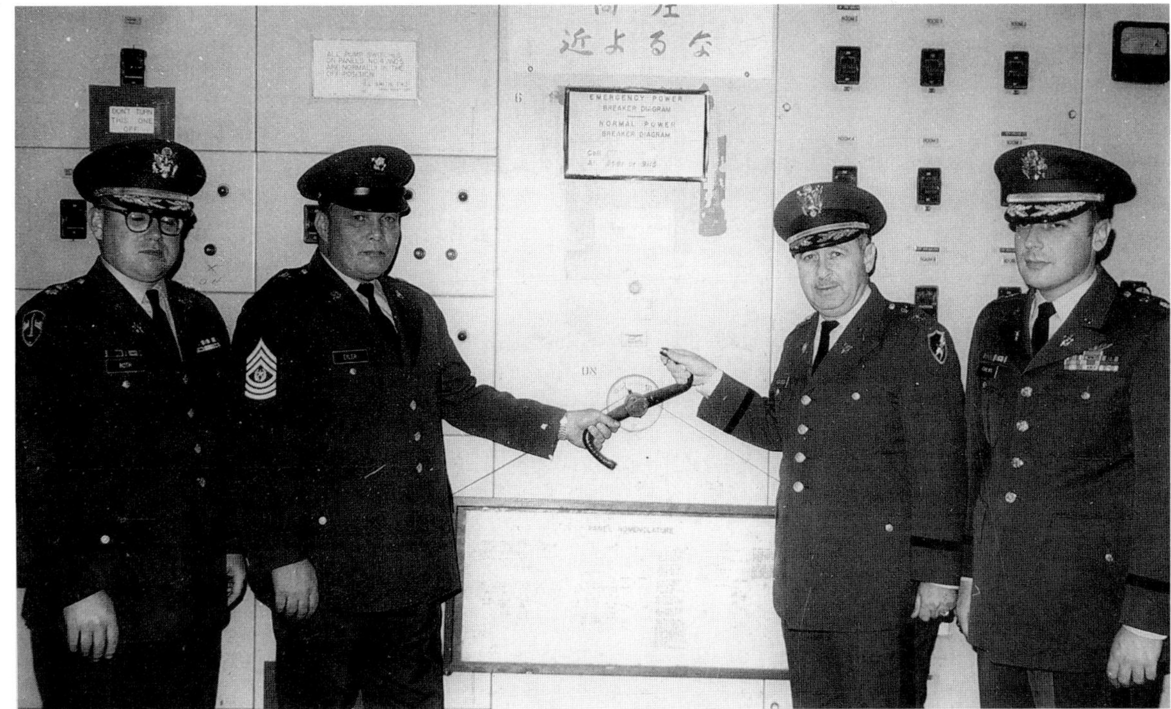

Turning out the lights. Officers prepare to turn off the main power switch of U.S. Army Security Agency Field Station Hakata, Japan, which was discontinued in 1972 as part of an overall ASA drawdown.

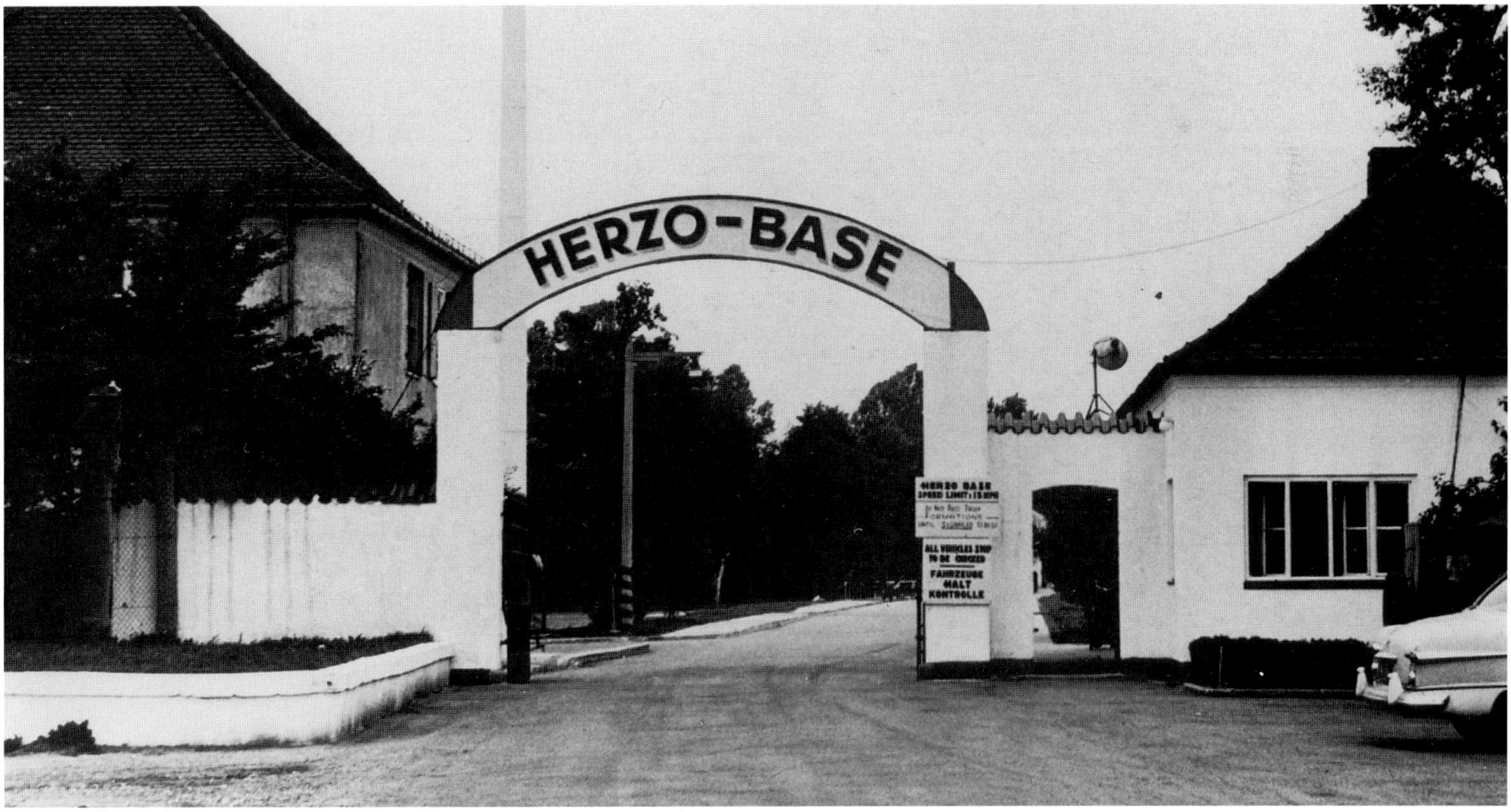

U.S. Army Security Agency Field Station Herzogenaurach was one of three ASA fixed sites in the Federal Republic of Germany to be discontinued in 1972. Missions were consolidated in a new facility at Augsburg.

The All-Volunteer Force

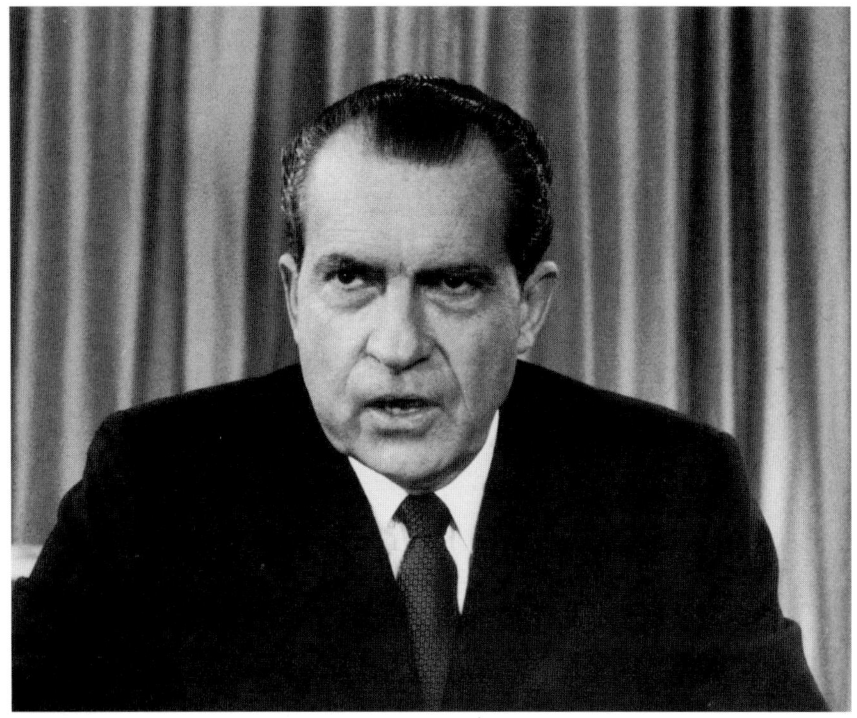

In 1972, President Richard M. Nixon recommended that Congress terminate the draft and institute an All Volunteer Force.

Ever since World War II, the United States had relied on Selective Service to fill the Army's ranks in peace and war. The abrupt transition to an All Volunteer Force posed particular challenges for MI.

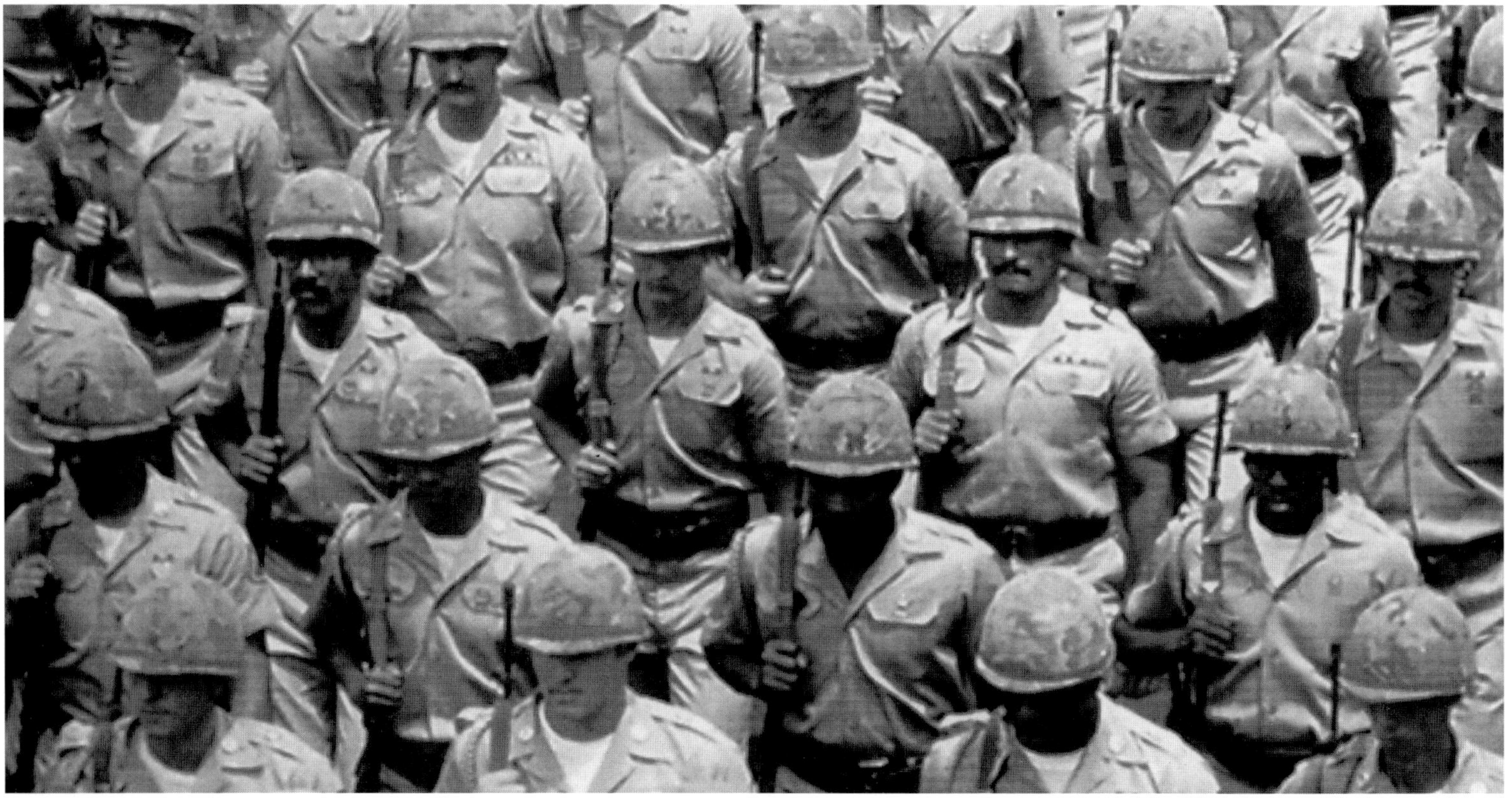

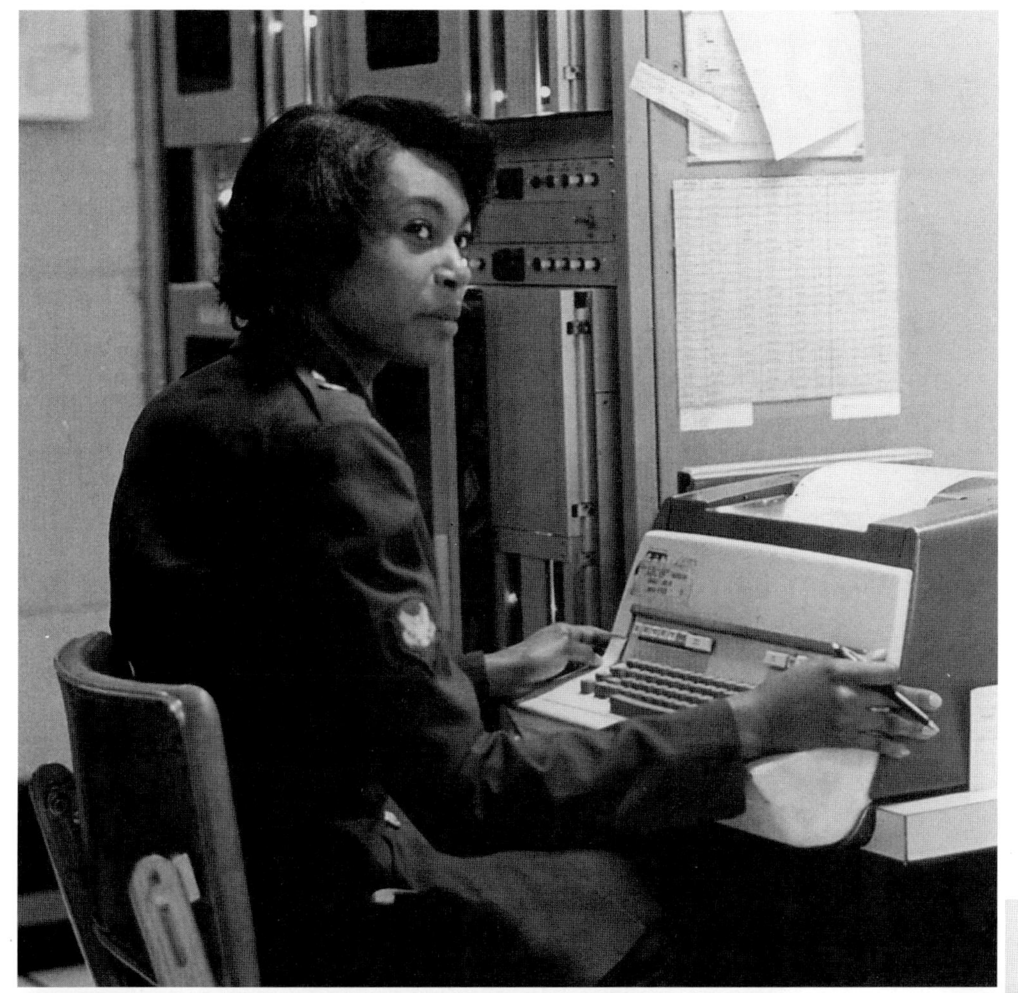

The Women's Army Corps was discontinued in 1976. Within MI, female soldiers began to take their place alongside their male counterparts as fully equal members of the Army team. A female intelligence specialist at Field Station Augsburg in 1977.

Creation of an all-volunteer force changed Army life-styles, as barracks were replaced by dormitories. The room of a female soldier of the CONUS Military Intelligence Group at Fort George G. Meade, Maryland.

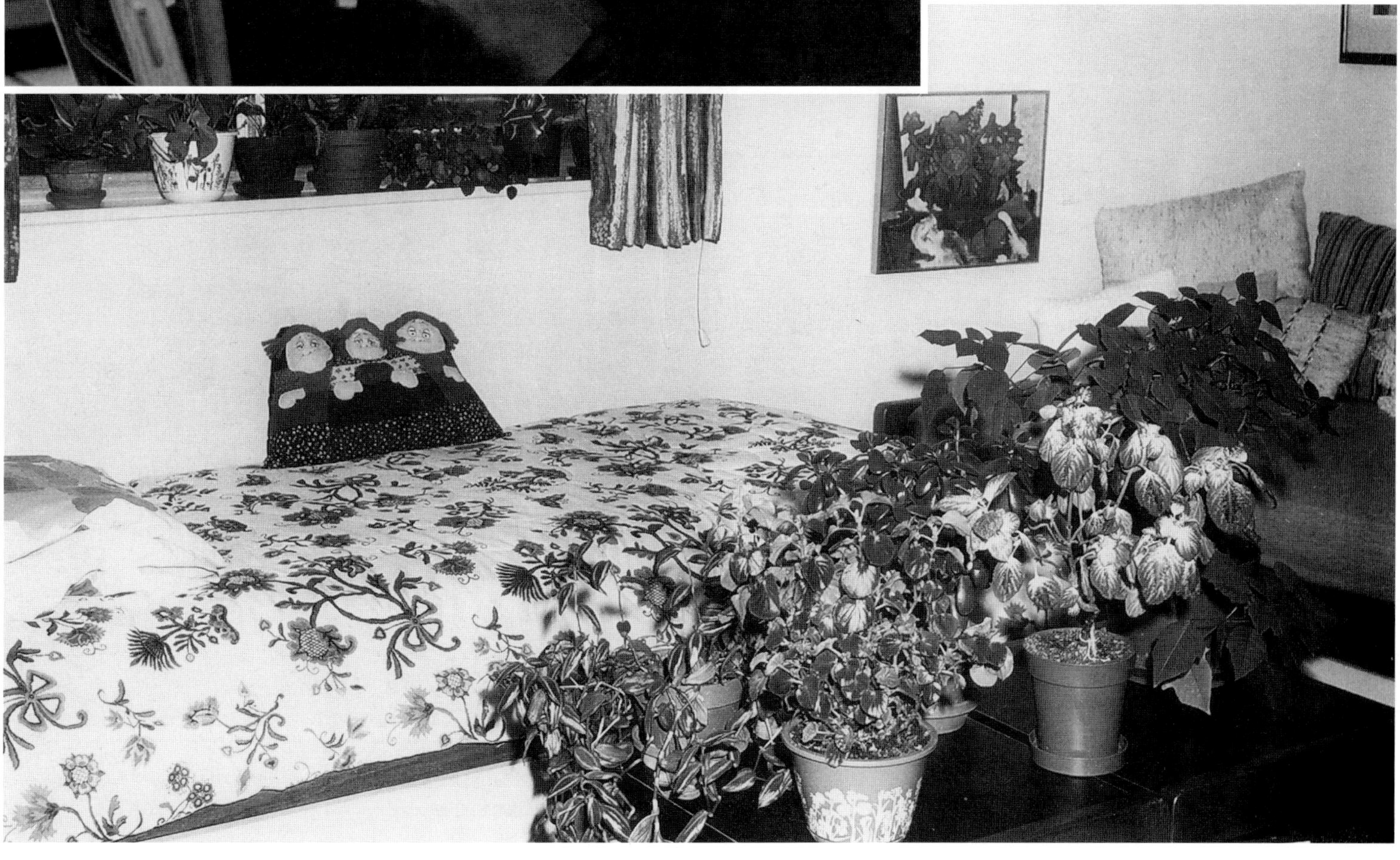

New Directions

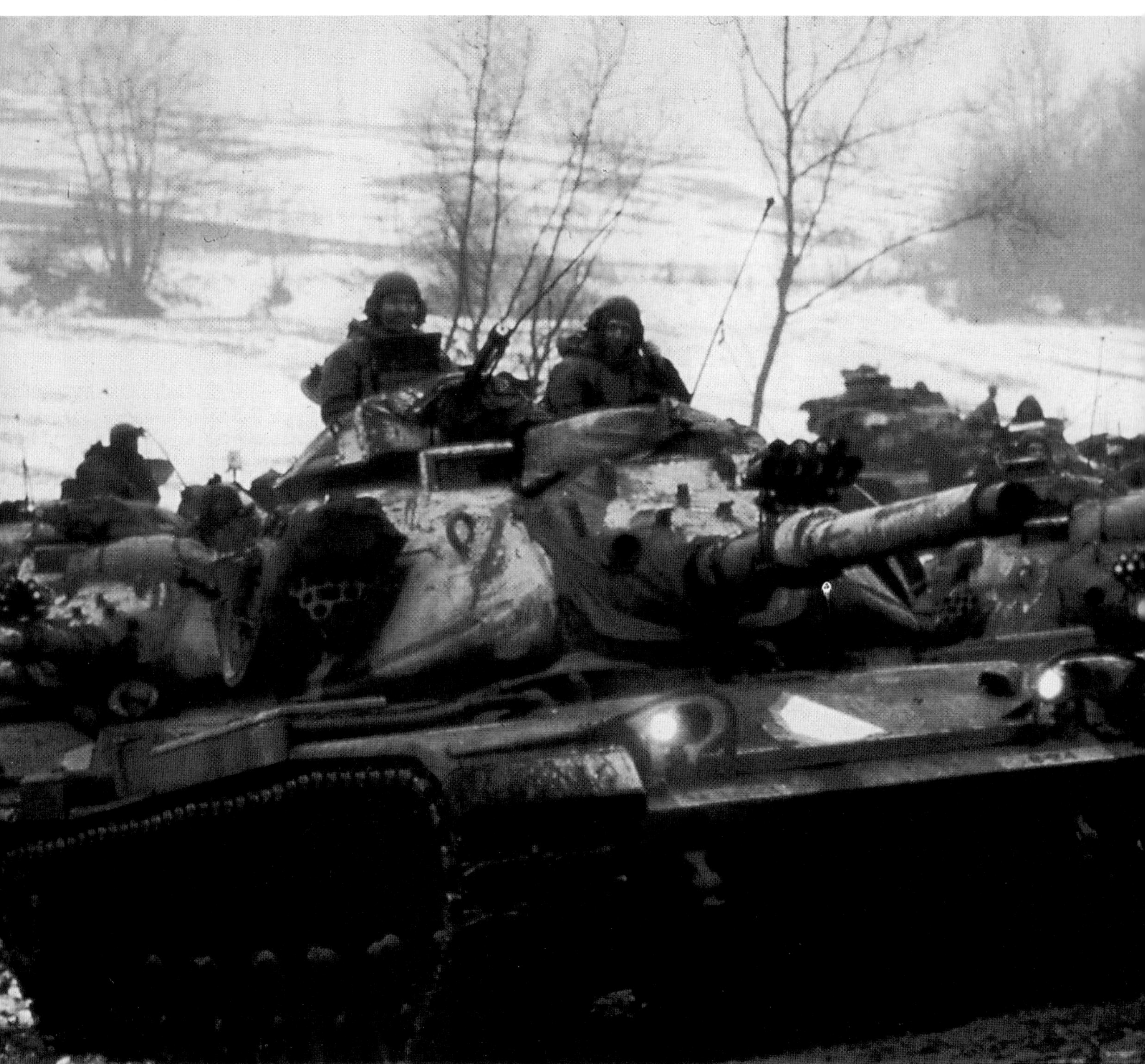

M–60 tanks on maneuver in Germany. Following the termination of the Vietnam conflict, the Army focused on the formidable challenge of meeting its NATO commitments by defending the European heartland against an overwhelming Warsaw Pact superiority.

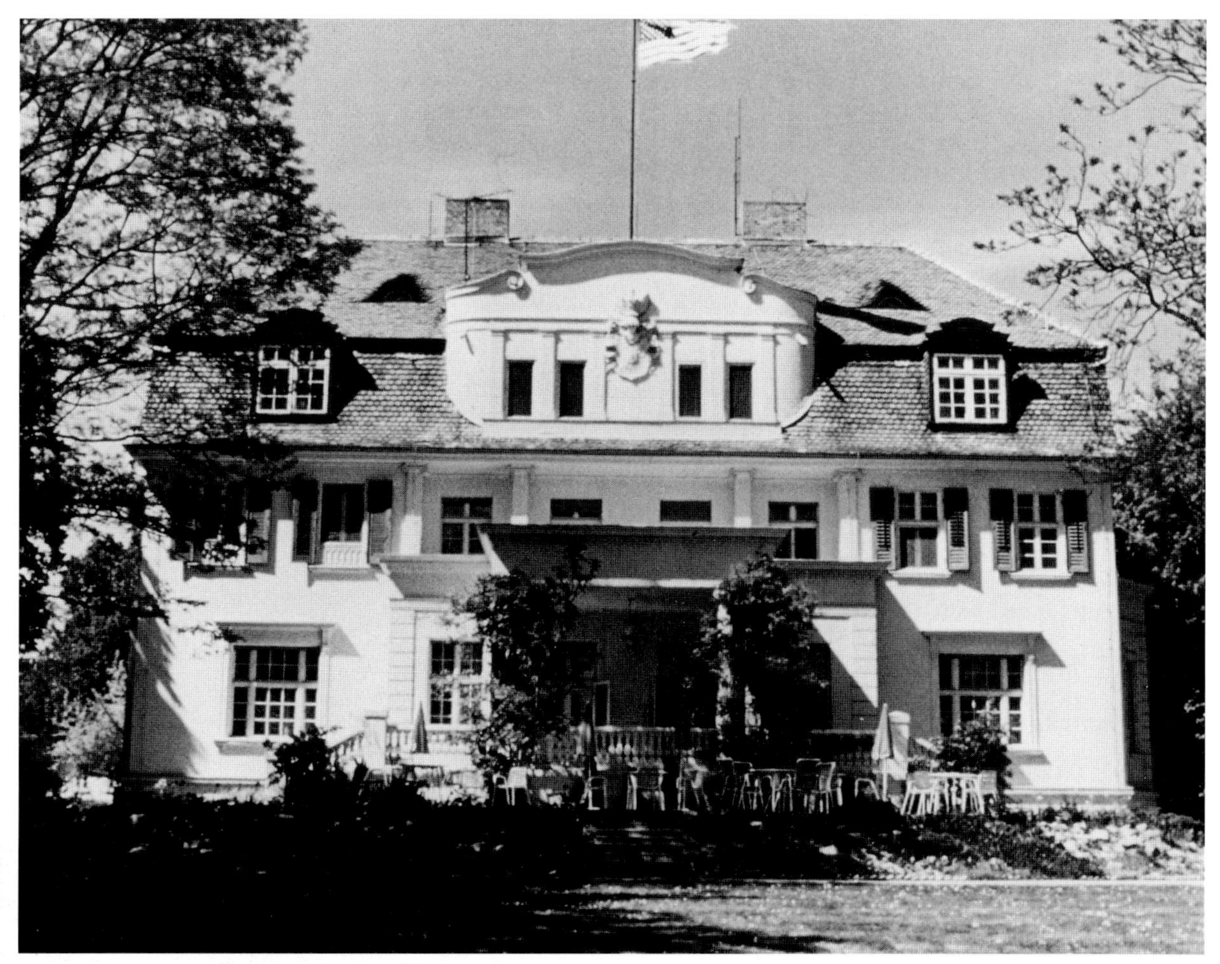

Headquarters of the U.S. Military Liaison Mission at Potsdam, German Democratic Republic. Established in 1947, the mission continued to provide the Army with a window behind the Iron Curtain throughout the course of the Cold War.

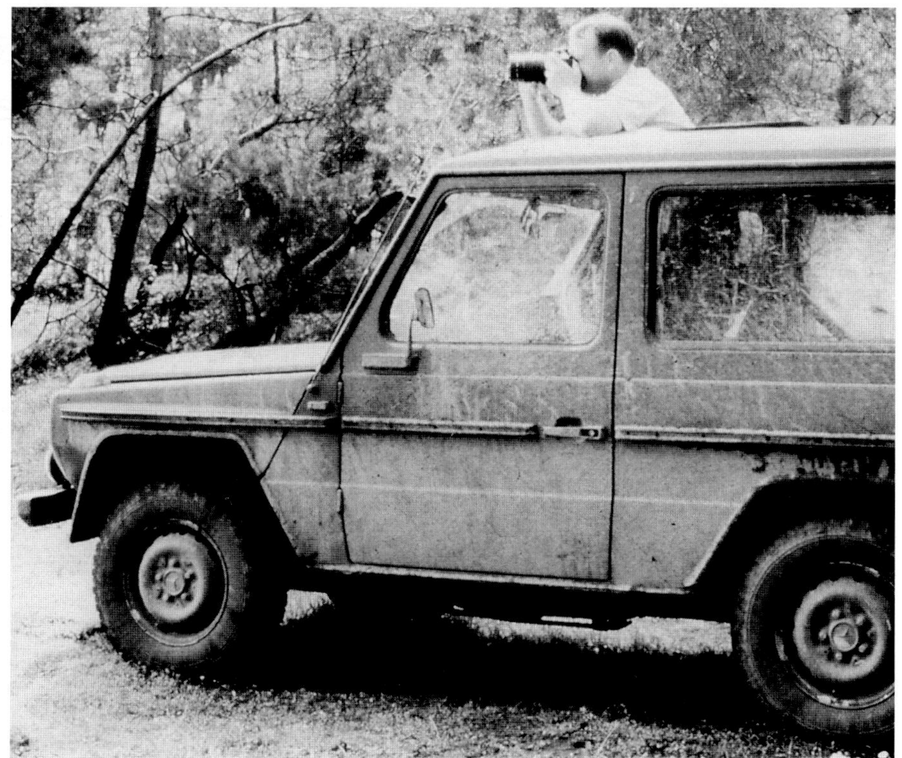

A member of the U.S. Military Liaison Mission conducts surveillance operations.

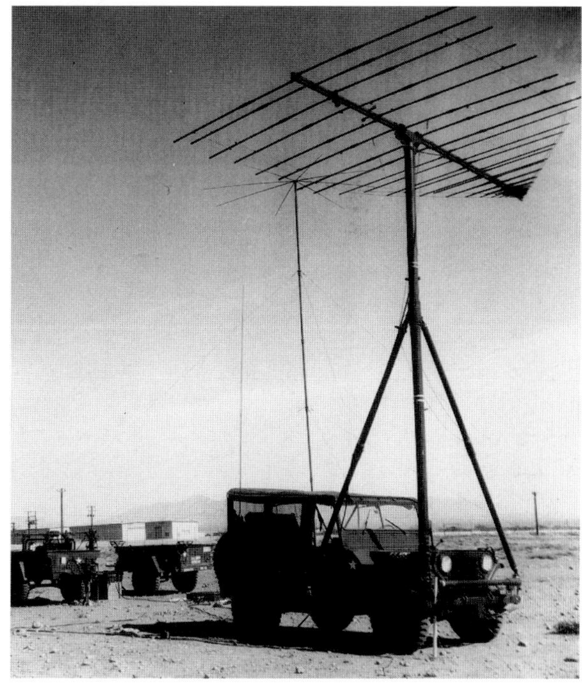

A TLQ–17 jammer fielded by the Army Security Agency. The Yom Kippur War of 1973 demonstrated to the Army the nature of high intensity war and especially the need for a greater emphasis on electronic warfare.

Rebuilding Military Intelligence

THE LARGEST SINGLE ELEMENT WITHIN Military Intelligence in the 1970's was the Army Security Agency (ASA). It had been established in 1945 to exercise centralized control over all Army cryptologic assets, and its responsibilities had been further enhanced in 1955 when it assumed the electronic warfare mission. In 1964, it became a major Army field command.

The U.S. Army Security Agency was a unique institution within the Army. ASA headquarters controlled all cryptologic installations, units, and personnel through a verticalized, "stovepipe" command structure. The agency conducted its own research and development, operated its own training school, and managed its own personnel system. All of this was done behind a high wall of secrecy, symbolized by the mythical "Green Door" that shielded ASA operations from the rest of the Army.

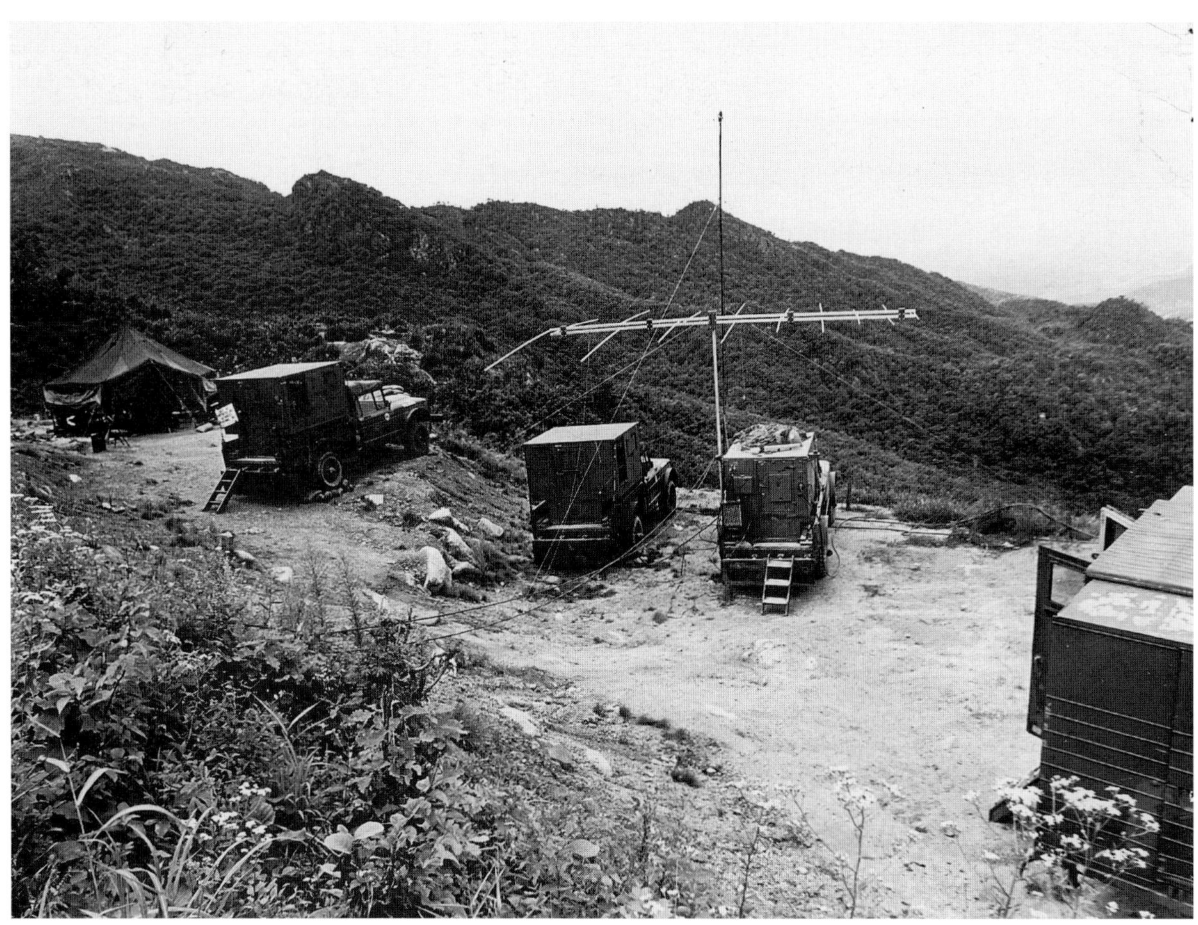

Field operations are conducted by Detachment M, U.S. Army Field Station Korea.

ASA

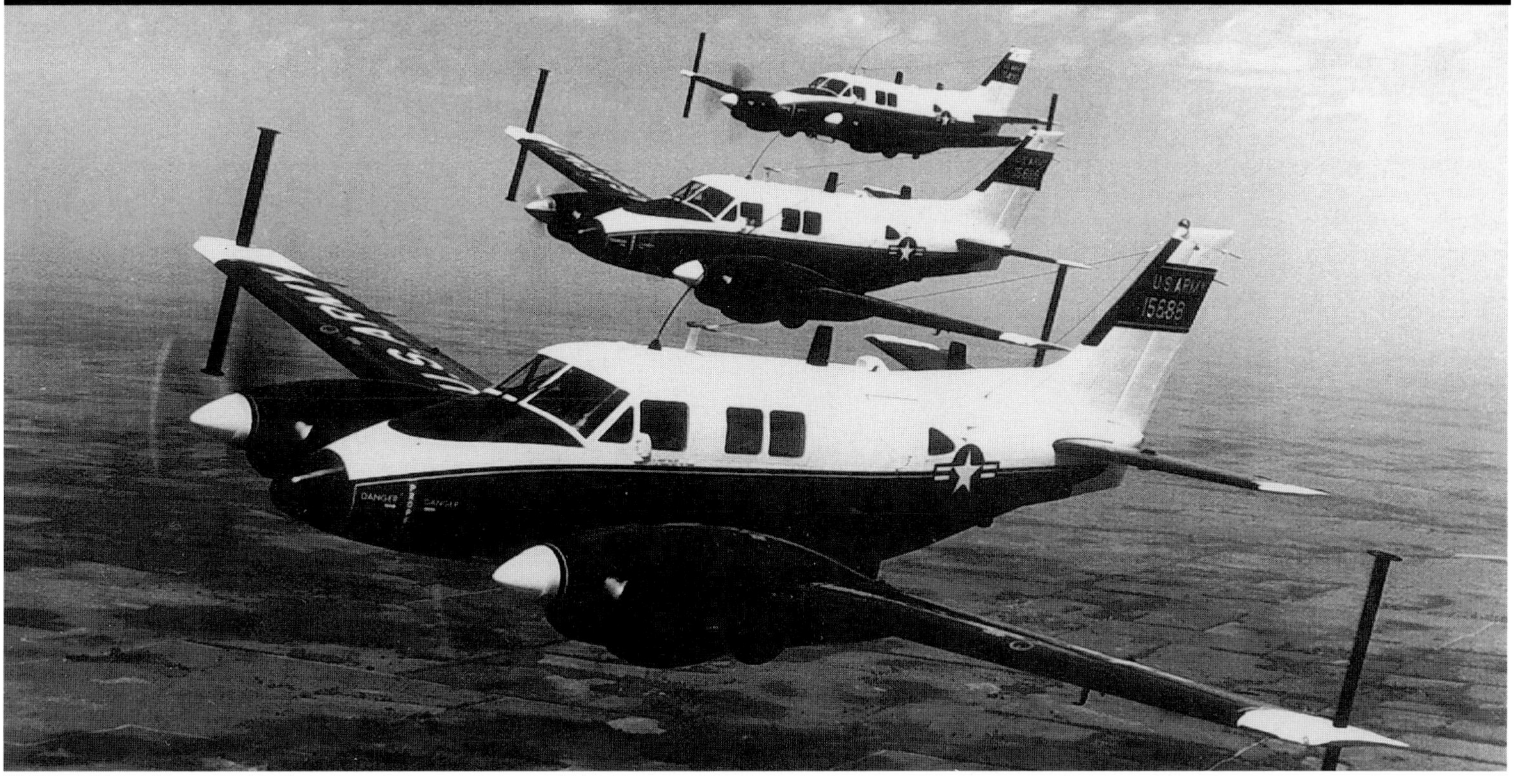

By the 1970's, ASA had taken to the skies. A flight of U–21 Special Electronic Mission Aircraft (SEMA) from the 156th ASA Company (Aviation).

An antenna array at U.S. Army Field Station Homestead.

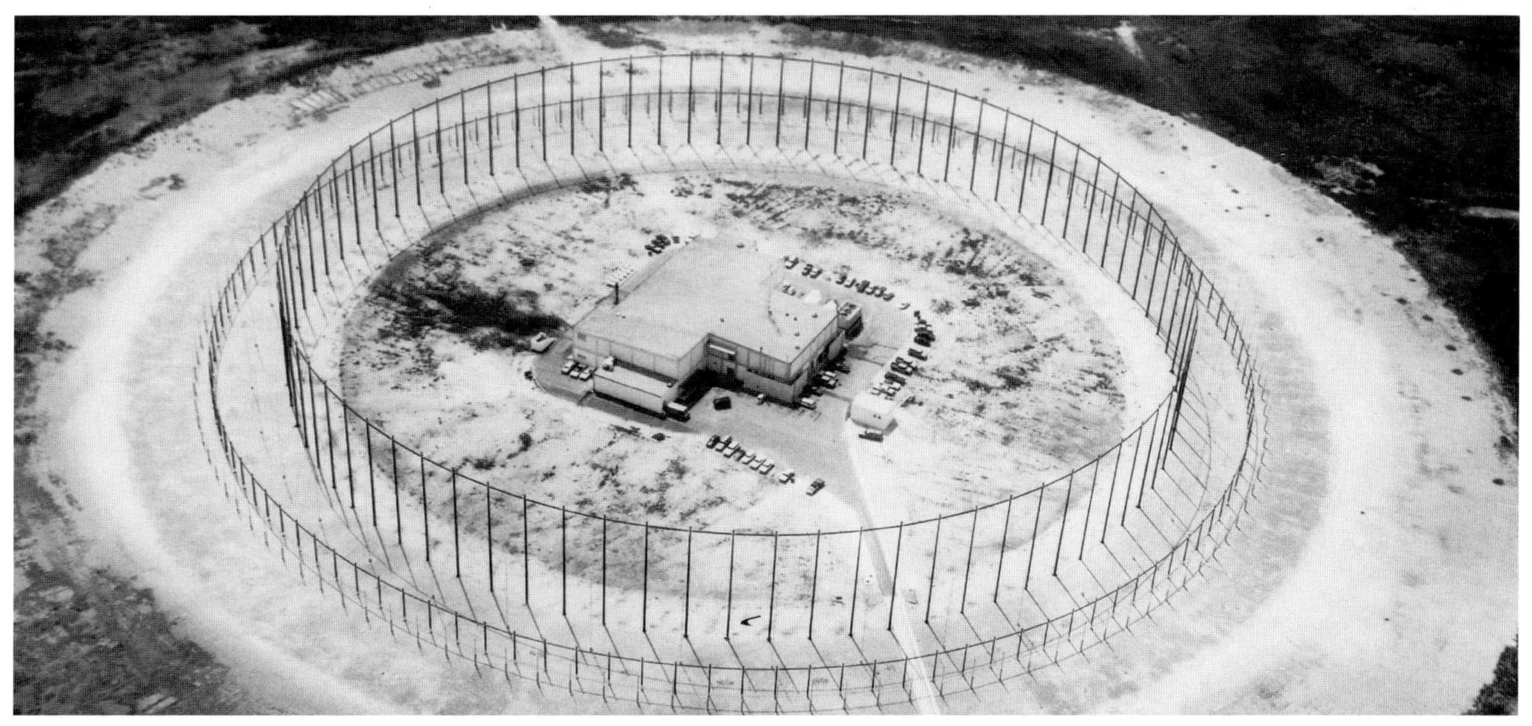

USAINTC/USAINTA

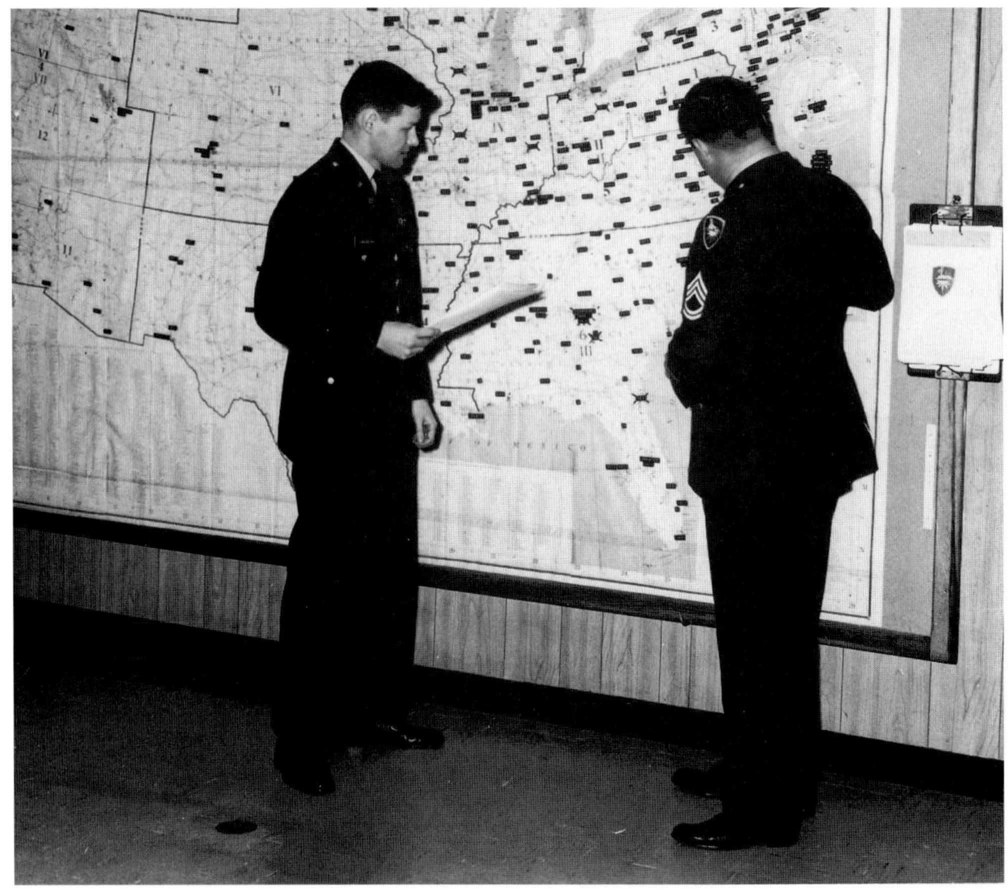

This operations room at USAINTC's Fort Holabird headquarters served as the command's nerve center in the troubled times of the 1960's. The command relocated to Fort George G. Meade, Maryland, in 1973.

THE ARMY'S PRINCIPAL COUNTERINTELLIGENCE and human intelligence organization in the Continental United States was the U. S. Army Intelligence Agency (USAINTA), a field operating agency operating under the control of the Assistant Chief of Staff for Intelligence. USAINTA was the successor organization to the larger U.S. Army Intelligence Command (USAINTC), which had been created in 1965 to control all Army counterintelligence operations in CONUS. During the course of the Vietnam War, near-chaotic conditions in inner cities and campuses had led the nation's political leadership to embark on the collection of domestic intelligence. When USAINTC's activities in this field became public in the early 1970's, there was a sharp and critical public reaction. The domestic intelligence program was discontinued, and a new civilian agency, the Defense Investigative Service, took over the mission of performing personnel background investigations which previously had constituted much of USAINTC's workload. Army counterintelligence activities in CONUS were retrenched to the point that they no longer warranted control by a major field command. Accordingly, USAINTC was discontinued in 1974, and replaced by USAINTA.

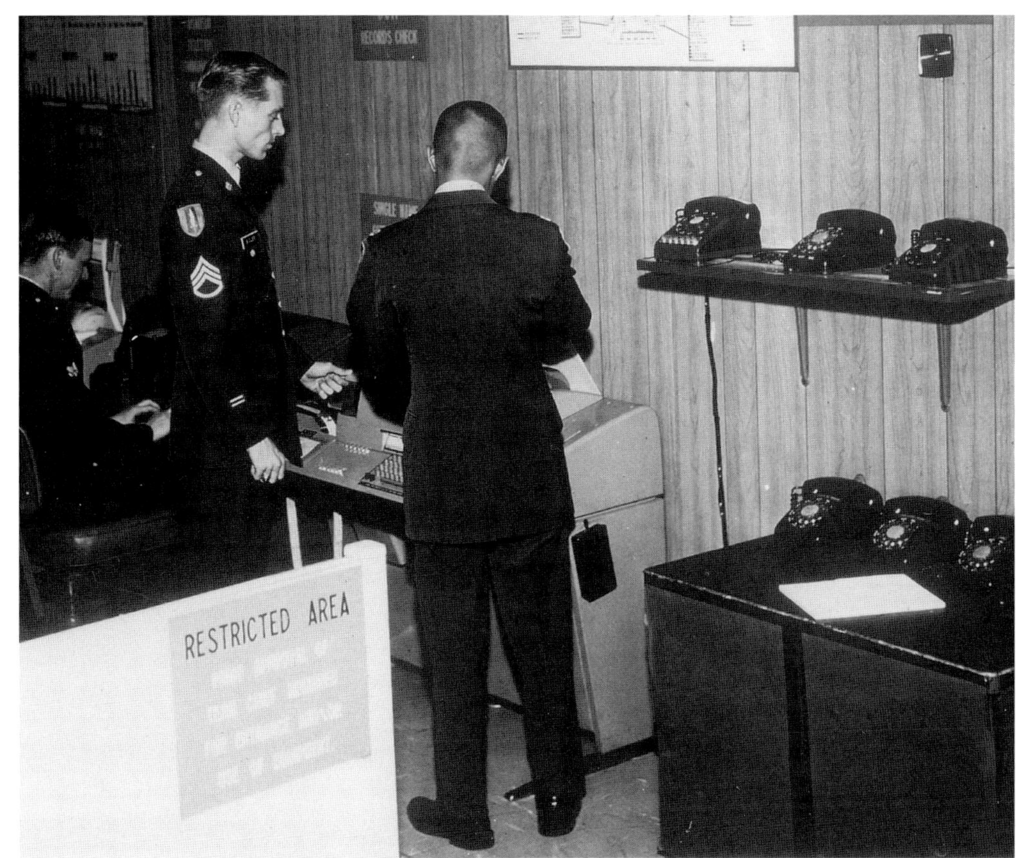

The USAINTC communications center linked headquarters with the Department of the Army and its seven subordinate counterintelligence groups in CONUS. By the time USAINTA was organized, all but two of the groups had been inactivated.

An Army counterintelligence agent checks in with his headquarters from an unmarked civilian vehicle.

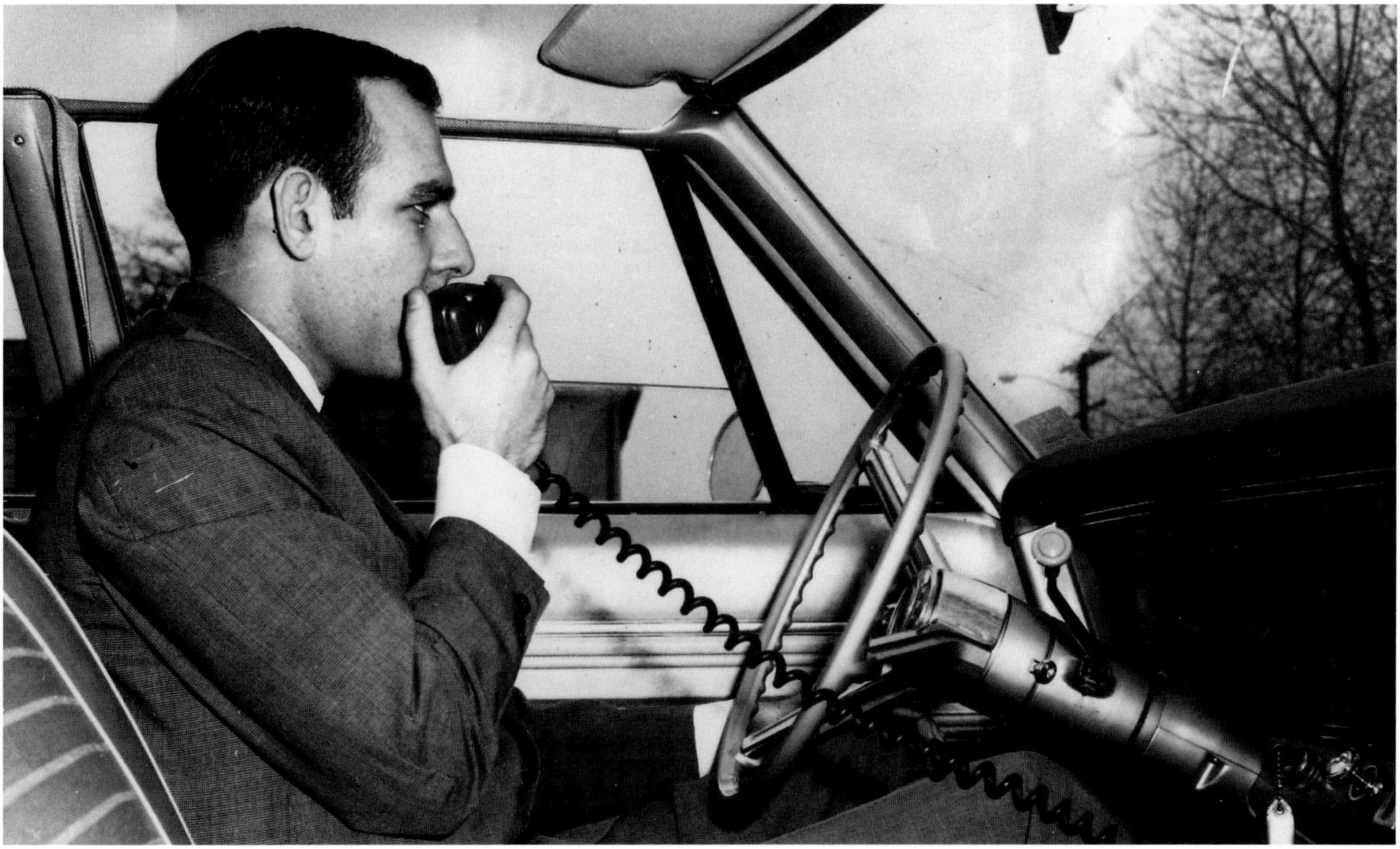

Training

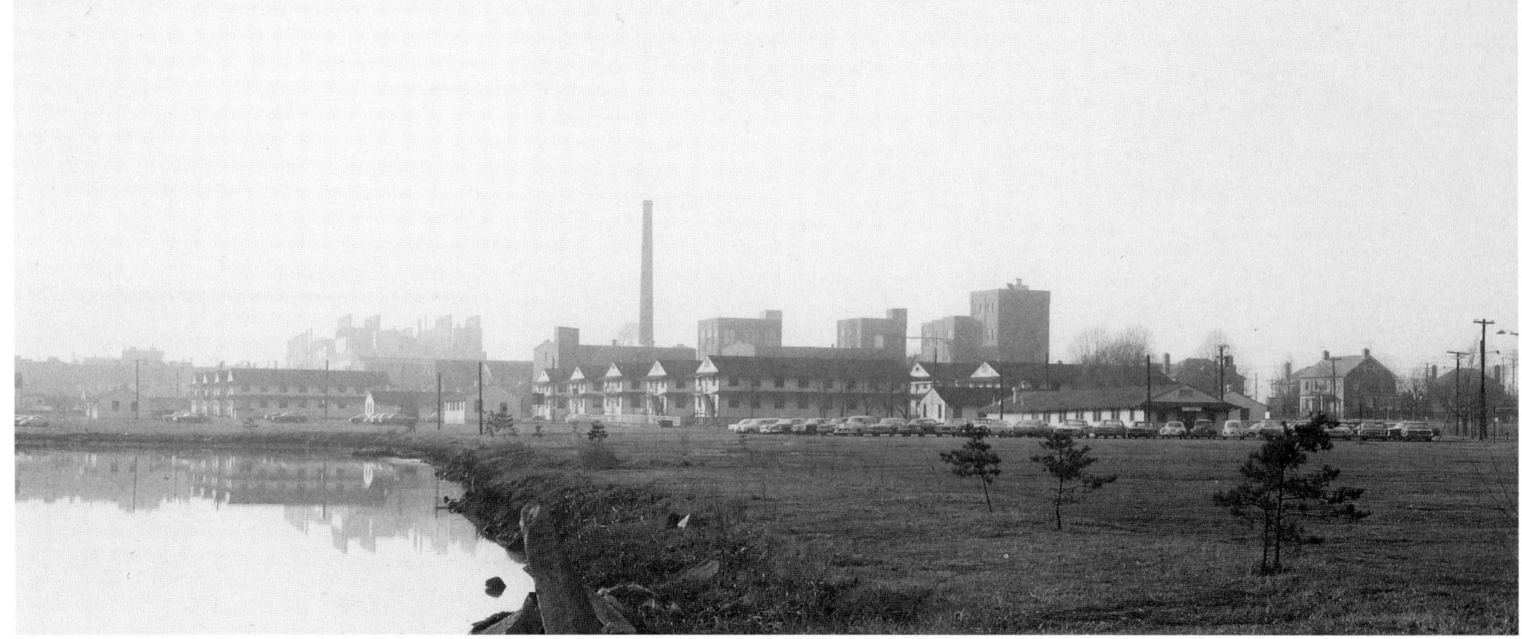

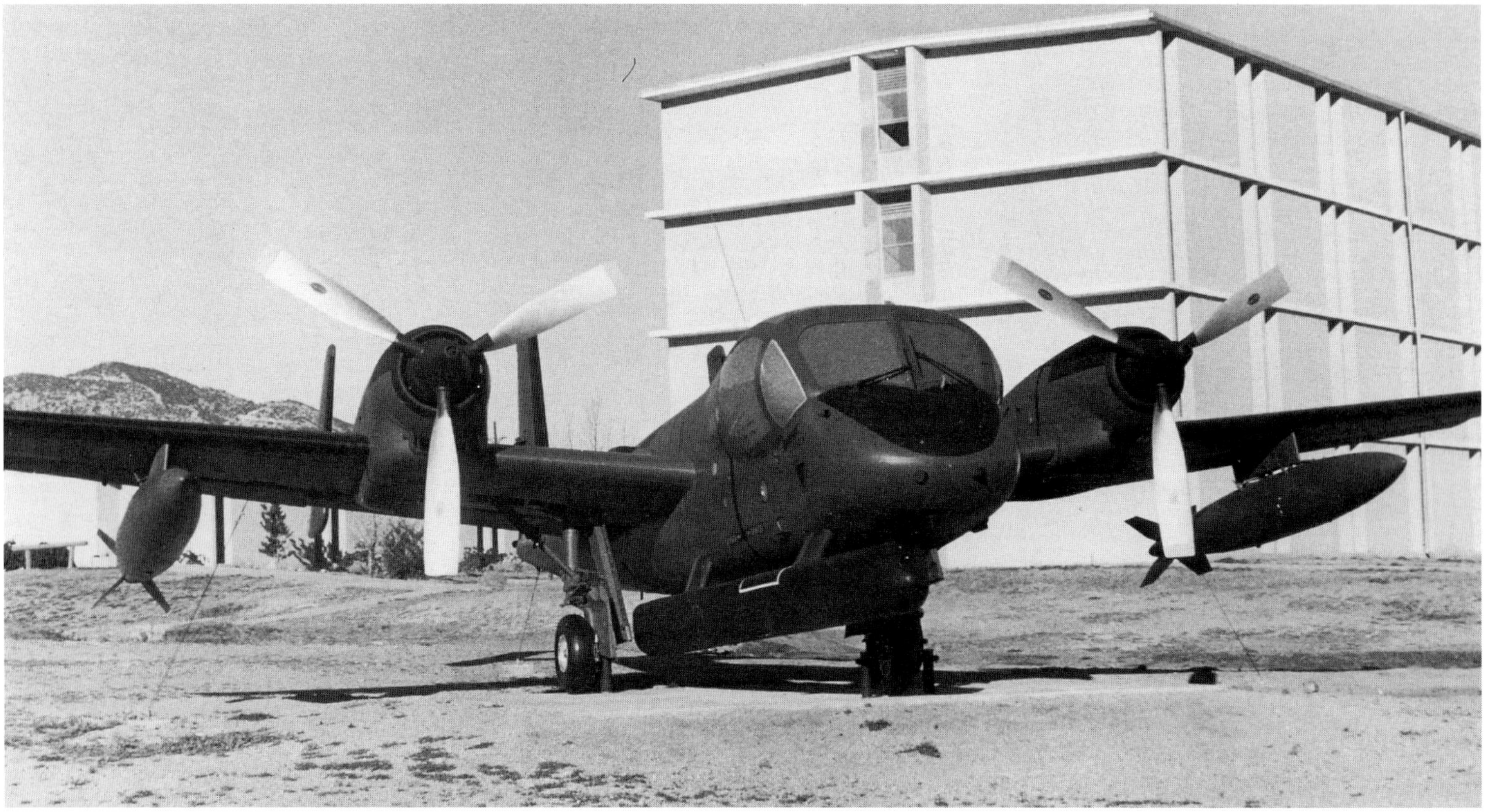

In 1971, the Army Intelligence School moved from its cramped quarters in an industrial suburb of Baltimore, Maryland, to new facilities at historic Fort Huachuca, high in the Arizona desert. Above, a view of Fort Holabird from the banks of Colgate Creek. Below, the new U.S. Army Intelligence Center and School. On display in the foreground is an Army OV-1 "Mohawk" surveillance aircraft.

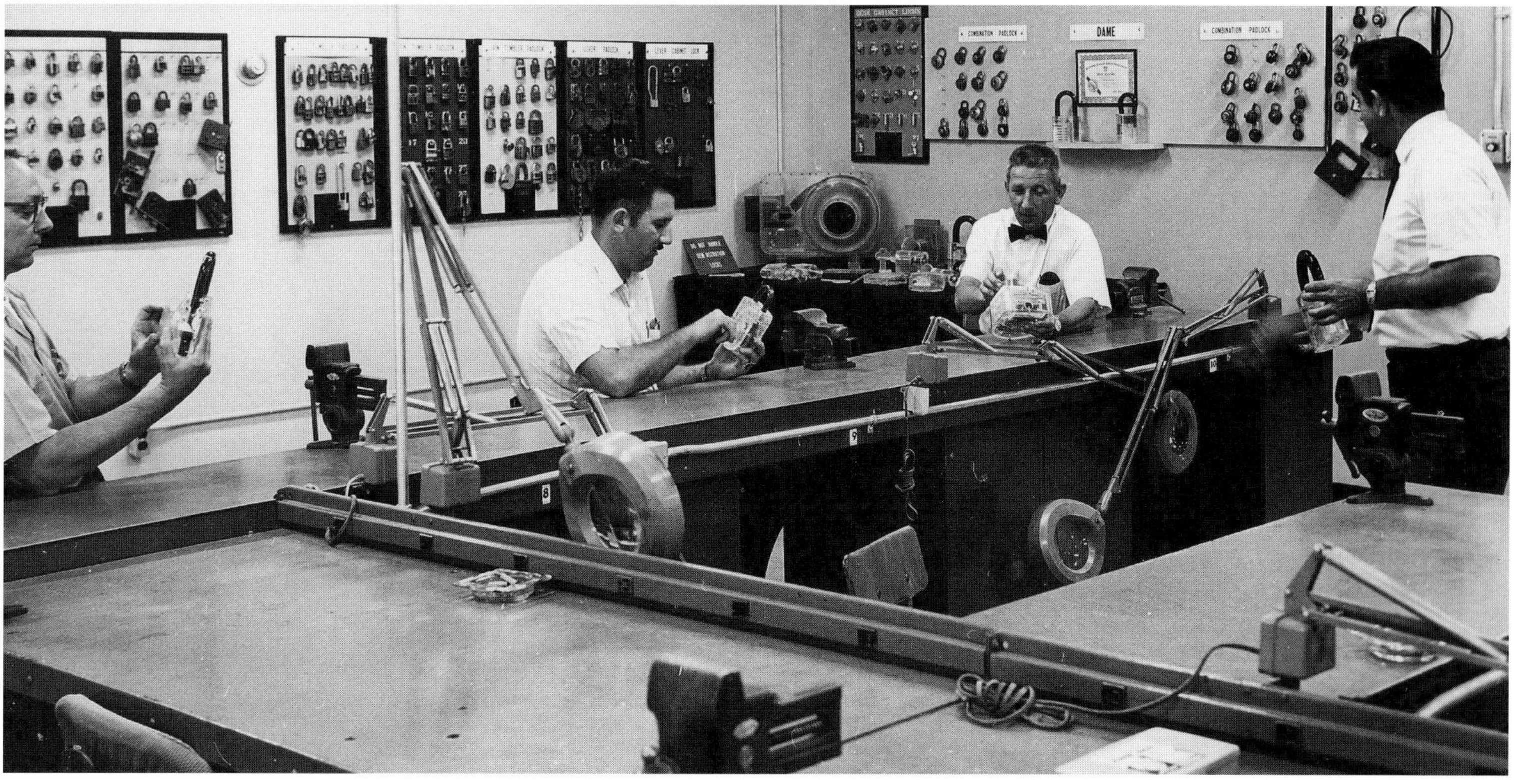

Students analyze locks in a Defense Against Methods of Entry (DAME) class at the Army Intelligence School.

A training class at the U.S. Army Security Agency Training Center and School at Fort Devens, Massachusetts, in 1972. ASA training was conducted independently from the Army Intelligence School.

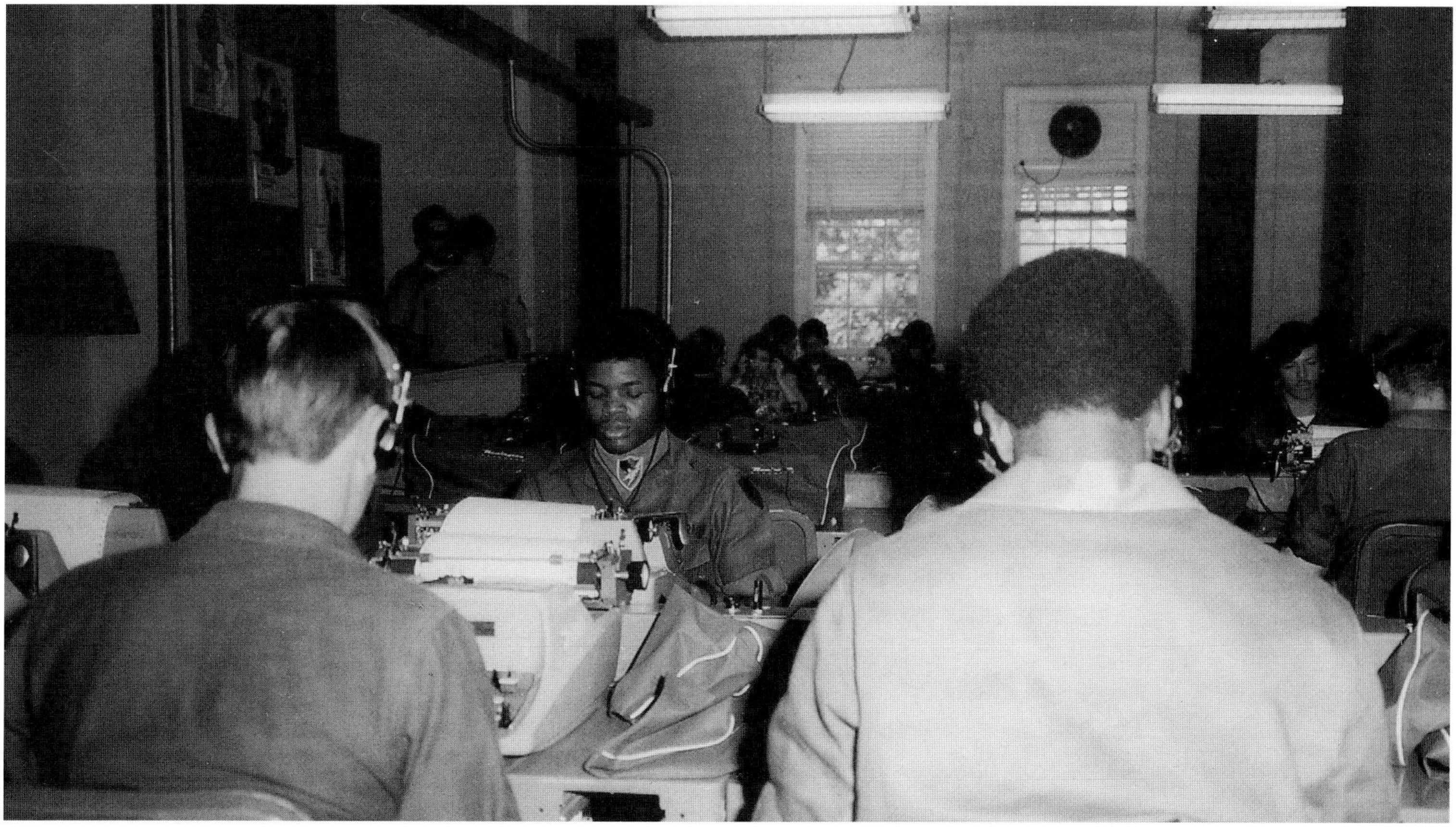

Organization and Stationing Study

In response to a request from the Secretary of the Army to analyze the structure of Military Intelligence, the Army Chief of Staff directed that the Army undertake a Intelligence Organization and Stationing Study (IOSS). The study was undertaken by a panel chaired by Major General James J. Ursano. The board released its report in 1975. Its findings were highly critical of the existing state of affairs within military intelligence. Army intelligence production, it concluded, was fragmented, and the Army's intelligence staff not properly aligned to meet its responsibilities. The panel was especially critical of ASA: the organization's compartmentalized and verticalized structure had artificially kept signals intelligence from the general intelligence flow, largely excluded the rest of the Army from involvement in the field of electronic warfare, and denied tactical commanders control of intelligence resources.

The Ursano board's recommendations, which were largely carried out by the Army Staff, fundamentally restructured Army intelligence. ASA, with its traditional vertical command structure, was broken up. Its school, research and development activity, and tactical units were resubordinated and integrated into the normal Army command structure. The remaining nucleus of ASA was merged with USAINTA and with a number of small intelligence production elements to form a new Major Army Command (MACOM), the U.S. Army Intelligence and Security Command (INSCOM). INSCOM, which became operational in 1977, was tasked with performing multi-discipline intelligence, security, and electronic warfare functions at the Echelon Above Corps (EAC).

At the tactical level, former ASA assets were merged with other military intelligence resources to form multi-discipline combat electronic warfare and intelligence (CEWI) units. The CEWI units were designed to give better support to commanders in the field by integrating all Army intelligence and security disciplines into single formations tailored to support divisions and corps. The new-type units simplified command arrangements, lessened the problem of artificial compartmentation of intelligence, and enhanced the Army's capabilities in the field of electronic warfare.

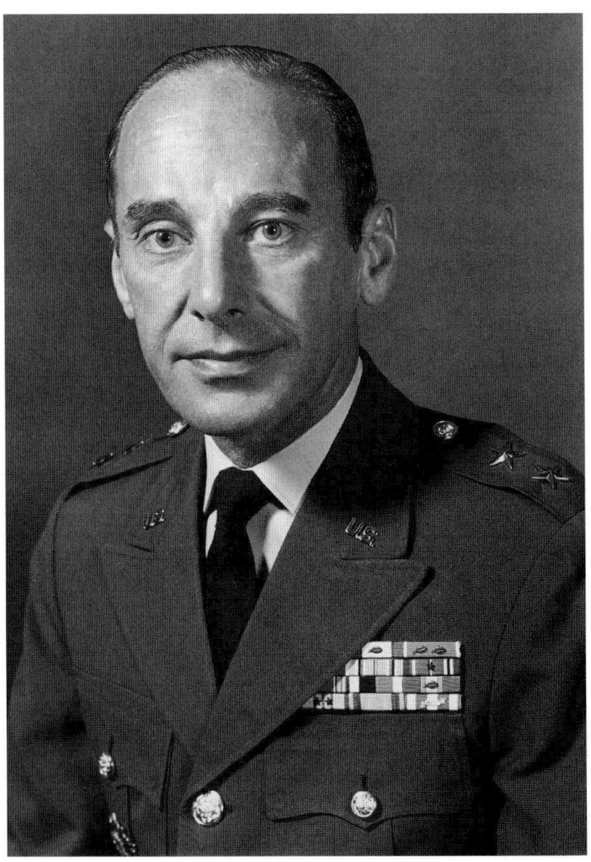

MG James Ursano led the Army study group that brought about the most sweeping rearrangement of Army intelligence assets in a generation.

INSCOM shoulder sleeve insignia.

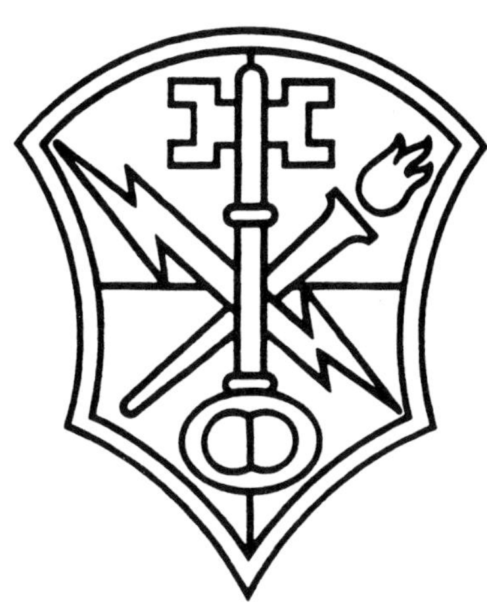

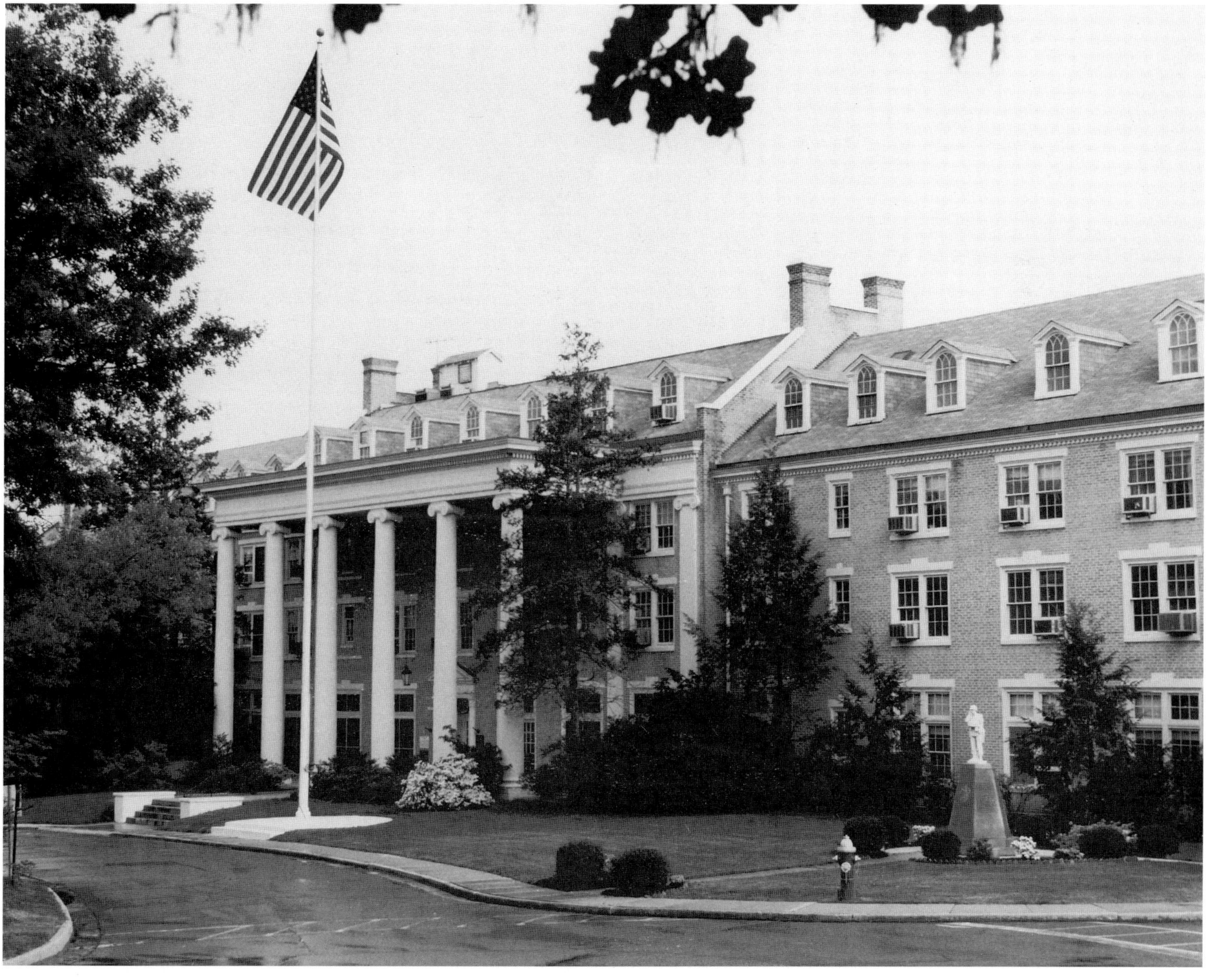

Centerpiece of the new reorganization was the U.S. Army Intelligence and Security Command (INSCOM). Above, INSCOM headquarters at Arlington Hall Station, Arlington, Virginia, a reconverted girls' school that had been associated with intelligence since World War II.

Modern Military Intellig

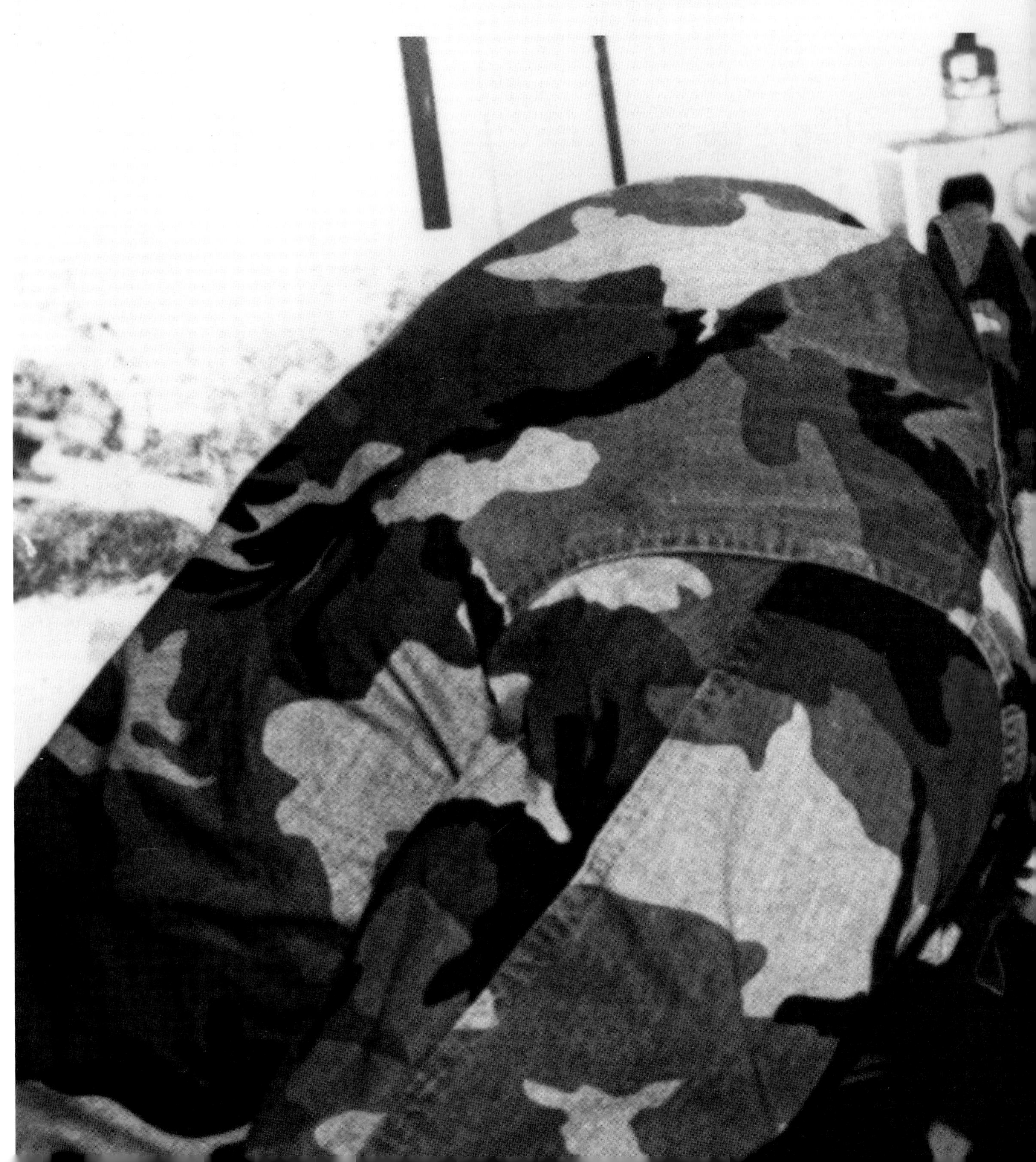

ace

Part III

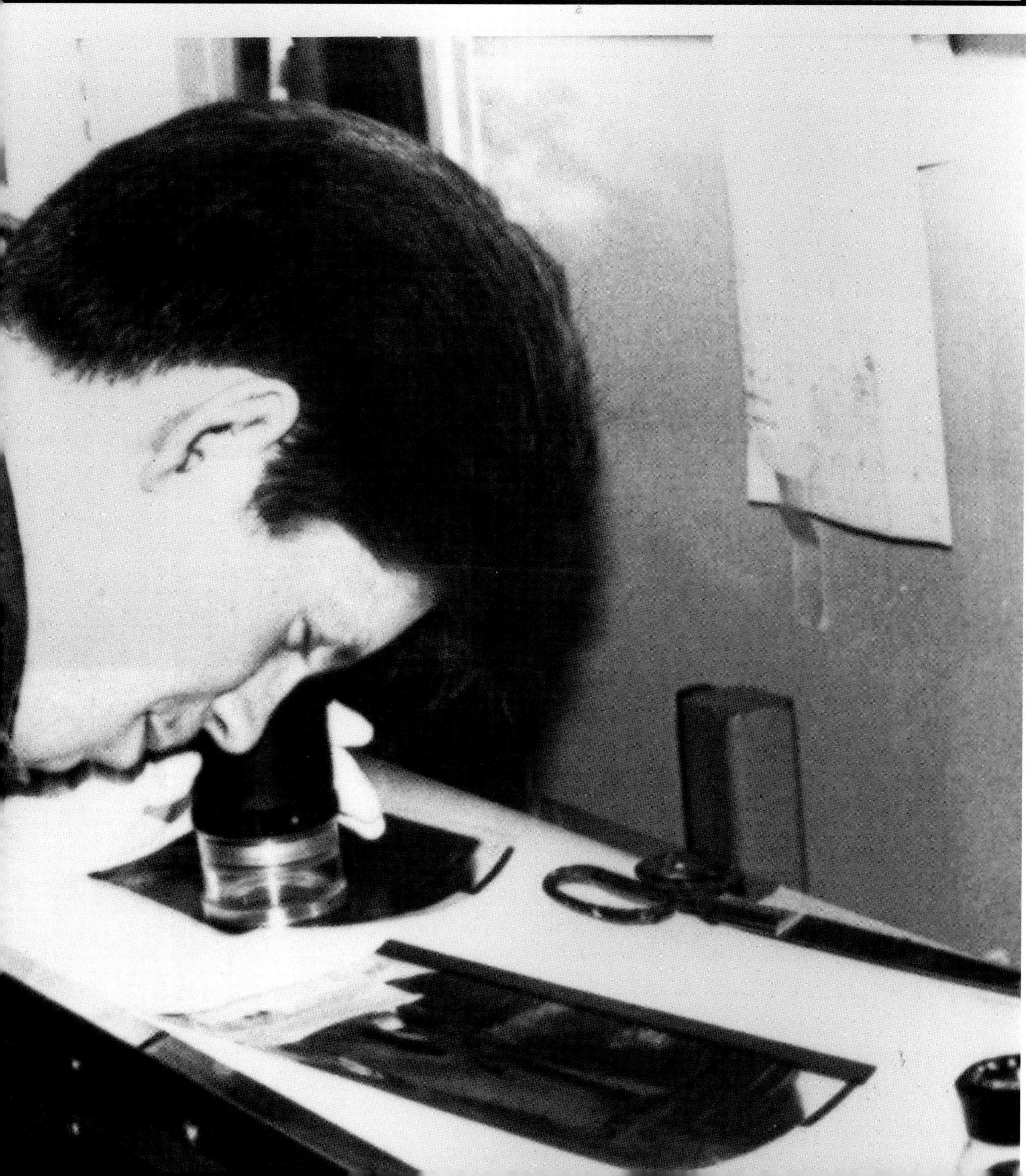

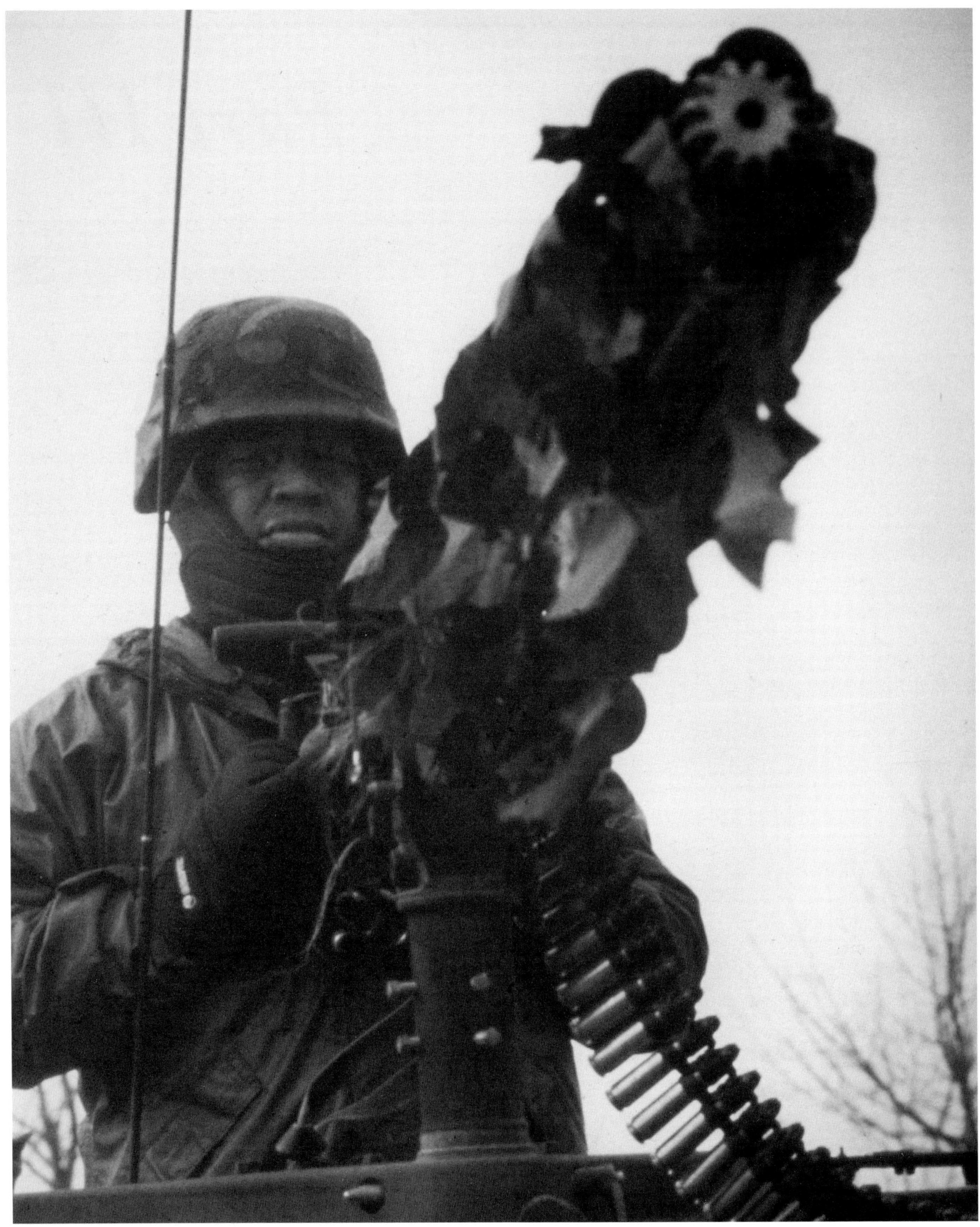

The American soldier. In the last analysis, the mission of Military Intelligence was to support the warfighter. To properly execute the mission, Military Intelligence had to transform itself from an exotic specialty to an integral part of the fighting Army.

At the time the Army put into effect the recommendations of its Intelligence Organization and Stationing Study, the sad outcome of the Vietnam conflict continued to cast a long shadow. The Army, underfunded and unpopular, was hard-pressed to fill its ranks with quality personnel without the stimulus of the draft. By the end of the decade, in the estimation of the Army's Chief of Staff, it had been run down to a point where it had become a "hollow army." However, even as he spoke, things began to look up. The Iranian hostage crisis, the Soviet invasion of Afghanistan, and continued instability in Central America gradually fostered a renewed interest in American security. From 1979 on, the country began to build up its defenses at an accelerating tempo. And the IOSS reforms, conceived in an environment of tight resources, continued to provide a viable architecture for Army intelligence in a period of plenty for the United States Army and for intelligence operations in general.

There were at least five major structural developments in Military Intelligence that took place in the decade that followed Army implementation of the Intelligence Organization and Stationing Study report. The Army intelligence staff was streamlined and integrated. In 1987, it finally attained the position of equality within the Army staff that it had lost in 1956: the position of ACSI was upgraded to Deputy Chief of Staff for Intelligence (DCSINT). Secondly, INSCOM, now the centerpiece of the Army's intelligence organization, steadily expanded and acquired new functions, assuming control of the U.S. Army Russian Institute in 1978 and the Special Security Group in 1980.

A third change came in the organization of the Army's production functions. In 1977, INSCOM had absorbed a number of small production elements from ACSI and formed them into an Intelligence and Threat Analysis Center. However, other major intelligence production organizations remained subordinated to the Army Materiel Command or to the Office of the Surgeon General. In 1984, the Army at last centralized all intelligence production under a new Army Intelligence Agency, a field operating agency under ACSI.

Fourthly, there was a great expansion of the Army's tactical intelligence organizations in the wake of IOSS. ASA, MI, and Special Security assets were melded into new Combat Electronic Warfare and Intelligence (CEWI) units. Each division was assigned a full battalion; corps were assigned groups (later brigades). Military Intelligence was now organized like the rest of the Army, and its members functioned as field soldiers.

Finally, the institutional position of the U.S. Army Intelligence Center and School was significantly enhanced. USAIC&S now directed intelligence training activities not only at Fort Huachuca, but also at what had now become the U.S. Army Intelligence School at Fort Devens, Massachusetts. USAICS soon absorbed intelligence agencies at Fort Huachuca, and then became proponent for the Military Intelligence Branch. As a result, the position of Commandant of USAIC&S was elevated to a major general's slot. In 1987, the Commandant would become the Chief of the whole Military Intelligence Corps, as Military Intelligence became part of the Army's regimental system.

Challenge and Response

At the end of 1979, the American public was jarred from its complacency and indifference to national defense by two successive shocks. In November, militant Iranian students, adherents of the radical fundamentalist Ayatollah Khomeini, seized the United States Embassy in Teheran and took its personnel hostage. After protracted and unsuccessful negotiations, the United States attempted a military rescue mission. This failed catastrophically. Meanwhile, the Soviet Union had invaded Afghanistan. As a result of these unexpected developments, the world no longer seemed to be a safe place for Americans. The nation took this as a call to arms.

In response to the disconcerting developments on the international scene, President Jimmy Carter initiated an expanded defense program at the end of his presidency. In turn, this program was still further expanded by Carter's successor, President Ronald Reagan. All of the armed services would benefit. A reinvigorated Army devised new battle doctrines, upgraded its personnel, fielded a new generation of sophisticated equipment, and created easily deployable light divisions to intervene in contingency situations. And Army intelligence refocused its priorities to give greater support to the warfighter.

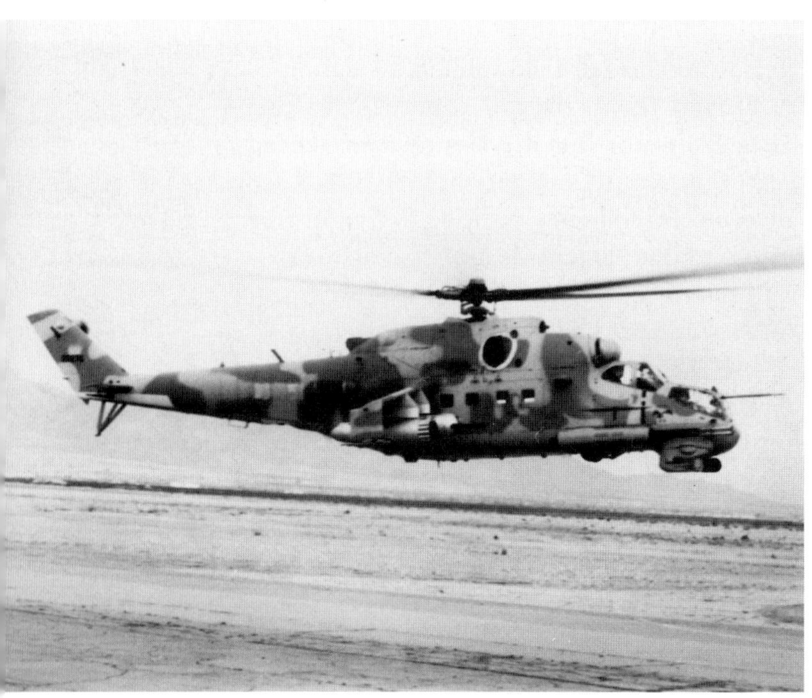

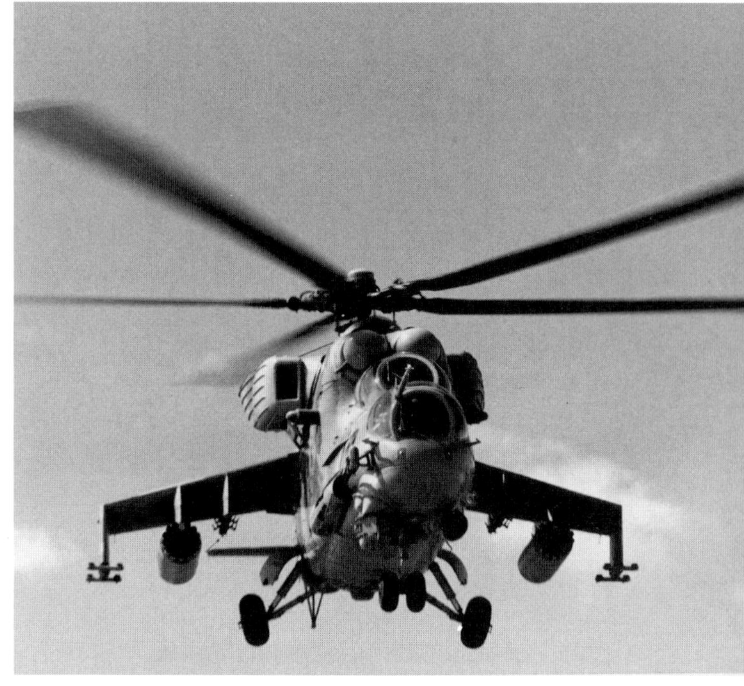

The Soviet invasion of Afghanistan in 1979 led to a ten-year guerrilla war. As one of their most effective weapons, the Soviets deployed attack helicopters such as this HIND.

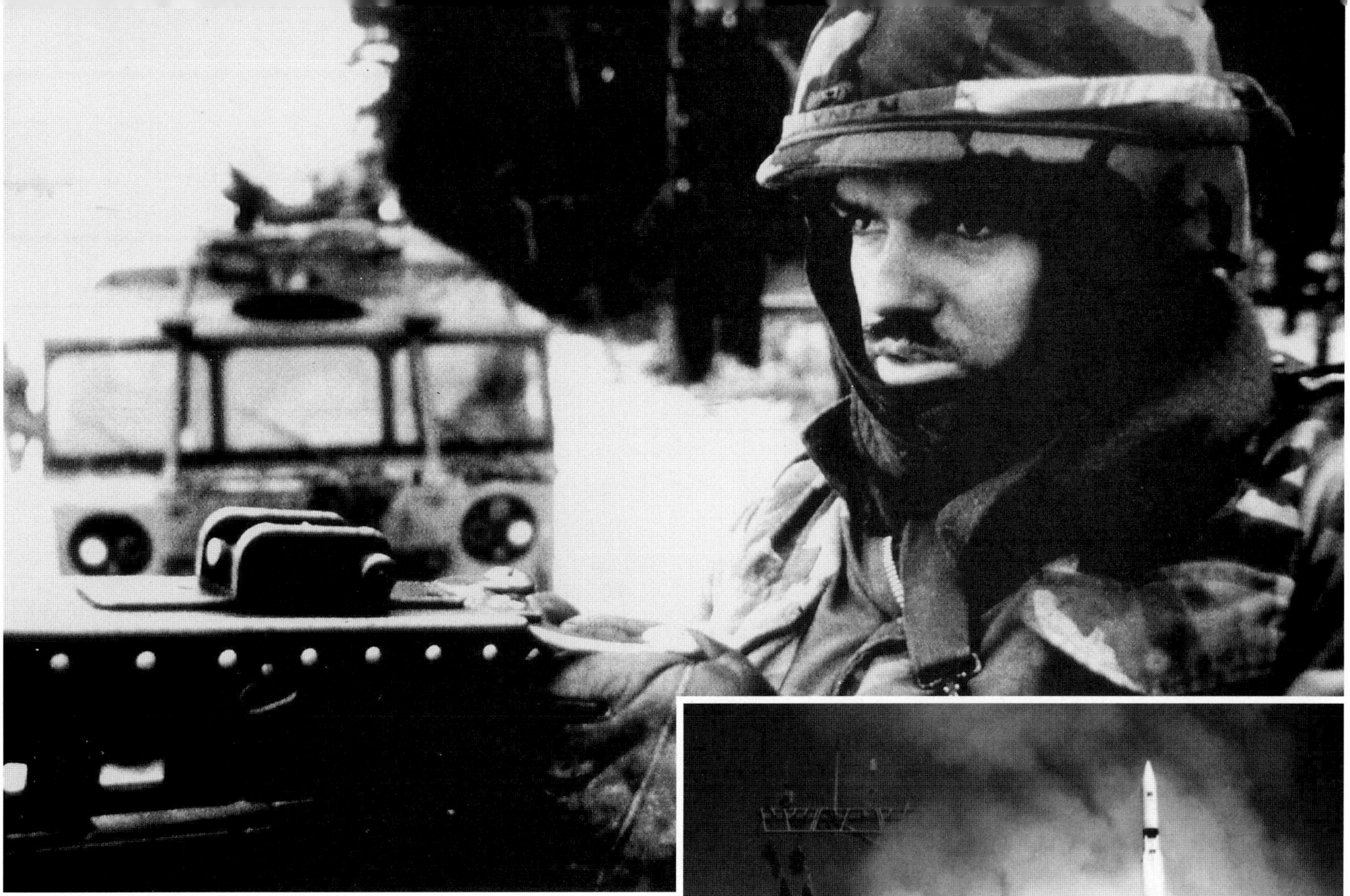

American troops on maneuvers in Germany. The 1980's would witness a steady qualitative improvement in the Army.

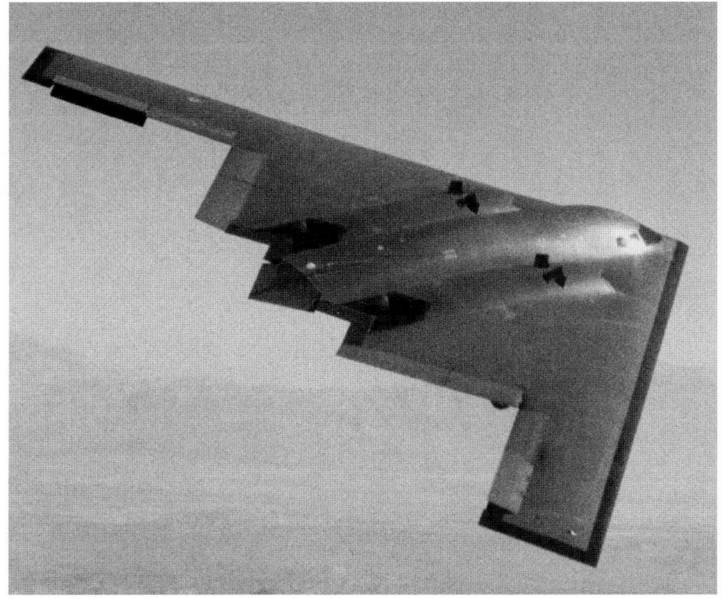

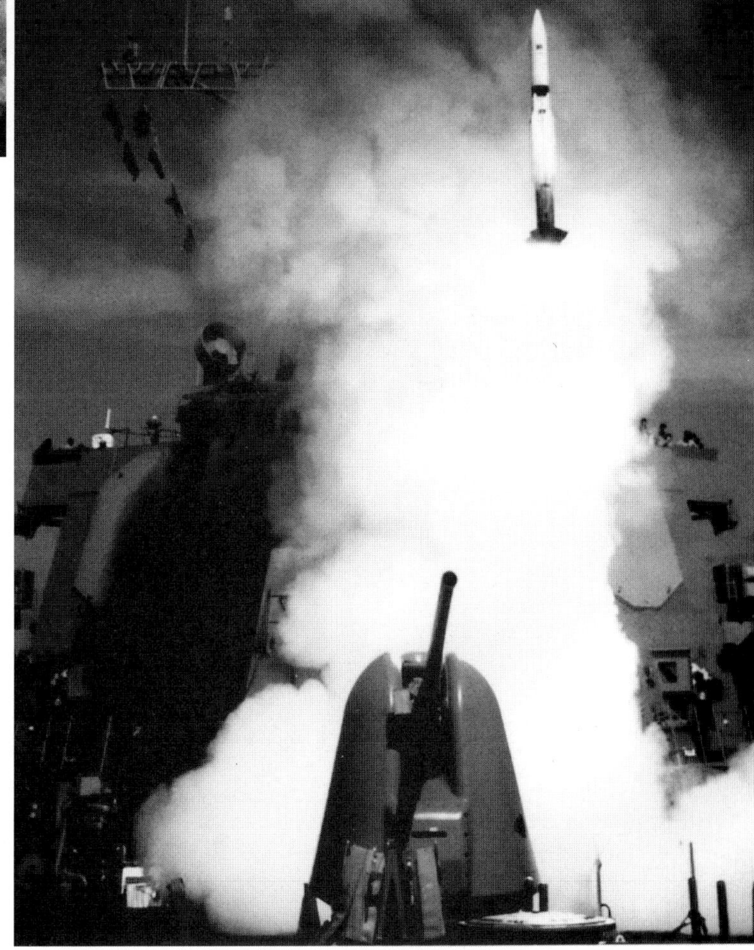

America increased its lead in technology during the 1980's. Left, the U.S. Air Force's B–2 bomber was designed to defeat radar detection systems. Right, an Arleigh Burke-class guided missile destroyer.

INSCOM:

As the new centerpiece of the Army's intelligence structure, INSCOM supported operations of two interdepartmental intelligence organizations at the Department of Defense level. As the Army's Service Cryptologic Element (SCE), the command was closely involved with the National Security Agency (NSA), which had managed the national cryptologic program since 1952. INSCOM also worked in collaboration with the Defense Intelligence Agency, created by Robert S. McNamara in 1961. Army personnel were assigned to both agencies, and the directorship of the agencies rotated among the services.

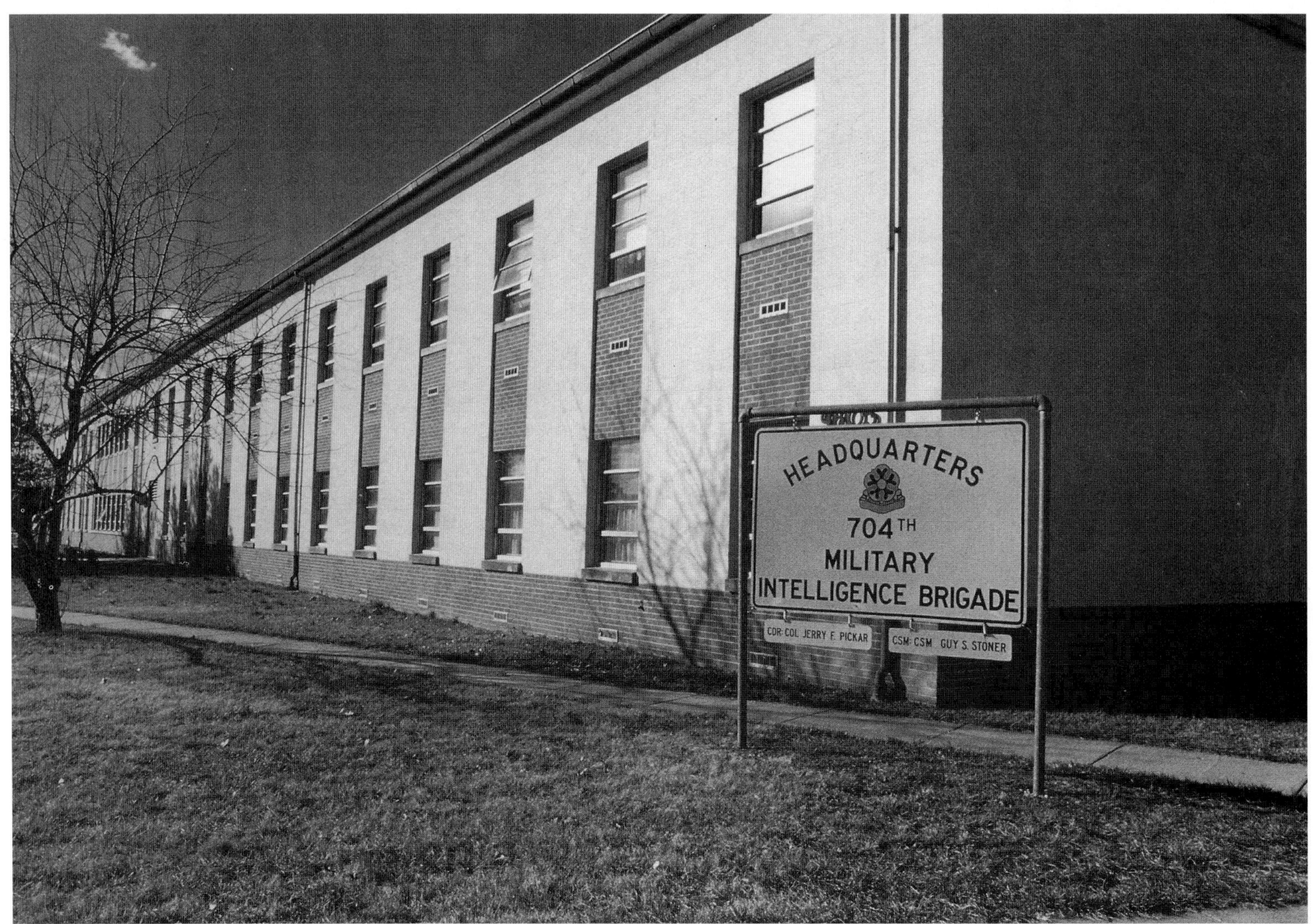

Headquarters of INSCOM's 704th MI Brigade at Fort Meade. Formerly known as the CONUS MI Group, the brigade furnished MI personnel to support NSA operations, as well as exercising command and control over numerous widely dispersed INSCOM elements.

Support to DOD

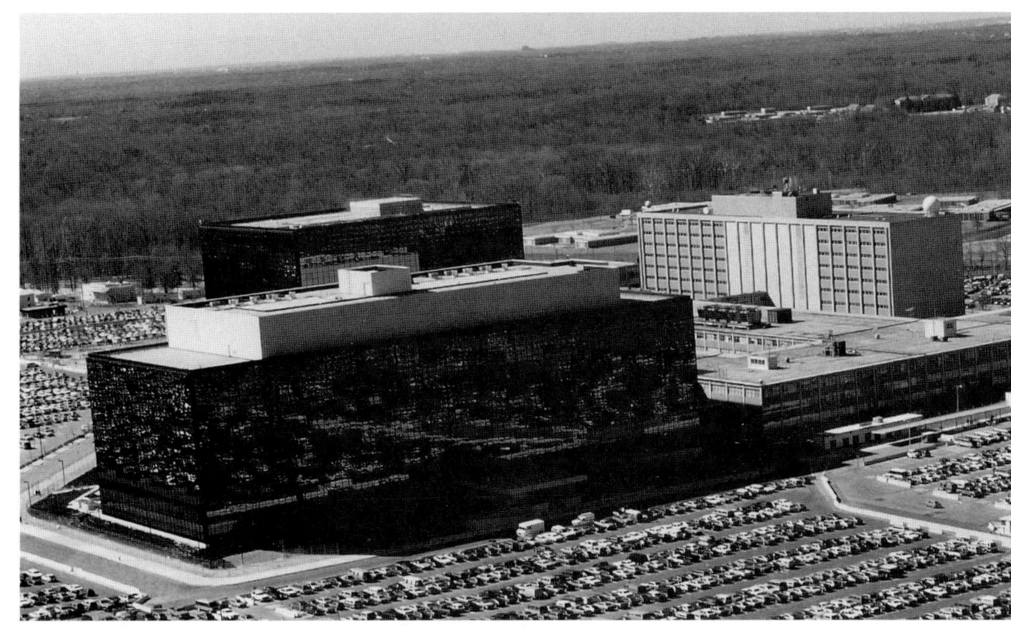

National Security Agency Headquarters at Fort George G. Meade, MD.

Secretary of Defense Richard Cheney presents the Travis Trophy for cryptologic excellence to the commander of Field Station Augsburg. NSA awards the trophy annually. To date, sixty percent of all trophies have gone to Army elements.

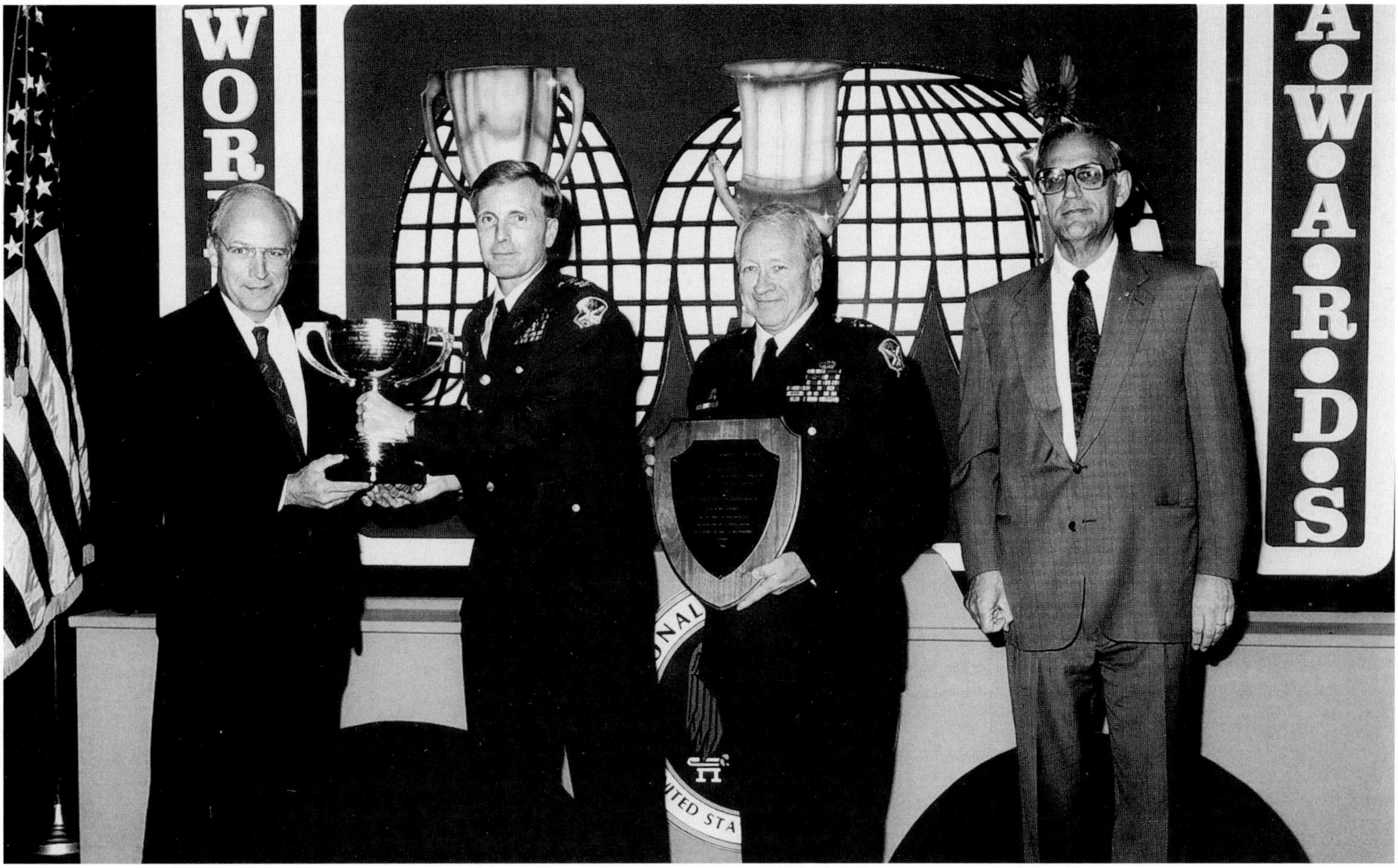

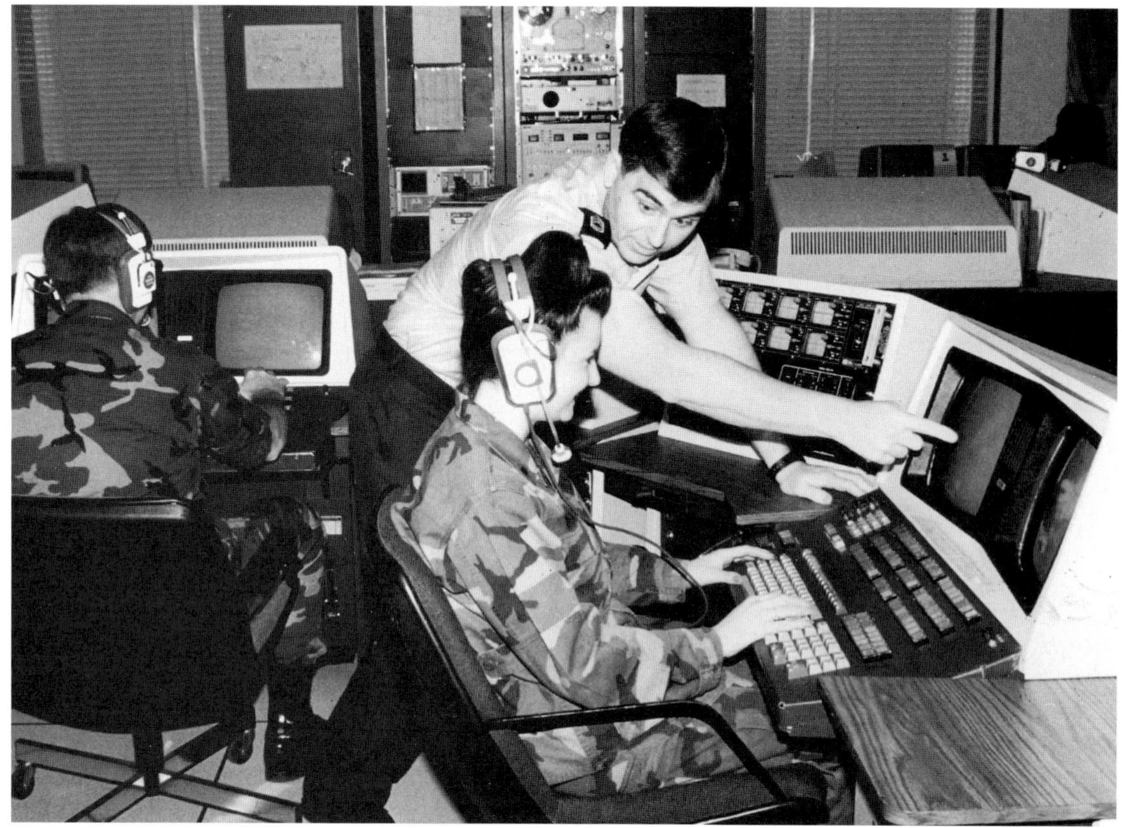

Operational personnel of the 704th MI Brigade man positions at the Fort Meade site. The TROJAN system shown below was used to provide troops in garrison with training opportunities.

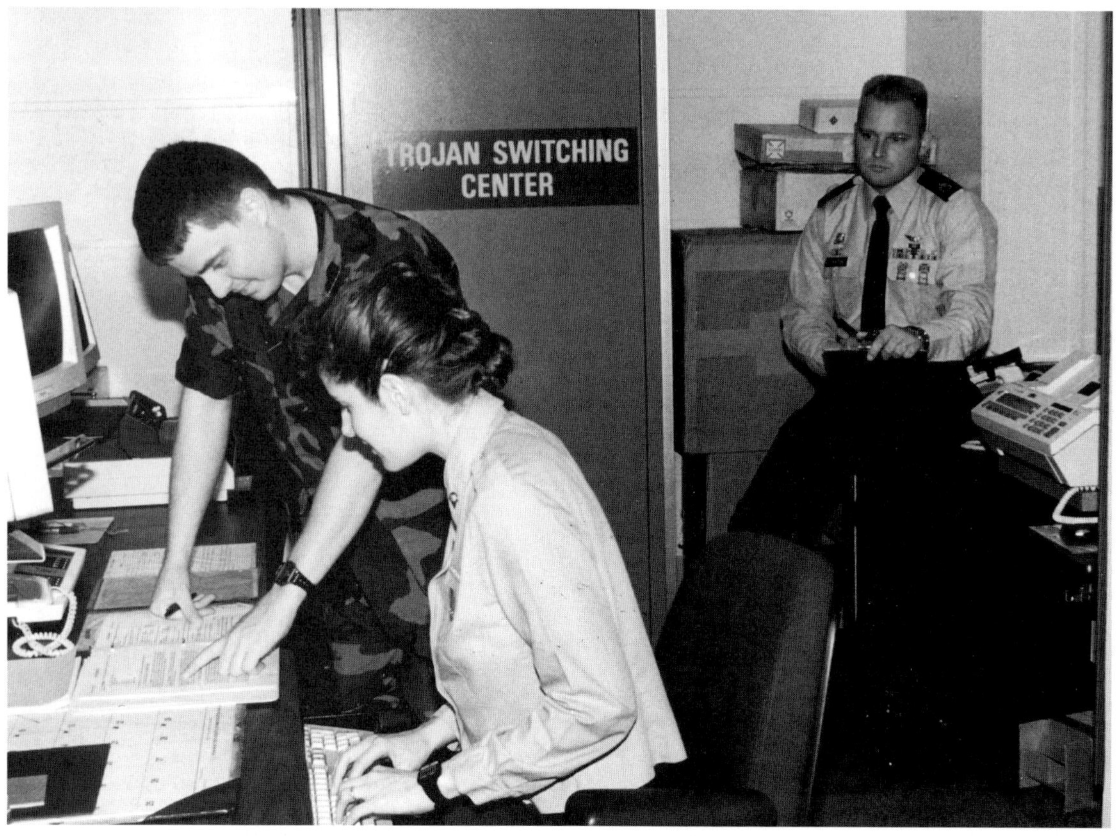

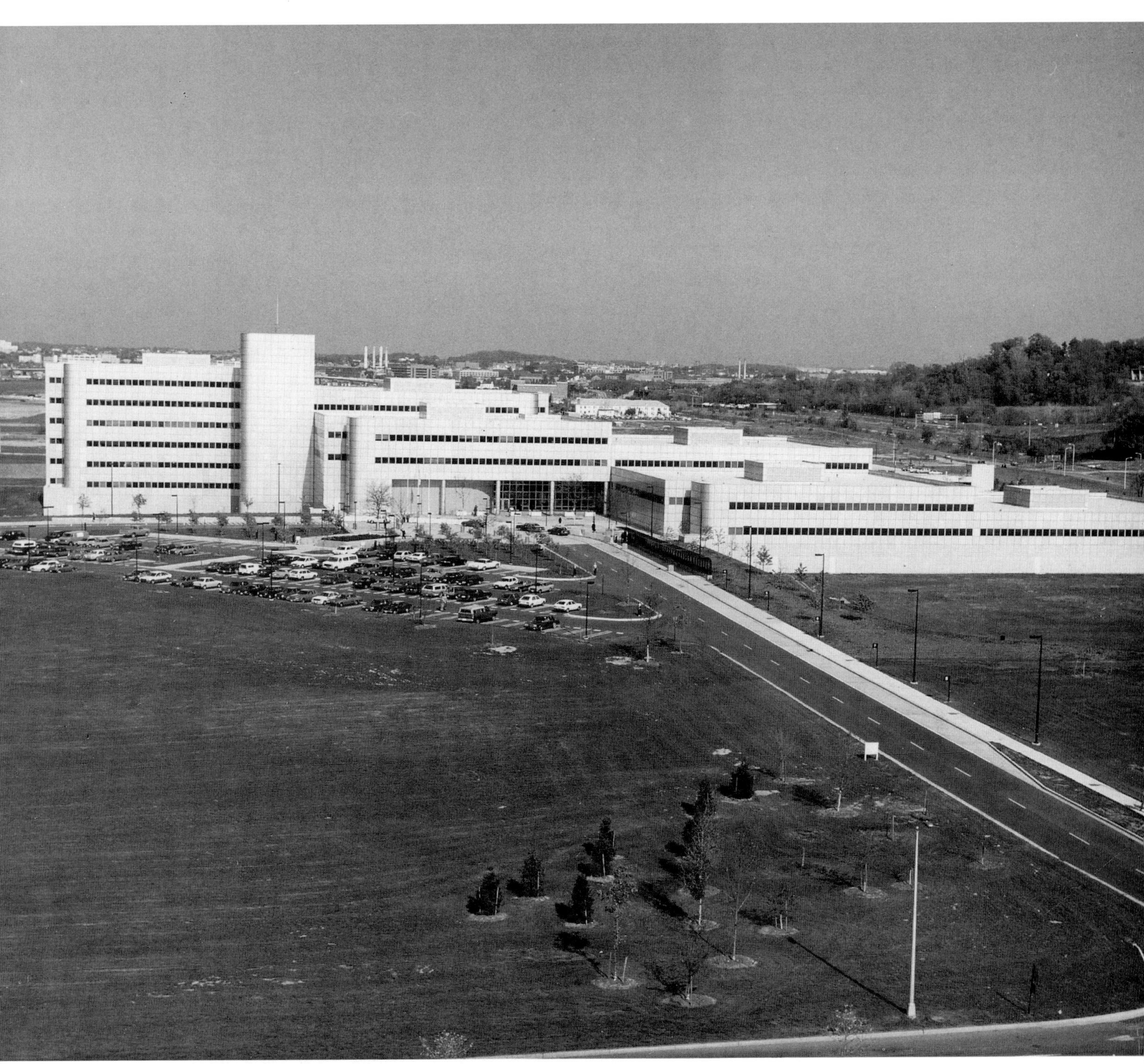

The Defense Intelligence Analysis Center at Bolling Air Force Base, Washington, D.C. Although DIA was established in 1961, it did not find a permanent home until 1986.

Fixed Sites

Among INSCOM's assets were a number of fixed installations inherited from the former Army Security Agency. Known as "field stations," these sites varied in size, but all housed suites of sophisticated communications equipment. At certain locations, soldiers worked side by side with personnel from the other armed services. INSCOM field stations were initially located at Berlin and Augsburg in Germany; Sinop, Turkey; Okinawa and Misawa, Japan; Pyongtaek, Korea; Key West, Florida; and San Antonio, Texas. During the course of the 1980's, additional field stations were organized at Kunia, Hawaii; and in Panama; and Field Station Okinawa was discontinued. In 1987, troops at selected field stations were organized into numbered MI units at brigade-level and below. This initiative was designed to enhance unit esprit and morale, and to provide these units with appropriate designations that would be more familiar to the Army as a whole.

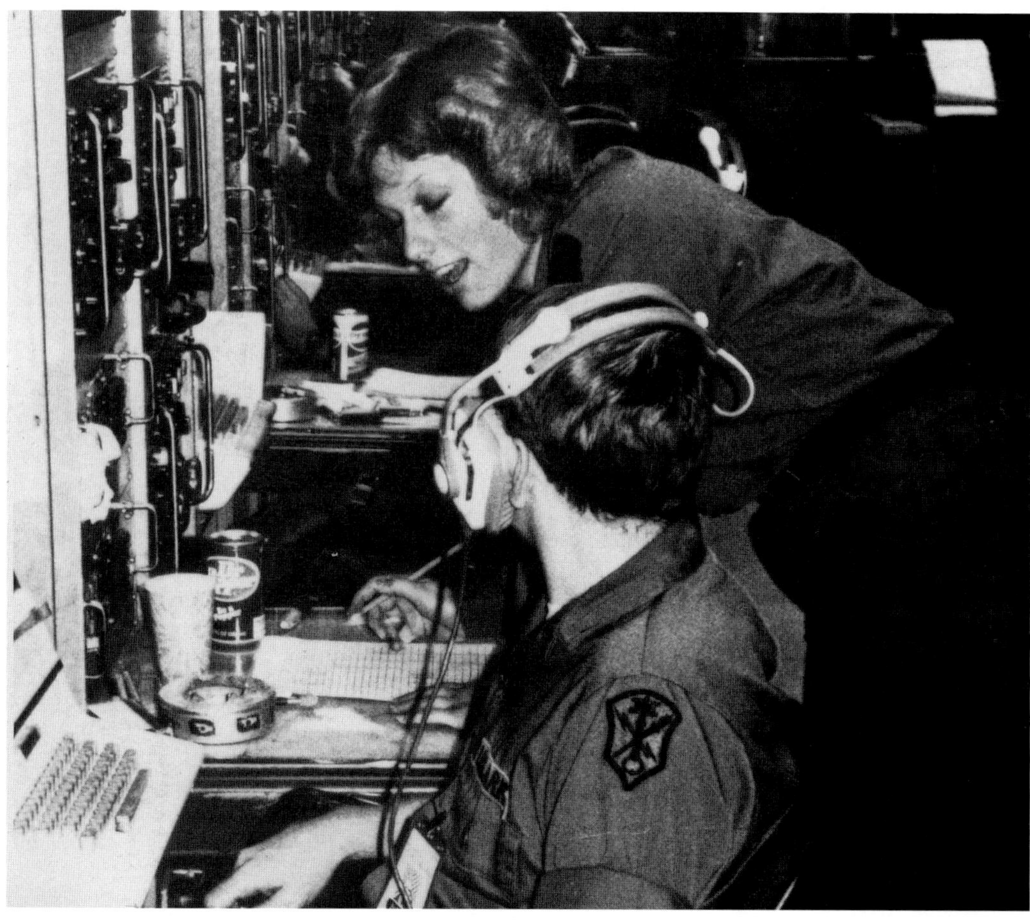

Operational personnel at a position at U.S. Army Field Station Misawa in 1982. The station was located in northern Honshu, Japan.

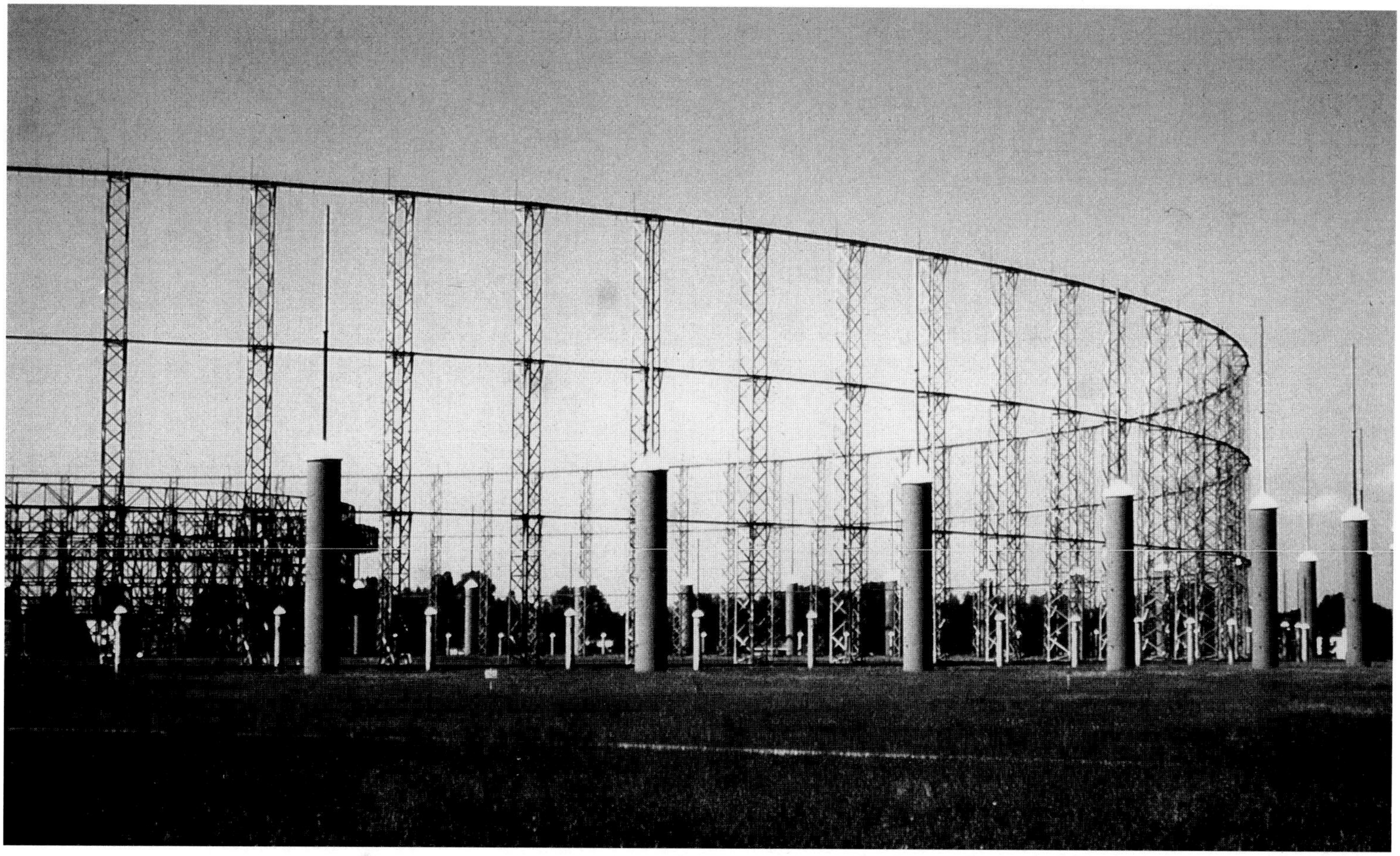

The AN/FLR–9 Circular Disposed Array Antenna at U.S. Army Field Station Augsburg. The enormous circular antenna covered 32 acres and was informally known as "The Elephant Cage."

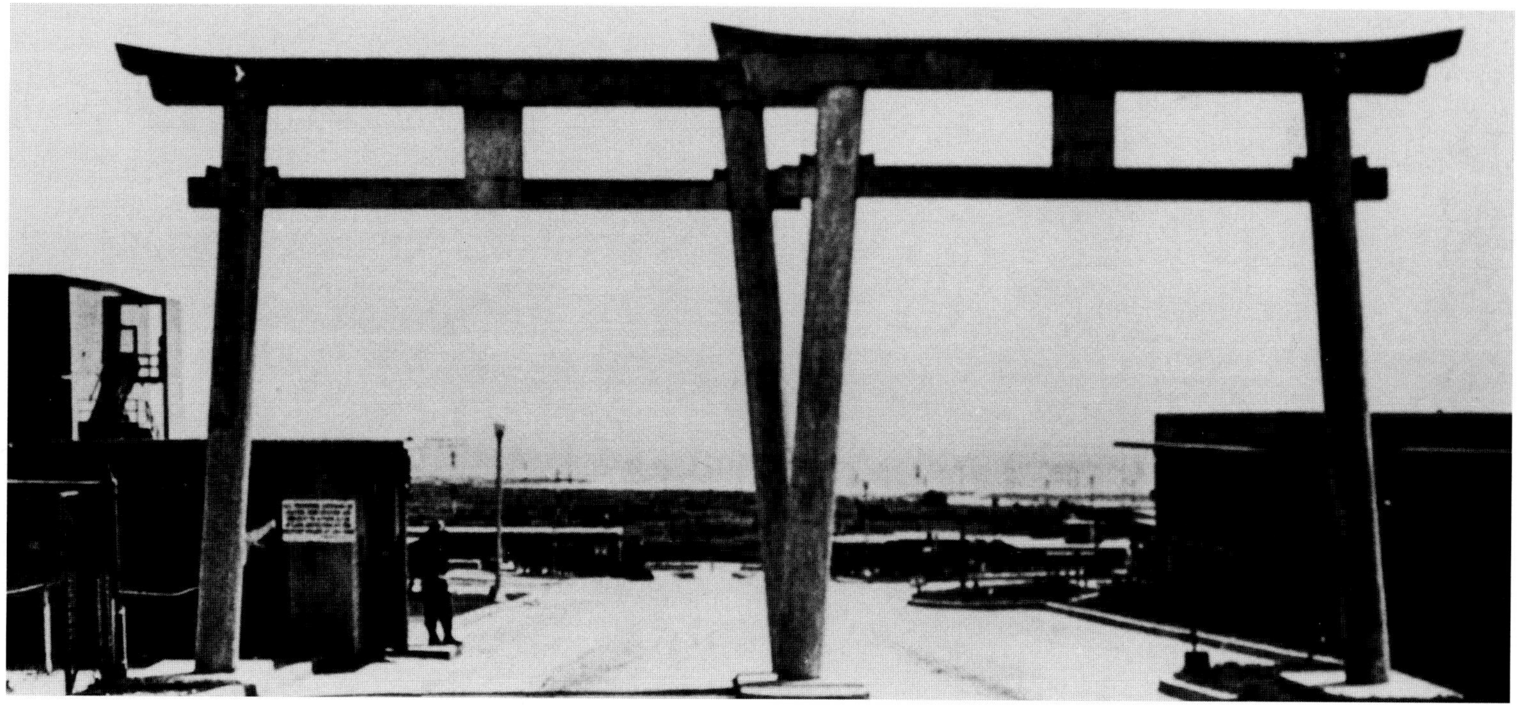

The torii gate at the entrance to U.S. Army Field Station Okinawa. The installation was discontinued in 1986.

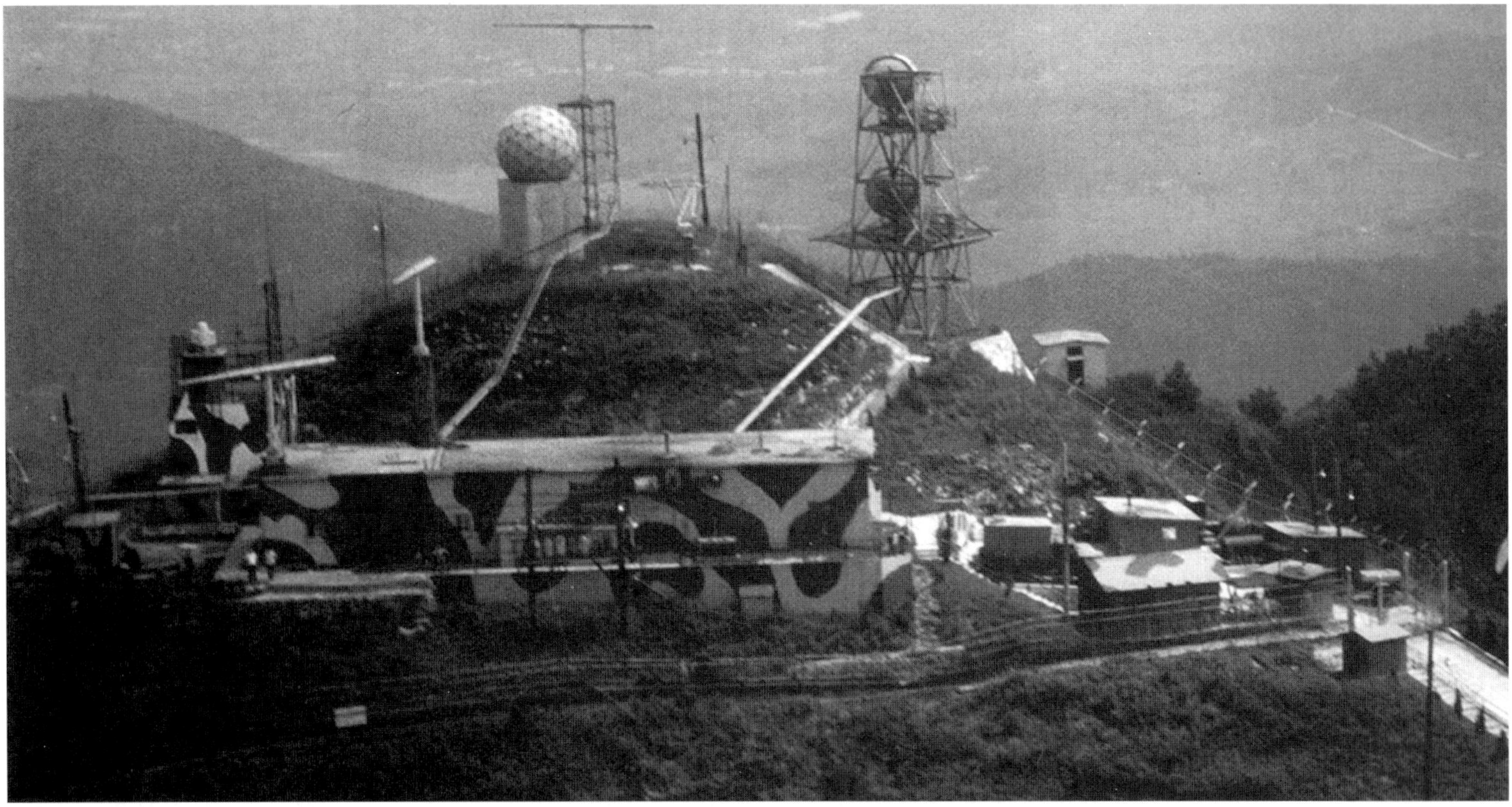

A border ADVENTURER site of U.S. Army Field Station Korea.

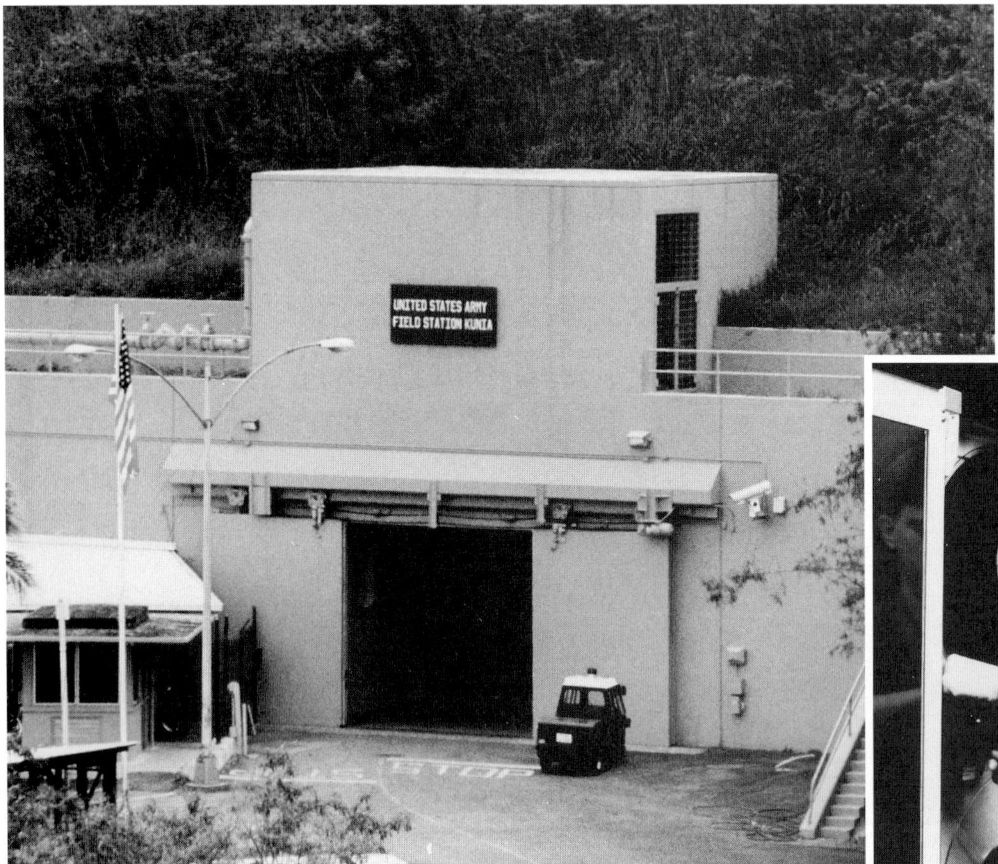

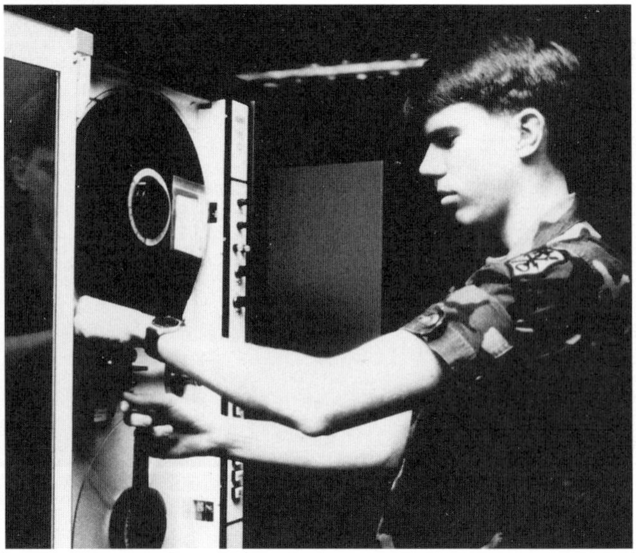

Tunnel entrance to Field Station Kunia on Hawaii. Established in 1980, the station made use of facilities originally built in World War II to house an underground aircraft assembly plant.

A computer operator of the 703d MI Brigade at Kunia.

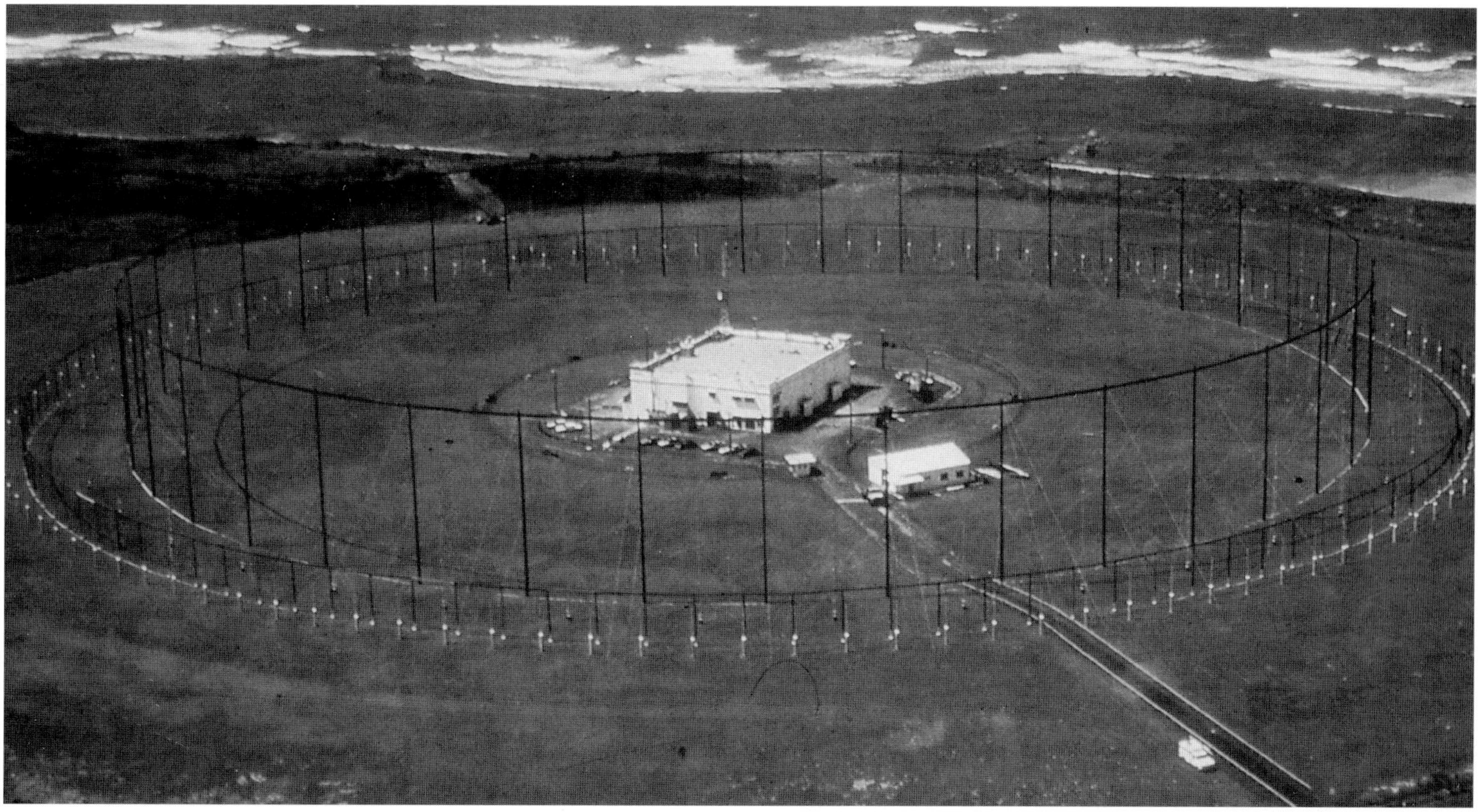

U.S. Army Field Station Panama on Galeta Island in the former Canal Zone. In 1987, the station's Army complement was redesignated as INSCOM's 747th MI Battalion. The battalion was discontinued in 1995.

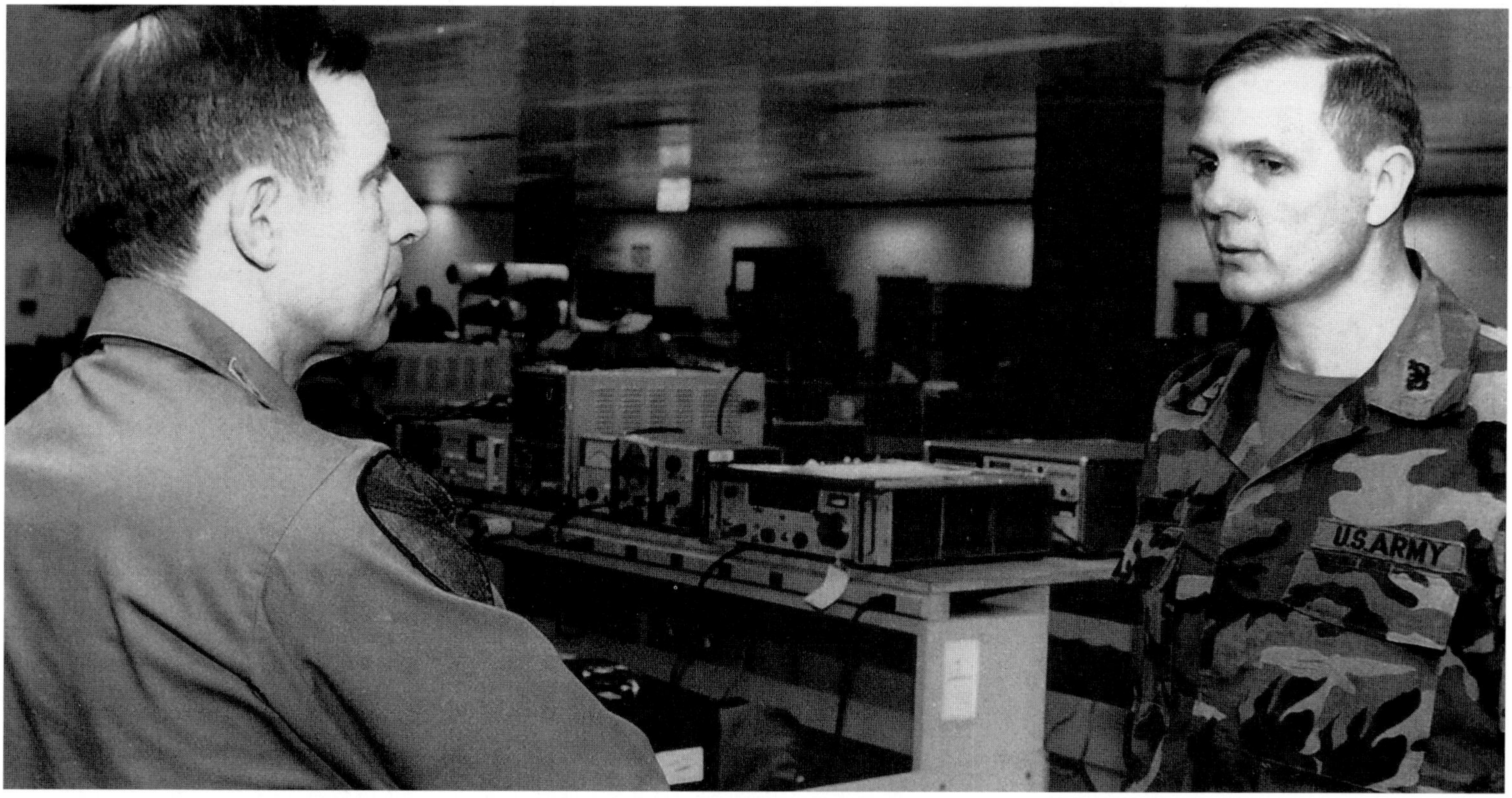

Army Chief of Staff GEN Edward C. "Shy" Meyer inspects the maintenance shop at U.S. Army Field Station Berlin in 1985.

Theater Support

To provide intelligence, security, and electronic warfare support at the Echelon Above Corps level to Army elements worldwide, INSCOM relied upon its multidisciplinary theater-level military intelligence groups. Originally, there were four of these: the 66th in Germany; the 470th in Panama; the 500th in Japan; and the 501st in Korea. Each group was sized and structured to support a theater-specific mission. In 1982, a new such unit, the 513th MI Group, was activated at Fort Monmouth, New Jersey, to support contingency operations. One of the 513th's subordinate units was the Army's only technical intelligence collection battalion. In 1986 and 1987, these MI groups were redesignated as brigades.

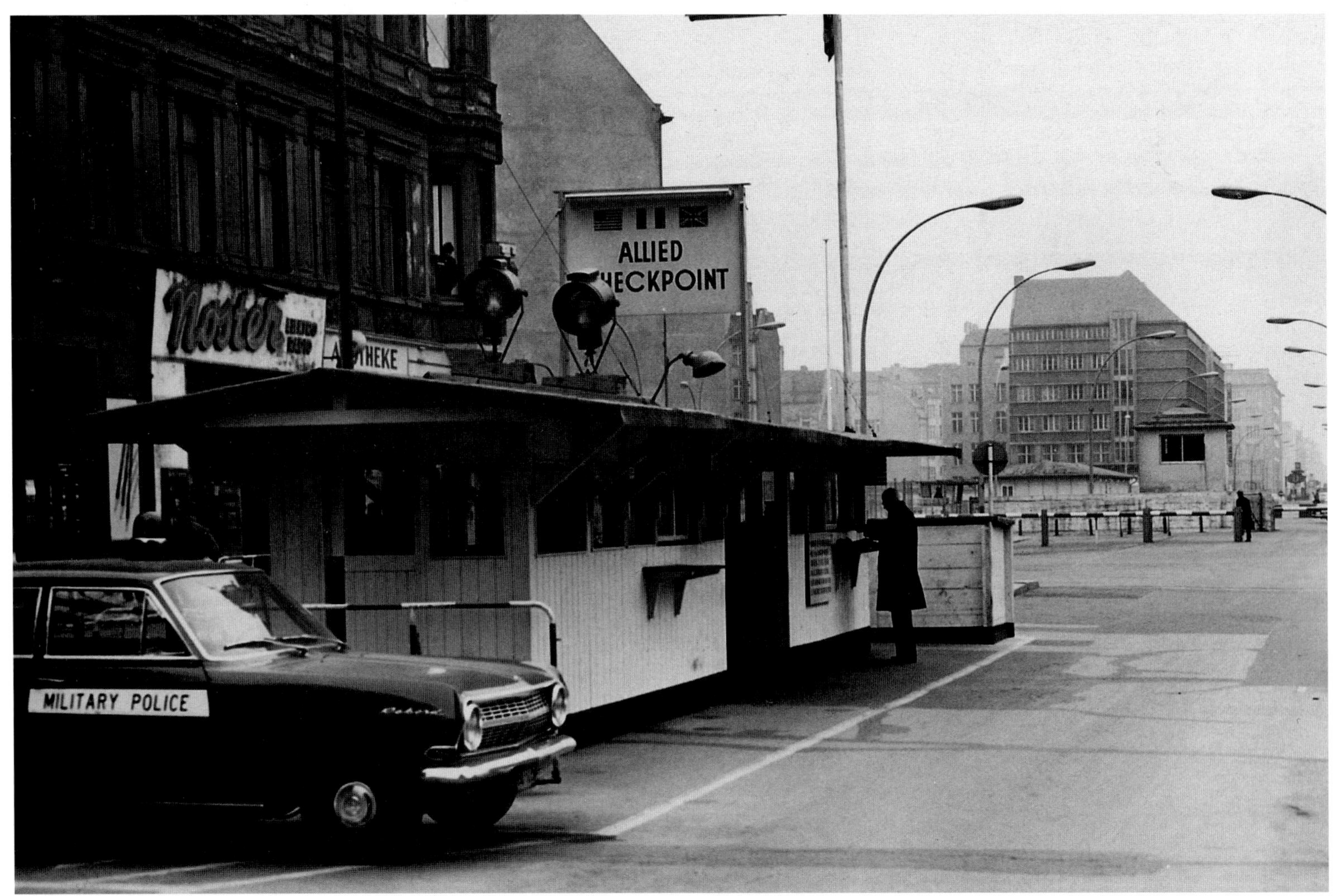

Check Point Charlie in Berlin, main entrance to the Soviet Zone. During the course of the Cold War, the 66th MI Brigade's 766th MI Detachment manned the front lines in West Berlin. The Detachment's motto was "Surrounded but Free."

Europe

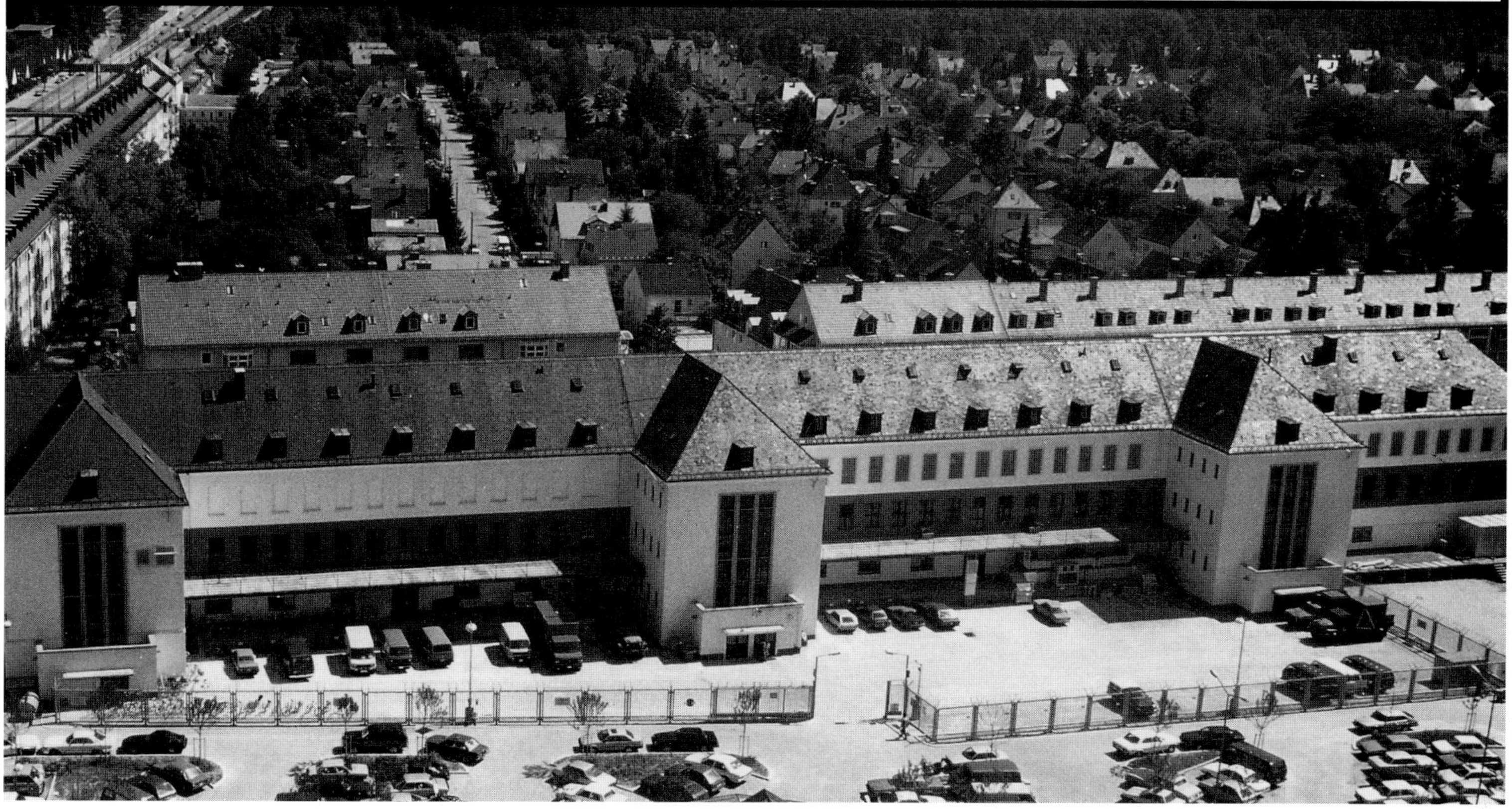

Headquarters of the 66th MI Brigade in Munich, Germany. With an assigned strength of 2500 personnel, the brigade would be INSCOM'S largest unit throughout the 1980's.

An intelligence officer of the 66th MI Brigade examines his files.

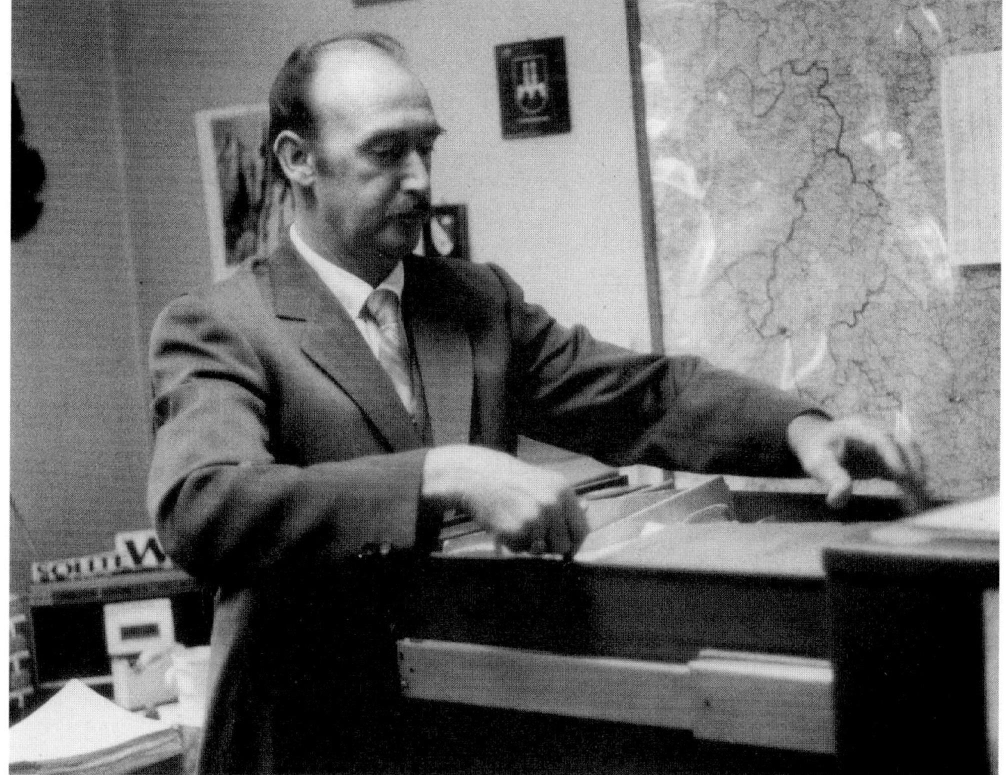

The Far East

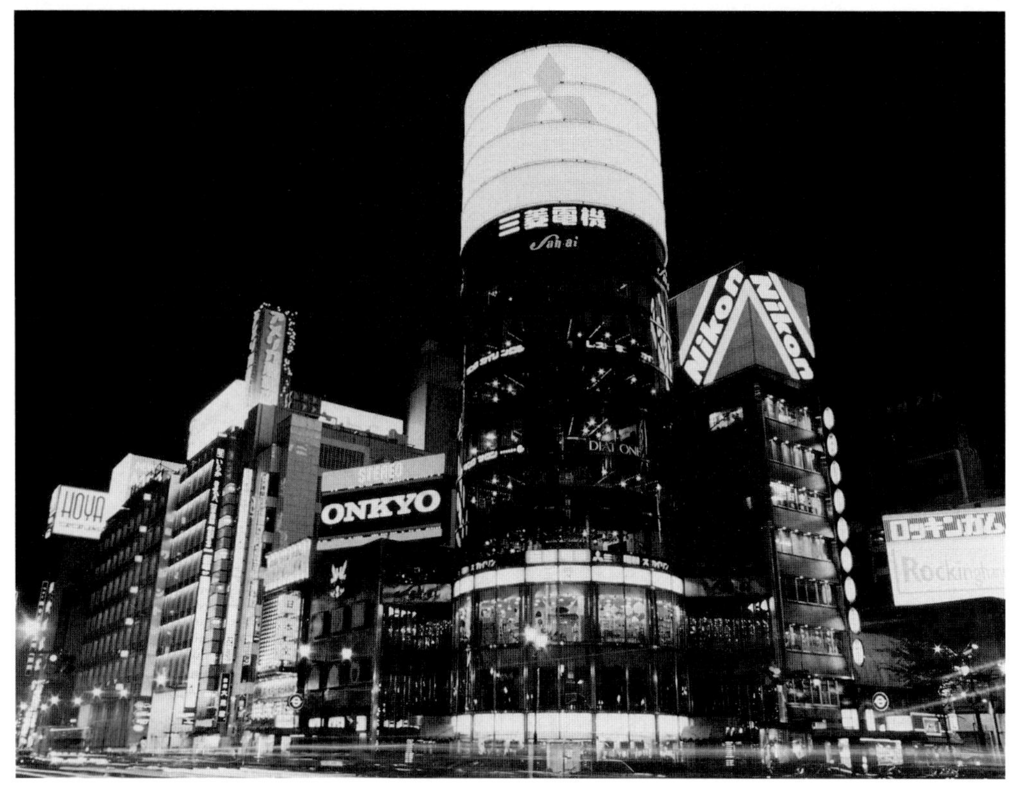

Tokyo, Japan. INSCOM'S 500th MI Brigade provided the Army's main intelligence presence in Japan. The brigade was headquartered at Camp Zama in the Tokyo suburbs.

COL Harry Fukuhara, U.S. Army retired, served as long-time head of the brigade's Foreign Liaison Office, which worked closely with Japanese military and intelligence elements.

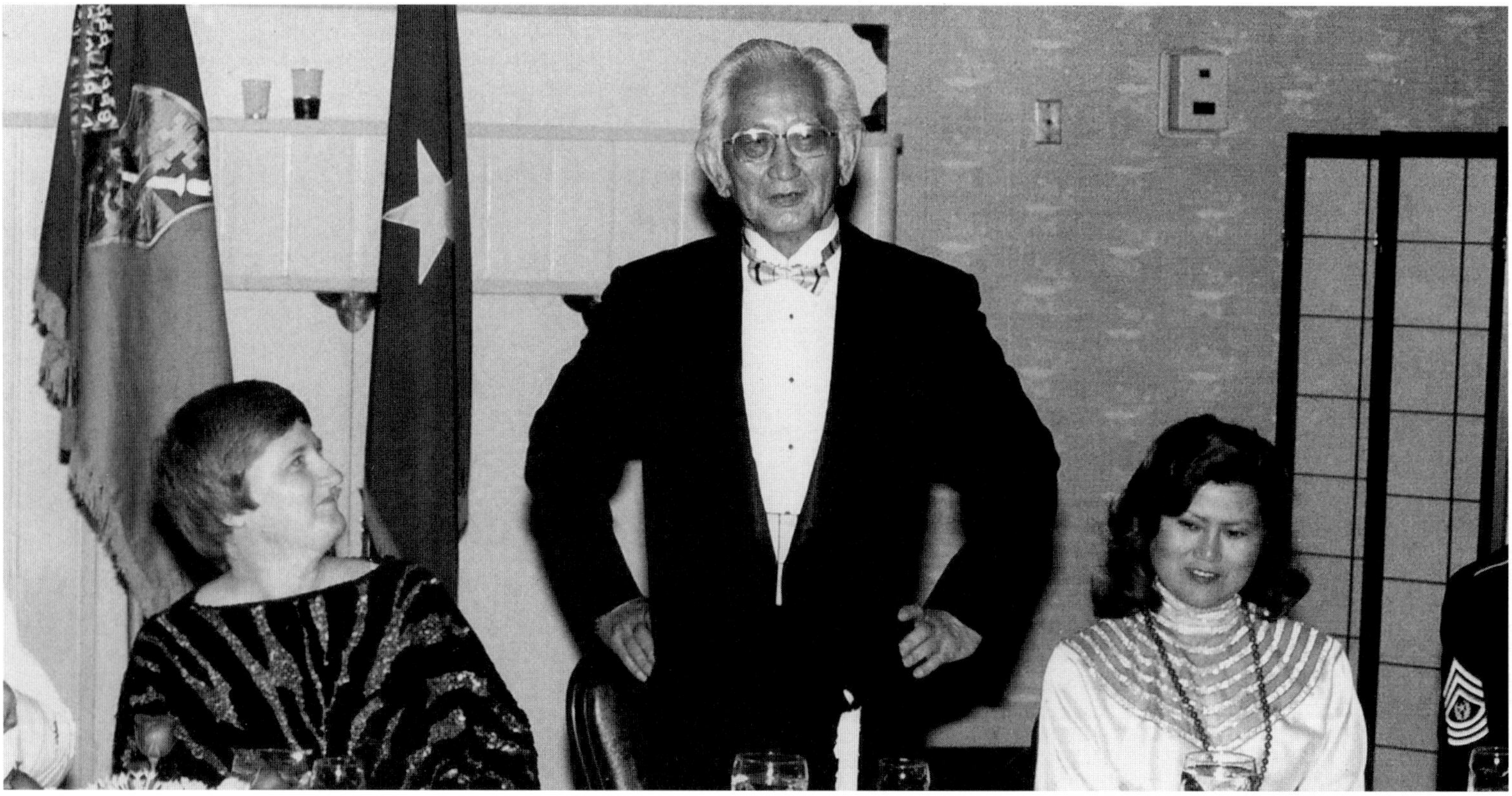

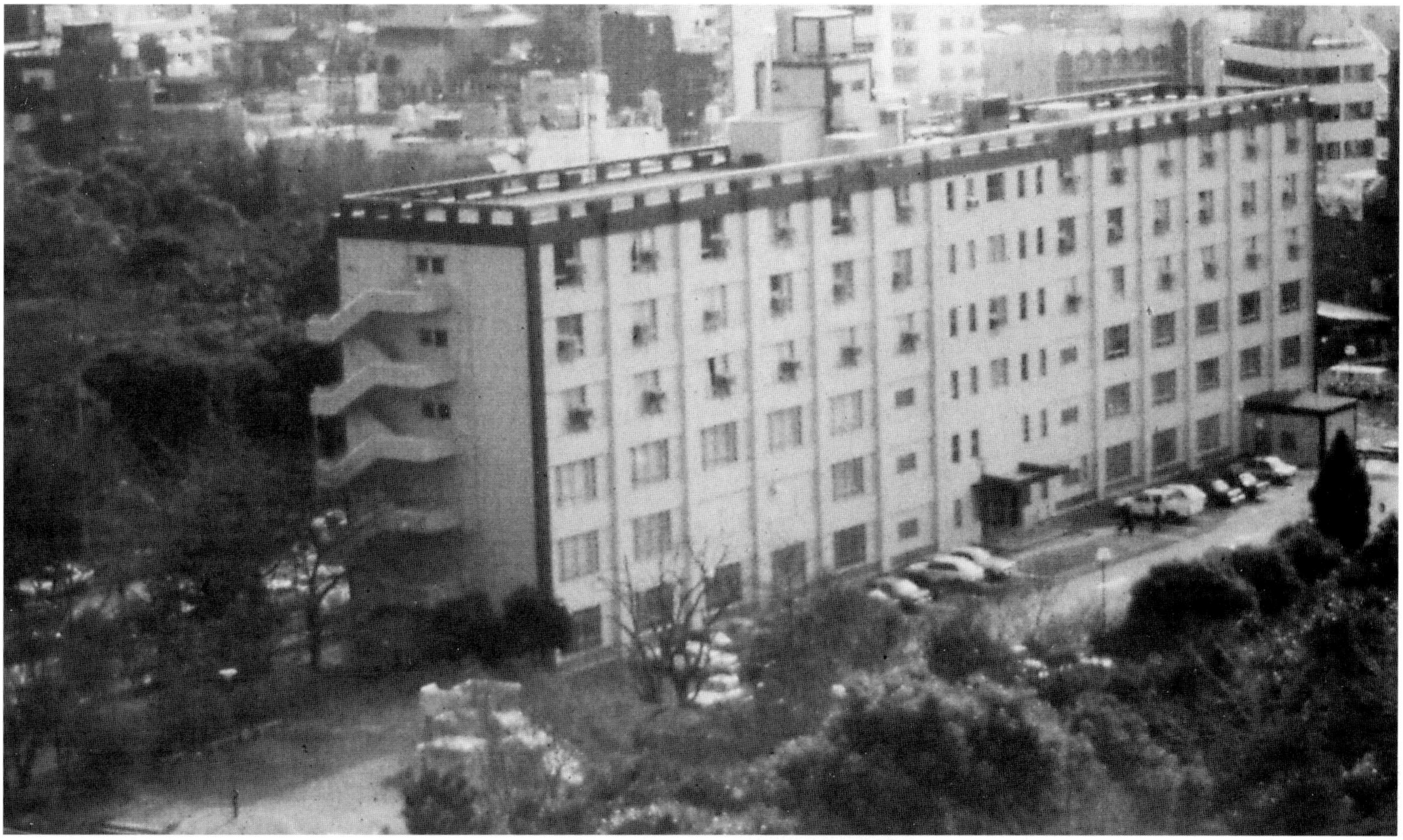

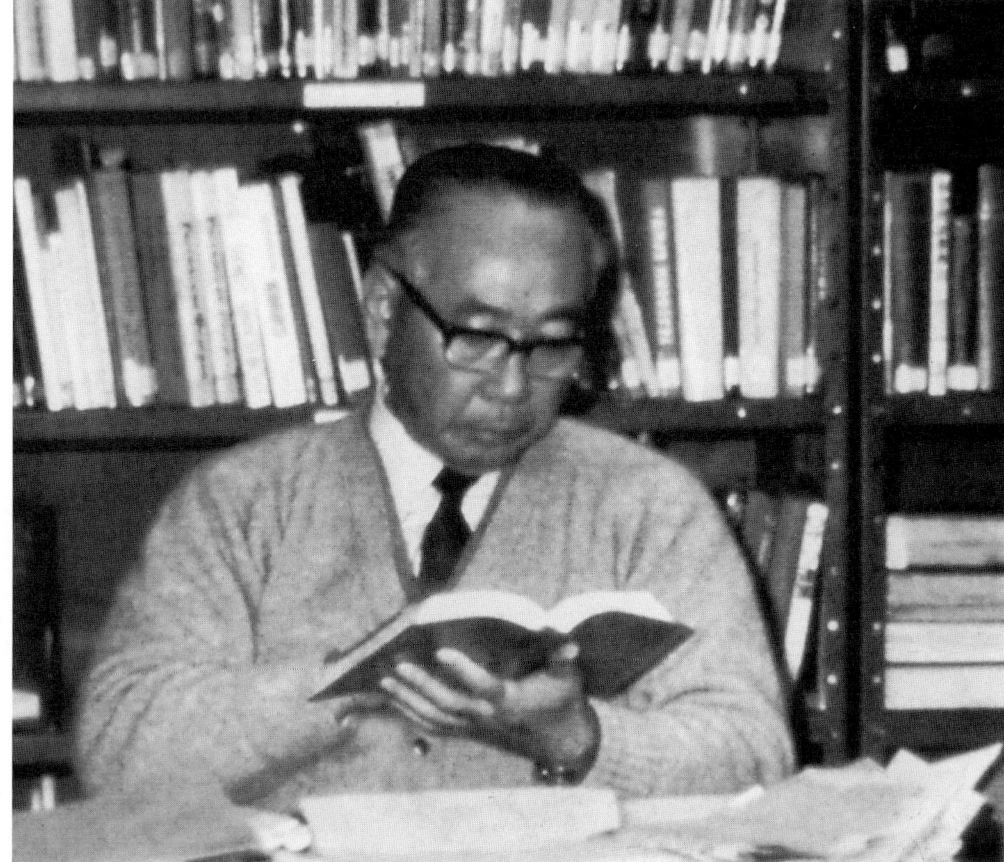

The Foreign Liaison Office was quartered in Hardy Barracks at Rappongi Circle in downtown Tokyo.

The 500th MI Brigade's Asian Studies Detachment at Camp Zama made use of the unique skills of retired Japanese Self Defense Force officers.

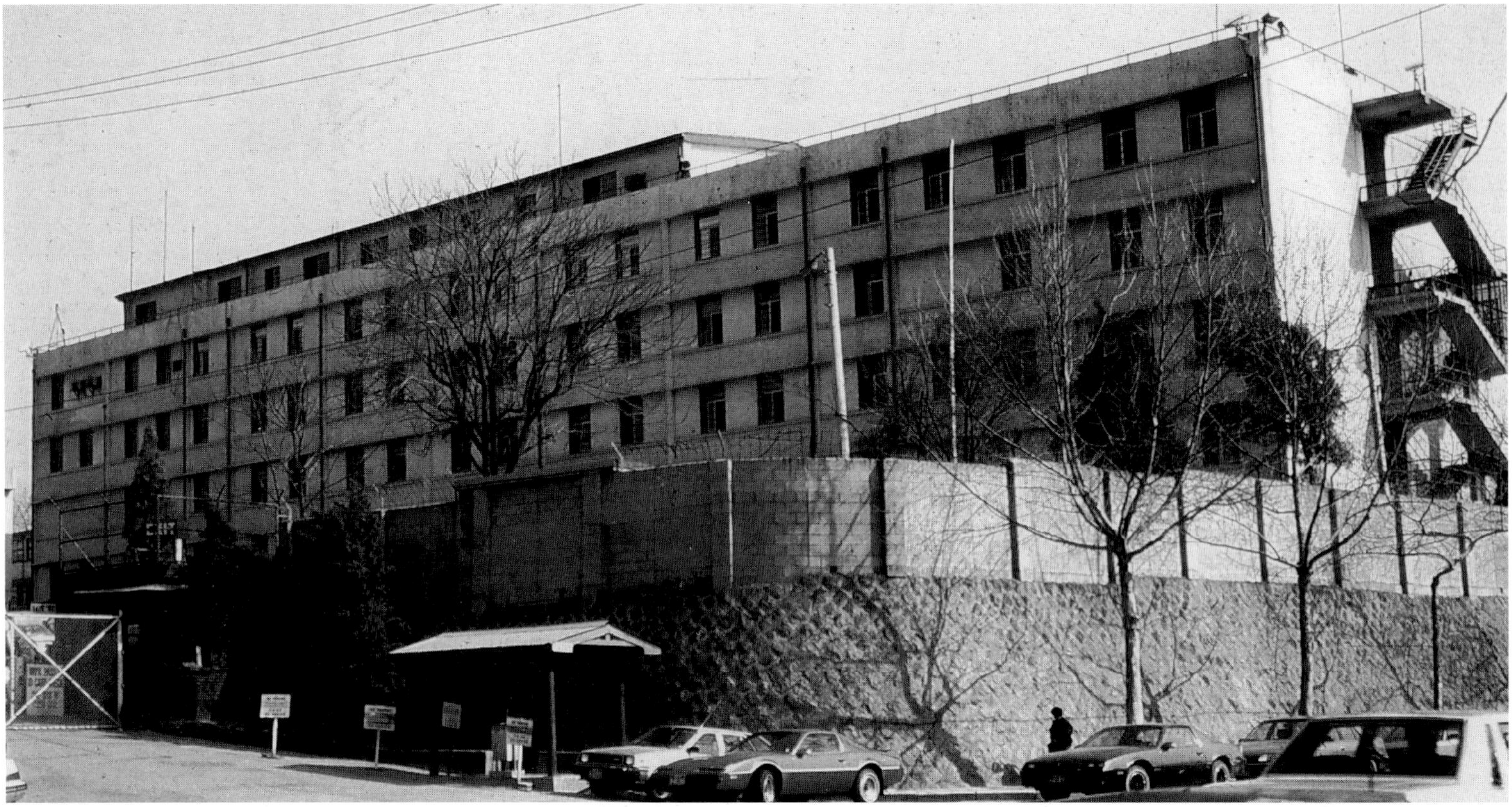

Headquarters of INSCOM'S 501st MI Brigade at Yongsan, Korea. The building formerly housed the Republic of Korea's Department of Defense.

The 501st provided intelligence support to the men and women of the Eighth U.S. Army in Korea. Below, soldiers of the 2d Infantry Division man a TOW missile launcher.

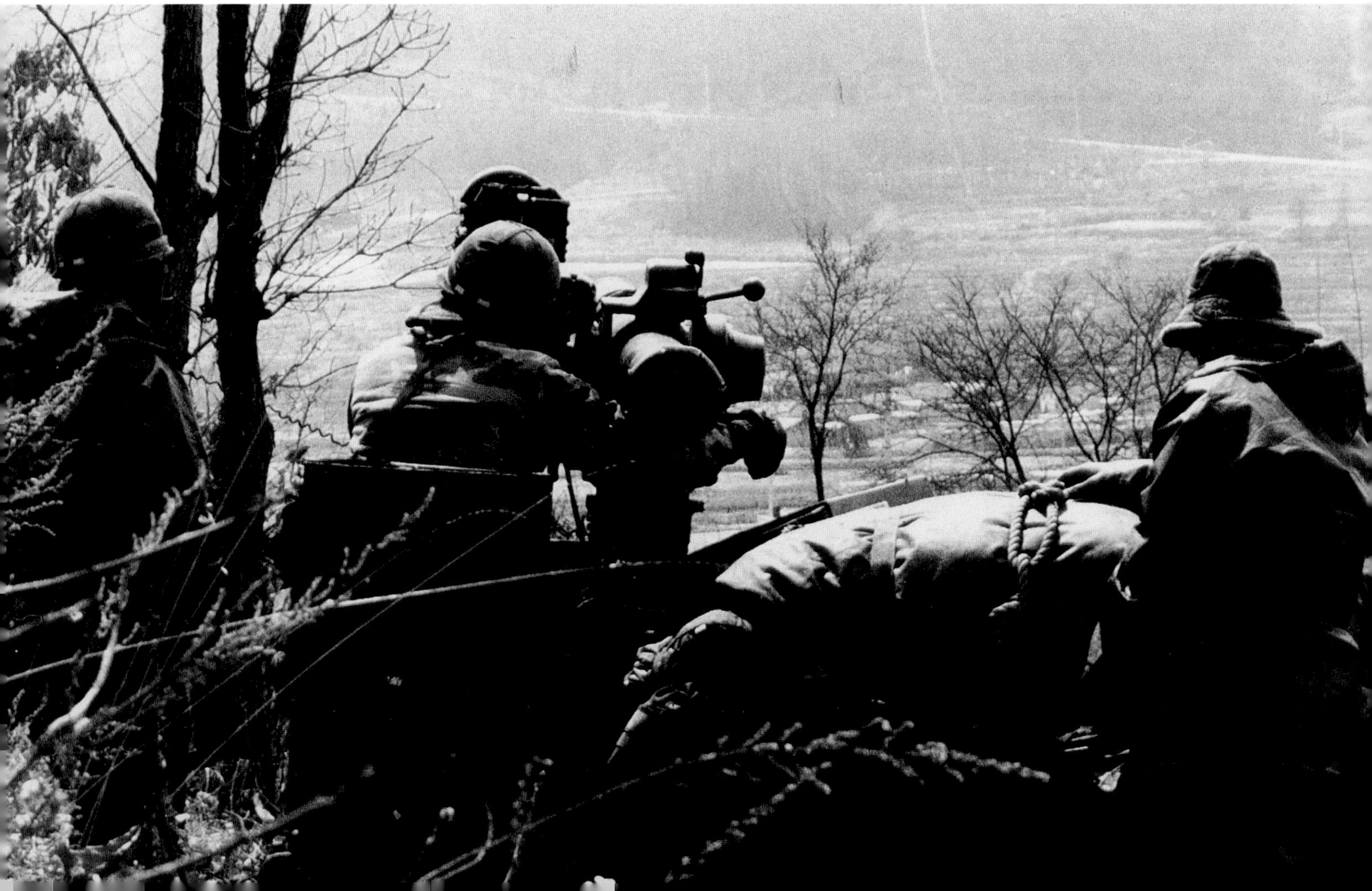

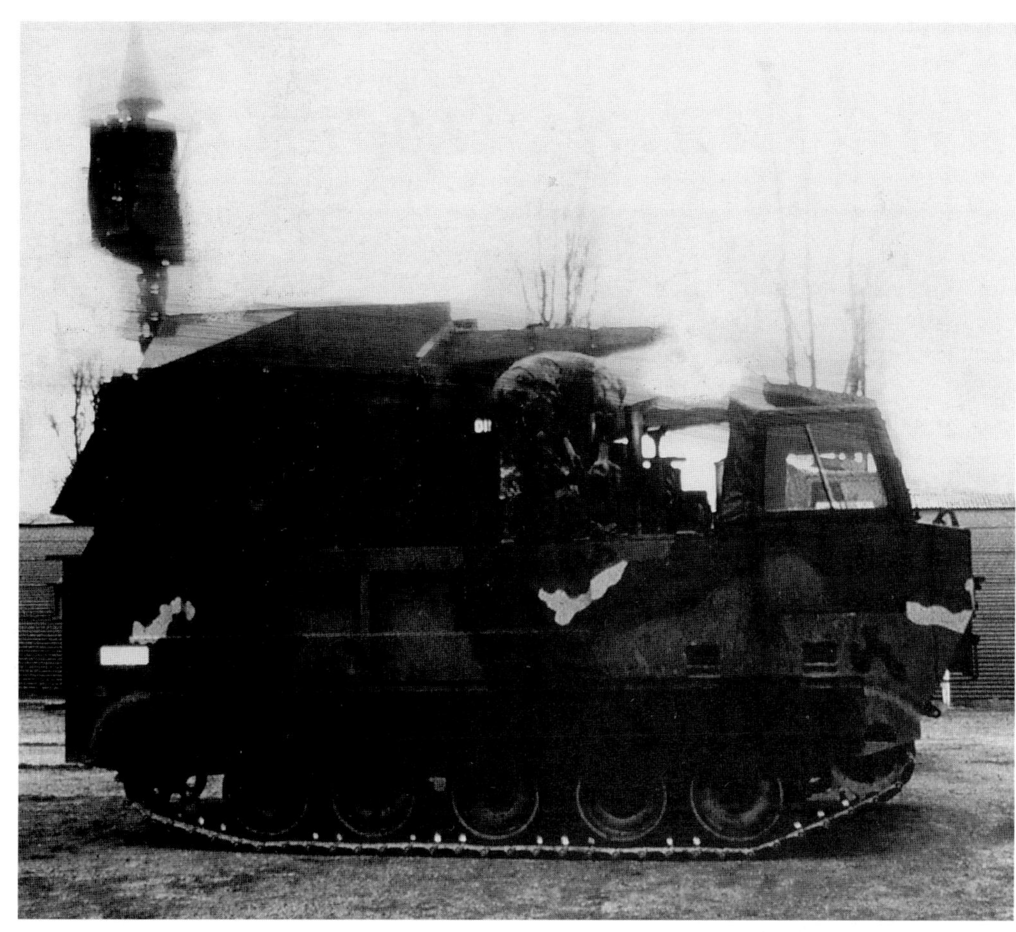

An MSQ–103 electronic intelligence collector of the 501st MI Brigade.

An officer of the 501st meets with personnel of the Republic of Korea (ROK) Army during the course of a joint exercise.

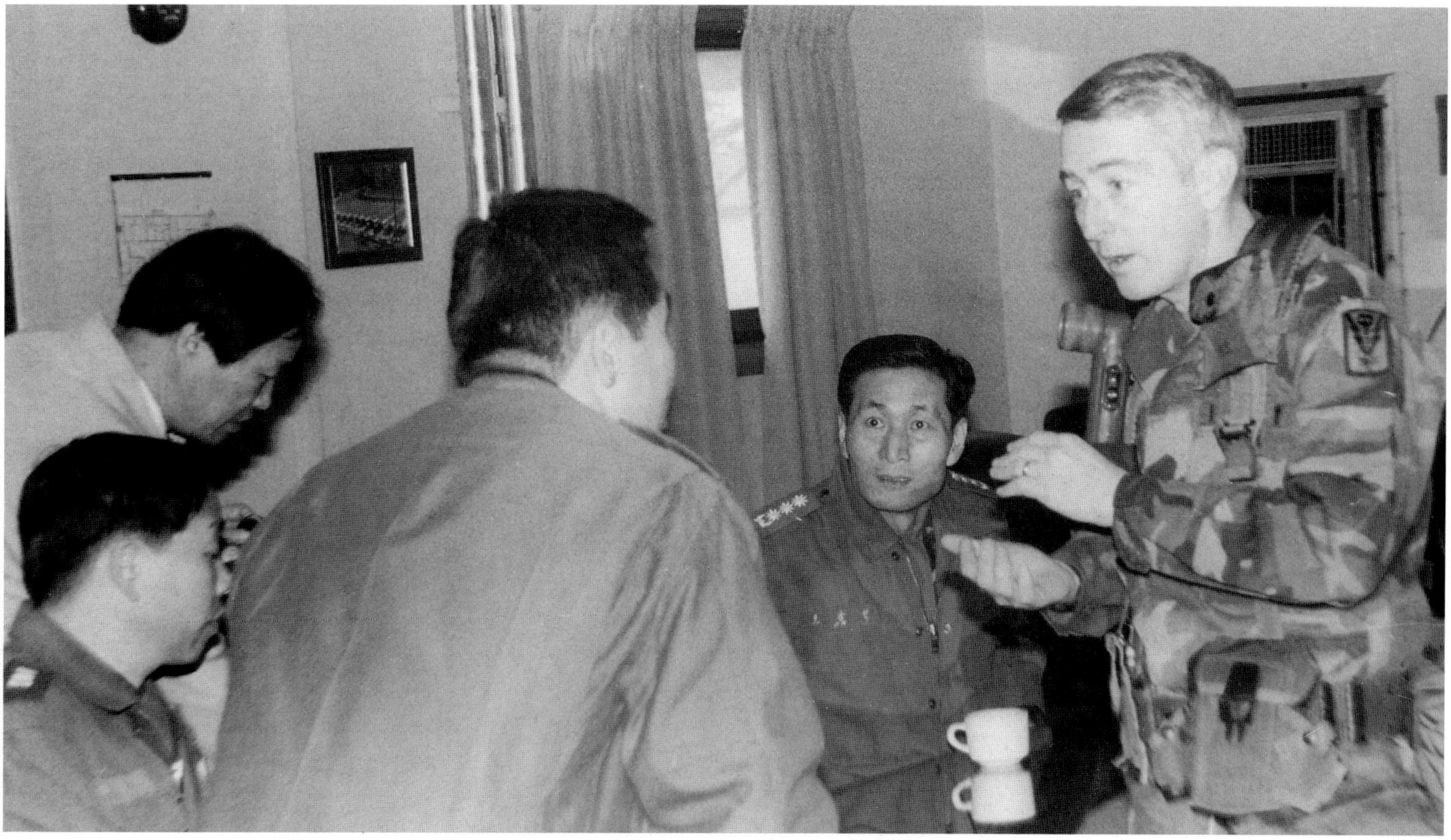

Central and Latin America

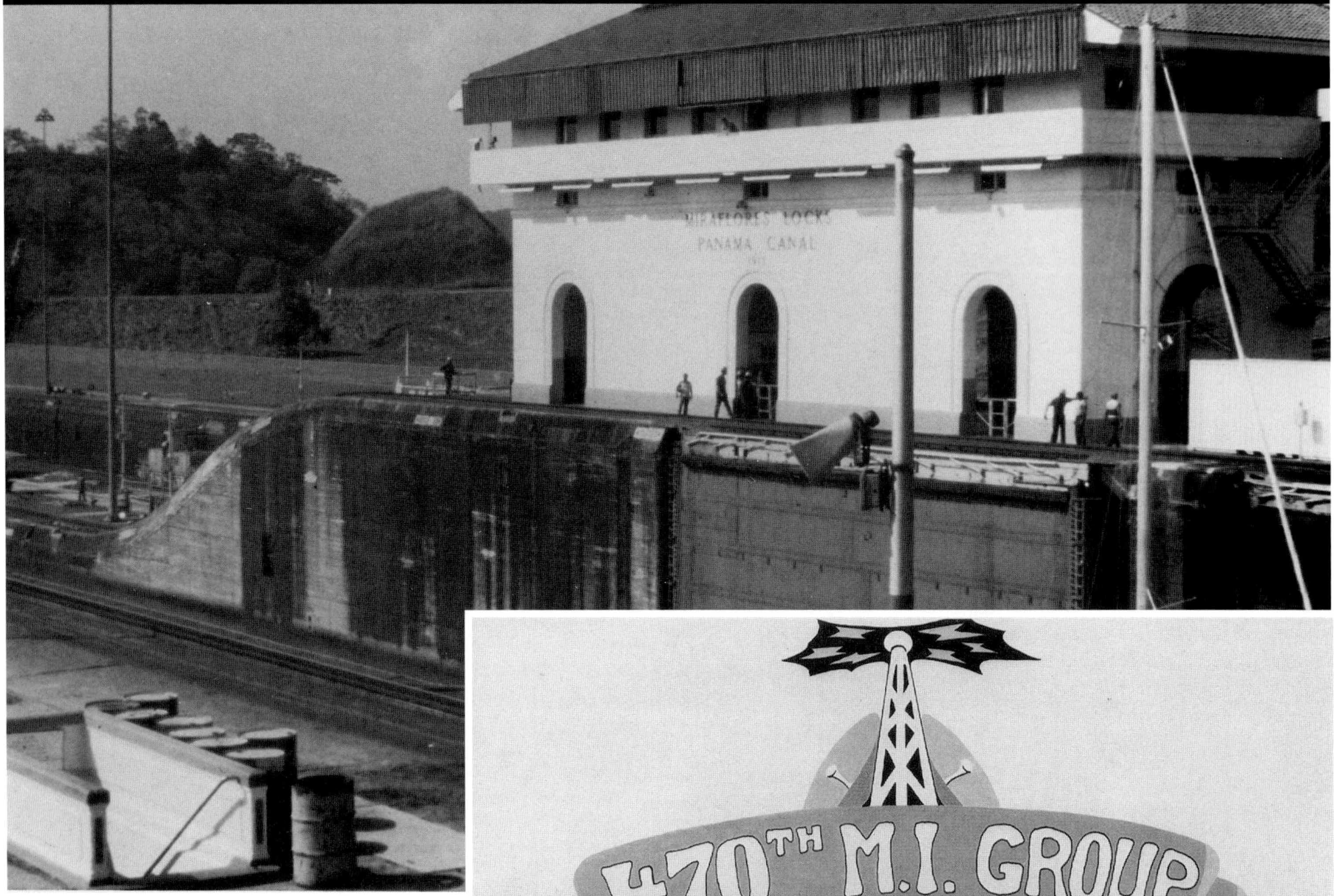

The Panama Canal. The need to defend the Canal led to a long-term American military presence in Panama. INSCOM'S 470th MI Brigade provided intelligence support to Southern Command and to the command's Army component, U.S. Army South.

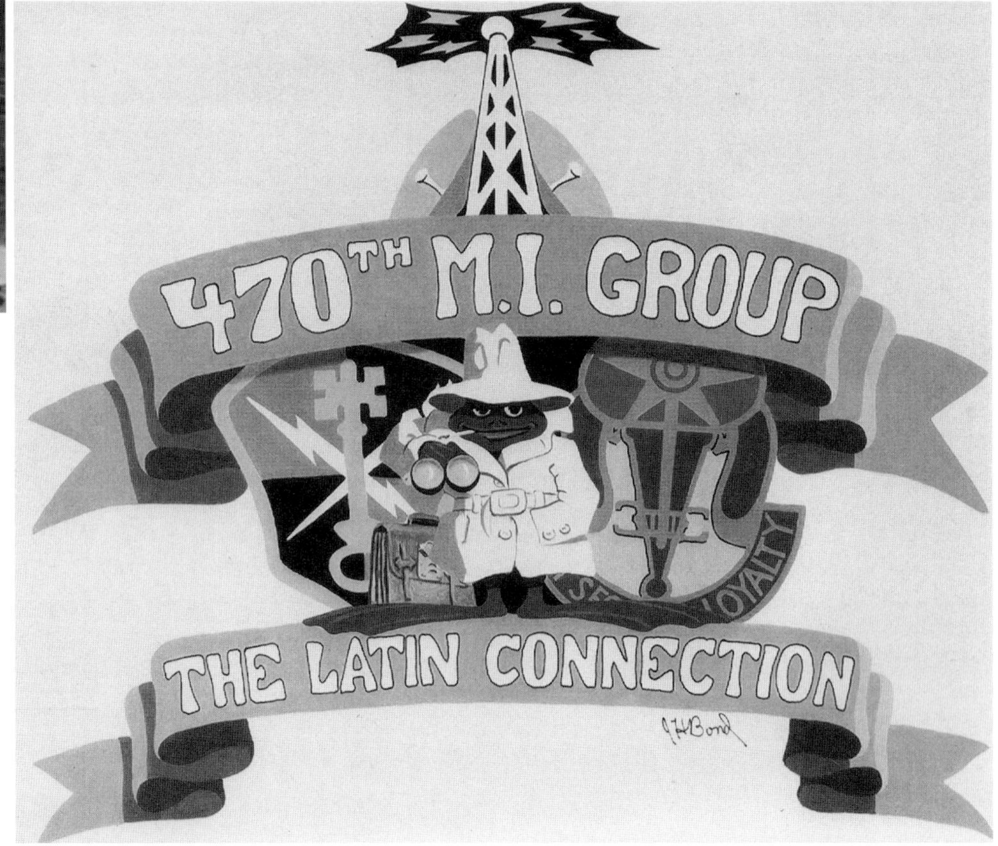

The 470th's informal logo.

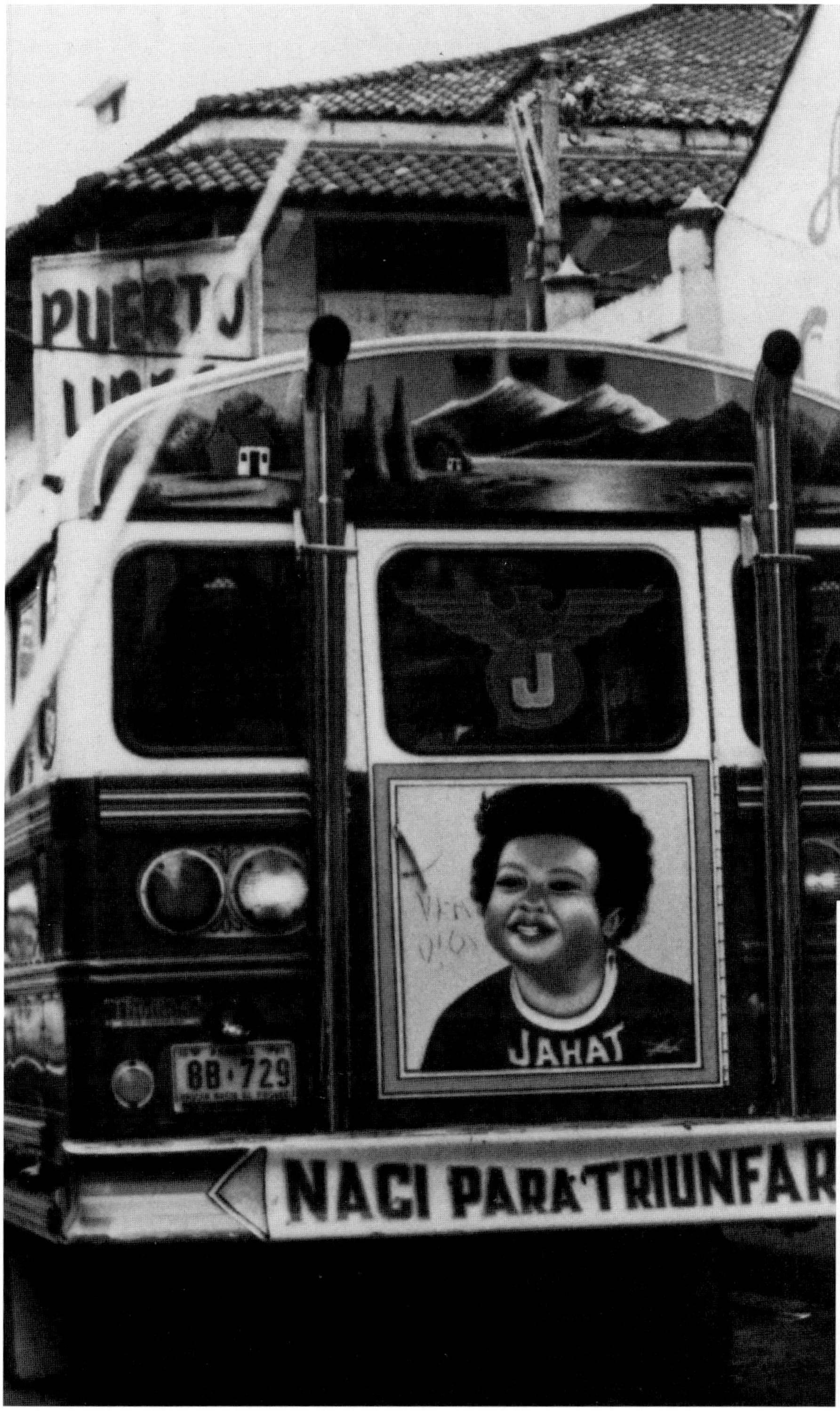

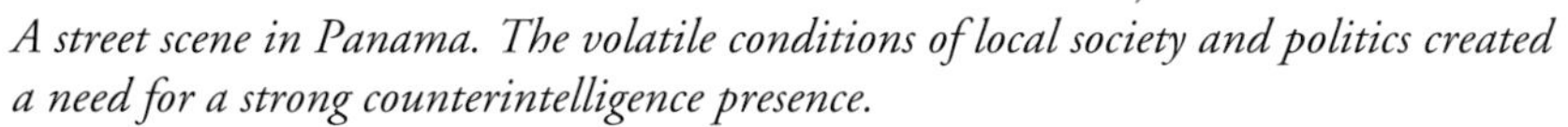

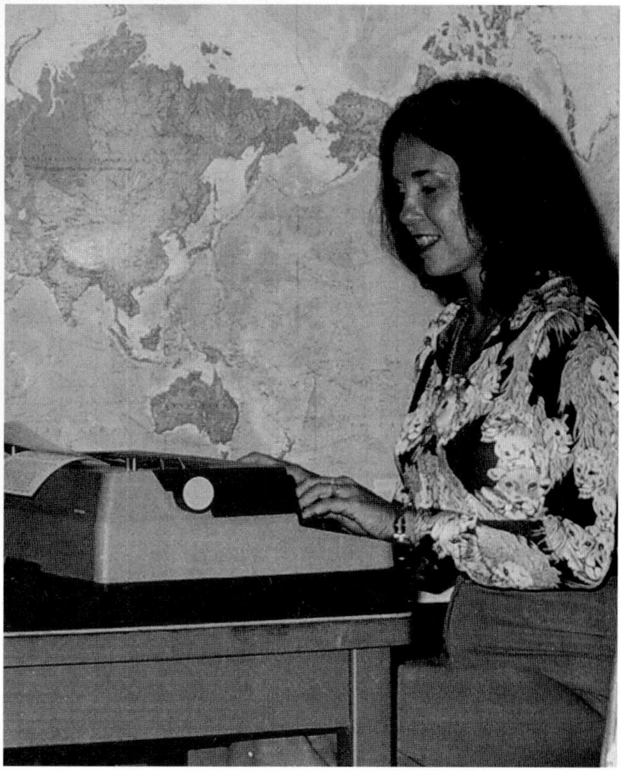

A street scene in Panama. The volatile conditions of local society and politics created a need for a strong counterintelligence presence.

A brigade intelligence assistant at Fort Clayton, Panama. As a result of threatened Communist penetration of the Western Hemisphere, the brigade's mission expanded to cover Central and Latin America during the course of the 1980's.

Central Command

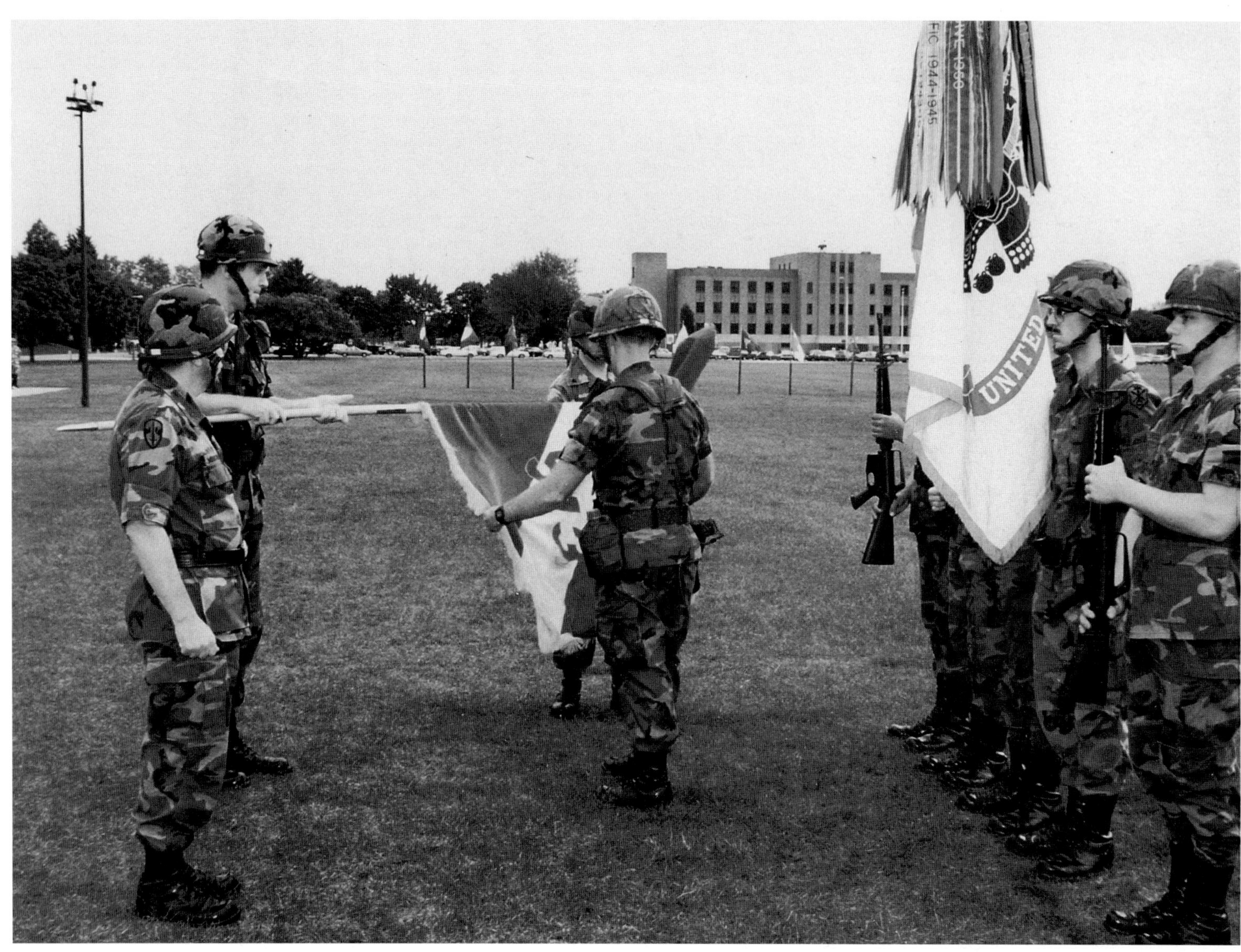

The 513th MI Group was activated in 1982 with the mission of providing the Army with intelligence support in contingency situations. Above, the group transitions to brigade status in 1987.

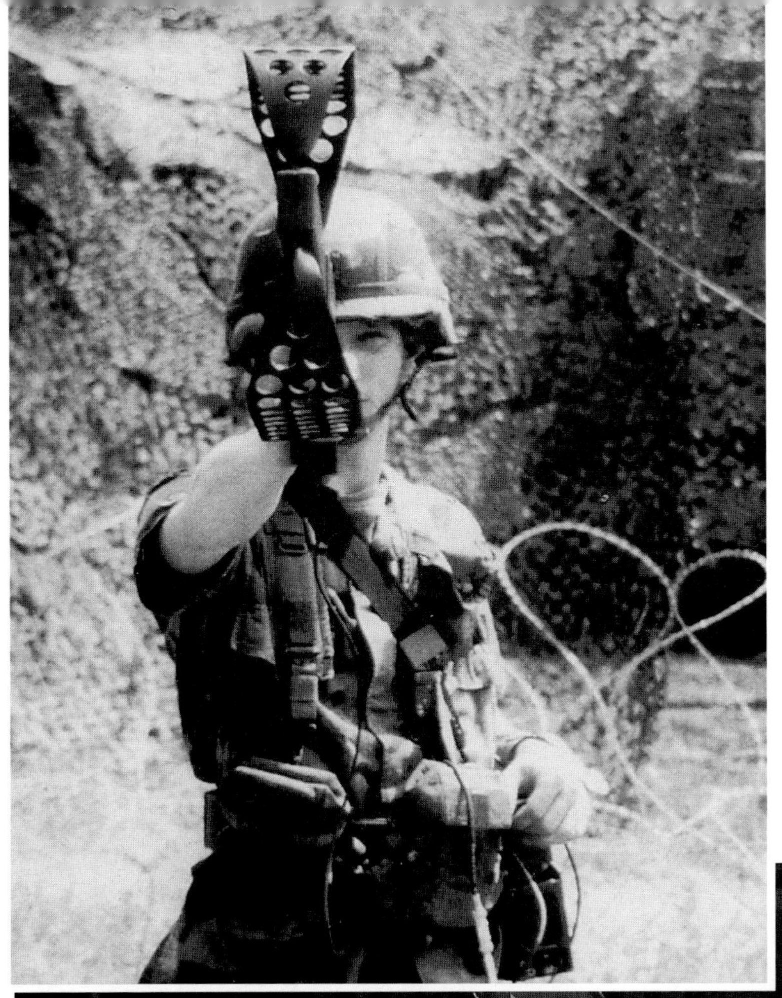

A 513th MI Brigade soldier demonstrates a new experimental man-carried radio direction-finding system.

A communicator transmits an intelligence report utilizing the TT–99 Teletype System.

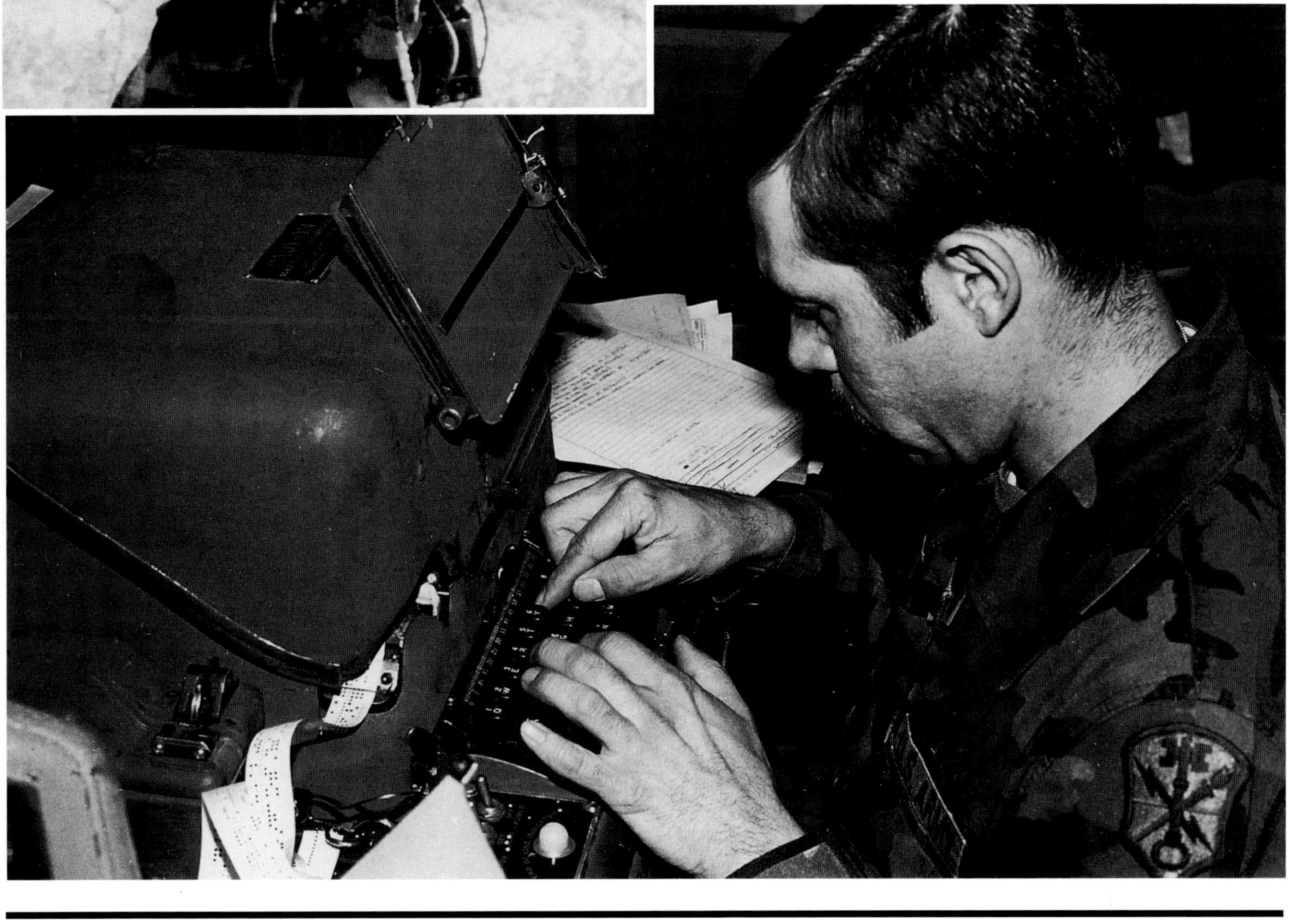

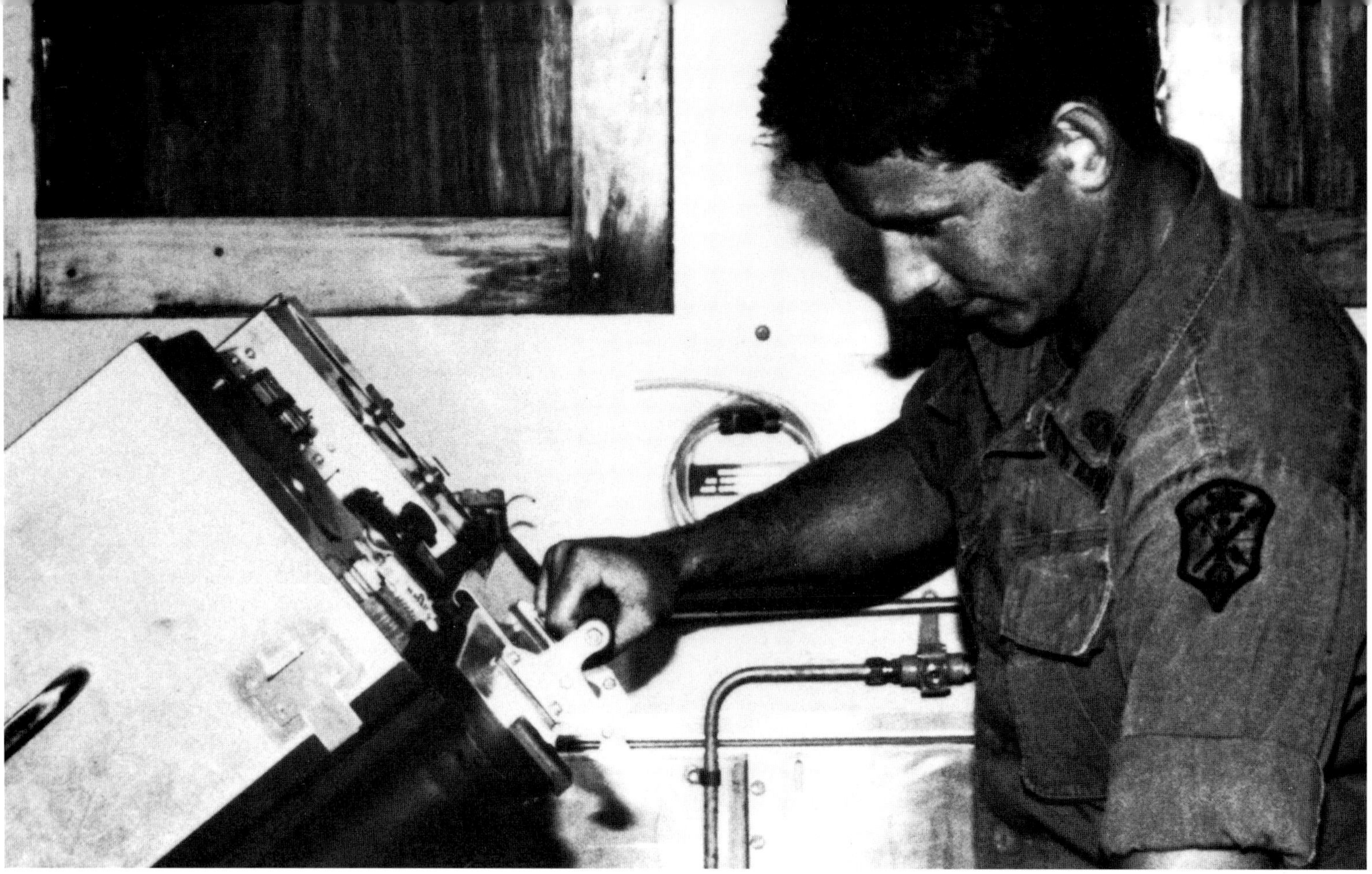

Photo interpreters of the 513th's 17th MI Company in 1982.

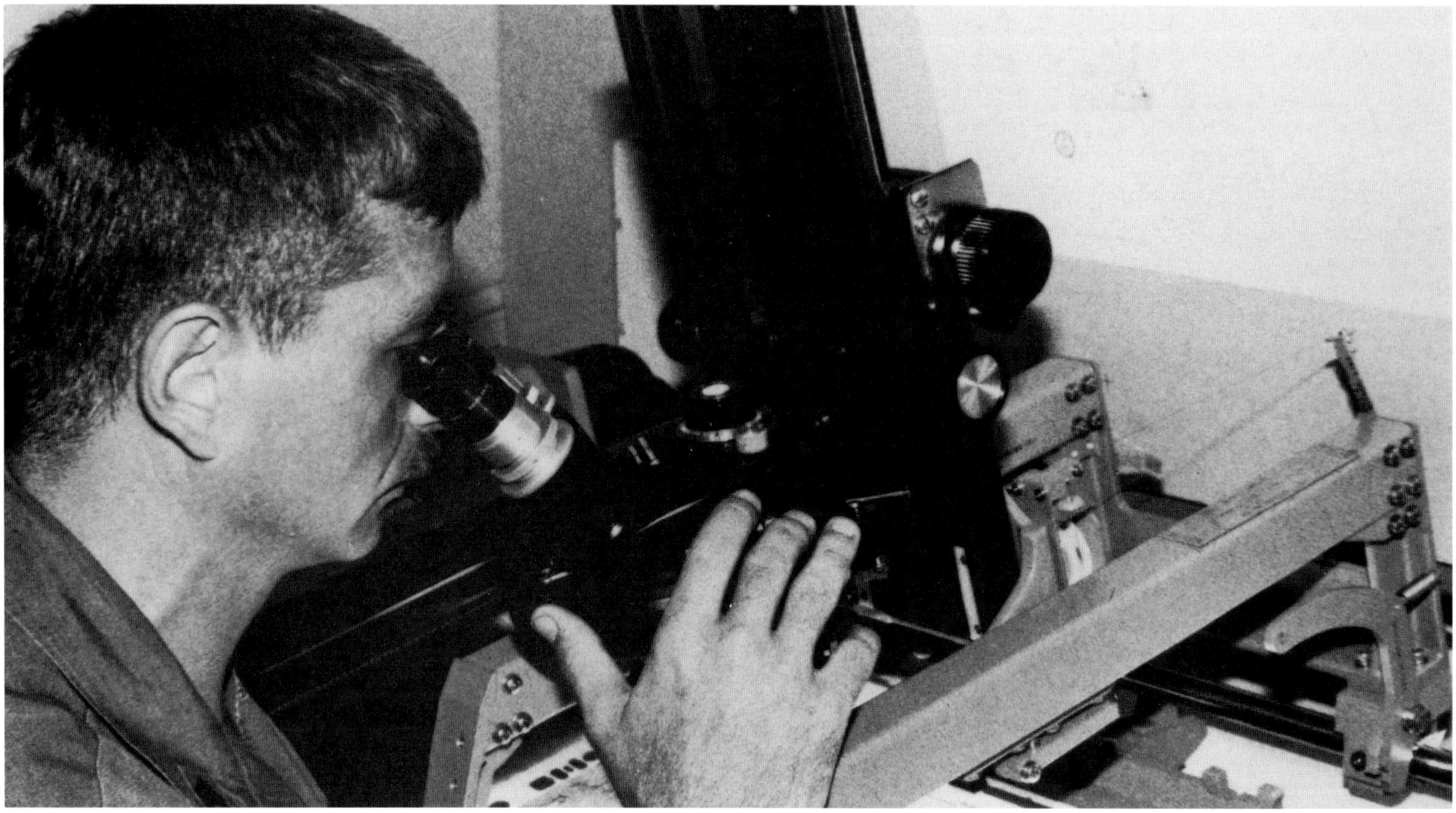

Technical Intelligence

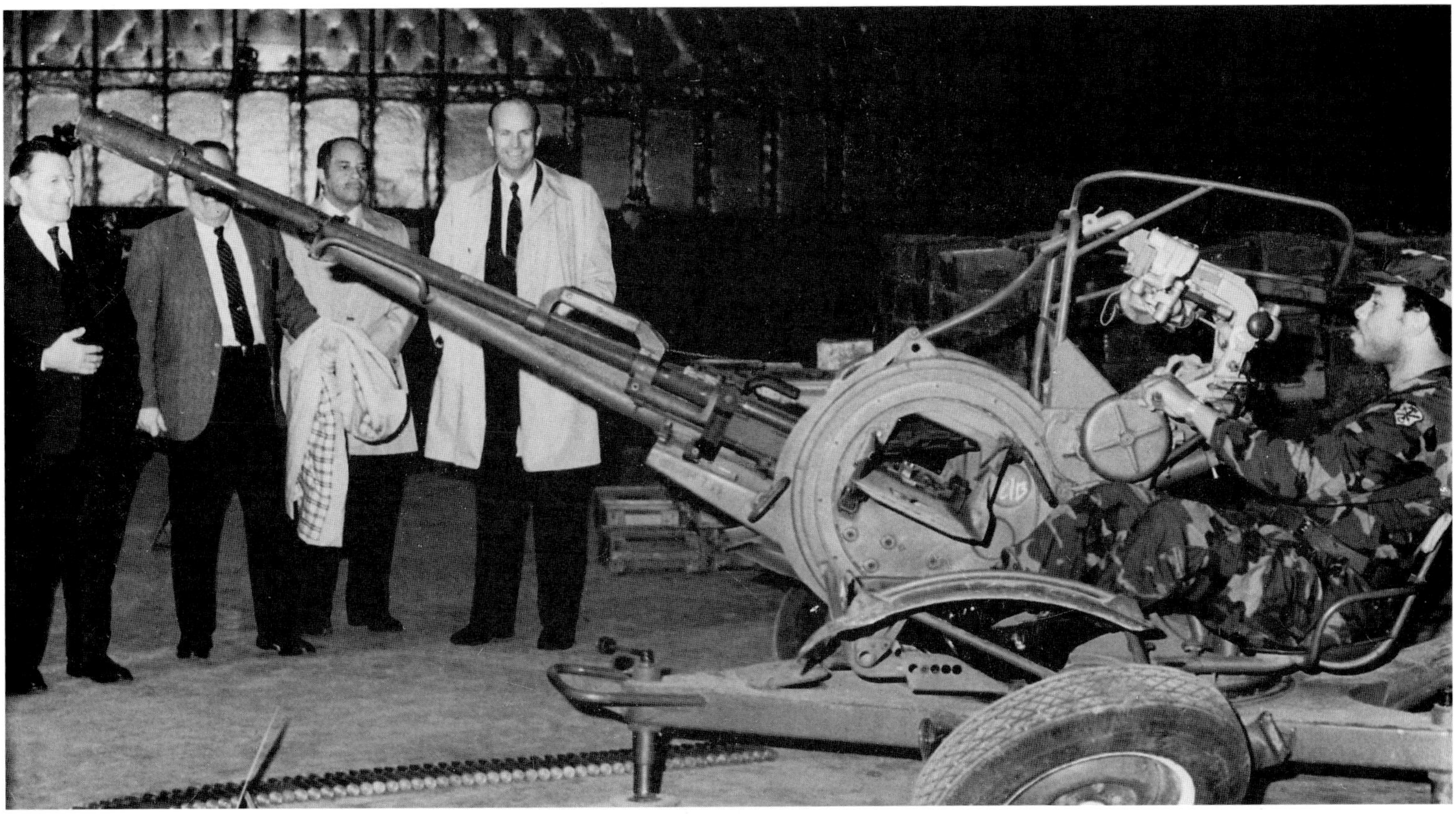

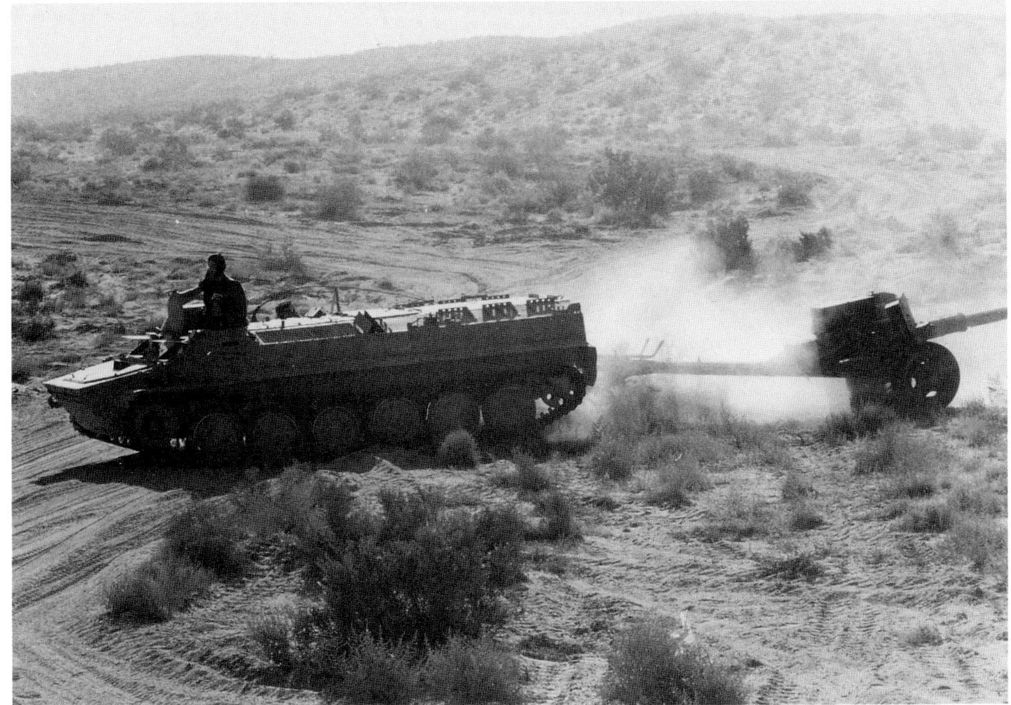

In the aftermath of Operation URGENT FURY, a soldier from the 513th demonstrates a Soviet-made antiaircraft gun captured on Grenada to Department of Defense officials in 1983. At extreme left, Secretary of Defense Casper Weinberger.

In addition to its contingency mission, the 513th's technical intelligence unit also was responsible for providing foreign materiel support to Army training needs under the Opposing Forces (OPFOR) program. Left, an OPFOR demonstration of Soviet-type weaponry.

Single Discipline Units

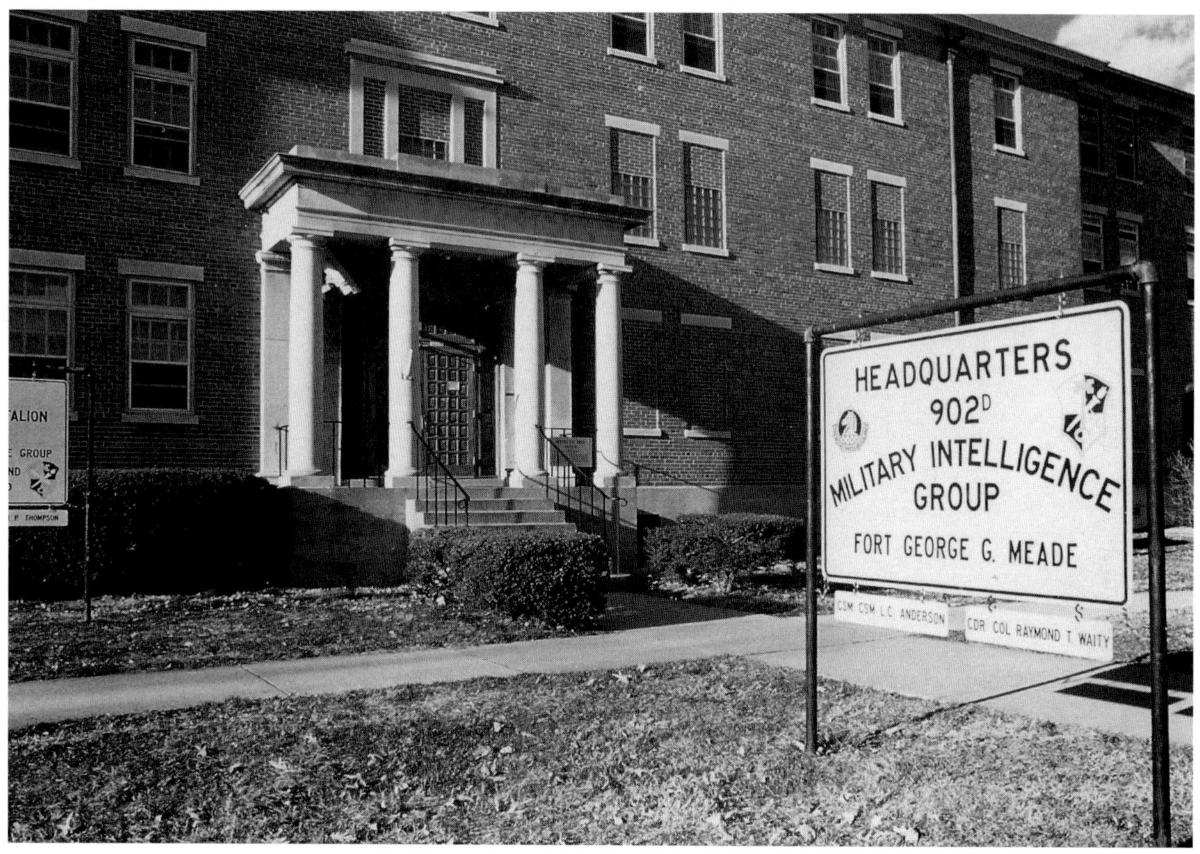

Counterintelligence support to the Army in CONUS was provided by INSCOM's 902d MI Group, with headquarters at Fort George G. Meade, Maryland. This post had been closely associated with Army intelligence since 1973.

In addition to its field stations and multidiscipline brigades, INSCOM also commanded a number of specialized, single discipline units. During the 1980's, these included the 902d MI Group, which provided counterintelligence support to CONUS; the Central Security Facility, which housed both the Army's Investigative Records Repository and INSCOM's Freedom of Information and Privacy Office; the Special Security Group, which controlled and disseminated Sensitive Compartmented Information to Army MACOM's; the U.S. Army Russian Institute; the Foreign Language Training Center, Europe; and specialized intelligence, counterintelligence, and support units.

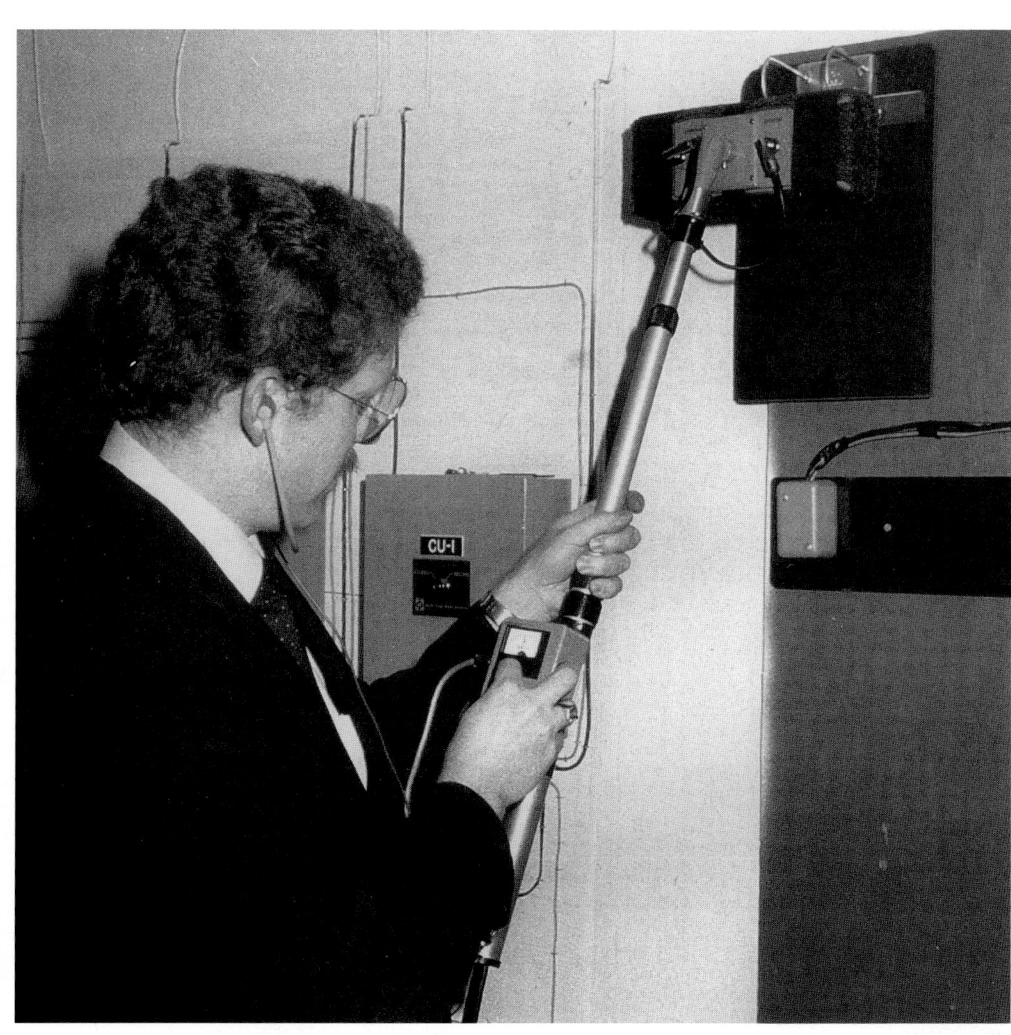

A technical surveillance countermeasures technician of the 902d sweeps a room for "bugs."

Counterintelligence personnel conduct a surveillance operation from a vehicle.

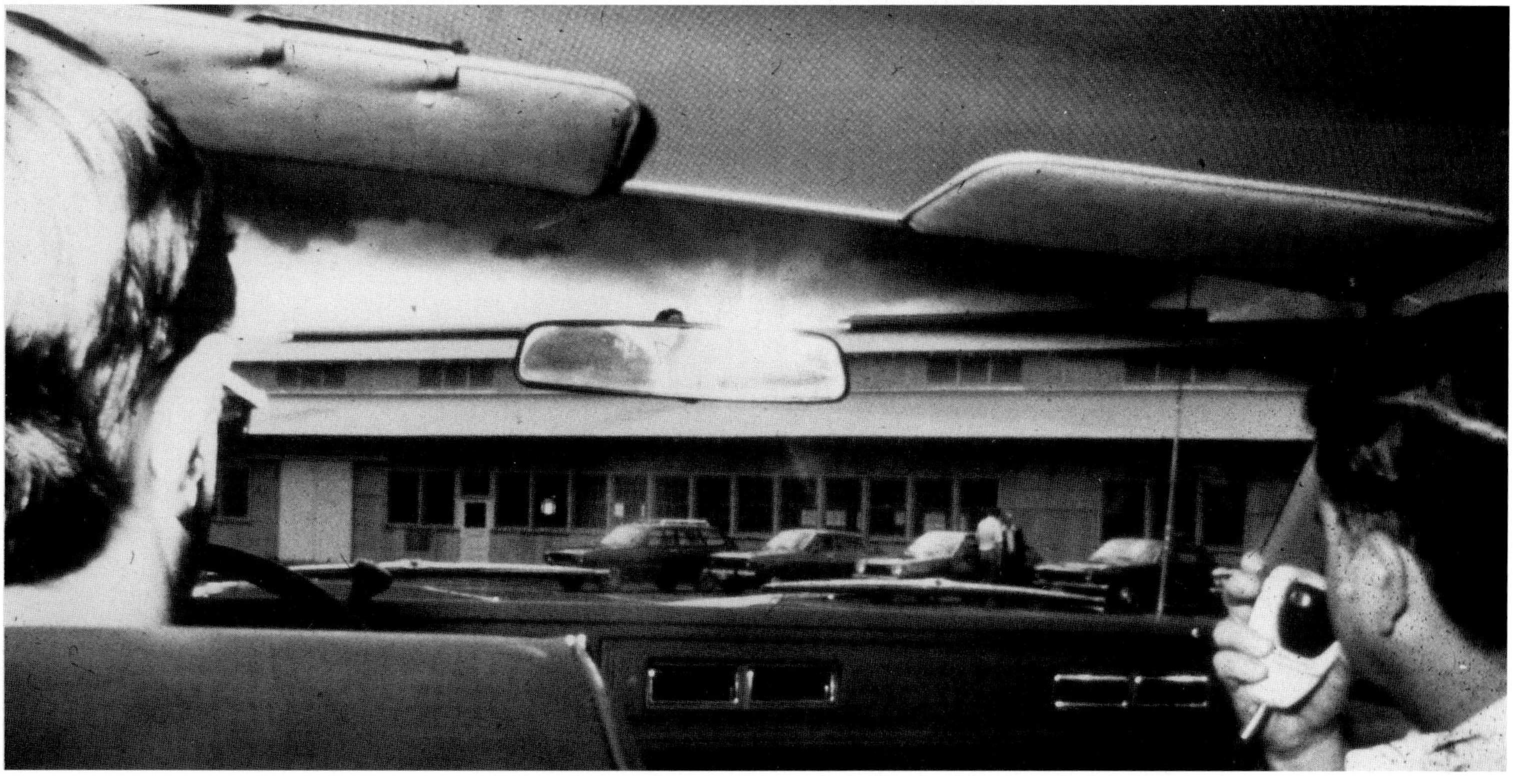

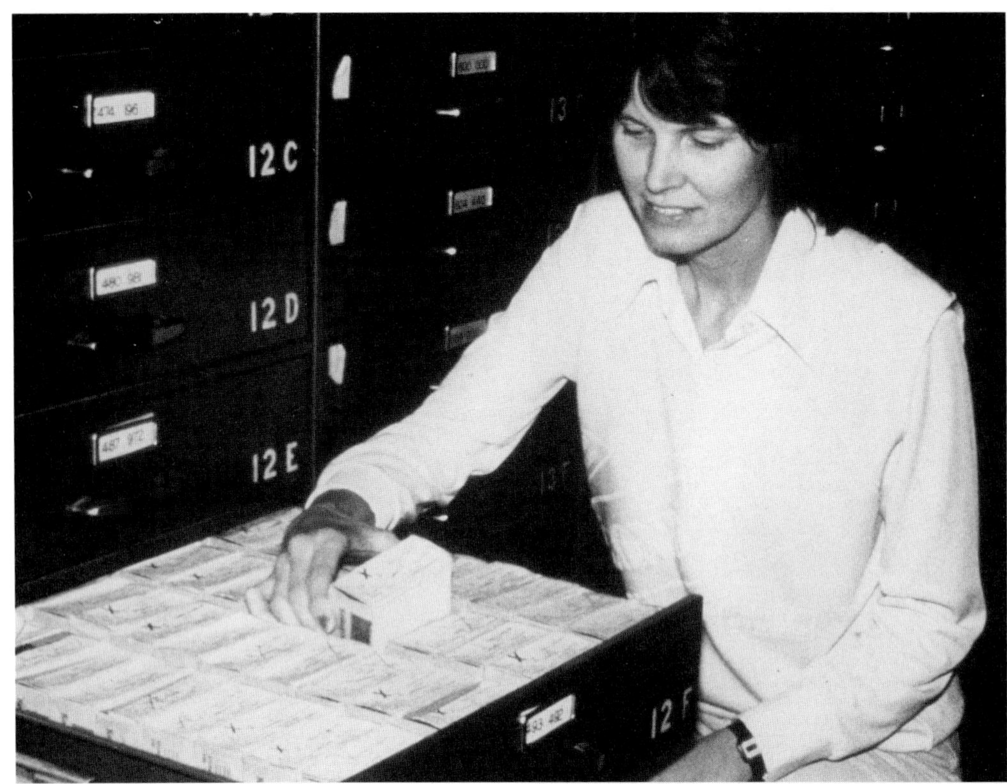

Army counterintelligence records were held by INSCOM's Central Security Facility, also located at Fort Meade. To reduce space, records were put on microfilm.

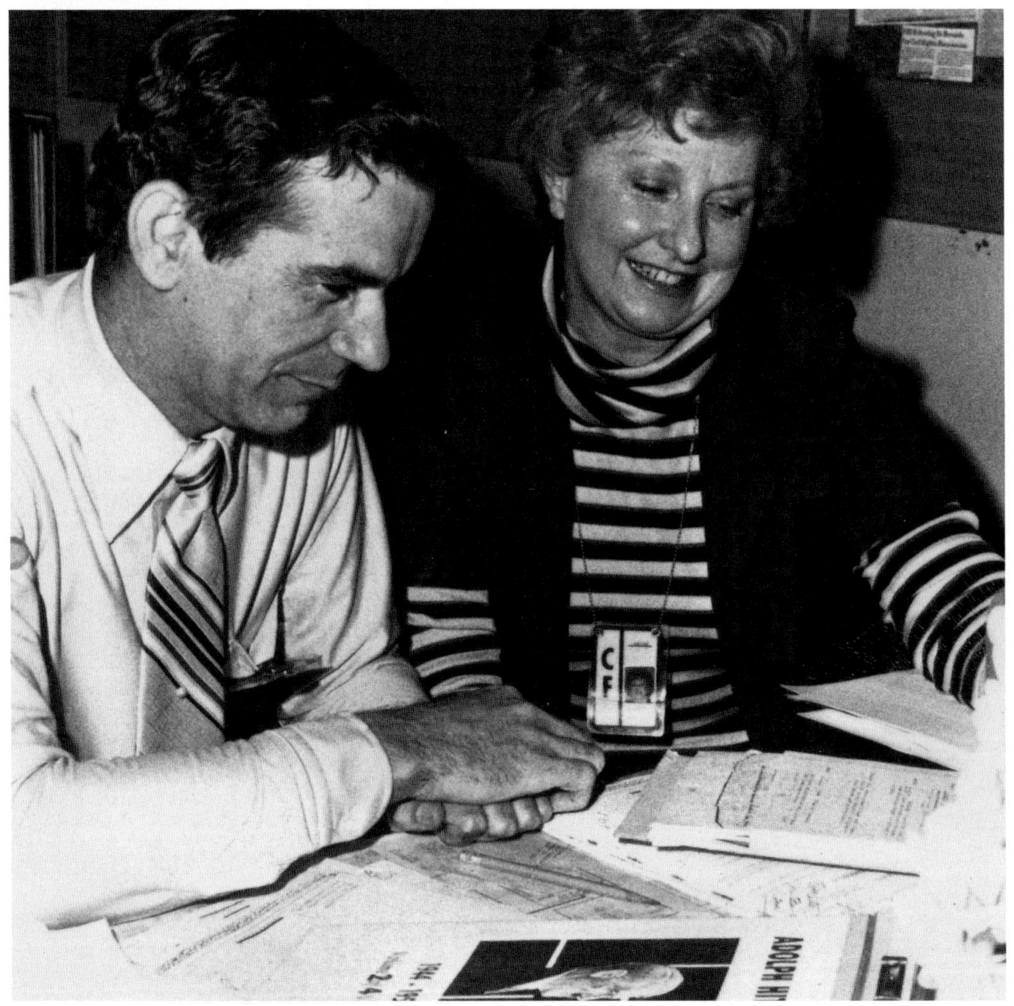

In addition to housing records, the Central Security Facility supervised the INSCOM Freedom of Information and Privacy Act Office, which responded to public information requests.

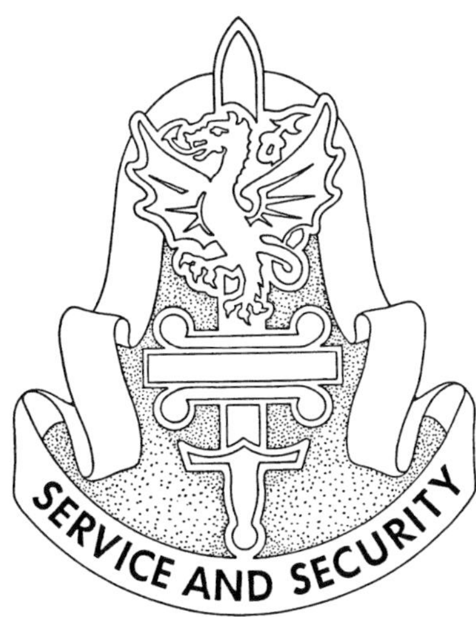

Insignia of the Special Security Group. The Group was a lineal descendant of the World War II Military Intelligence Service's Special Branch, charged with the secure dissemination of sensitive compartmented information.

A Sensitive Compartmented Information Facility (SCIF). Accreditation and supervision of such facilities was one of the Special Security Group's missions.

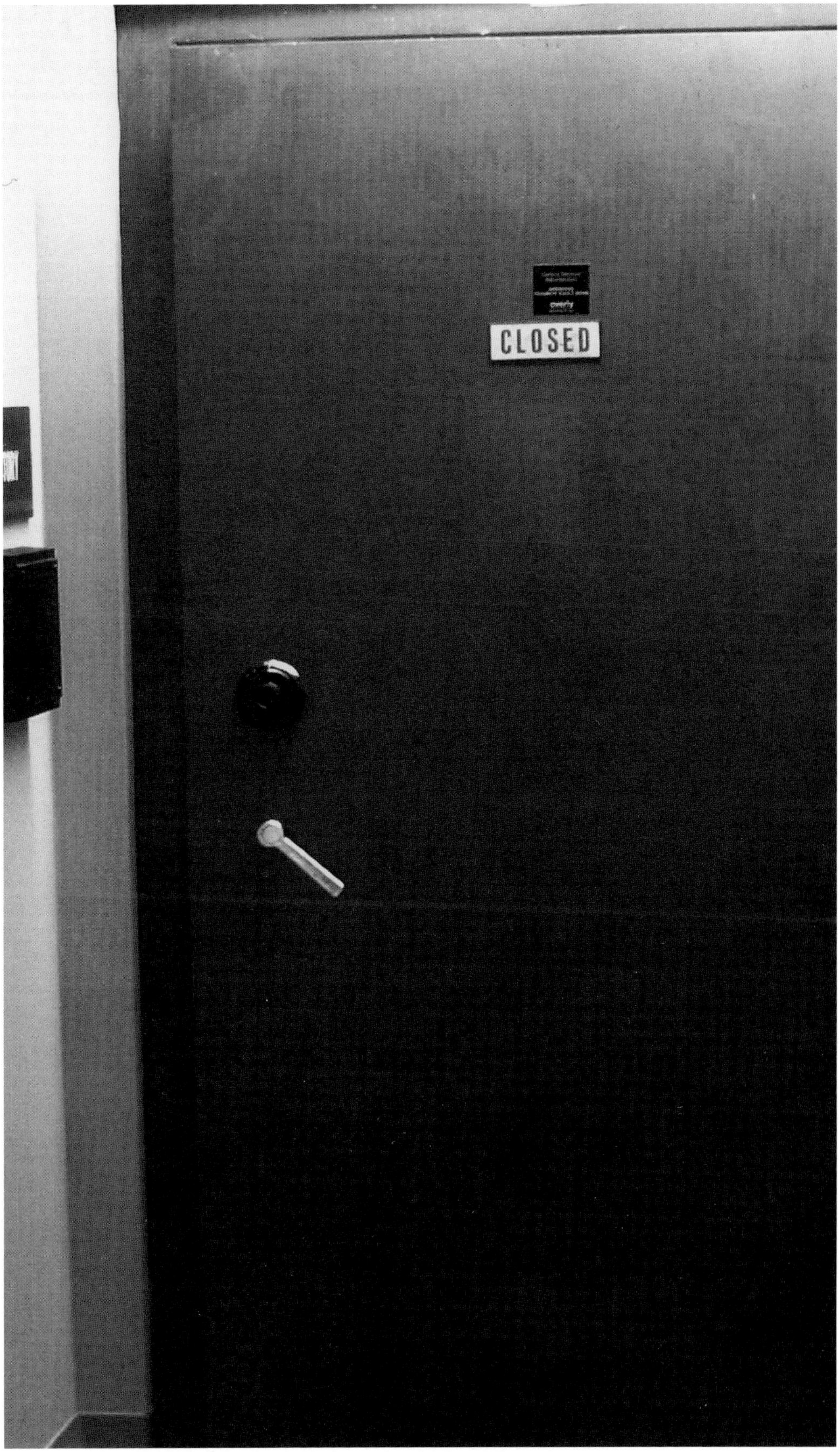

Tactical Support

As a result of implementation of the Intelligence Organization and Stationing Study, military intelligence units for the first time were assigned to Army tactical units rather than being attached. Each division was assigned a Combat Electronic Warfare and Intelligence (CEWI) Battalion. These battalions amalgamated former MI, Army Security Agency, and ground surveillance assets. As initially configured, each battalion had a headquarters, headquarters and operations company and three line companies. The headquarters company included collection management, counterintelligence, interrogation, and aviation personnel; the line companies respectively carried out functional missions of collection and jamming, ground surveillance through radars and sensors, and service support.

To provide equivalent support at the corps level, CEWI-type Military Intelligence Groups were activated; these were upgraded to brigade status in 1985. Finally, the Army reorganized and redesignated all of its Active Component Military Intelligence Battalions (Aerial Reconnaissance Support) as Military Intelligence Battalions (Aerial Exploitation). These new units integrated imagery interpretation with aerial surveillance capabilities and provided a suitable management framework for various types of airborne collection platforms.

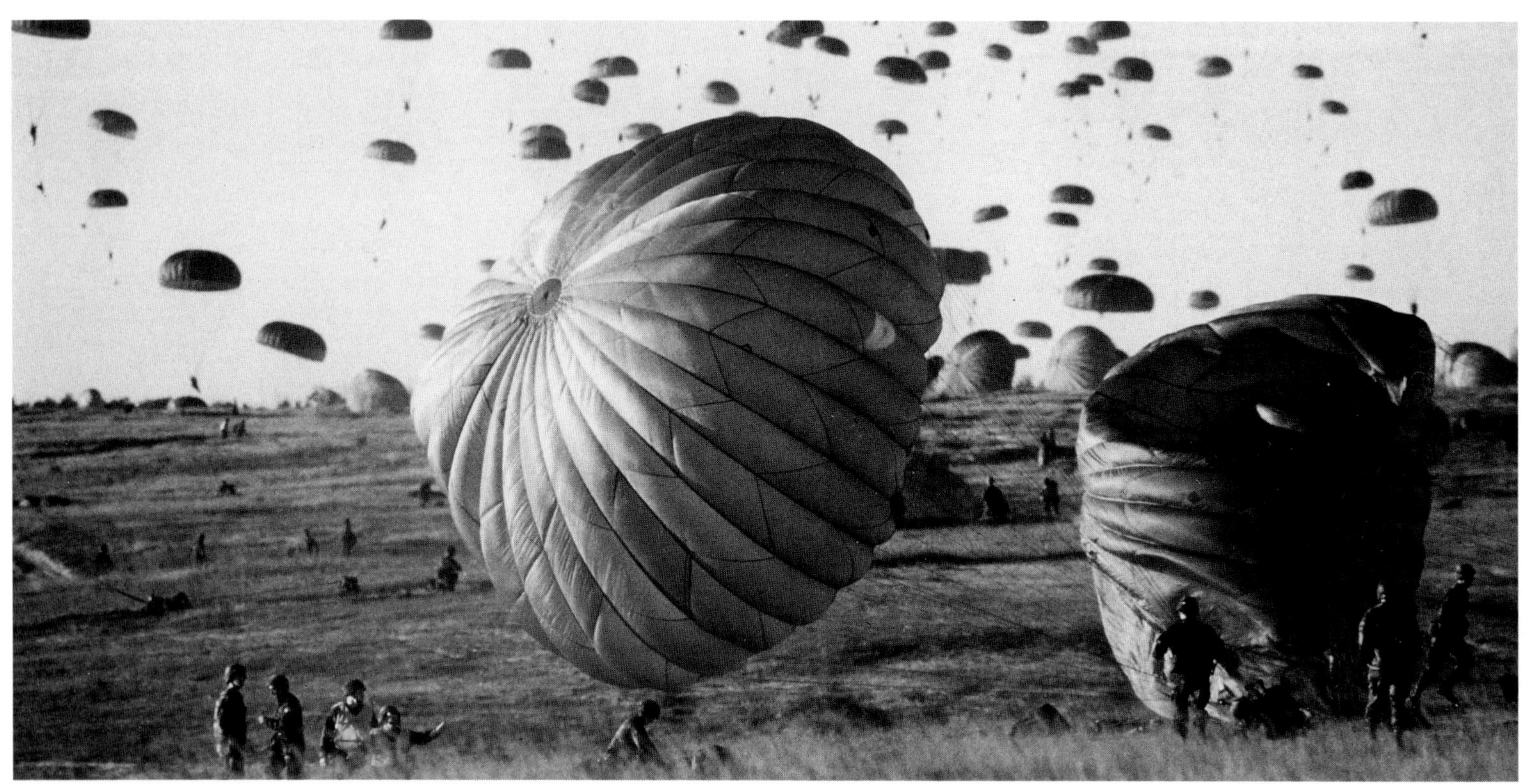

America's fire-brigade. Troopers of the 82d Airborne Division, the core of the Army's rapid-reaction forces, make a mass jump at Fort Bragg, North Carolina. The division received its intelligence support from the 313th MI Battalion.

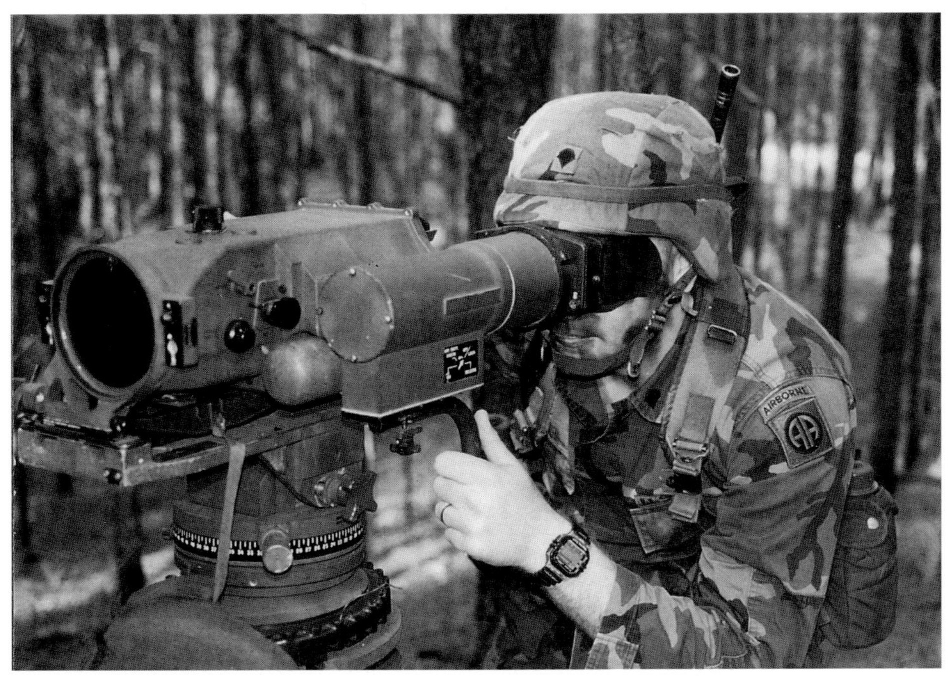

A soldier of the 313th MI Battalion with the TAS–6 optical scanner.

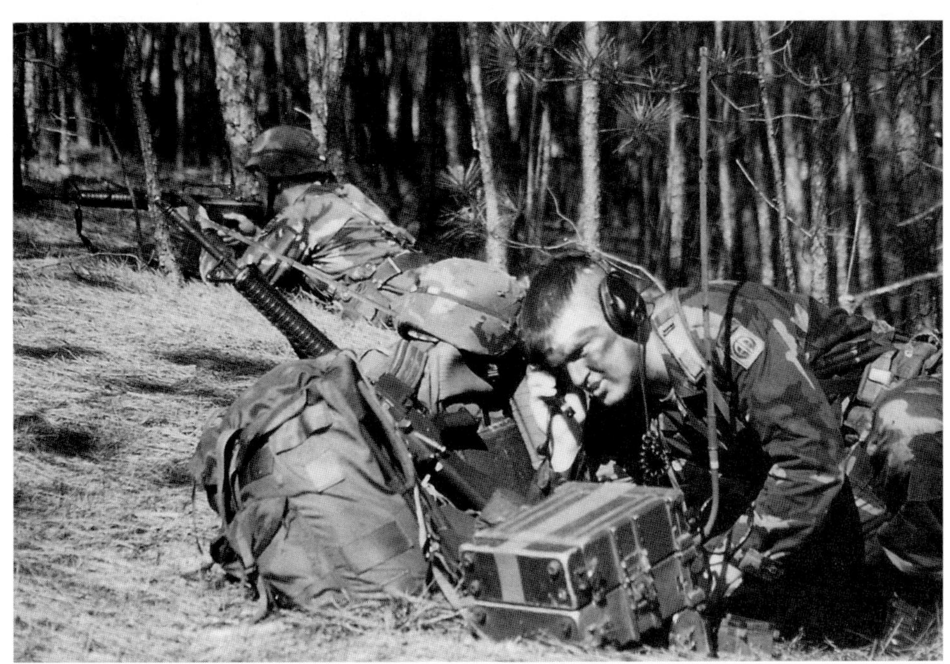

A non-commissioned officer of the 313th MI Battalion submits a Tactical Report (TACREP) summarizing intelligence data.

SIGINT/EW

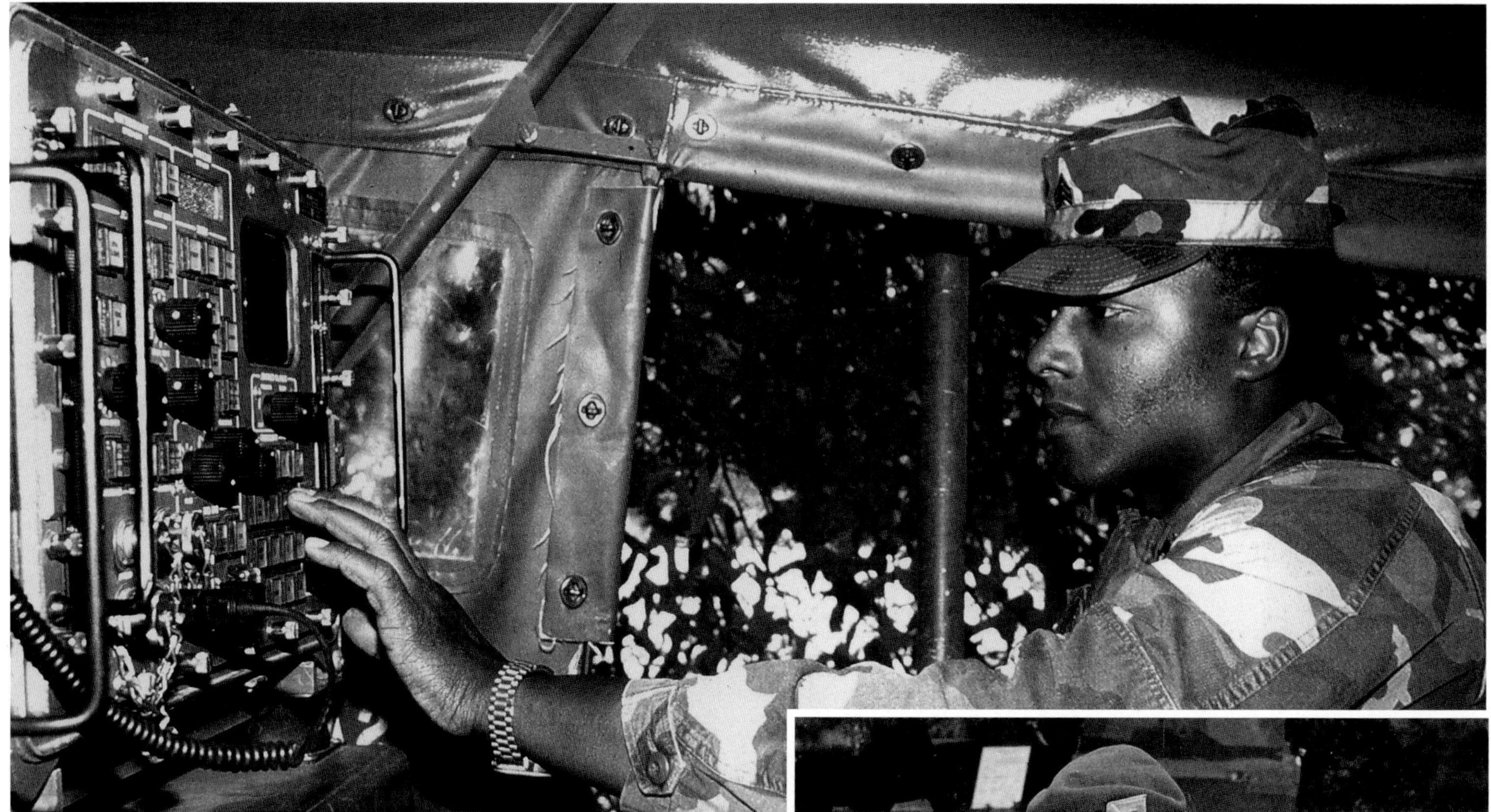

Electronic warfare was an integral part of the CEWI unit mission. Here, a soldier monitors a TLQ–17A electronic countermeasures system used for communications jamming.

A soldier of the 519th MI Battalion adjusts a PRD–11 radio direction finder.

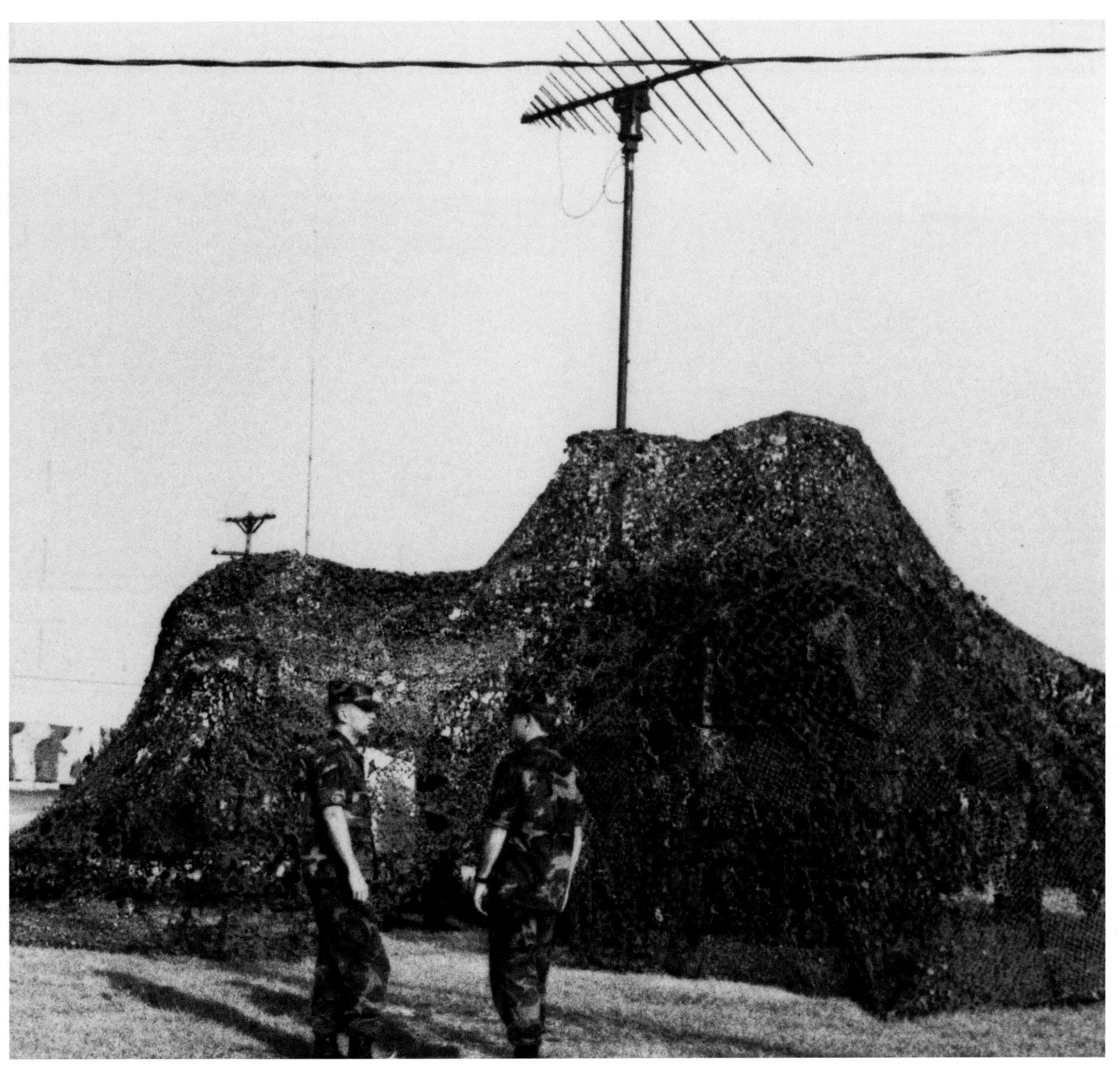

C Company, 163d MI Battalion, during a field deployment at the Consolidated Security Operations Center in San Antonio, Texas.

Sensors

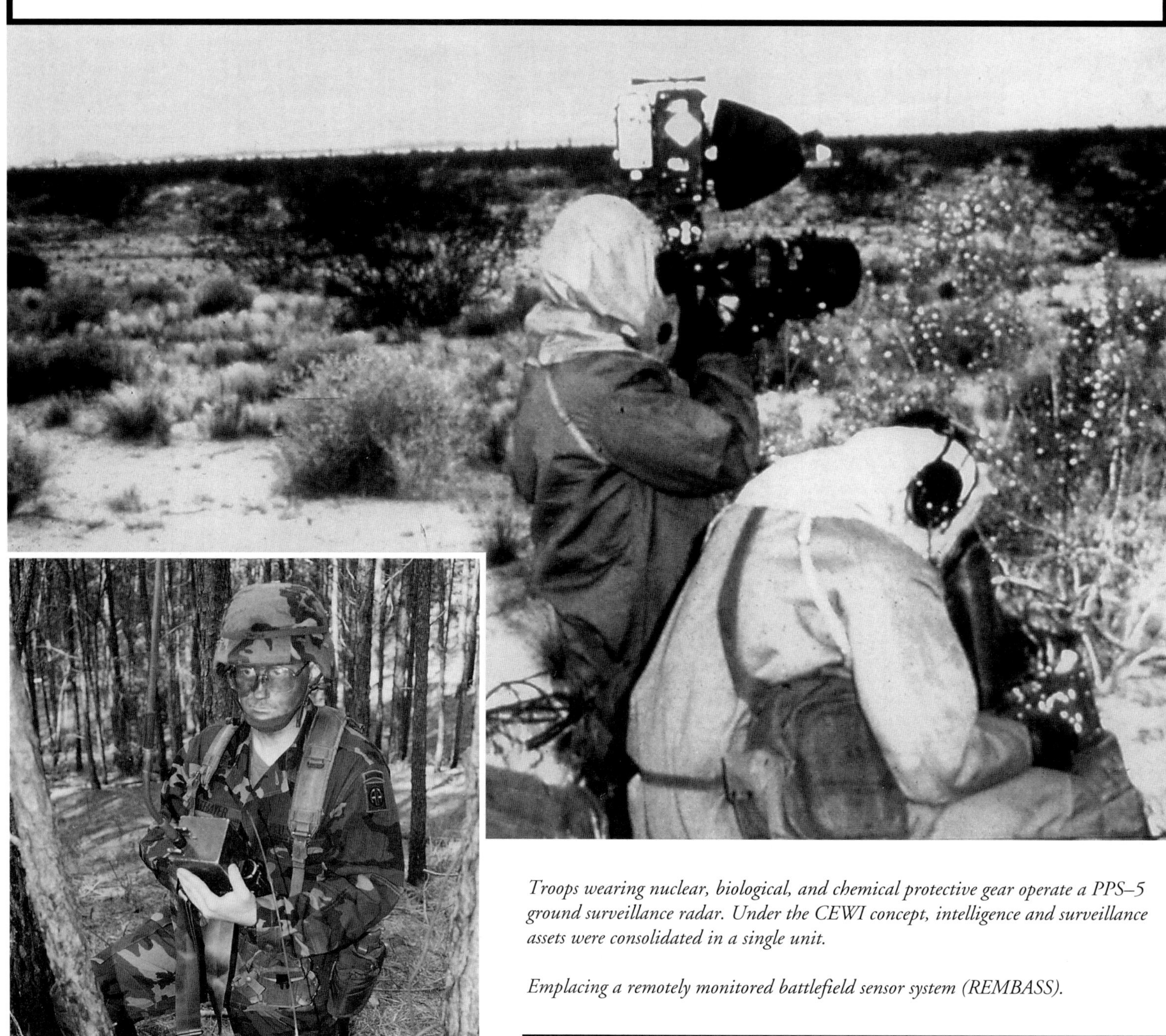

Troops wearing nuclear, biological, and chemical protective gear operate a PPS–5 ground surveillance radar. Under the CEWI concept, intelligence and surveillance assets were consolidated in a single unit.

Emplacing a remotely monitored battlefield sensor system (REMBASS).

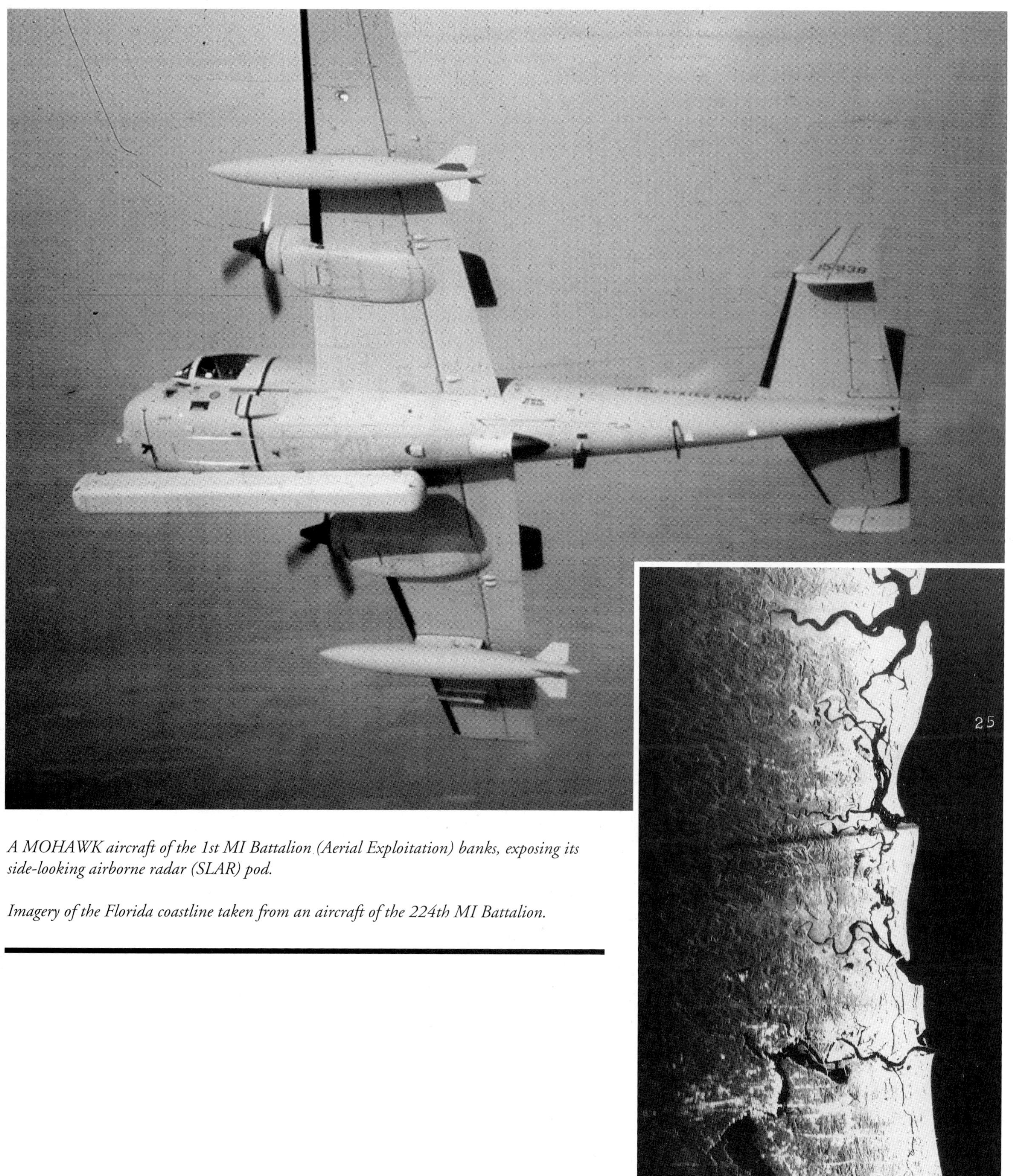

A MOHAWK aircraft of the 1st MI Battalion (Aerial Exploitation) banks, exposing its side-looking airborne radar (SLAR) pod.

Imagery of the Florida coastline taken from an aircraft of the 224th MI Battalion.

Training the Force

As a result of the implementation of IOSS, the former U.S. Army Security Agency Training Center and School at Fort Devens, Massachusetts, was redesignated as the U.S. Army Intelligence School, Devens and resubordinated to USAINTC&S at Fort Huachuca, Arizona, together with former ASA training detachments at Goodfellow Air Force Base, Texas, and Corry Station, Florida.

In 1983, the Commanding General, U.S. Army Intelligence Center and School, was given proponency over the Military Intelligence Branch and assumed the title of Chief, Military Intelligence.

Meanwhile, the U.S. Army Russian Institute in Germany, a unique facility that trained officers in Russian language and Soviet studies, had been resubordinated from ACSI to INSCOM.

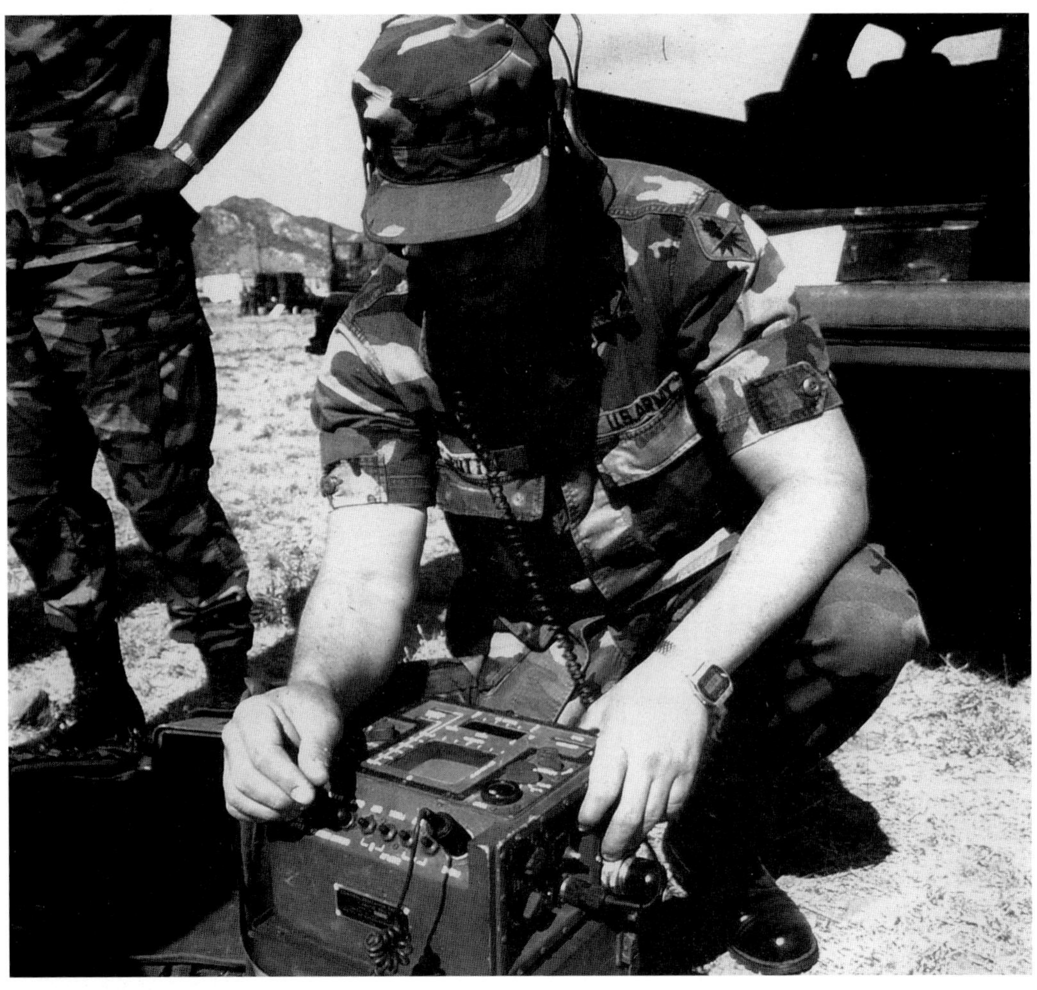

Field training at the U.S. Army Intelligence School and Fort Huachuca. An instructor demonstrates the central monitoring station used to correlate data provided by ground sensors.

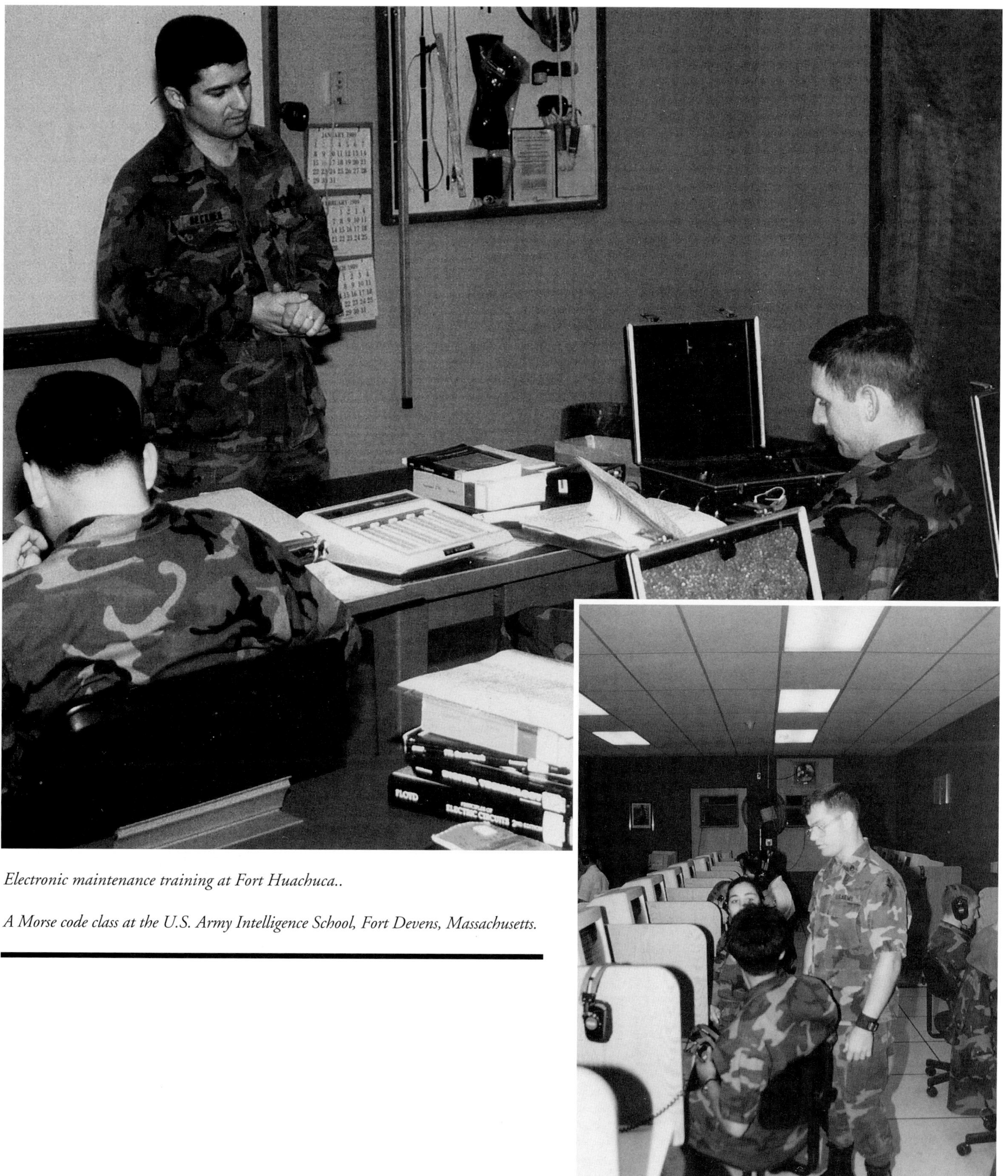

Electronic maintenance training at Fort Huachuca..

A Morse code class at the U.S. Army Intelligence School, Fort Devens, Massachusetts.

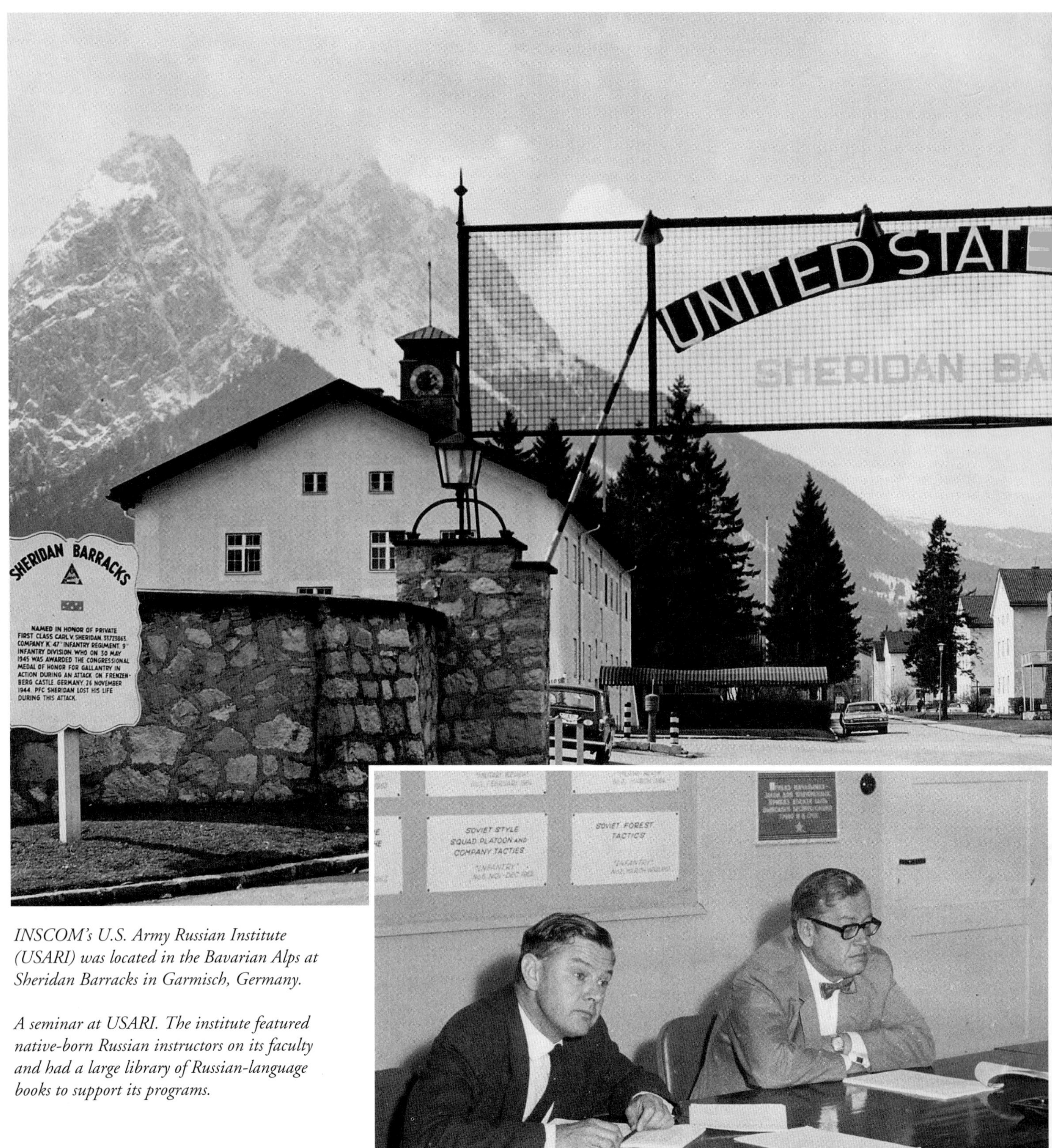

INSCOM's U.S. Army Russian Institute (USARI) was located in the Bavarian Alps at Sheridan Barracks in Garmisch, Germany.

A seminar at USARI. The institute featured native-born Russian instructors on its faculty and had a large library of Russian-language books to support its programs.

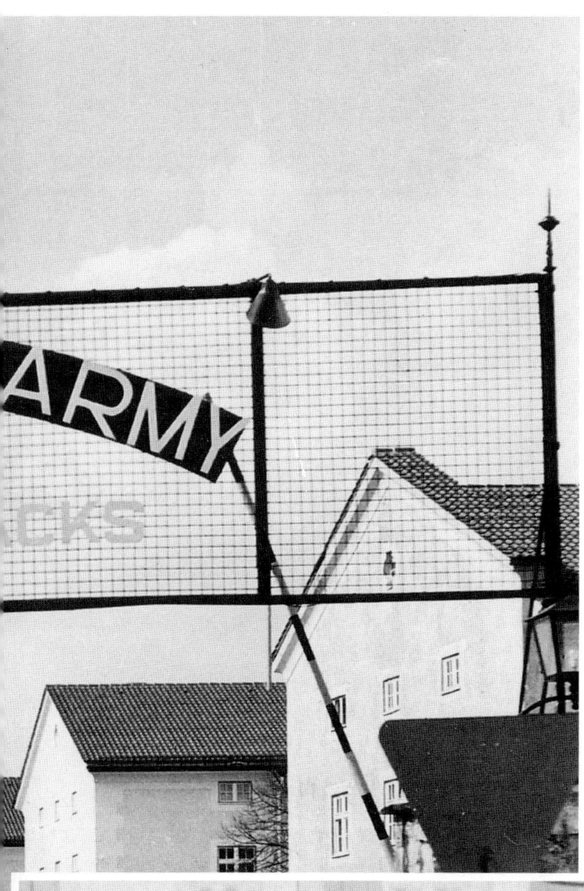

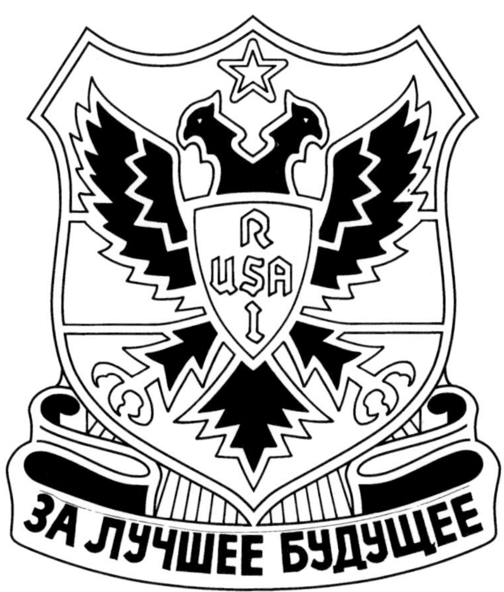

USARI Distinctive Unit Insignia.

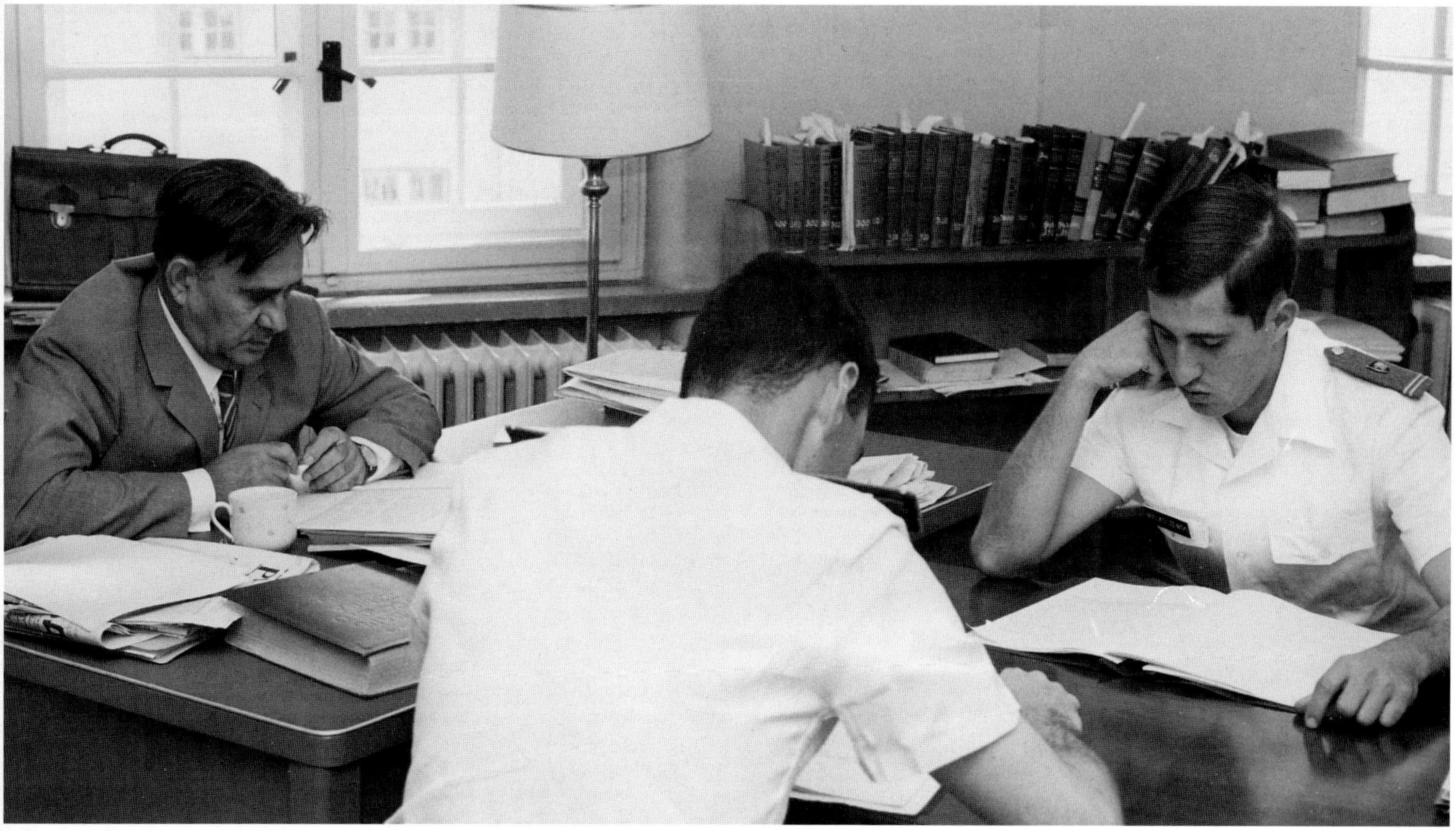

In addition to its regular program for Army officers, the Institute also held a summer program for students of the service academies.

Readiness

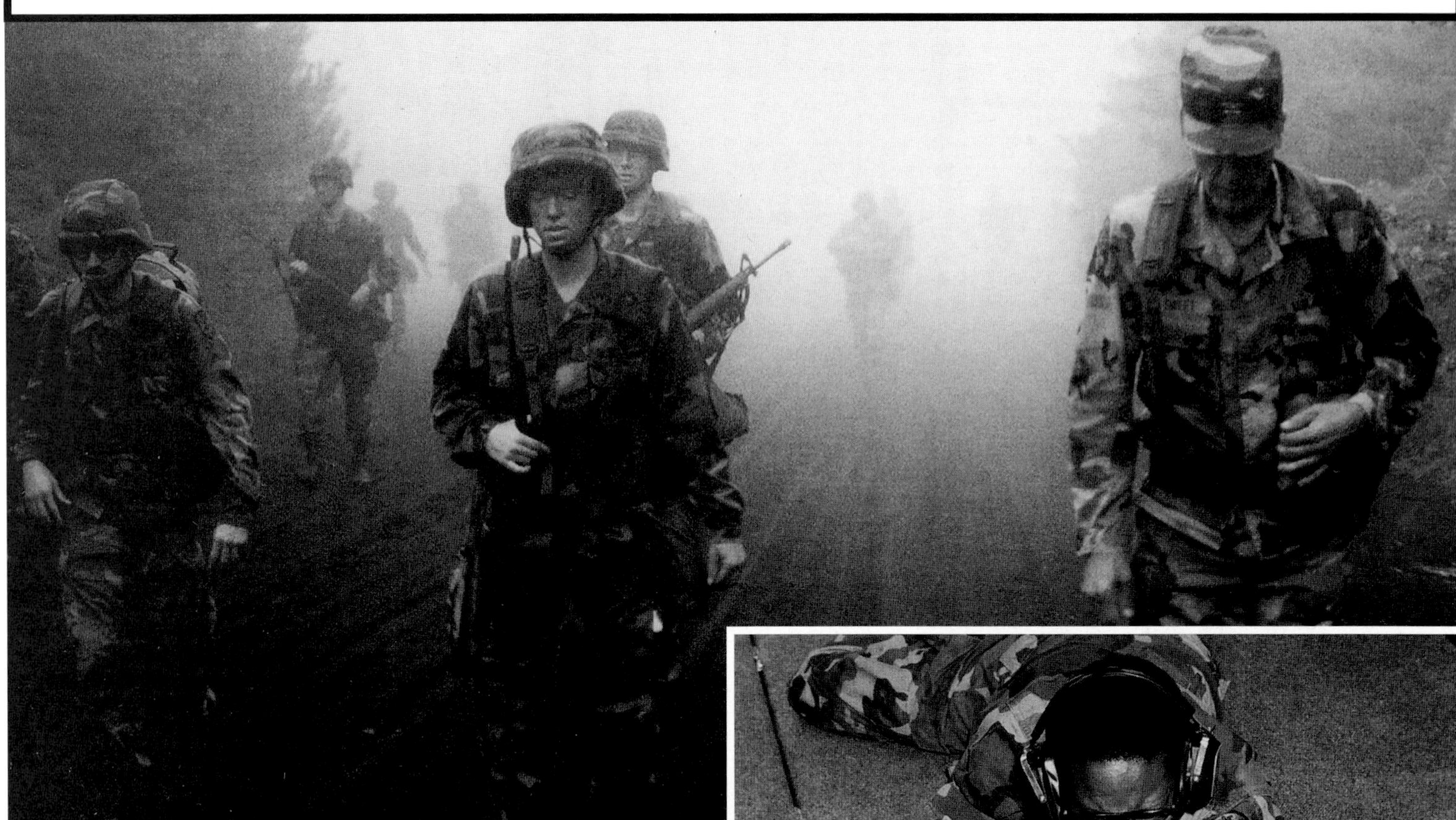

Men and women of MI are soldiers first and specialists second. Troops of the 500th MI Brigade march through the mists of Mount Fuji, Japan, on a training exercise.

An INSCOM soldier practices marksmanship on the WEAPONEER System at Field Station Misawa.

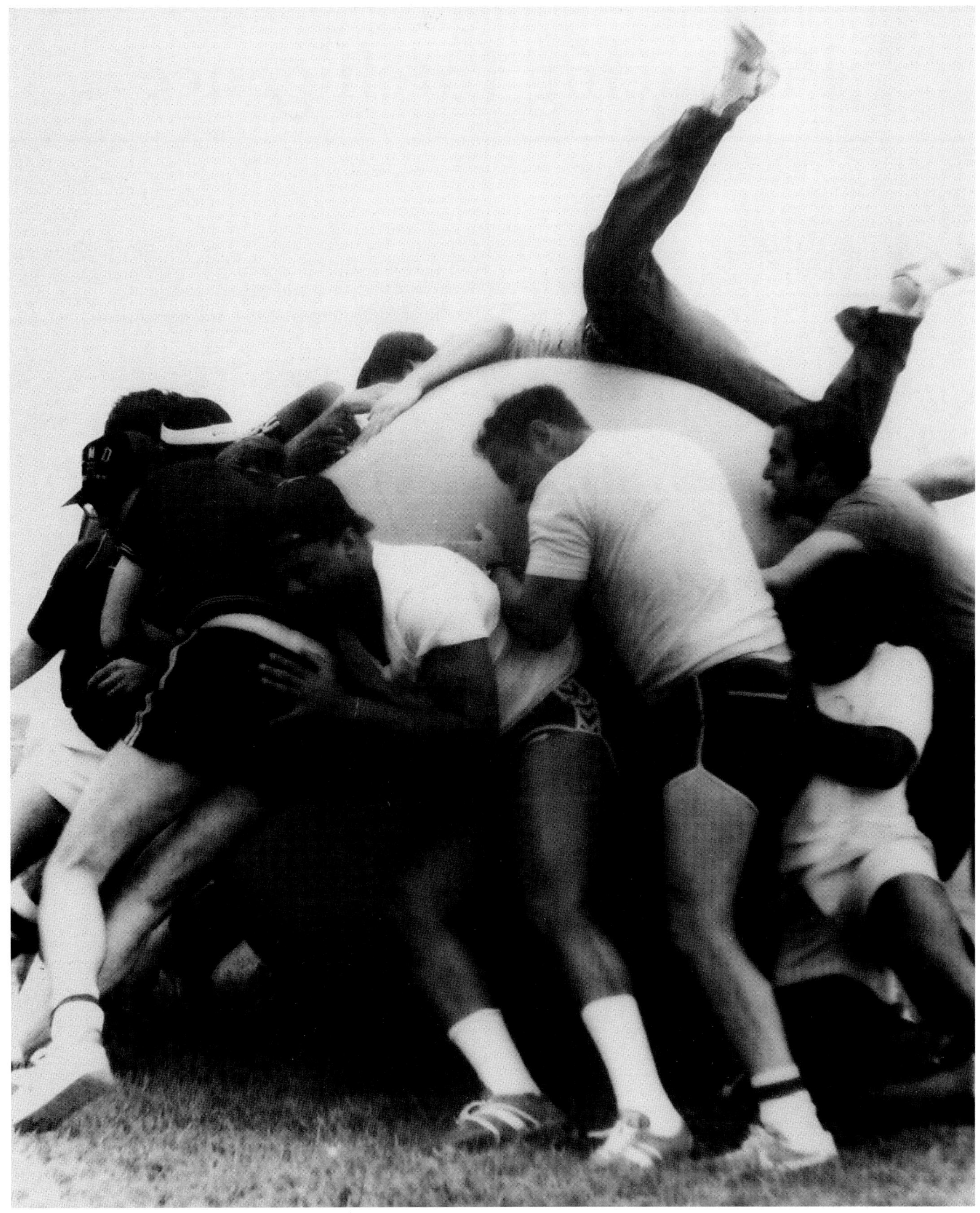

Physical fitness remained an Army and MI priority. Troops from Field Station Okinawa compete vigorously during Organization Day games in 1983.

Producing Intelligence

In partial conformity with the recommendations of IOSS, a number of Army production elements were consolidated into an Intelligence and Threat Analysis Center (ITAC) under INSCOM. However, the Army Materiel Command continued to control the Army's Foreign Science and Technology Center and Missile and Space Intelligence Center. In 1984, the Army consolidated all three centers under the Army Intelligence Agency, a Field Operating Agency of ACSI.

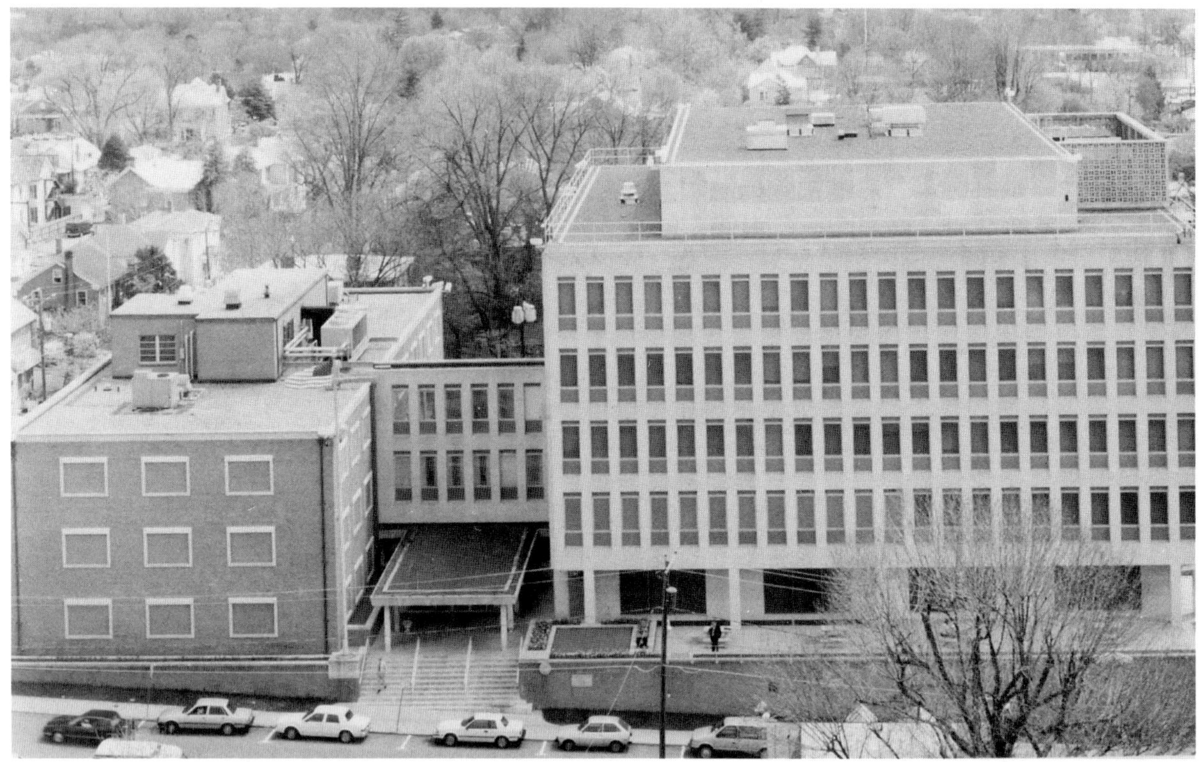

The Foreign Science and Technology Center (FSTC) in Charlottesville, Virginia.

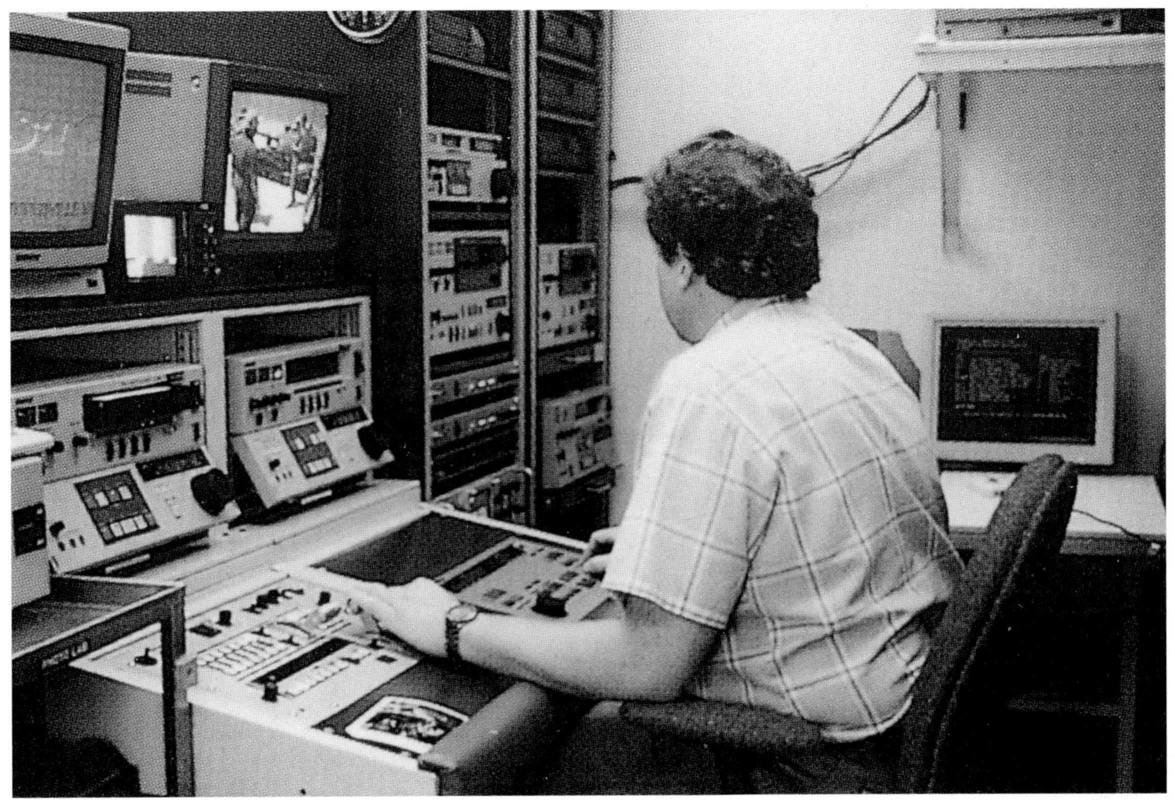

High technology assisted in the analysis of foreign systems at the FSTC. Above, the Center's video production facility; below, a signals intelligence analyst.

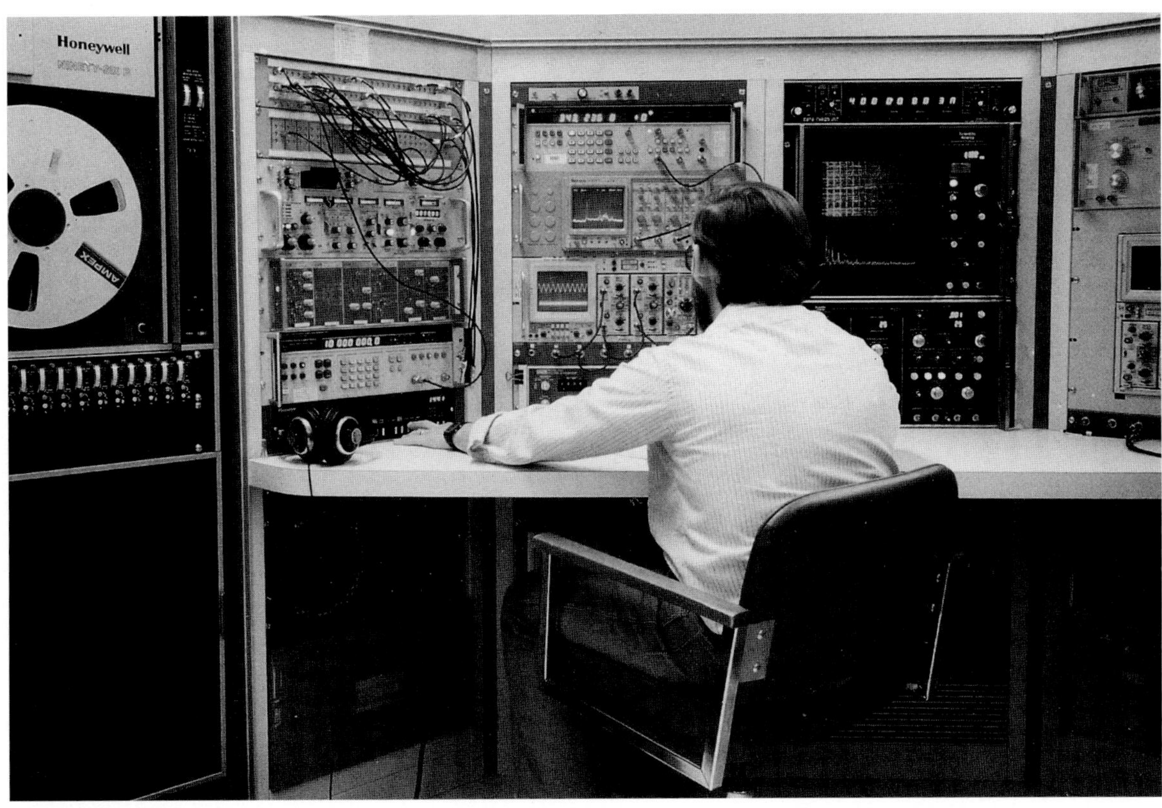

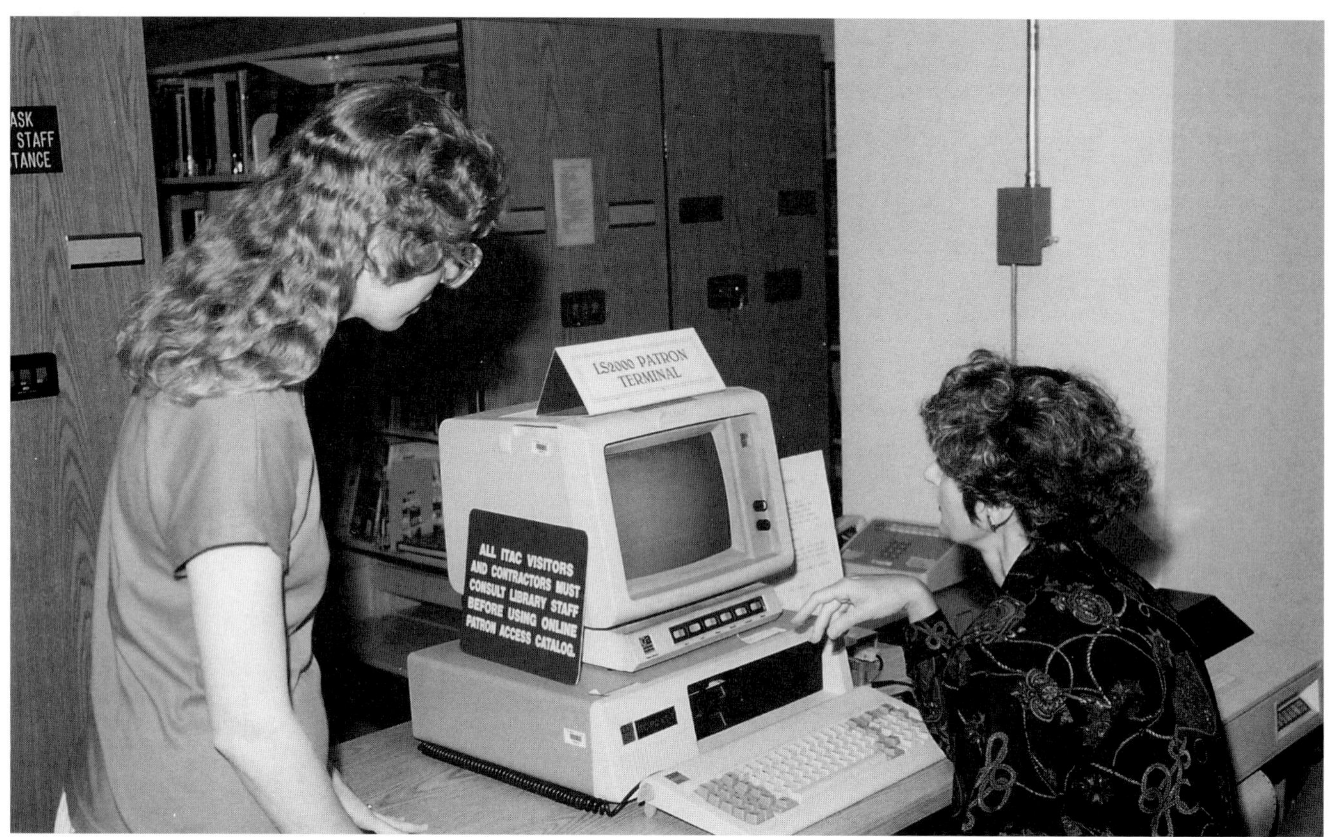

Computers and skilled intelligence librarians provided analysts at the Intelligence and Threat Analysis Center (ITAC) with access to classified and commercial data bases.

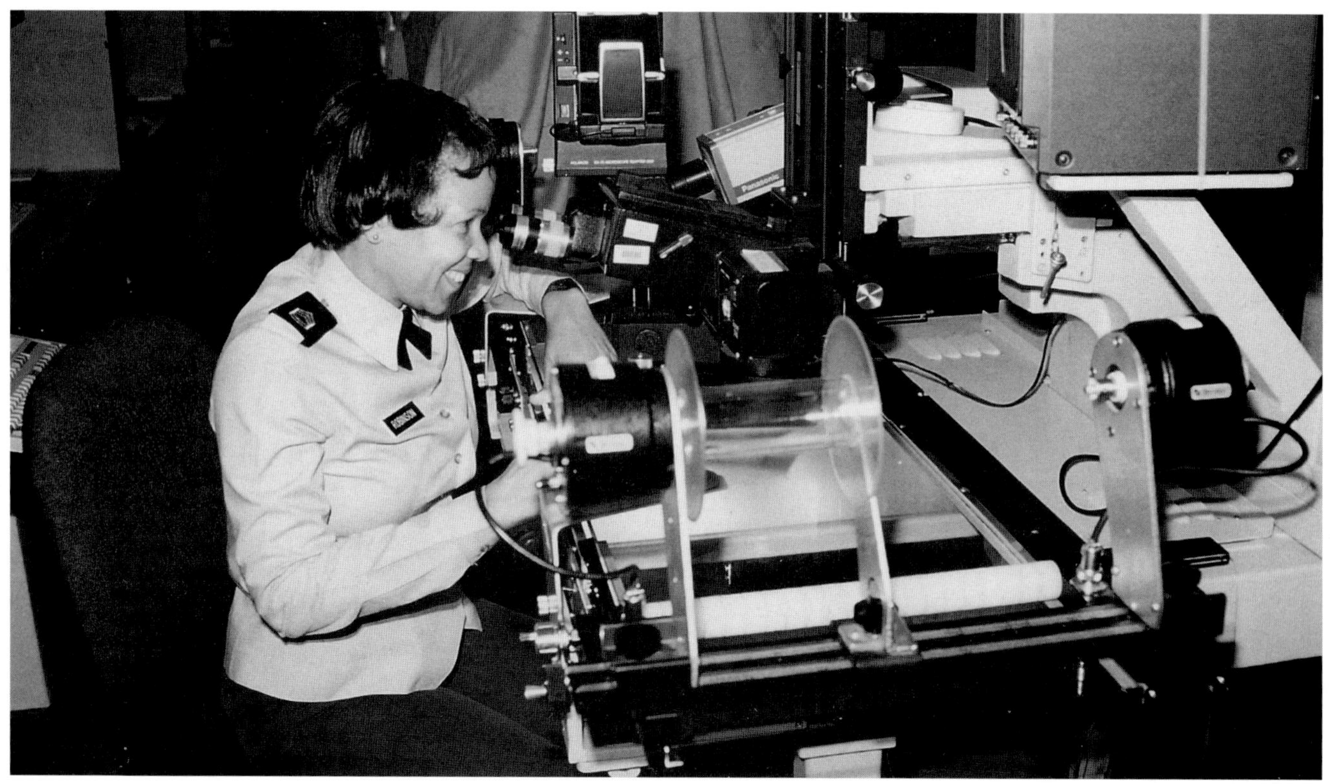

An ITAC imagery interpreter performs exploitation at ITAC headquarters in the Washington Navy Yard.

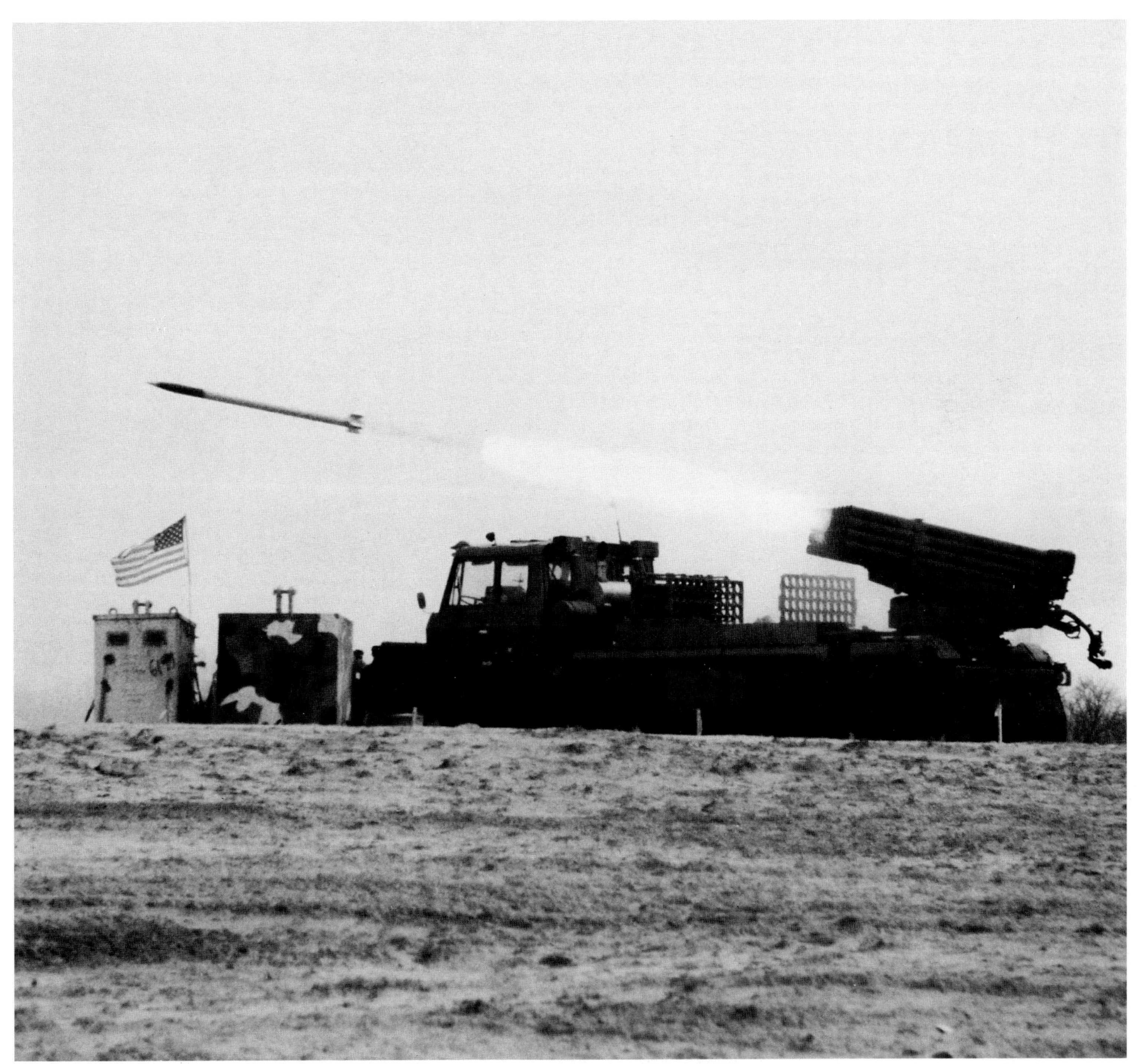

Experts at the FSTC use a hands-on approach as they test a Soviet-model RM–70–85 rocket launcher system at Aberdeen Proving Grounds, Maryland.

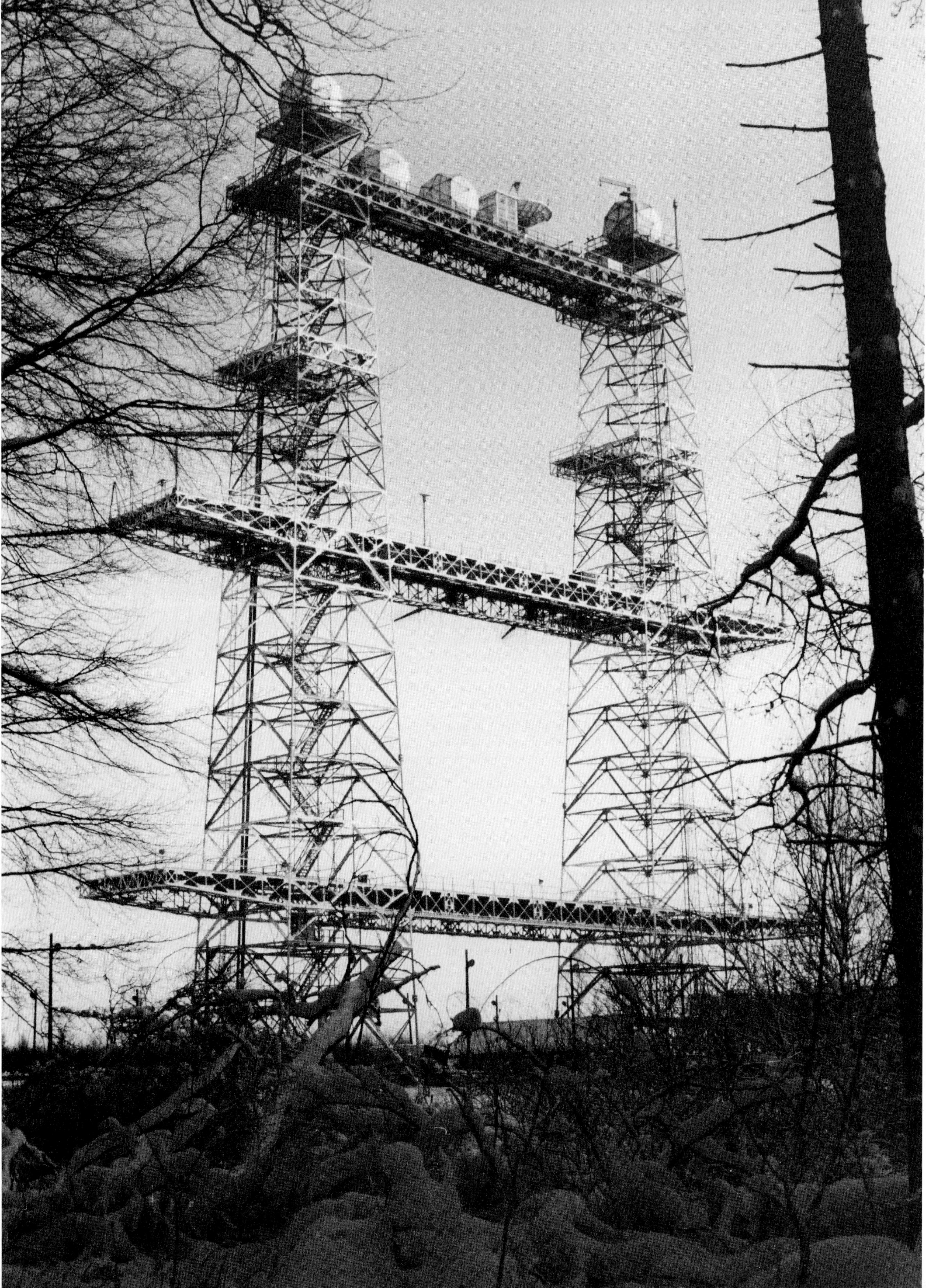

The March of Technology

THE DEVELOPMENT OF MODERN TECHNOLOGY had begun to impact upon military intelligence operations as far back as the Civil War. By the 1980's, the growth of new technologies had begun to affect every existing intelligence discipline, and even to create new ones. Synergistic use of a number of techniques to measure the distinct profiles displayed by an assortment of target "shooters, movers, and emitters" created the new intelligence discipline of Measurement and Signature Intelligence (MASINT). At the tactical level of intelligence, unattended ground sensors and radars supplemented human reporting, and a variety of airborne platforms collected information that could not feasibly be gathered on the ground. At the strategic level, use of new technologies meant that Army analysts could now draw upon a variety of theater and national resources to generate all-source intelligence. The computer allowed intelligence specialists to create and manipulate enormous masses of data, and improved communications systems allowed this information to be disseminated down to the field. Moreover, computers could now perform functions as diverse as translating documents and enhancing imagery.

Technology was not only an intelligence asset, but a vulnerability. Since emanations from unshielded electronic equipment could be acquired and analyzed by foreign intelligence services, Army counterintelligence was forced to develop the so-called TEMPEST program to counter such radiation hazards. Additionally, counterintelligence specialists now had to concern themselves with the possibility that computers could be penetrated by unauthorized "hackers" and that information could be destroyed by unauthorized computer "viruses." Moreover, sophisticated technologies now provided more tools for spies, ranging from specialized miniature cameras to various inconspicuous "bugging" devices, creating additional problems for the counterintelligence agent.

The "Torii Tower" at Wobeck was constructed in 1971 along the East German border. Its overview of a major Soviet training area provided the Army with unique collection opportunities.

Analysis and Automation

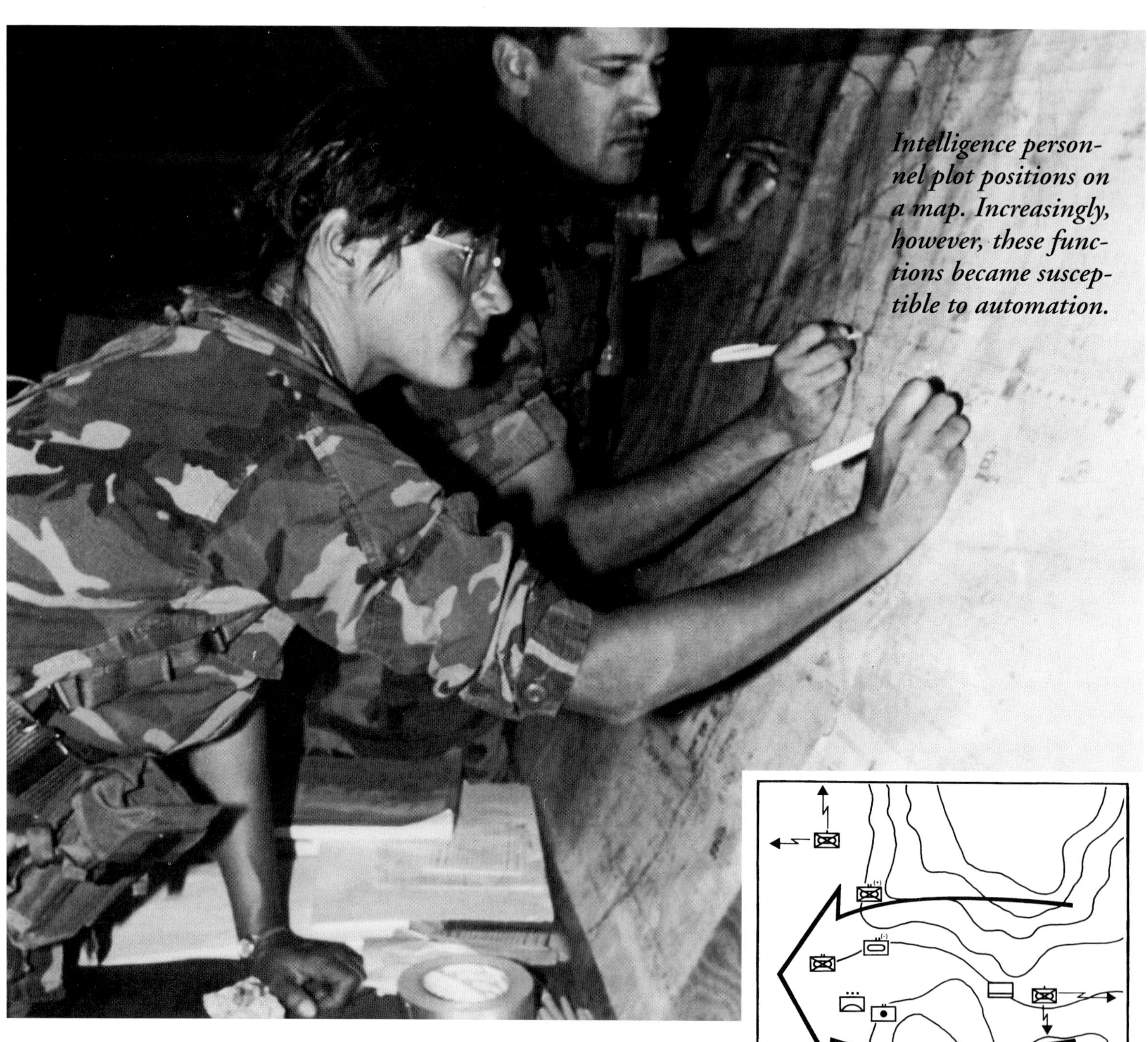

Intelligence personnel plot positions on a map. Increasingly, however, these functions became susceptible to automation.

An example of the Intelligence Preparation of the Battlefield approach now utilized by Army intelligence. Templates overlaid on a terrain map provide commanders and intelligence officers with a graphic overview of terrain, weather, and threat conditions.

Figure 4-35. Situation template: Type deployment for an MRR.

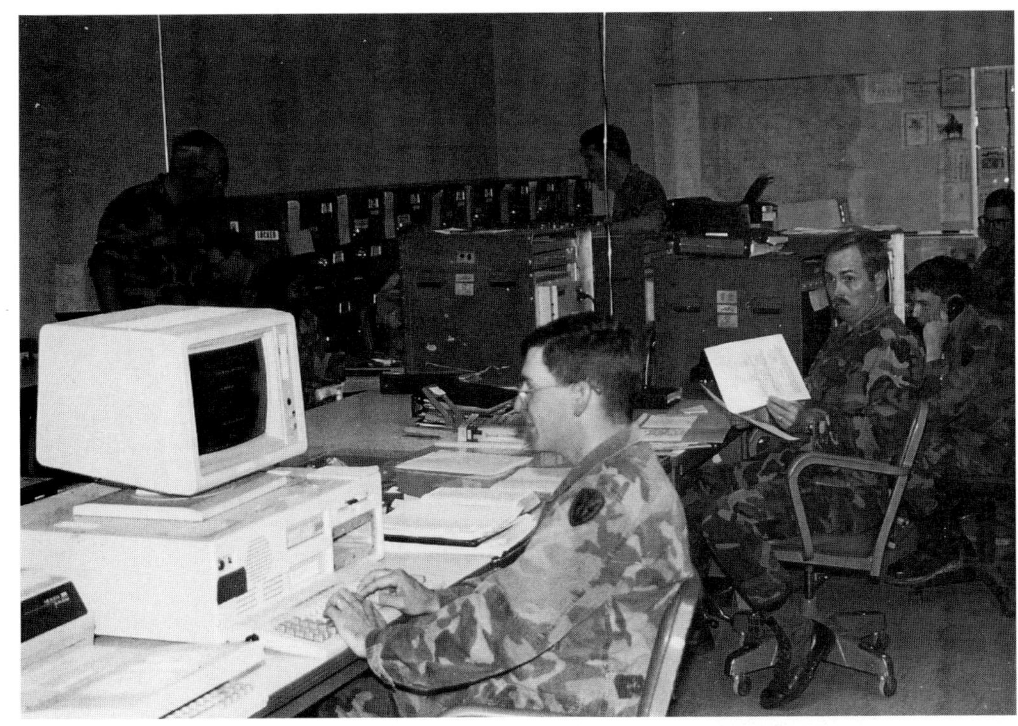

Introduction of computerized data into the field proved to be a key intelligence breakthrough. Personnel of the 504th MI Battalion man the All Source Analysis System (ASAS).

A computer programmer at the automated data processing facility of the 500th MI Brigade's Asian Studies Detachment..

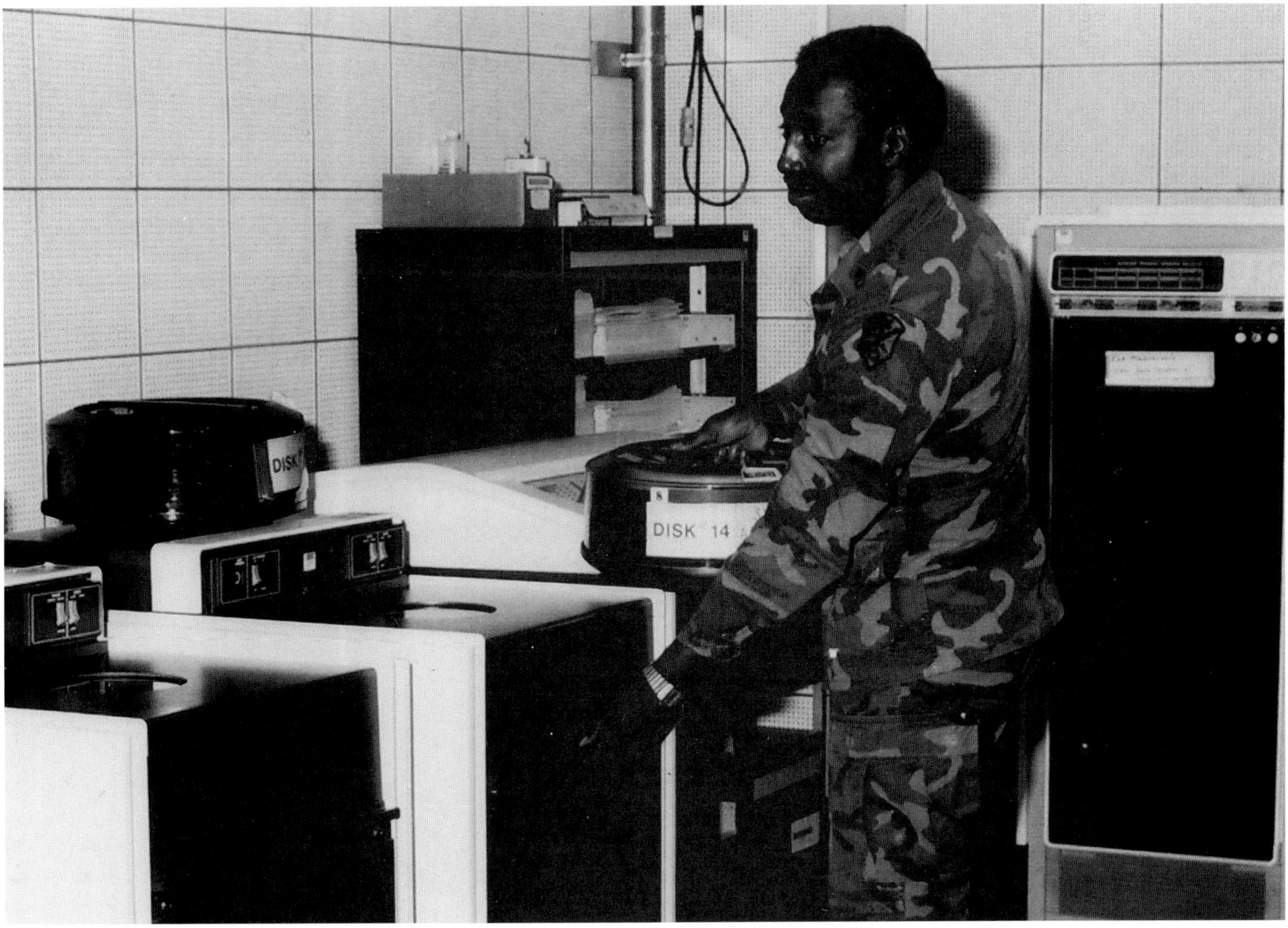

Counterintelligence

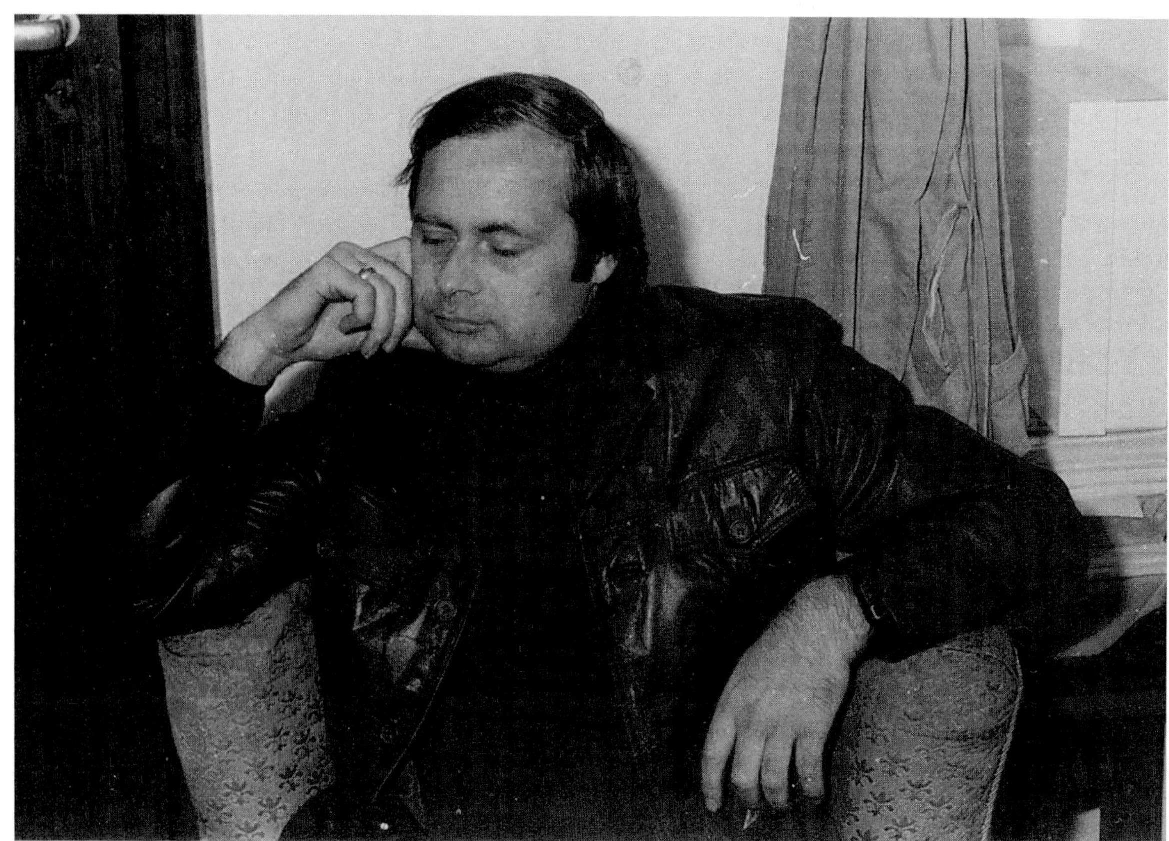

An agent of the Soviet KGB apprehended by 766th MI Detachment personnel in Berlin. Technology could enhance the effectiveness of both spies and counterspies.

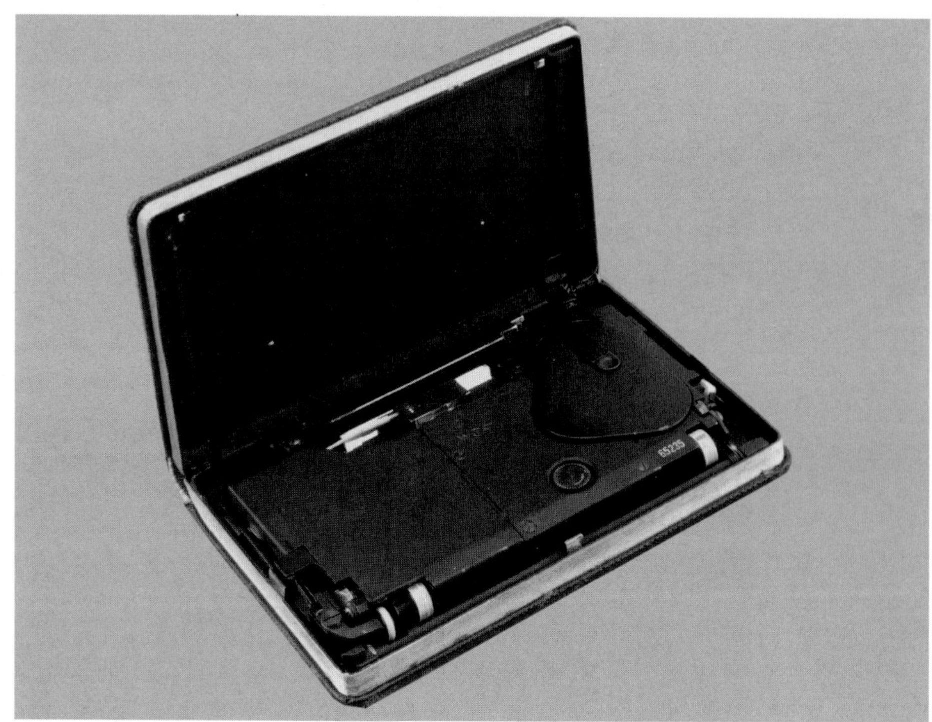

New tools for spies. This camera, ingeniously fabricated by the KGB, allowed documents to be copied by simply rolling the opened camera over the pertinent pages.

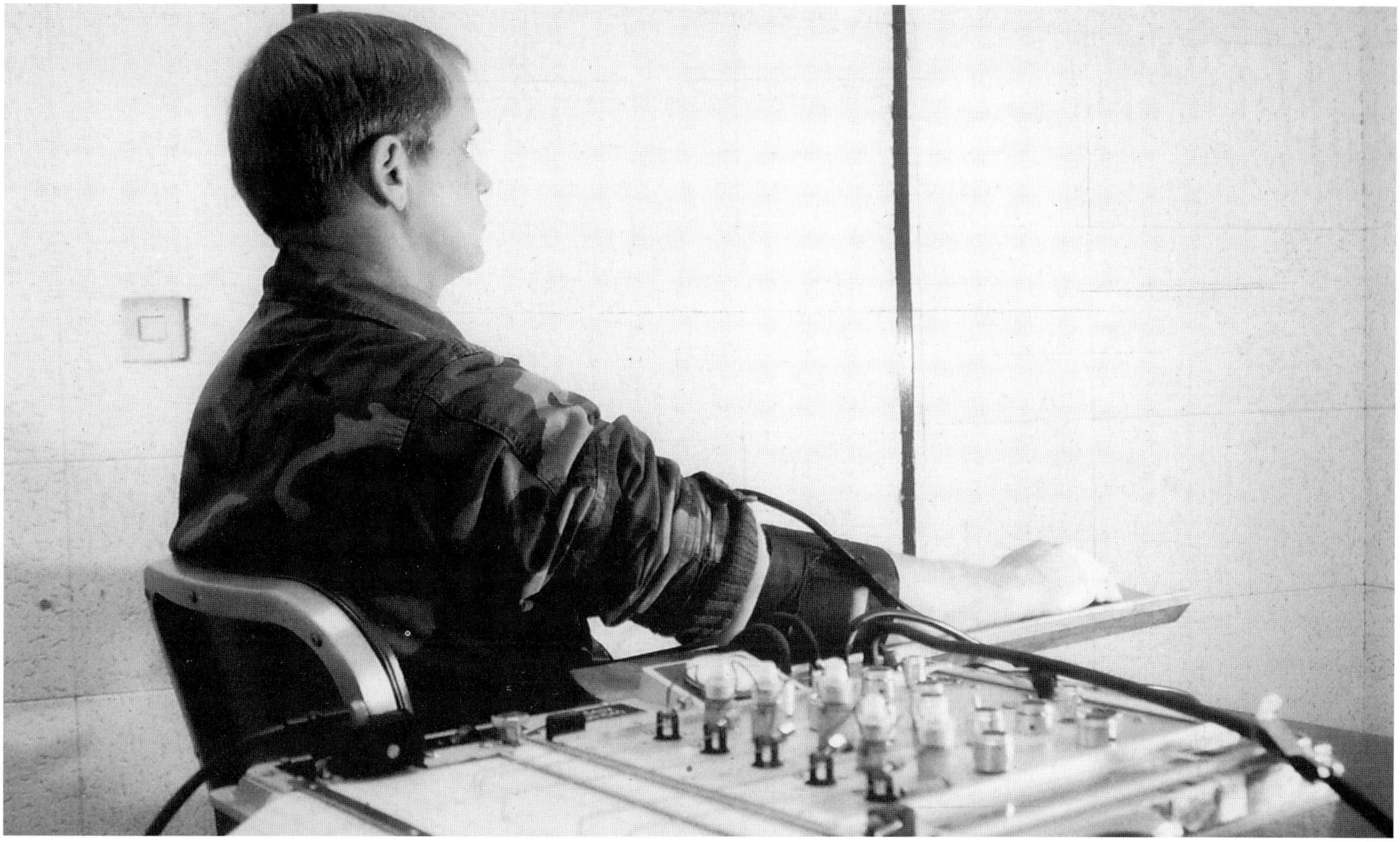

The polygraph was one item of counterintelligence technology which served as a formidable deterrent. However, it was not infallible.

This electronic test system allowed counterintelligence personnel to detect compromising emanations that might come from electronic equipment. The effort was known as the TEMPEST program.

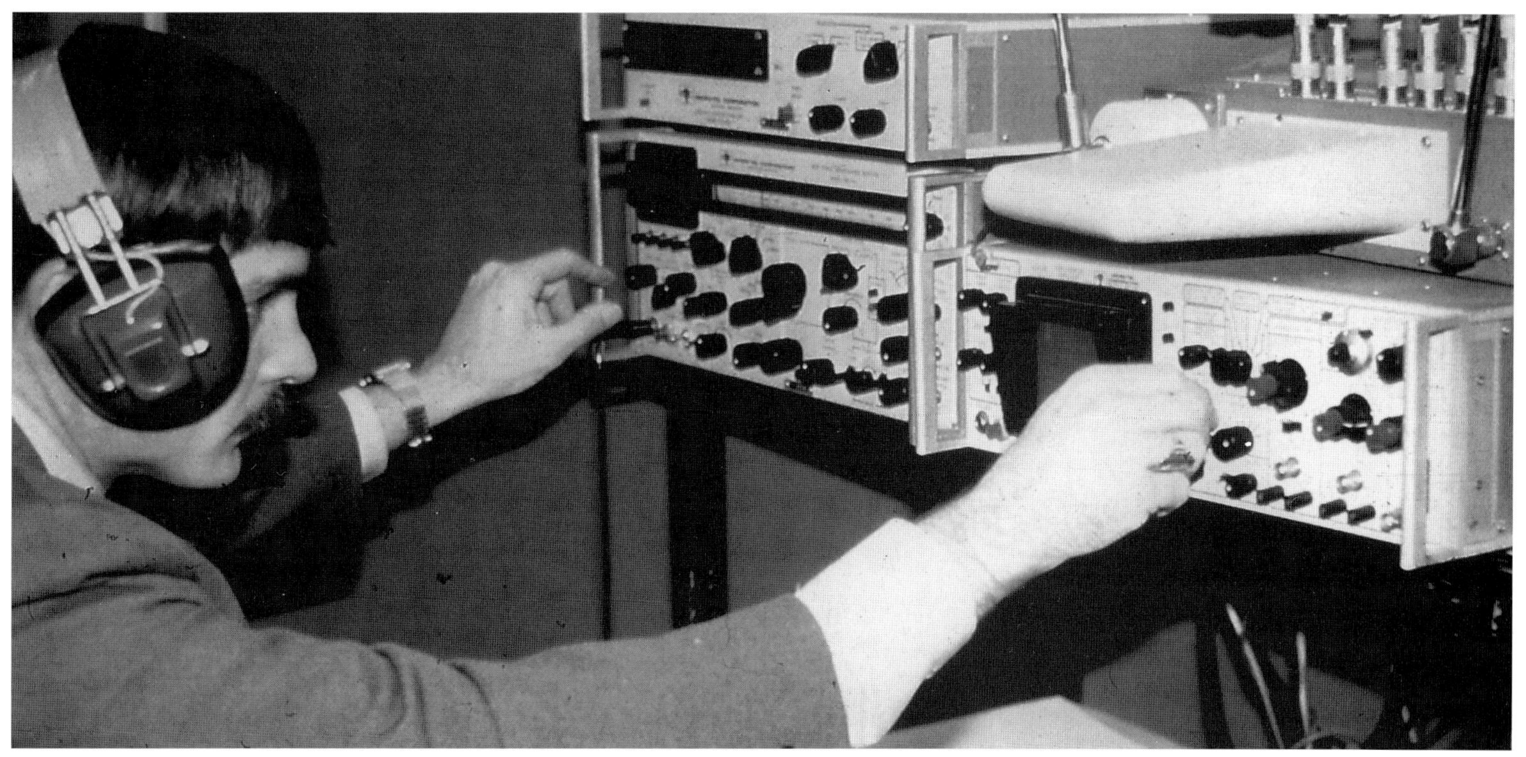

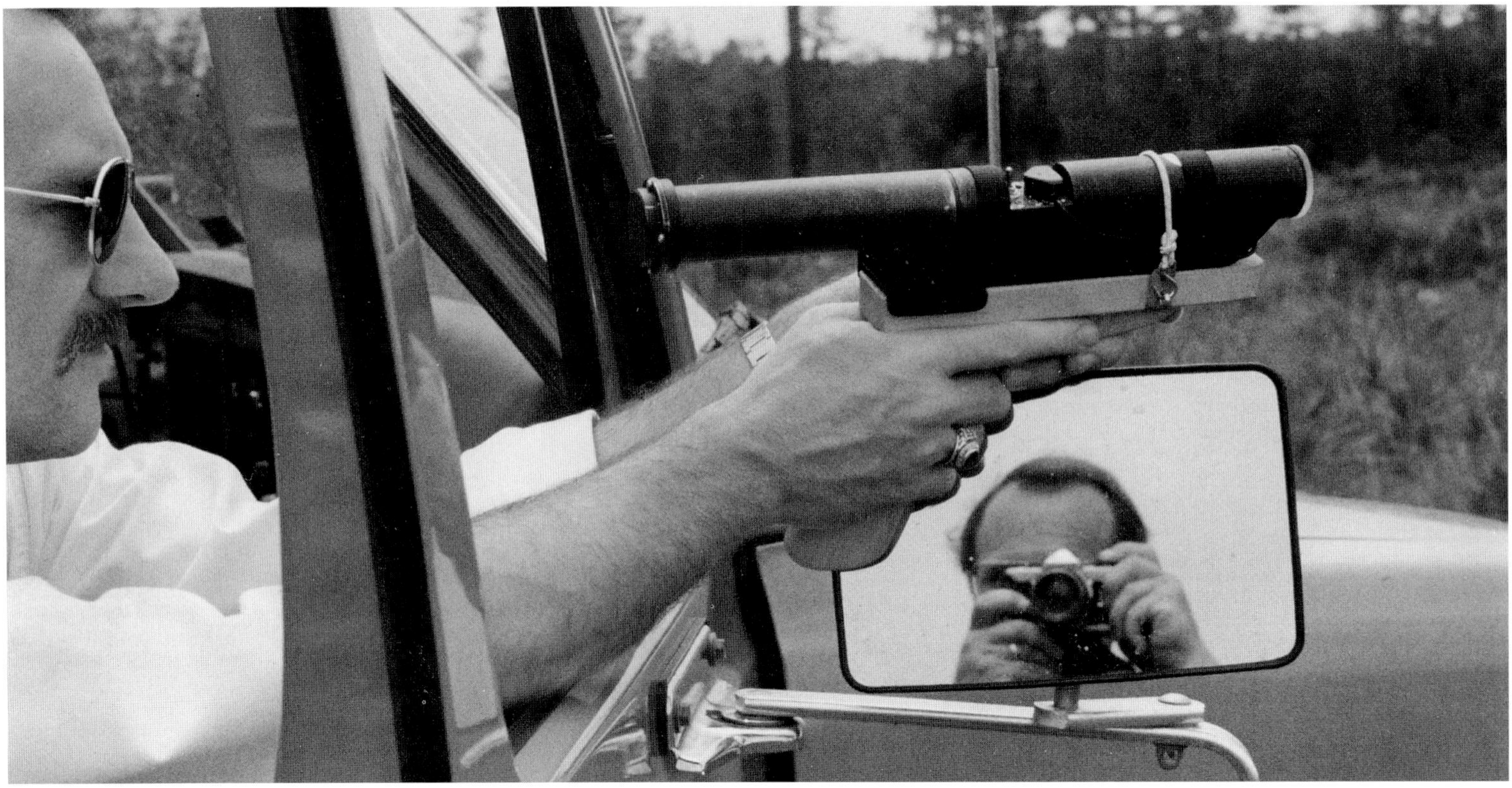

IRON SPIKE, prototype model of a hand-held laser detector.

The CANTICLE BOAT collection system.

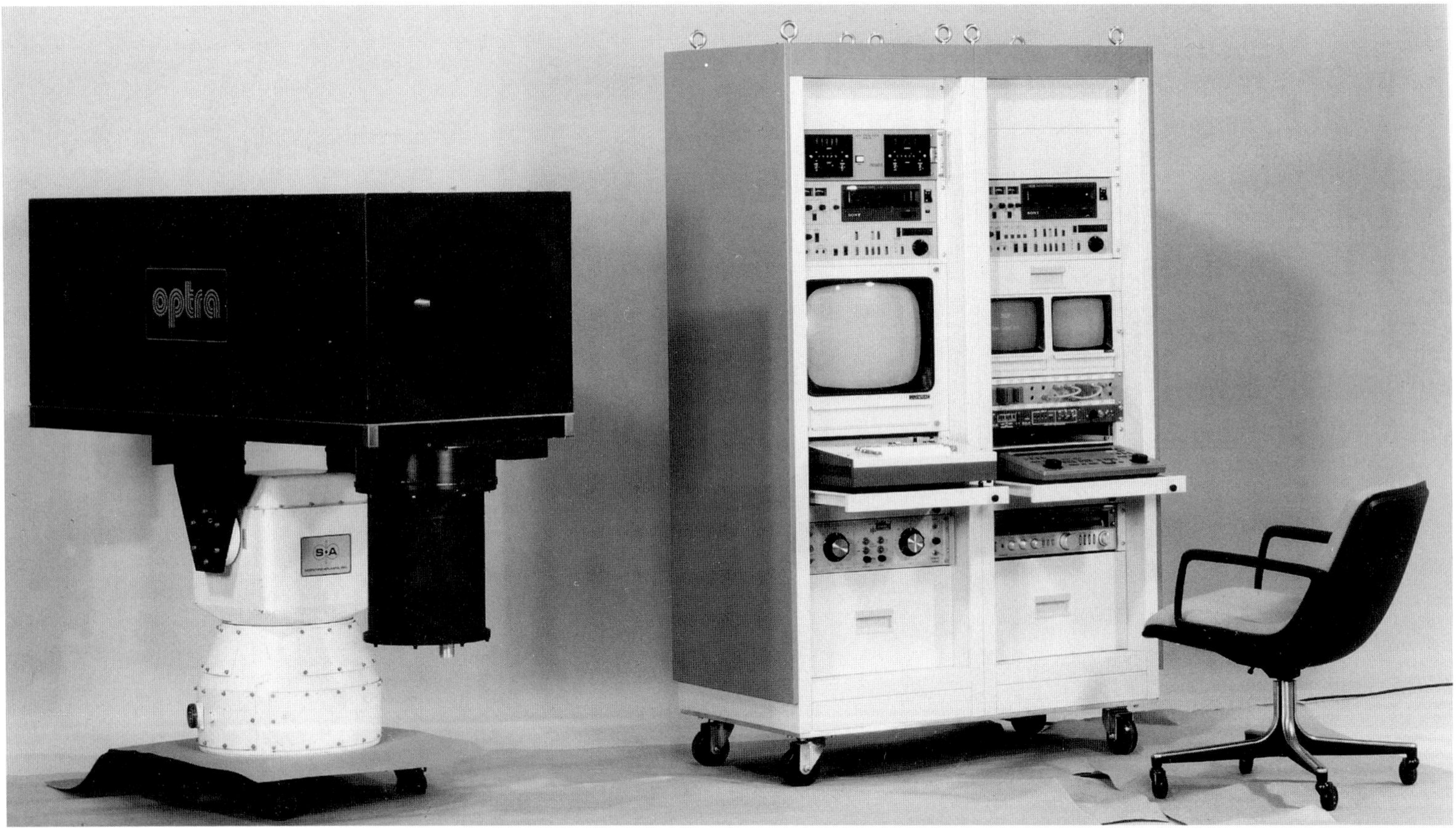

MASINT

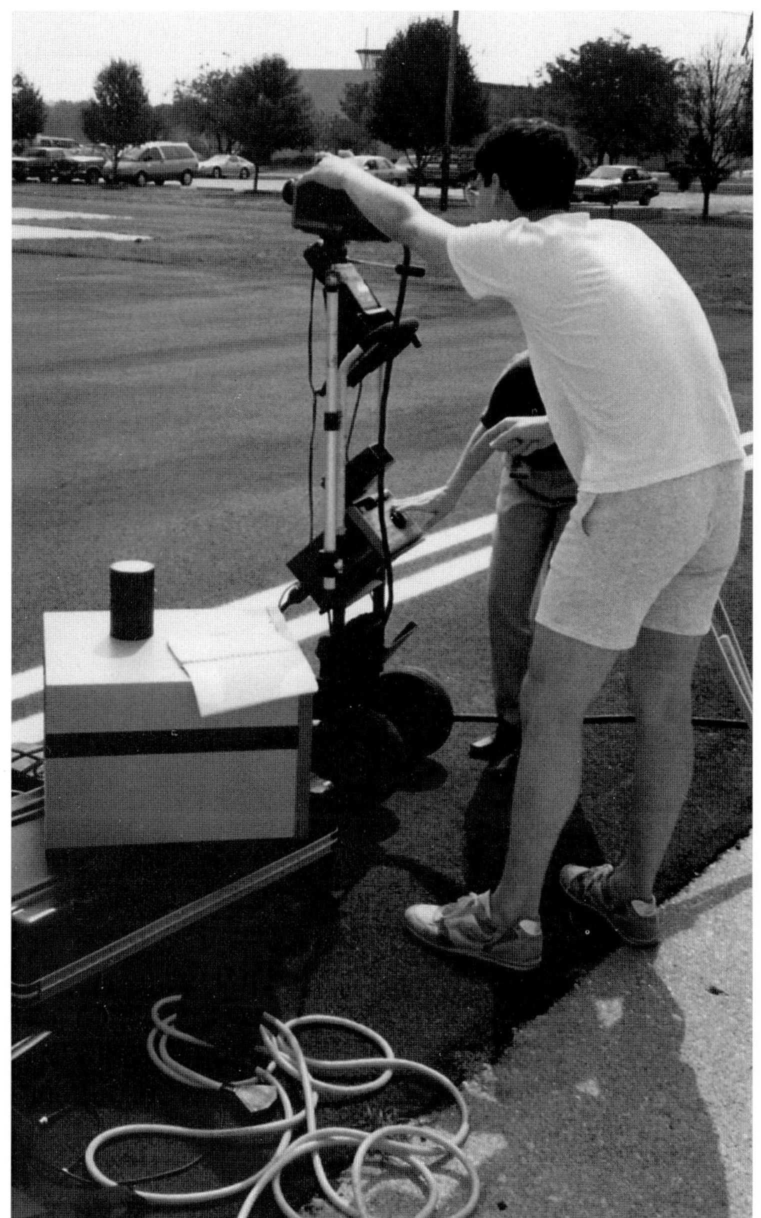

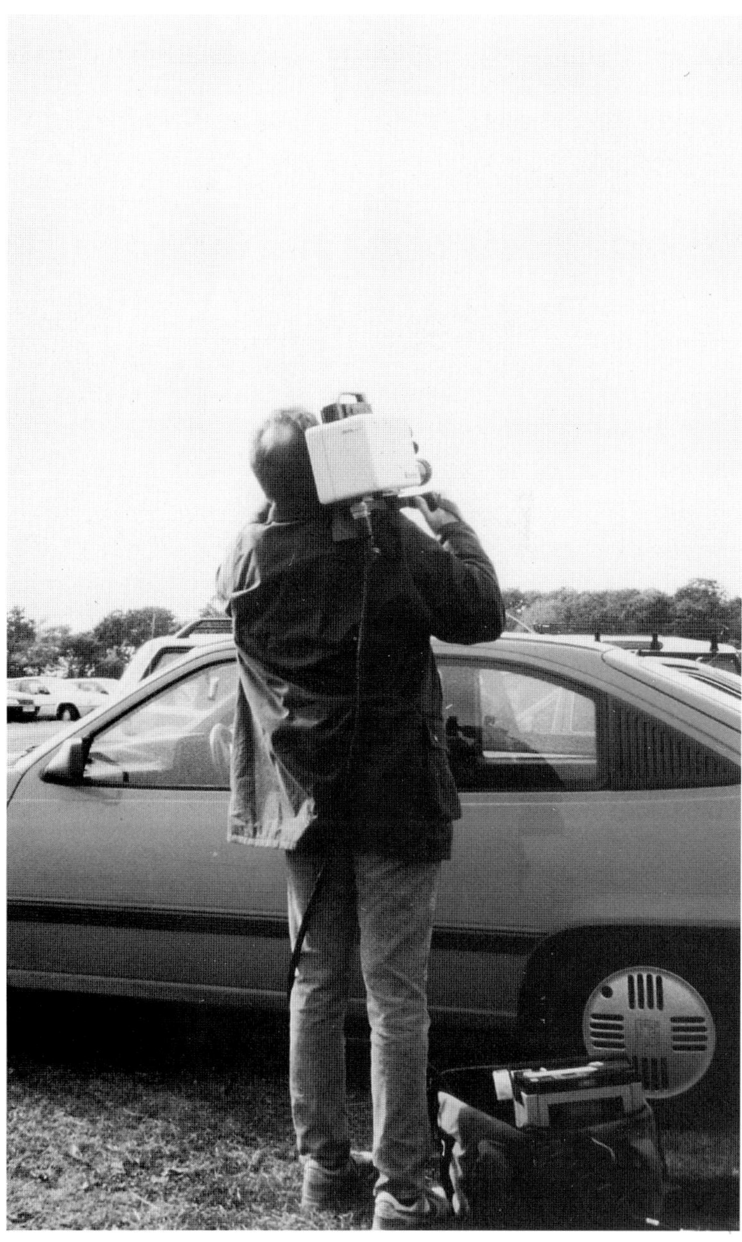

MASINT collection operations in the field.

Aerial Platforms

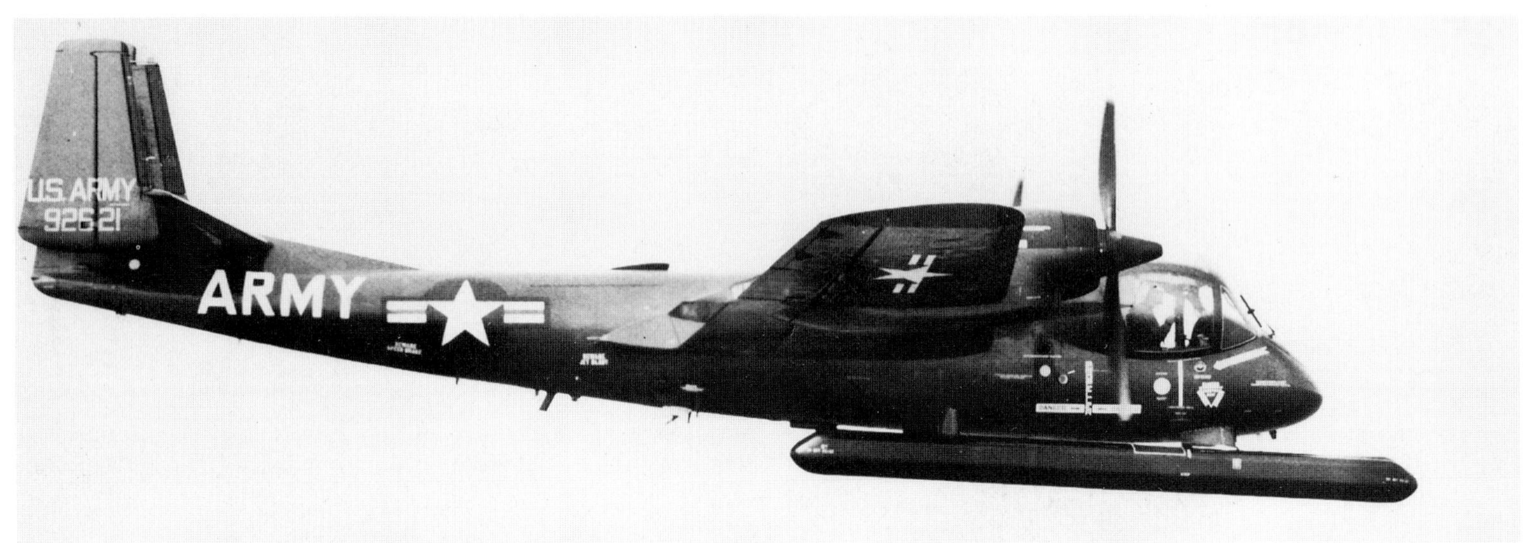

The venerable OV–1 Mohawk was part of the Army Intelligence inventory from 1962 to 1996.

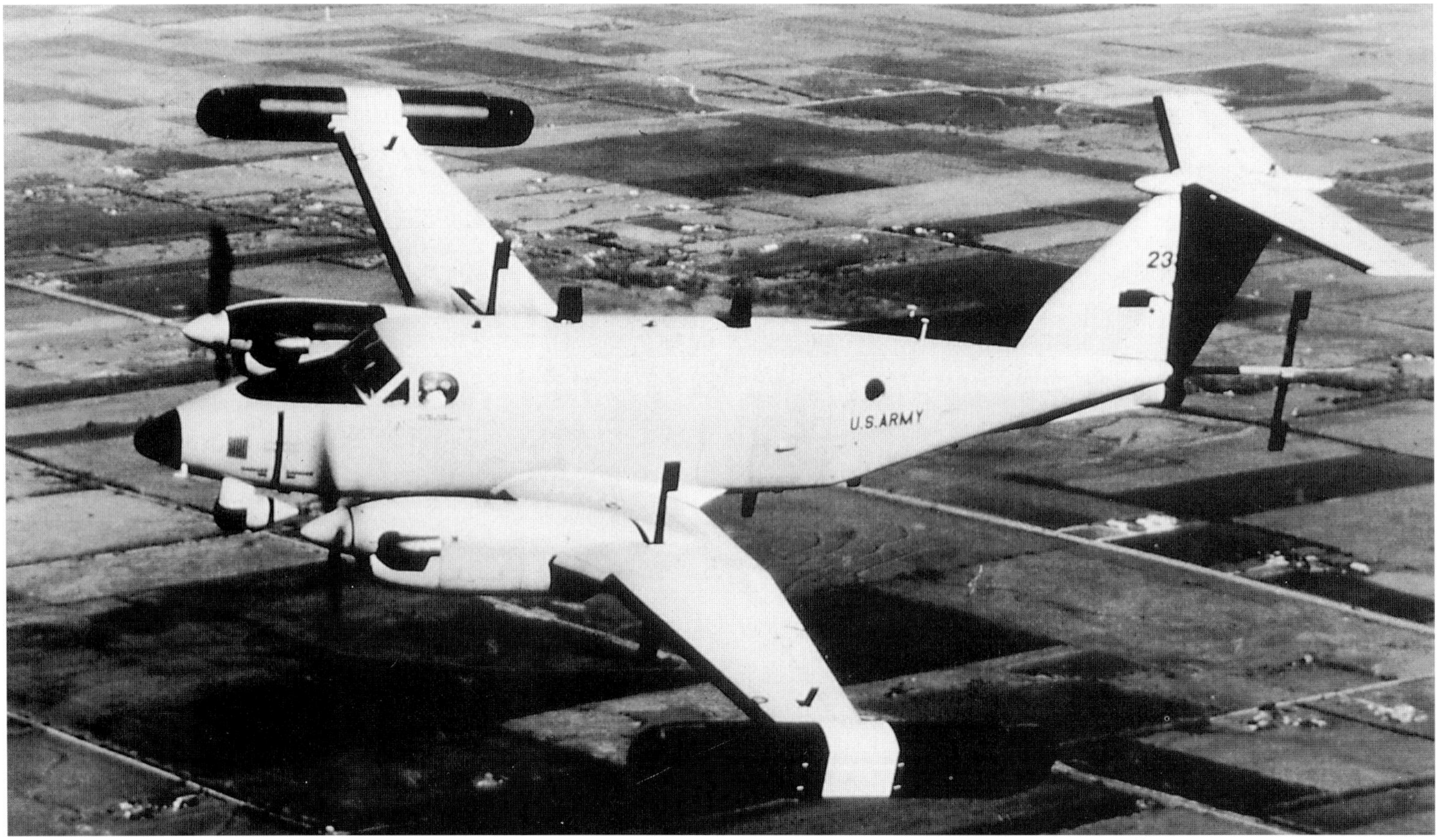

An RC–12 Special Electronic Mission Aircraft.

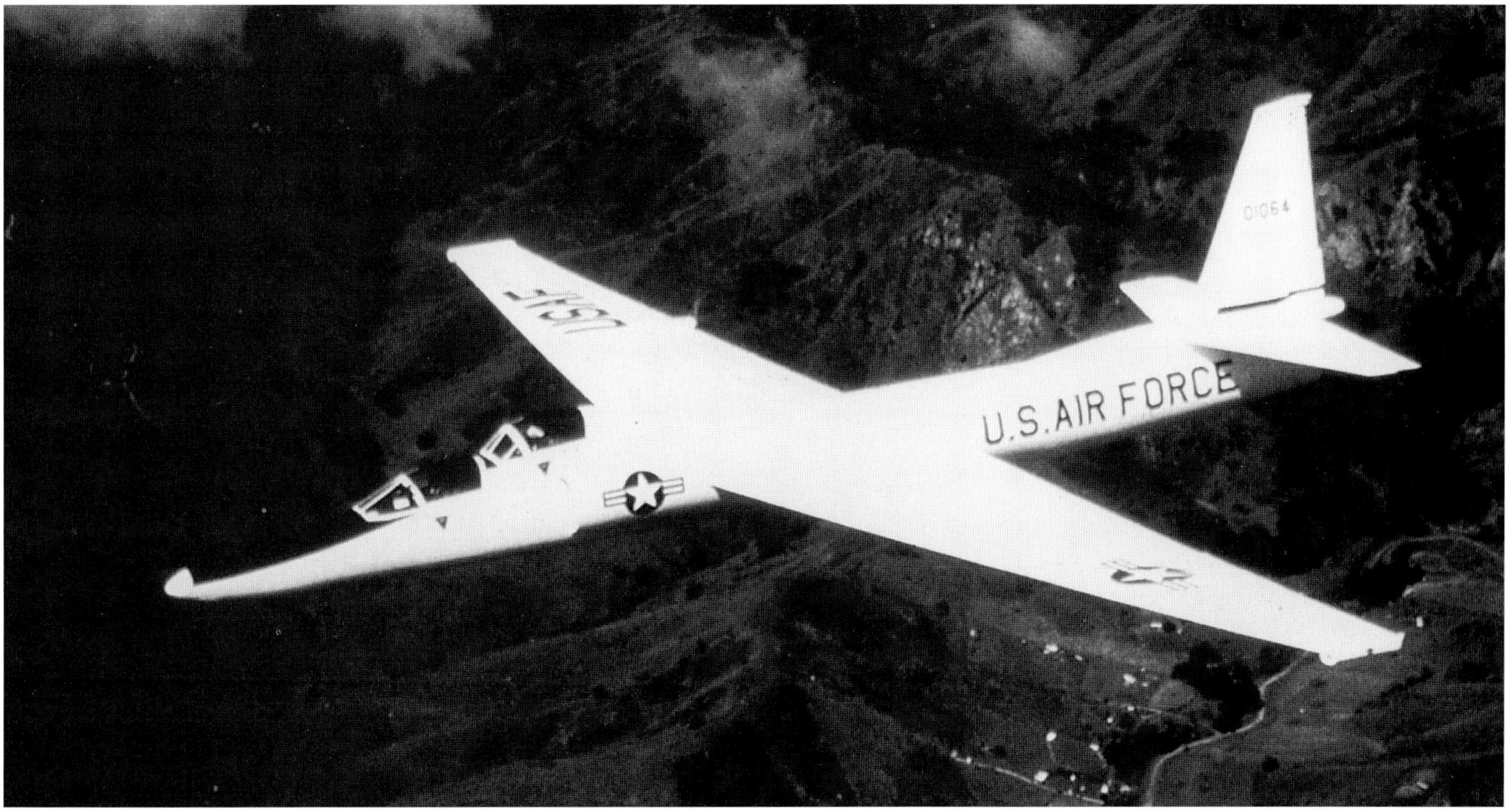

Air Force platforms continued to supply the Army with imagery during the 1980's. Above, the TR–1, a successor to the fabled U–2. Below, the SR–71 "Blackbird," fastest aircraft in the world.

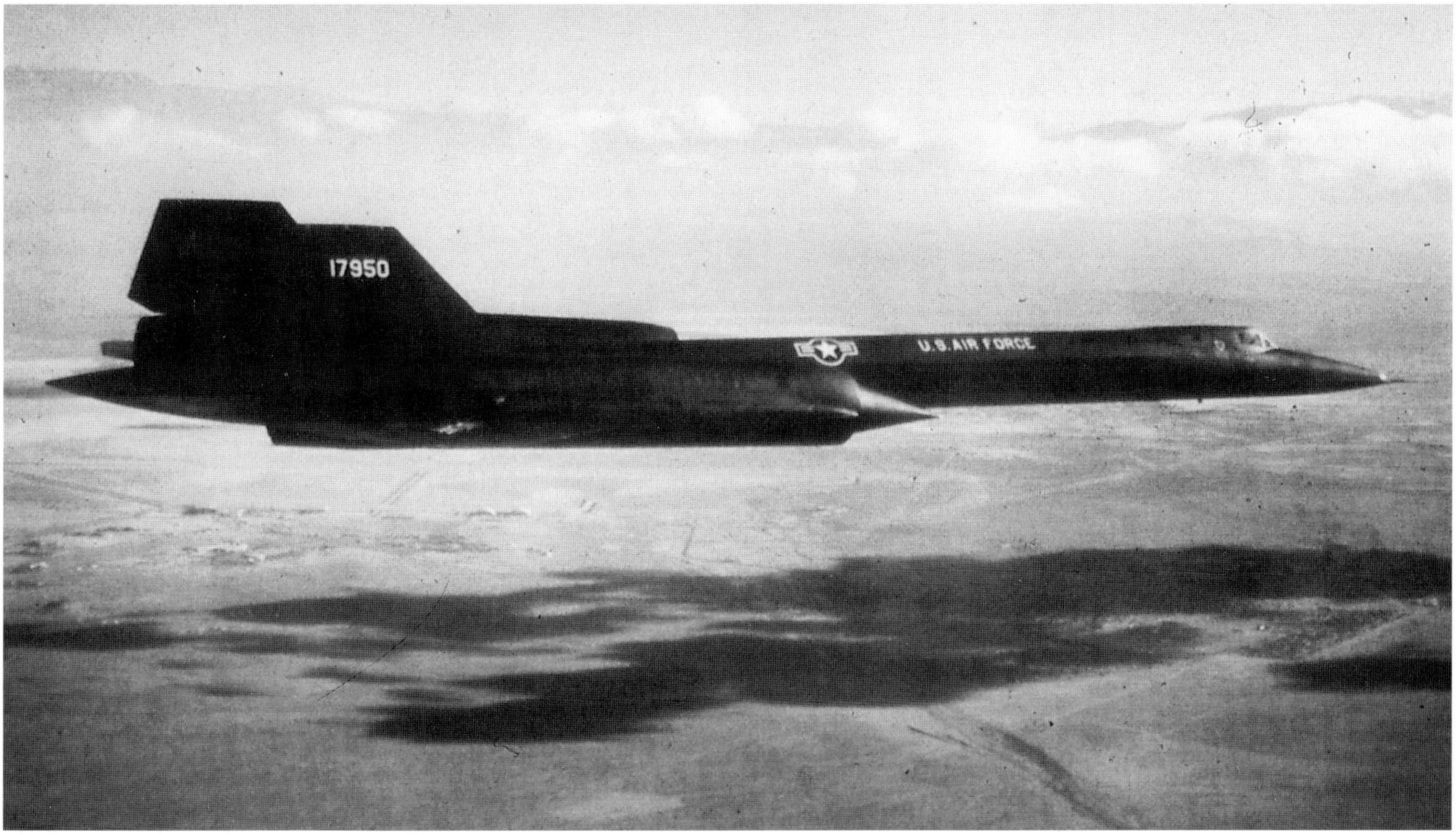

The High Frontier

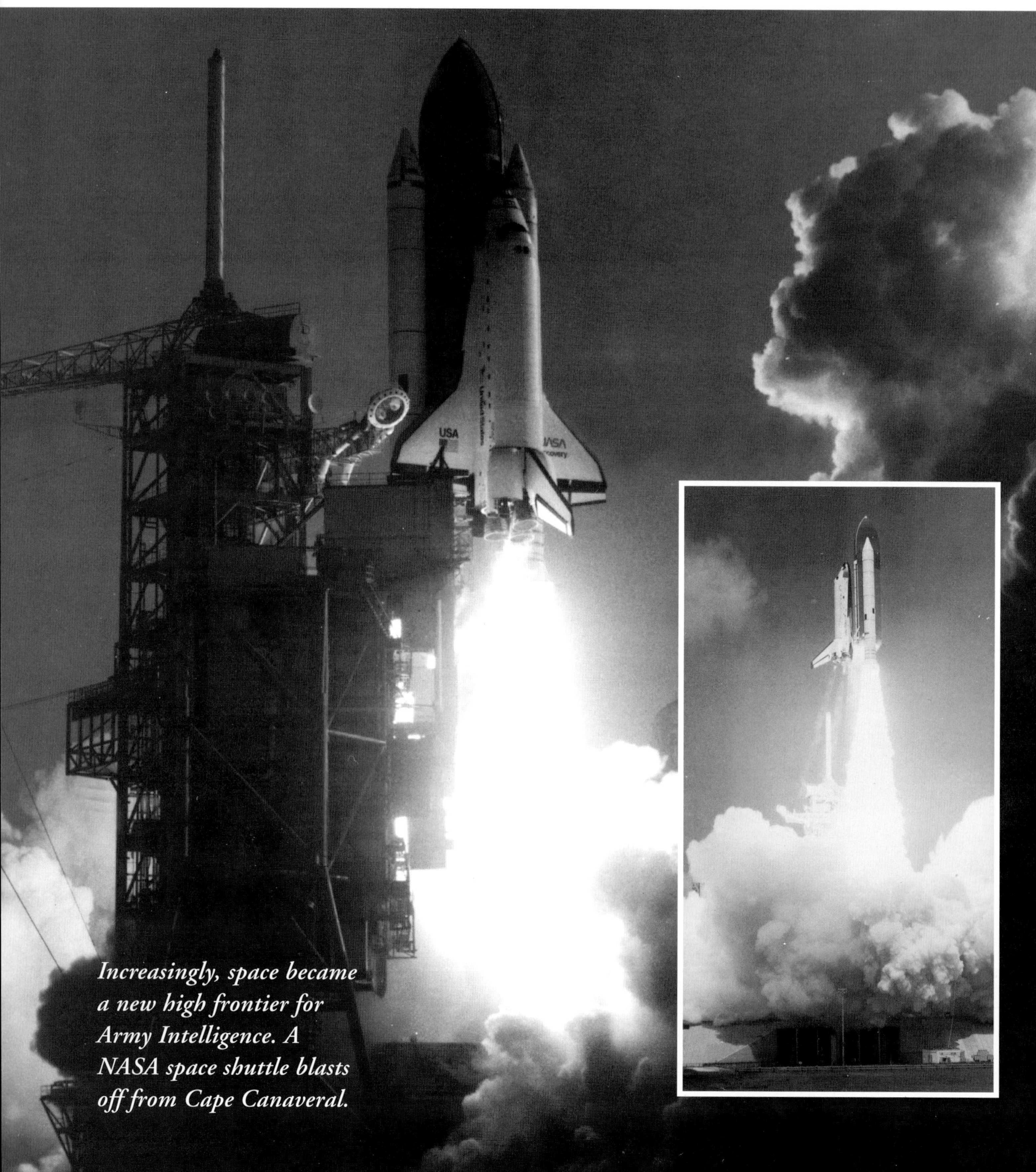

Increasingly, space became a new high frontier for Army Intelligence. A NASA space shuttle blasts off from Cape Canaveral.

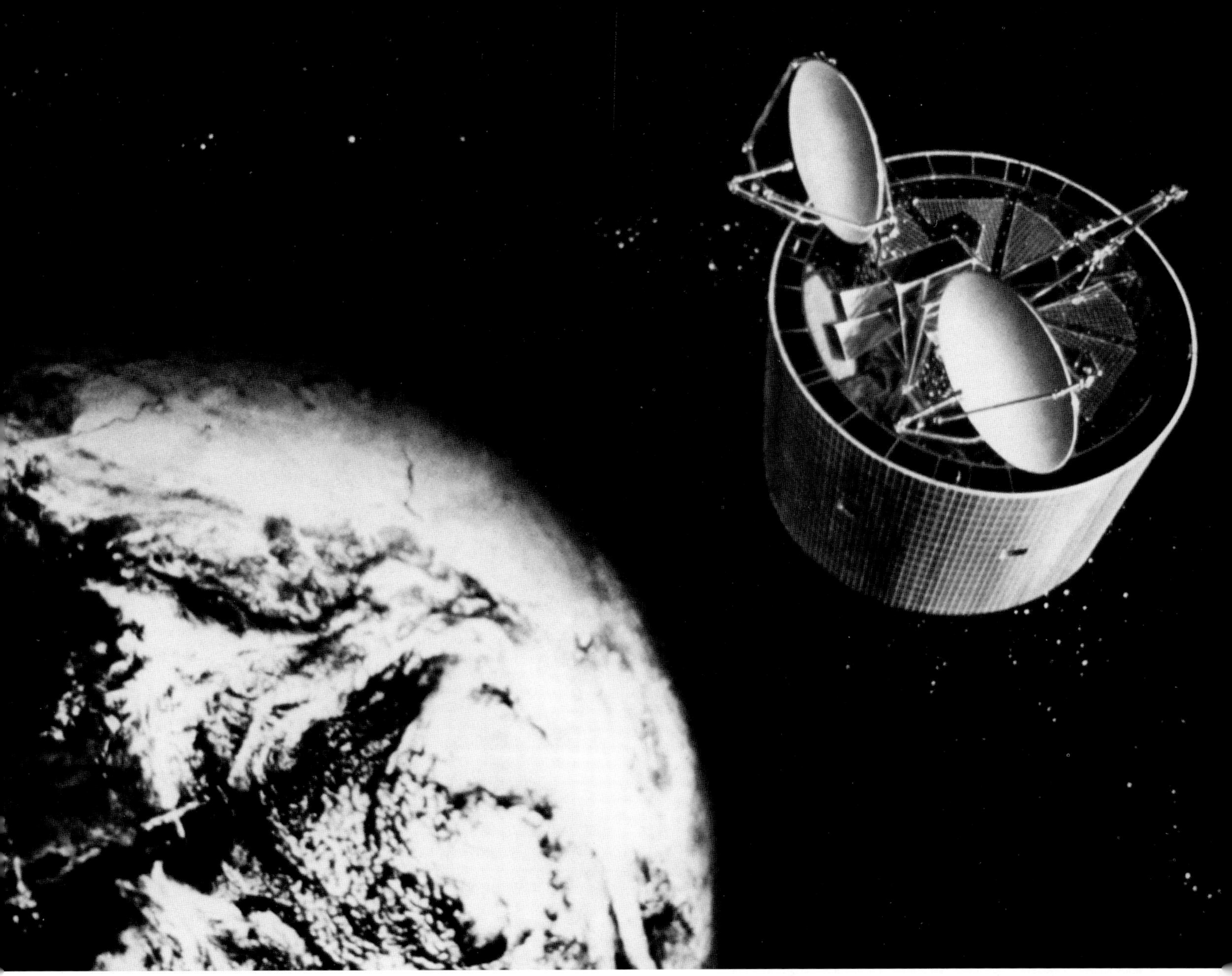

A communications satellite in geo-synchronous orbit hangs high above Planet Earth.

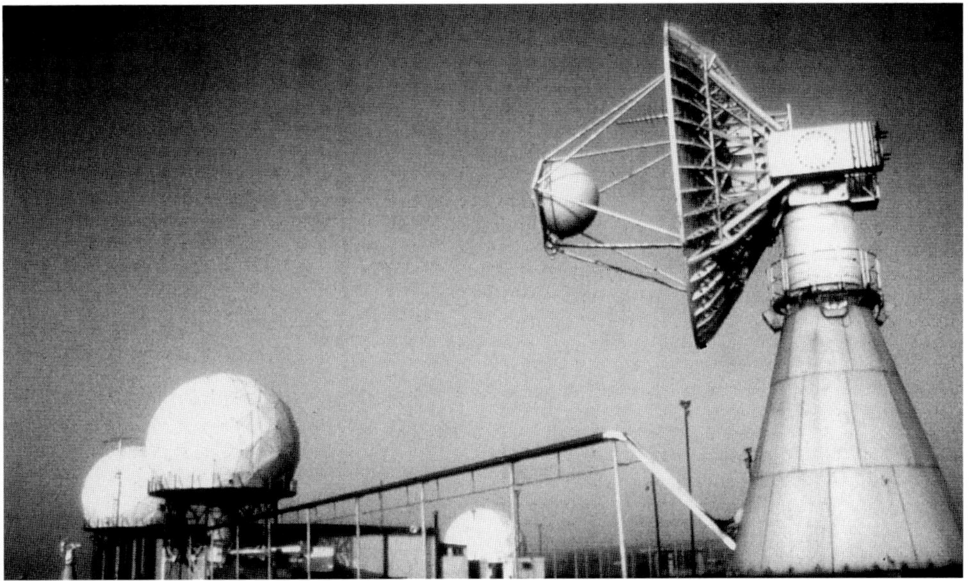

Space-based communication systems provided Army intelligence with global linkage. An Earth Satellite Terminal at Field Station Sinop.

"MI Has Arrived"

THE YEAR 1987 WITNESSED THREE significant milestones in the history of MI. In May, the position of ACSI was upgraded to Deputy Chief of Staff for Intelligence (DCSINT), a change that ended the position of organizational inferiority to which the intelligence function had been relegated since 1956. Lieutenant General Sidney T. Weinstein became the Army's first DCSINT. Subordinate to the DCSINT were directorates for foreign intelligence, intelligence policy and operations, intelligence plans and integration, counterintelligence and security management, and foreign liaison, along with separate offices dealing with intelligence oversight, personnel management, intelligence program and budget matters, and automation.

That same year, Army intelligence became part of the regimental system that had embodied the traditions of the U.S. Army ever since the Army itself had come into being. On July 1, 1987, the 25th anniversary of the establishment of intelligence as a Regular Army Branch, all Army intelligence personnel became part of a single large regiment, the Military Intelligence Corps. As Major General Julius Parker, the first Chief of the Military Intelligence Corps, observed, the step was "a recognition and celebration of our evolution from a plethora of diverse and separate intelligence agencies into the cohesive MI community we enjoy today. In short, it symbolizes the fact that Military Intelligence has truly arrived."

Finally, the Army gave new and coherent direction to Military Intelligence when it released an Army Intelligence, Electronic Warfare, Target Acquisition Master Plan (AIMP). The AIMP articulated a single integrated investment strategy for the planned evolution of Army intelligence, electronic warfare, and target acquisition systems and organizations at all levels. Factoring in projected threats, demonstrated and anticipated technological capabilities, and current and future Army intelligence requirements, the Master Plan provided the rationale for a massive modernization and procurement program. The new systems fielded as a result of the AIMP would revolutionize Army intelligence.

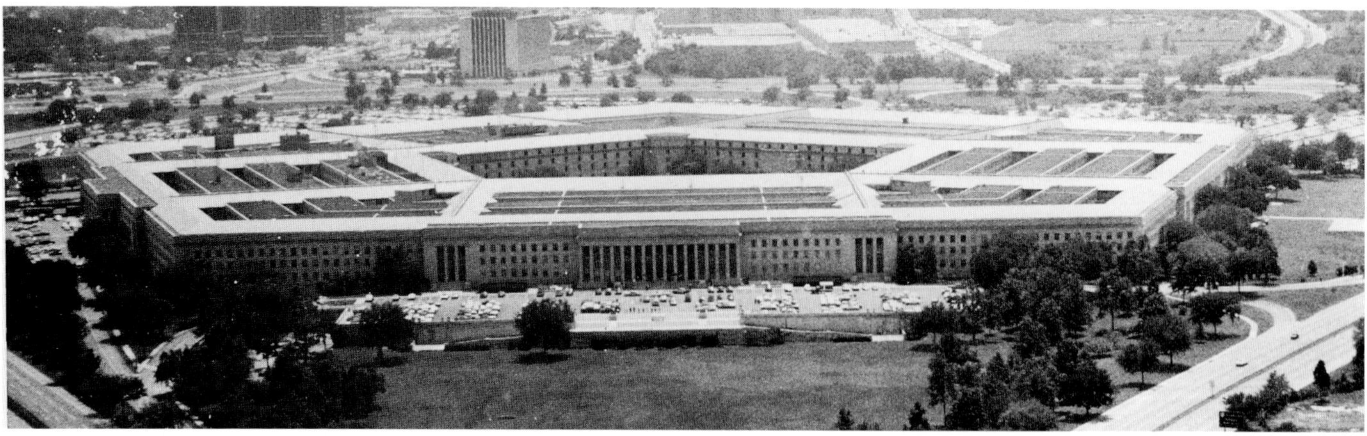

In 1987, intelligence at last regained equality with other Army Staff elements in the Pentagon, as the position of ACSI was upgraded to Deputy Chief of Staff for Intelligence with the rank of lieutenant general.

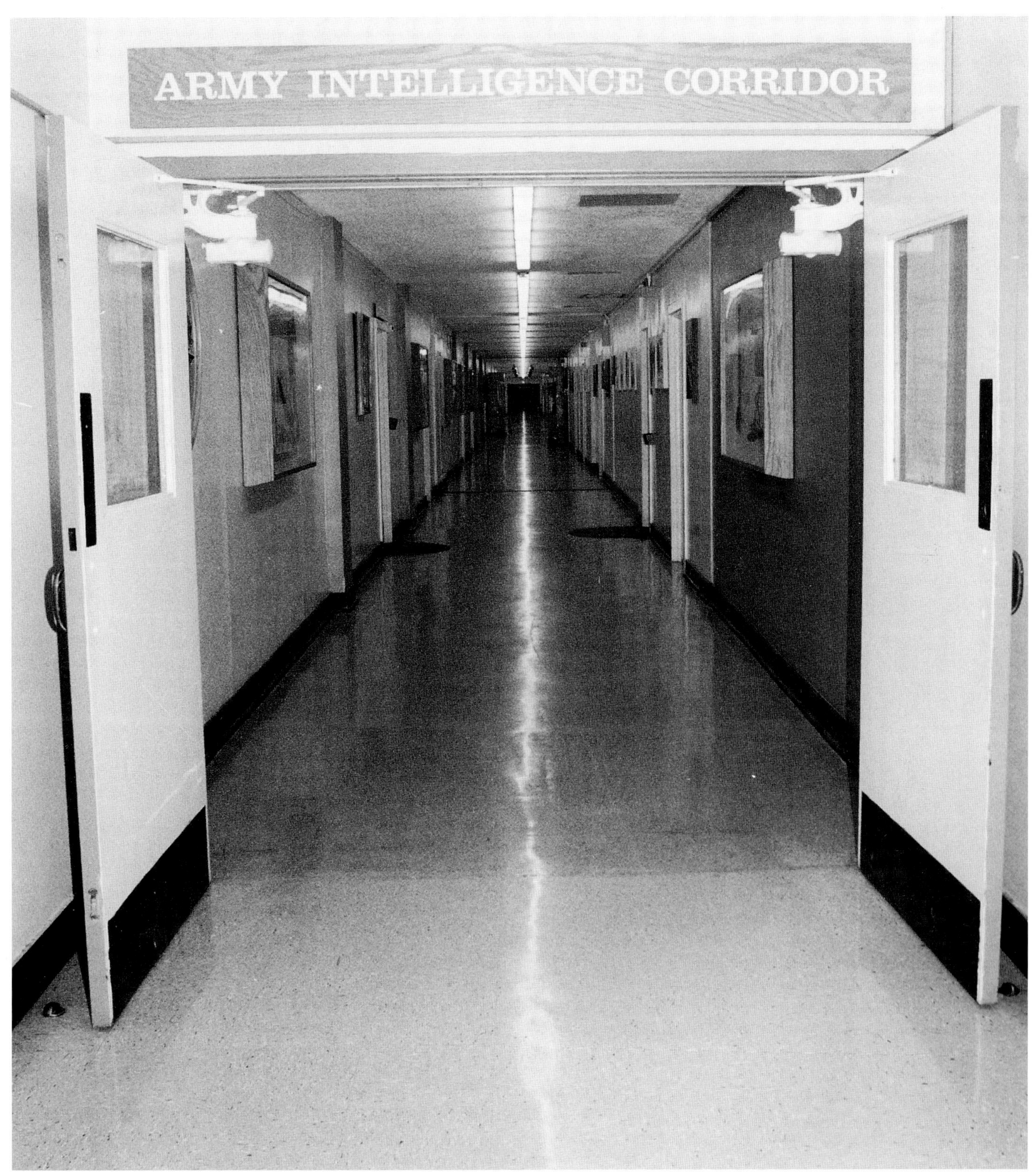

The Army Intelligence Corridor in the Pentagon houses offices of the Deputy Chief of Staff for Intelligence.

The MI Corps

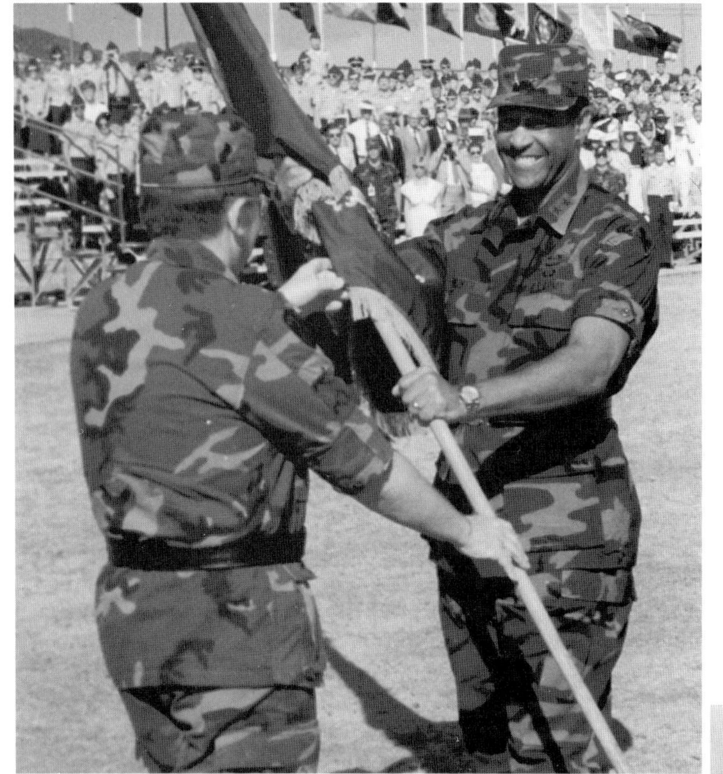

MG Julius Parker, first Chief of Military Intelligence, accepts the colors of the MI Corps from LTG Sidney T. Weinstein, the Army's first DCSINT.

Artillery booms out a salute at Fort Huachuca, Arizona, to commemorate the inauguration of the Military Intelligence Corps.

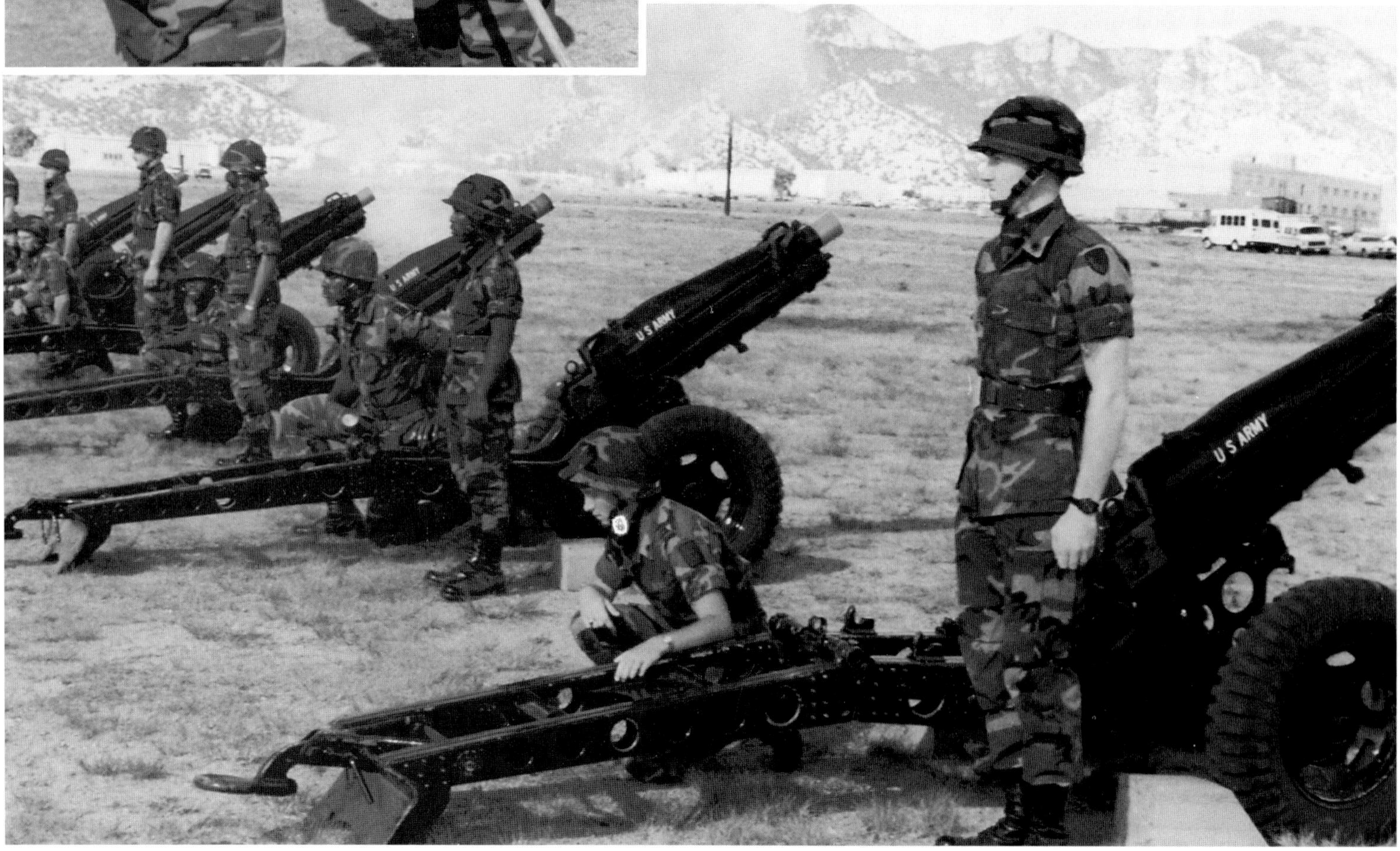

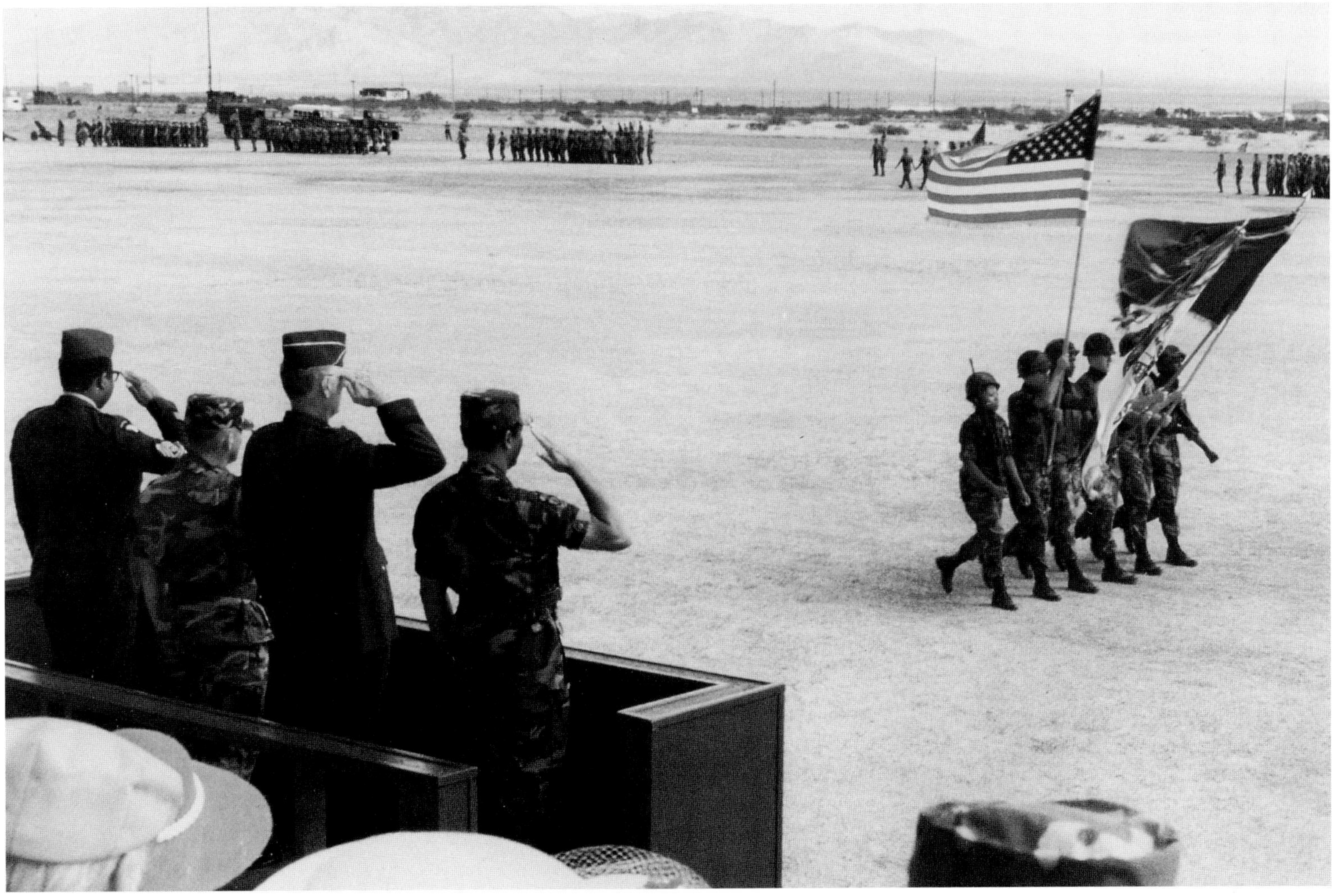

The MI Corps colors pass in review at Organization Day ceremonies at Fort Huachuca.

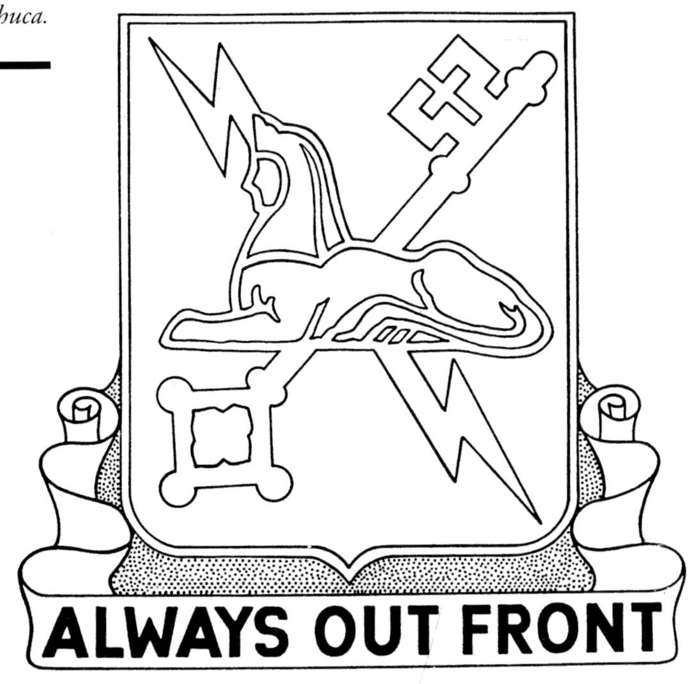

MI Corps Insignia.

A New Beginning

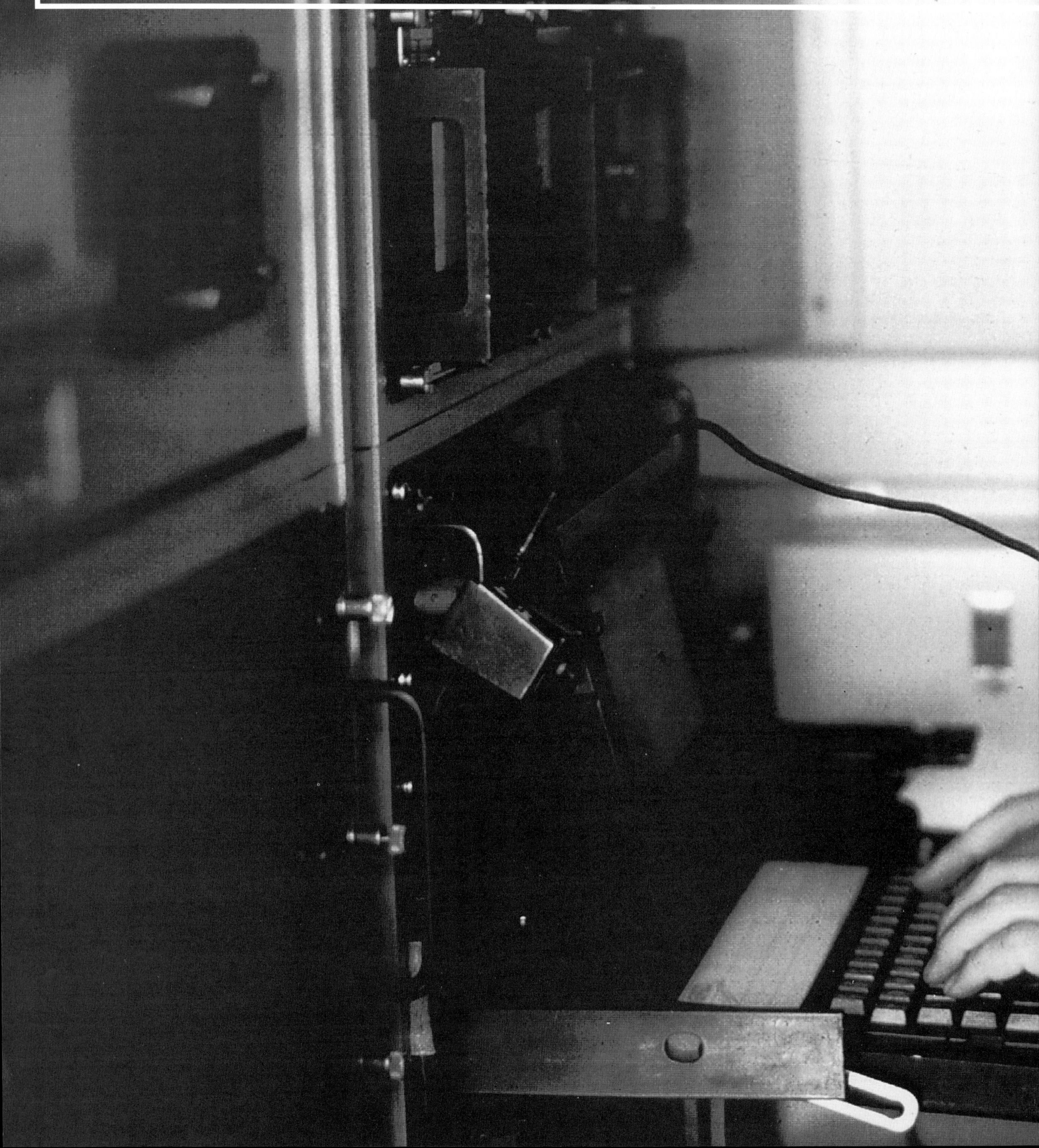

Part IV

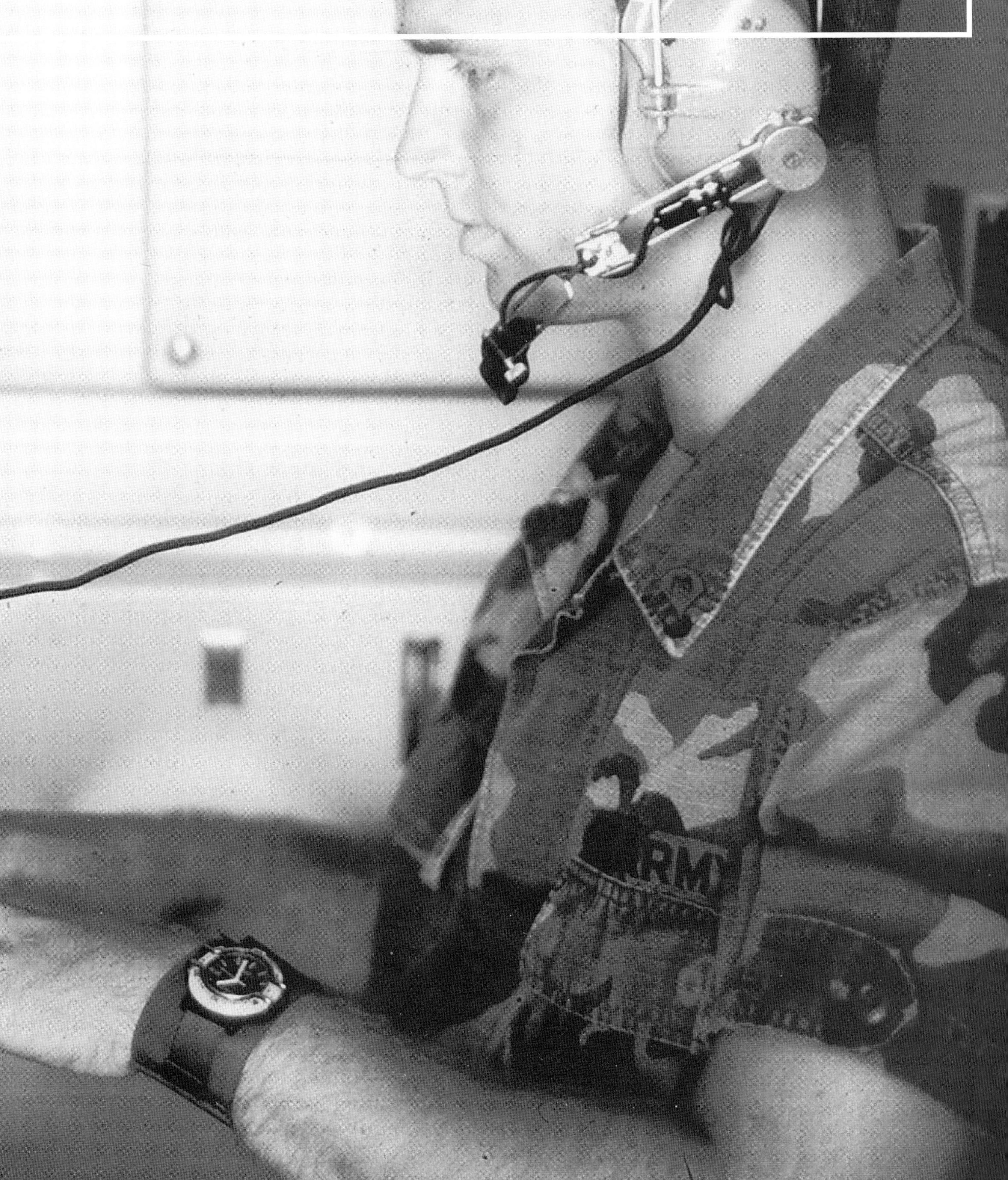

Culminations and Crises

The year 1989 marked the beginning of a startling transformation of the international scene that would have profound implications both for the Army and the nation which it served. That year witnessed the collapse of Communism throughout Eastern Europe, the fall of the Berlin Wall, and the demise of the Warsaw Pact which had linked the Soviet Union and its satellites behind the Iron Curtain. The Soviet threat that had loomed

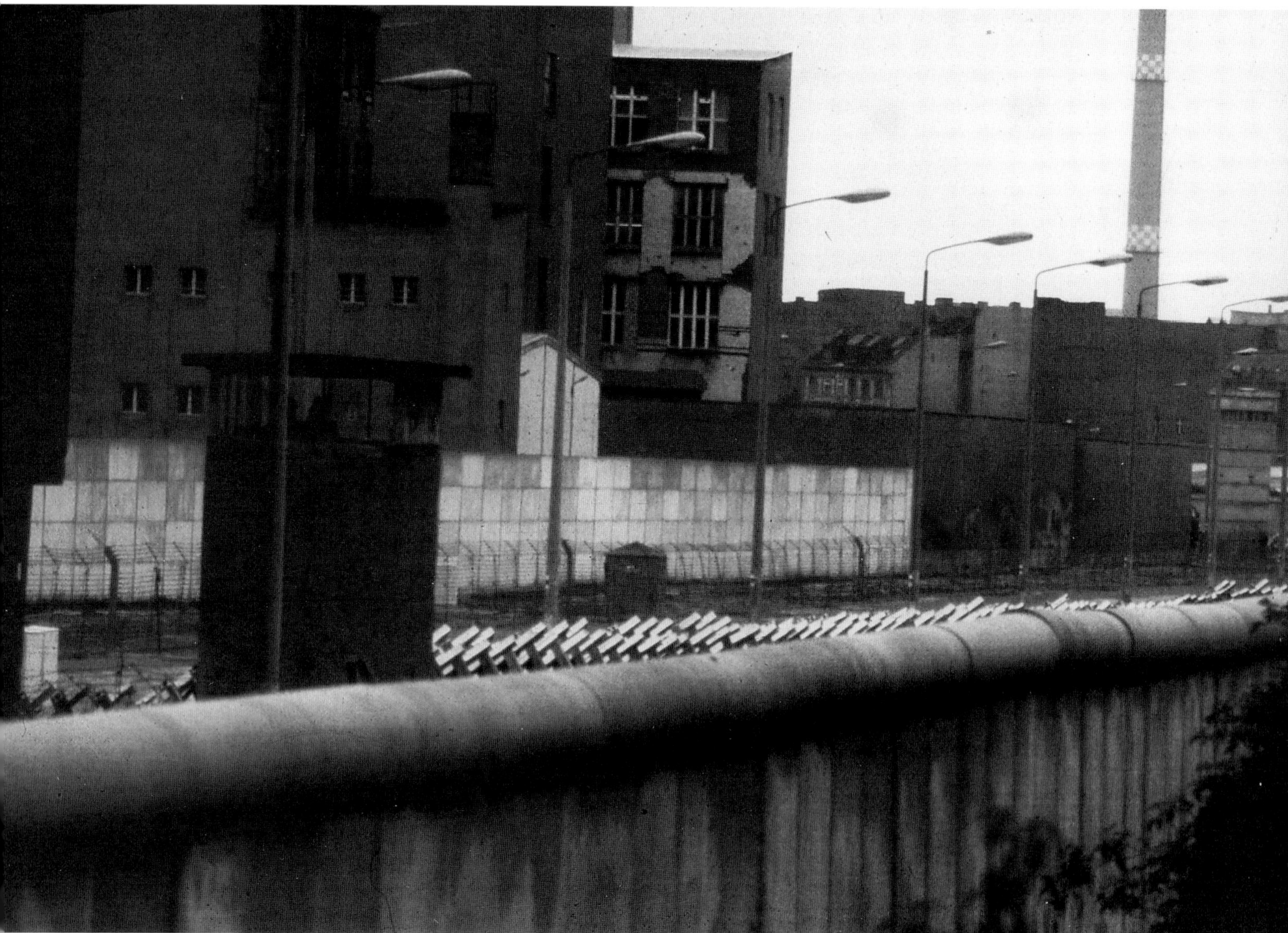

A watchtower on the Berlin Wall that sealed East from West for almost a generation. The collapse of the wall in 1989 was followed by the dissolution of East Germany. The end of the Cold War would force a massive reorientation of U.S. intelligence.

over Europe for so many years seemed to have vanished into thin air. Now that there was nothing to defend against, some policy makers hoped to find a "peace dividend" to restore the nation's battered finances.

This hope proved to be a little premature. Instead, the United States quickly found itself involved in two unanticipated armed conflicts. Growing tensions between Panamanian strongman General Manuel Noriega and the United States led to American military intervention in Panama in December 1989. Eight months later, Iraqi dictator Saddam Hussein seized the oil-rich Emirate of Kuwait and precipitated a major global crisis. The United States initially deployed major forces to protect the vital oil-fields of Saudi Arabia from further Iraqi aggression, and then drove Iraqi forces from Kuwait in a brilliant air and ground campaign when Hussein re-fused to yield to international sanctions.

Operation DESERT STORM—the liberation of Kuwait—proved to be a stunning success for American arms and a particular triumph for Military Intelligence. Three MI brigades supported the operation, along with numerous ancillary MI units, both Active and Reserve. The new generation of intelligence and electronic warfare systems fielded by the Army proved its worth, even though many were still in a developmental stage. Unmanned Aerial Vehicles (UAV's) and the airborne, ground-linked Joint Surveillance and Target Attack Radar System (JSTARS) allowed commanders an unprecedented overview of the battlefield. A communications network provided by the TROJAN Single Purpose Integrated Remote Intelligence Terminal (SPIRIT) linked commanders and intelligence officers in the front lines to intelligence production centers back in the United States via satellite. Army electronic warfare came into its own.

However, no sooner had the triumphant forces finished their victory parades than plans began to be implemented for a general drawdown of U.S. forces worldwide. The existing Army force structure had been overtaken by events. The reunification of Germany in October 1990 eliminated the need for a substantial troop presence to guard the Fulda Gap. These trends were further accelerated by the sudden collapse of the Soviet Union itself in 1991. What had formed the main target of Army intelligence for a generation now disappeared almost overnight. Planning guidance now called for the Army to be reduced in strength, falling to troop levels not seen since the general demobilization that followed World War II. The bulk of the Army's forces would no longer be forward deployed, but concentrated in the United States and utilized for power projection in any contingency situation. Inevitably, these major changes would have a dramatic impact on the Army's intelligence component.

As a result, the Army instituted an MI Relook in 1991 to reassess its Army Intelligence Master Plan. The MI Relook took into account the disappearance of the Soviet threat in Europe; the proliferating dangers elsewhere in the world; the Army's new force posture; and the impact of new technologies. It concluded that the Army would have to realign its intelligence production, and focus on providing warfighters with a "jointly interoperable and seamless" intelligence system. To bring this about, Intelligence Support Elements would be positioned at Joint Intelligence Centers and corps headquarters. Loss of direct access to targets by Army tactical commanders would be offset by leveraging national systems and by providing improved communications and secondary imagery dissemination to forces once they had deployed. Tactical MI assets would be restructured to enhance their counterintelligence and human resource intelligence capabilities, and greater emphasis would be given both to the MI reserves and the role of linguists. The new approach was reflected in the Army's 1993 revision of the AIMP.

Just Cause

In Panama, relations between the United States and Panamanian strongman General Manuel Noriega had quickly deteriorated after an American grand jury indicted the general for involvement in the narcotics traffic. Growing tensions presented an intolerable threat to American citizens in Panama and led to Operation JUST CAUSE, a massive intervention by American forces in December 1989. Overwhelming military force quickly smashed the Panama Defense Force that formed Noriega's power base, and the general himself was soon apprehended and returned to the United States to stand trial. Intelligence support to the operation was provided by INSCOM'S 470th MI Brigade and its attached 29th MI Battalion.

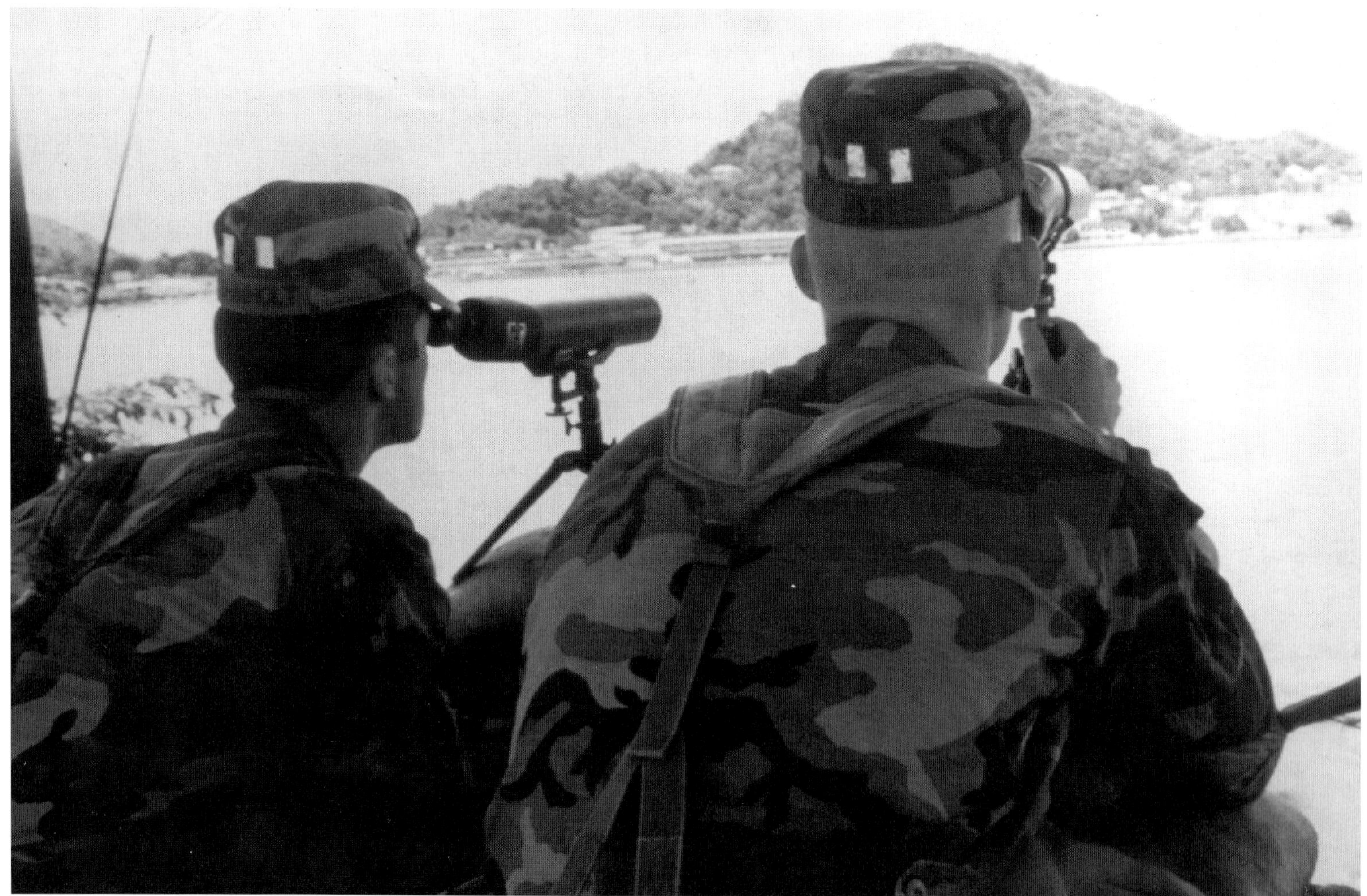

On the eve of JUST CAUSE, soldiers of the 193d Infantry Brigade use an M–49 observation scope to maintain surveillance over the Commandancia, headquarters of Noriega's Panama Defense Force.

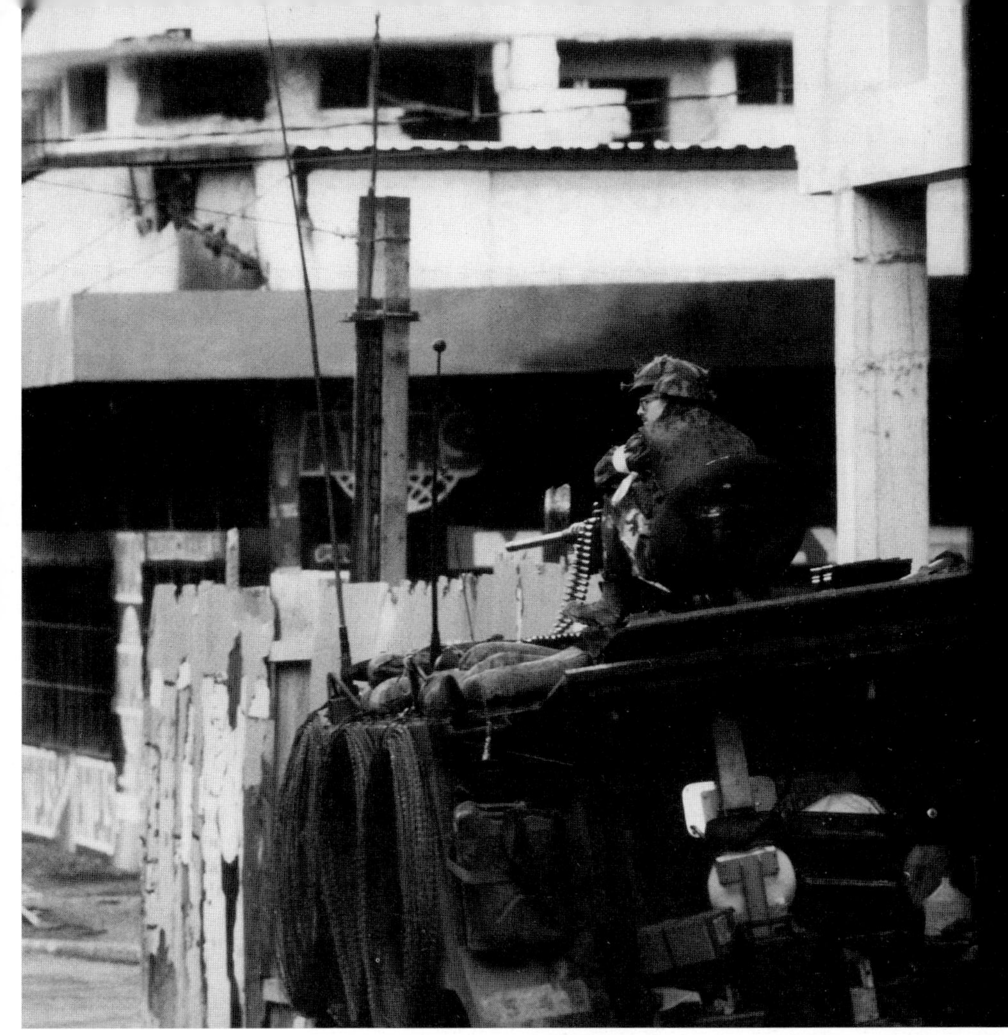

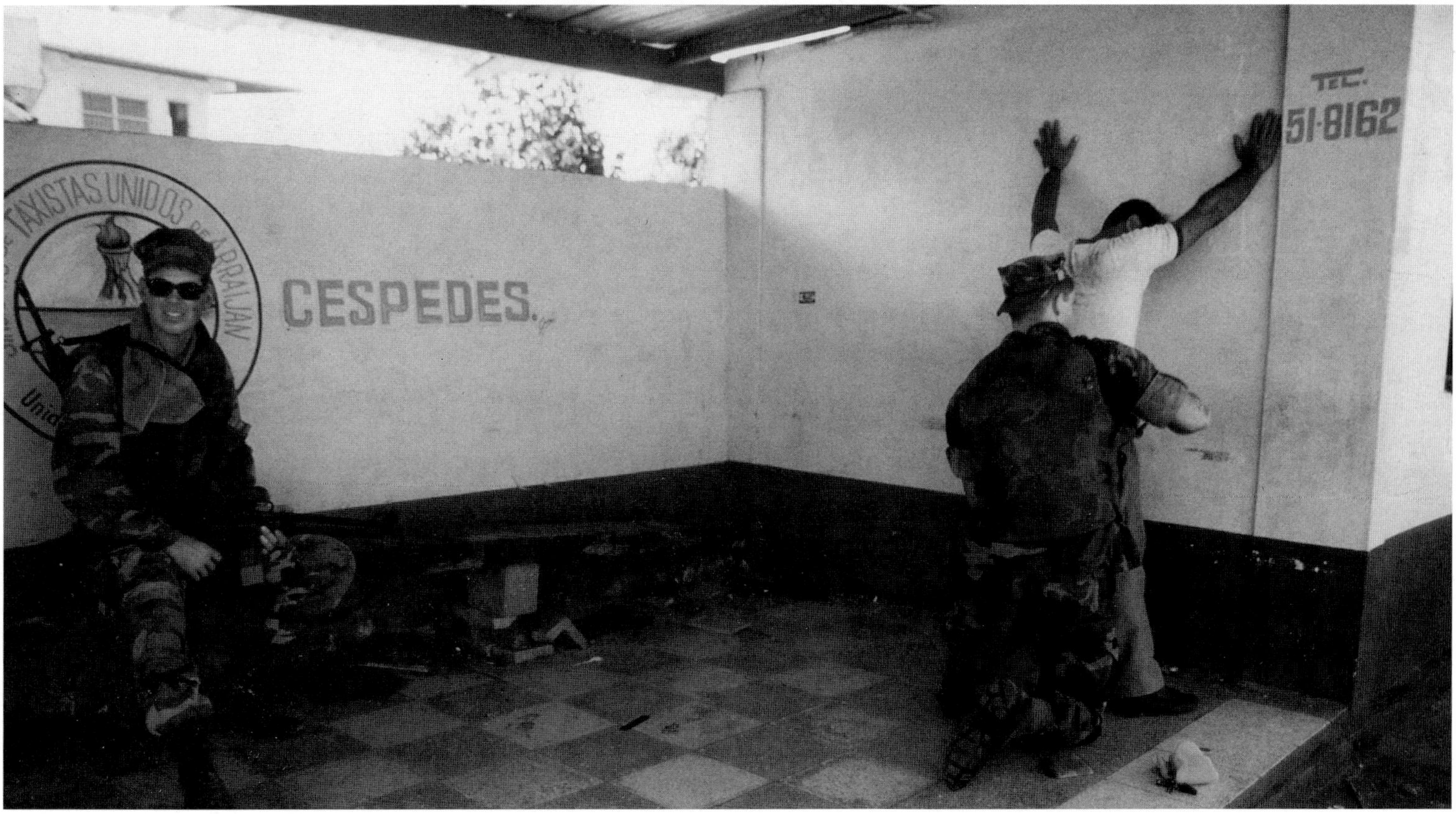

An M–113 armored personnel carrier (APC) takes up position in a Panama street in support of JUST CAUSE. Excellent intelligence helped to bring about quick victory.

Troops search Panamanian civilians in the aftermath of JUST CAUSE. Apprehended Panamanians of high-level intelligence interest were interrogated in a Joint Interrogation Center.

Desert Storm

In August 1990, Iraqi dictator Saddam Hussein launched a surprise attack on the neighboring Emirate of Kuwait, a tiny but oil-rich territory in the Persian Gulf. Hussein's actions threatened the stability of the whole Middle East, especially since his forces were now in a position to threaten the key oil-fields of Saudi Arabia. The United States was quick to react. As part of Operation DESERT SHIELD, troops were rushed to Saudi Arabia and the United States rallied world opinion against this aggression through the United Nations. When neither Security Council orders nor international sanctions proved effective in forcing Saddam Hussein to relinquish his prey, President George Bush reinforced the troops already committed to Saudi Arabia, calling up reservists and redeploying an army corps from Germany. In January 1991, an American-led Allied coalition launched the air phase of Operation DESERT STORM, the liberation of Kuwait. In February, this was followed up by a lightning ground attack that overwhelmed the Iraqis in 100 hours of fighting.

America's quick, decisive, and relatively bloodless victory in the desert ended the long malaise produced by the unhappy results of the Vietnam conflict and restored American pride and confidence in the armed forces. In addition to being a triumph for American arms and logistics, DESERT STORM also proved to be a milestone in the history of military intelligence. New technologies allowed commanders unprecedented surveillance of the entire Kuwaiti Theater of Operations, while enhanced satellite communications permitted intelligence produced in Washington to be relayed down to divisions in the field almost instantaneously. The Third United States Army that fought in the desert received intelligence support from three military intelligence brigades and numerous ancillary intelligence units. And in line with the Total Army concept, reserve MI units were deployed in the desert to assist the active component.

One of the best testimonies to the success of Military Intelligence in DESERT STORM was provided by a captured Iraqi officer. "We had a great appreciation of your intelligence system; we knew from our experience in the Iranian War that at all times you could see us during day and night and knew where we were on the ground. If we communicated, you could both hear us and target us, and if we talked too long, you would target us and destroy us with your ordnance. On the other hand, as we looked at our intelligence system, we had no idea where you were on the ground, we had no intelligence system capabilities to see what your dispositions were, and we had no way to monitor your communications. We knew you were going to attack only when you overran our front line positions. . . ."

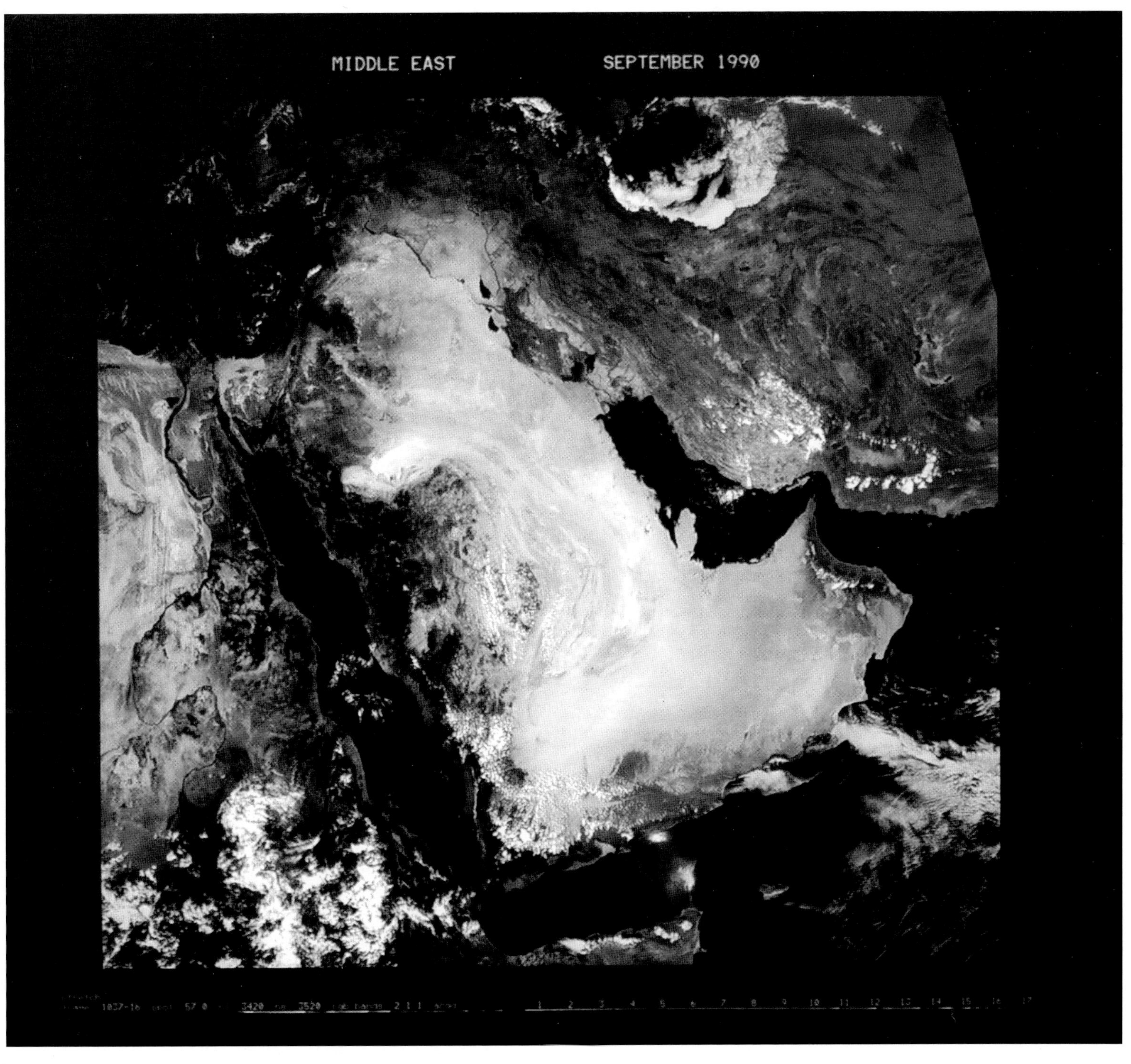

The arena of war. Overhead imagery of the Arabian peninsula produced by a weather satellite.

MI in the Desert

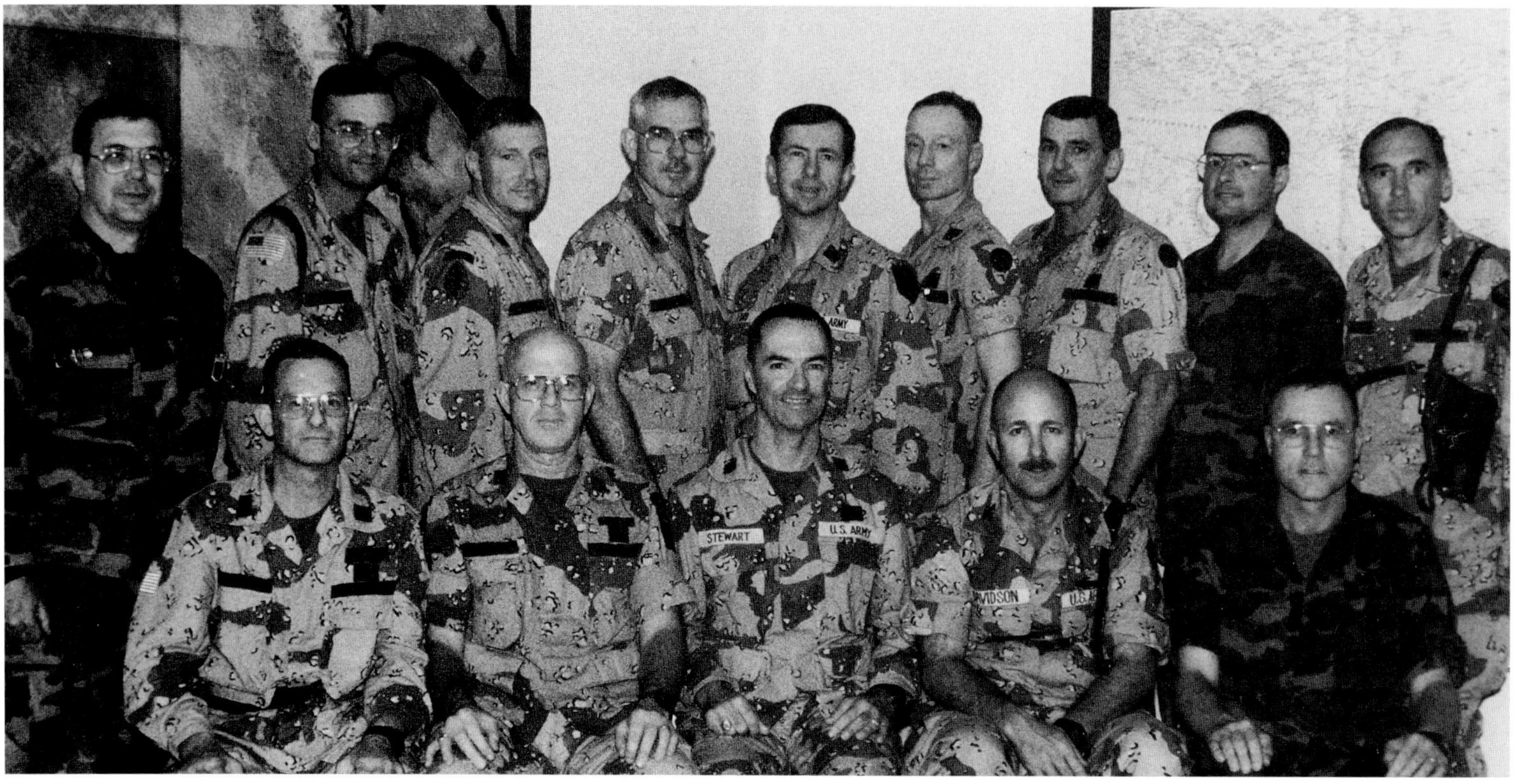

BG John F. Stewart, G–2 of Third U.S. Army, poses with the senior MI officers involved in Operation DESERT STORM.

Headquarters of Third U.S. Army and the 513th MI Brigade at Eskan Village, Riyadh, Saudi Arabia.

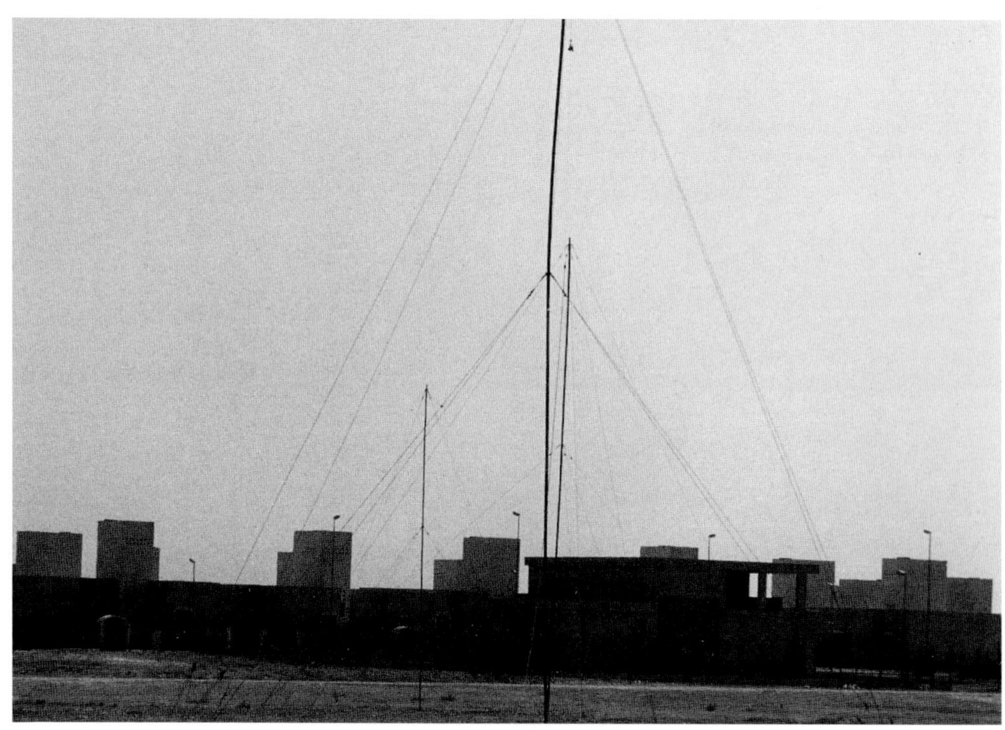

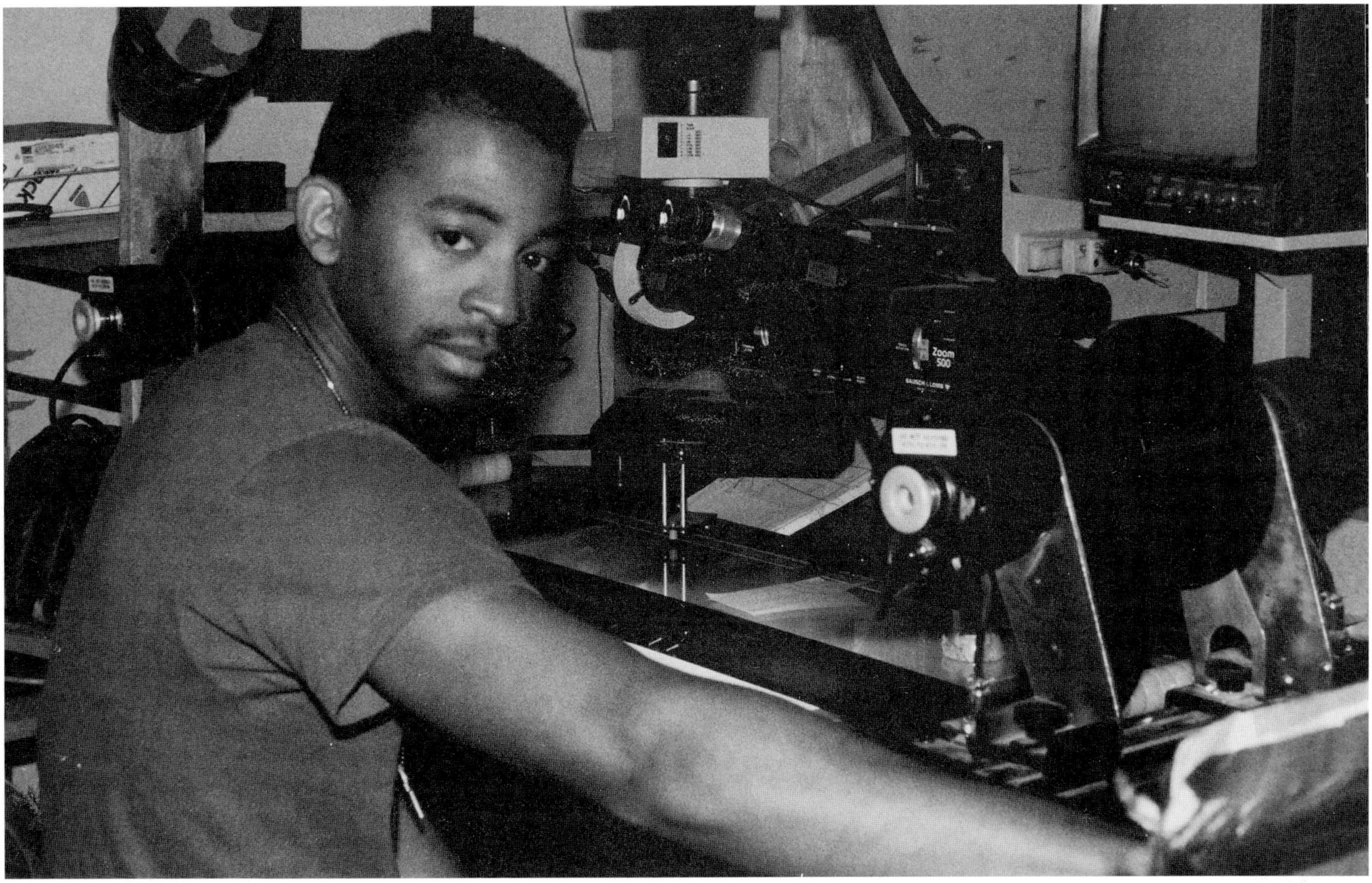

Because of the nature of the desert war, IMINT was the key intelligence discipline in the prosecution of DESERT STORM. An imagery interpreter of the 513th MI Brigade.

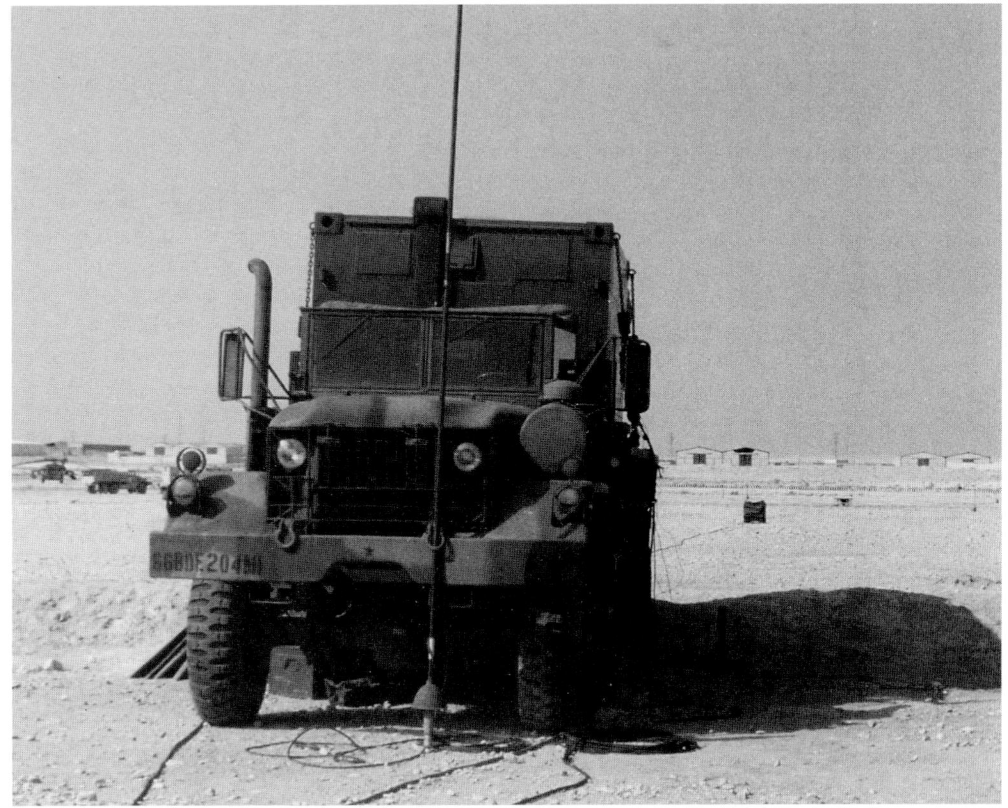

To bolster U.S. Army signals intelligence assets in the Gulf, INSCOM deployed elements of the 204th MI Battalion from Europe.

Electronics at War

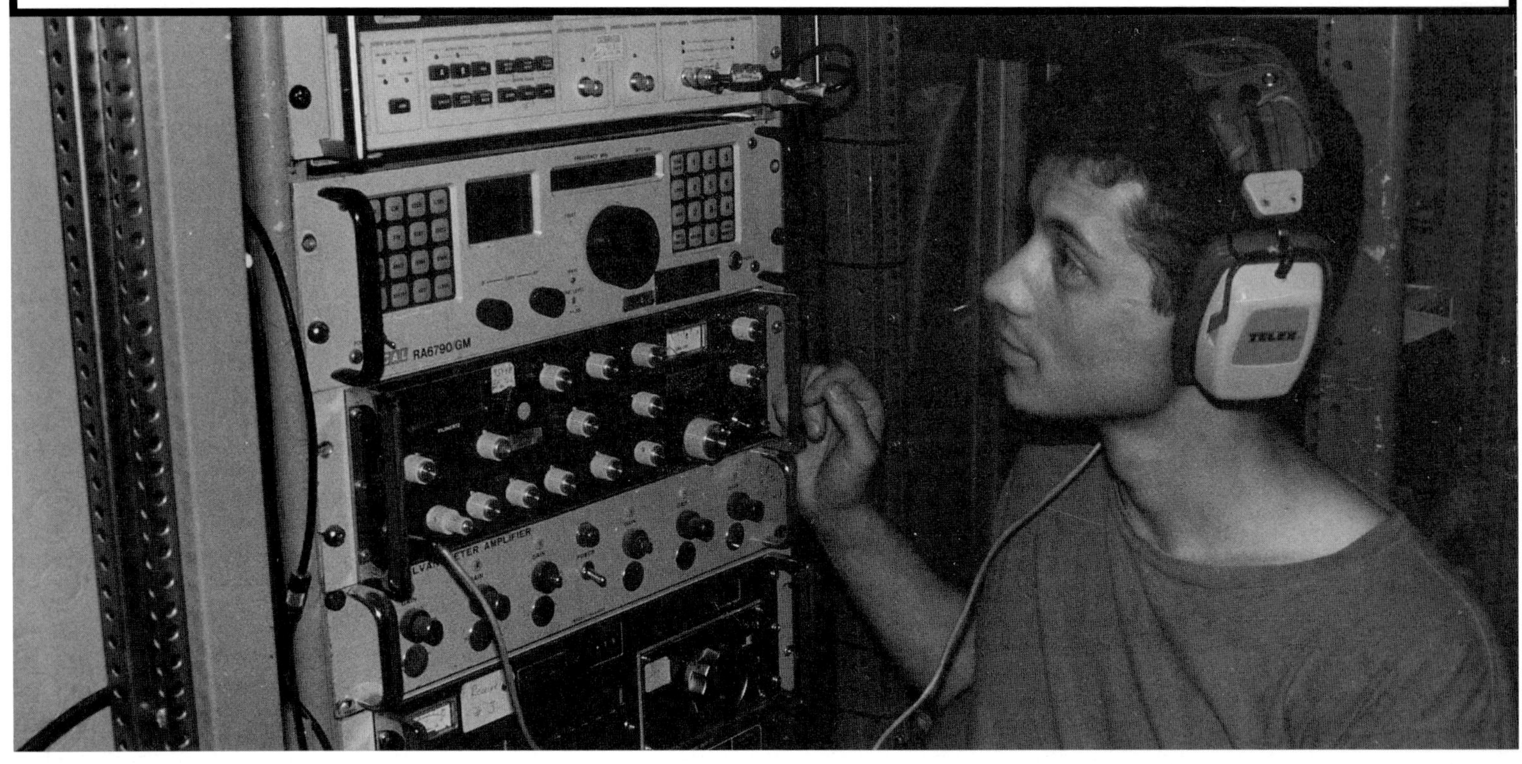

Top, monitoring operations in the desert. Bottom, a soldier of the 201st MI Battalion mans a radio direction finder.

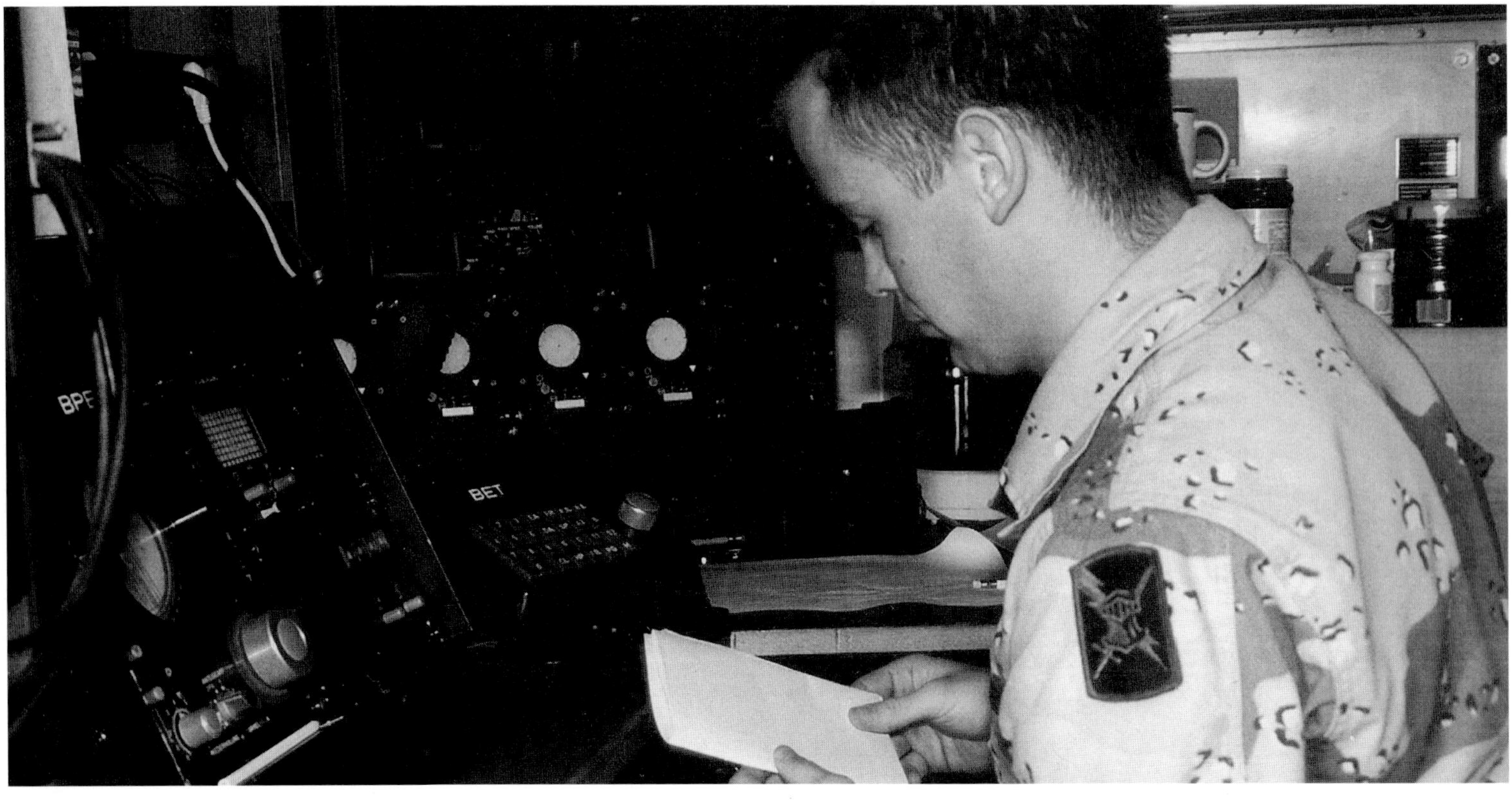

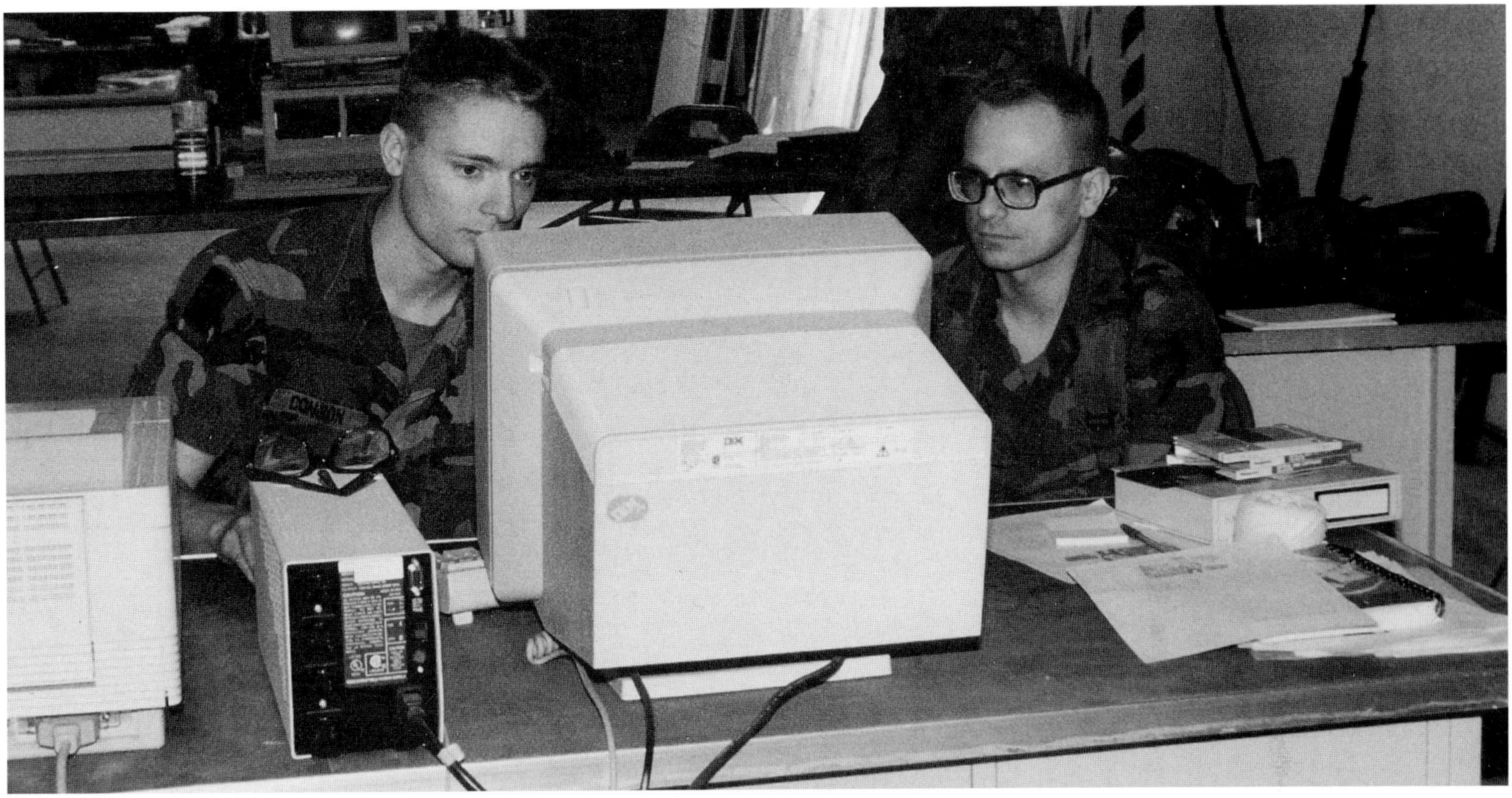

Advances in automation meant that intelligence operations could now be supported by computers even in the field.

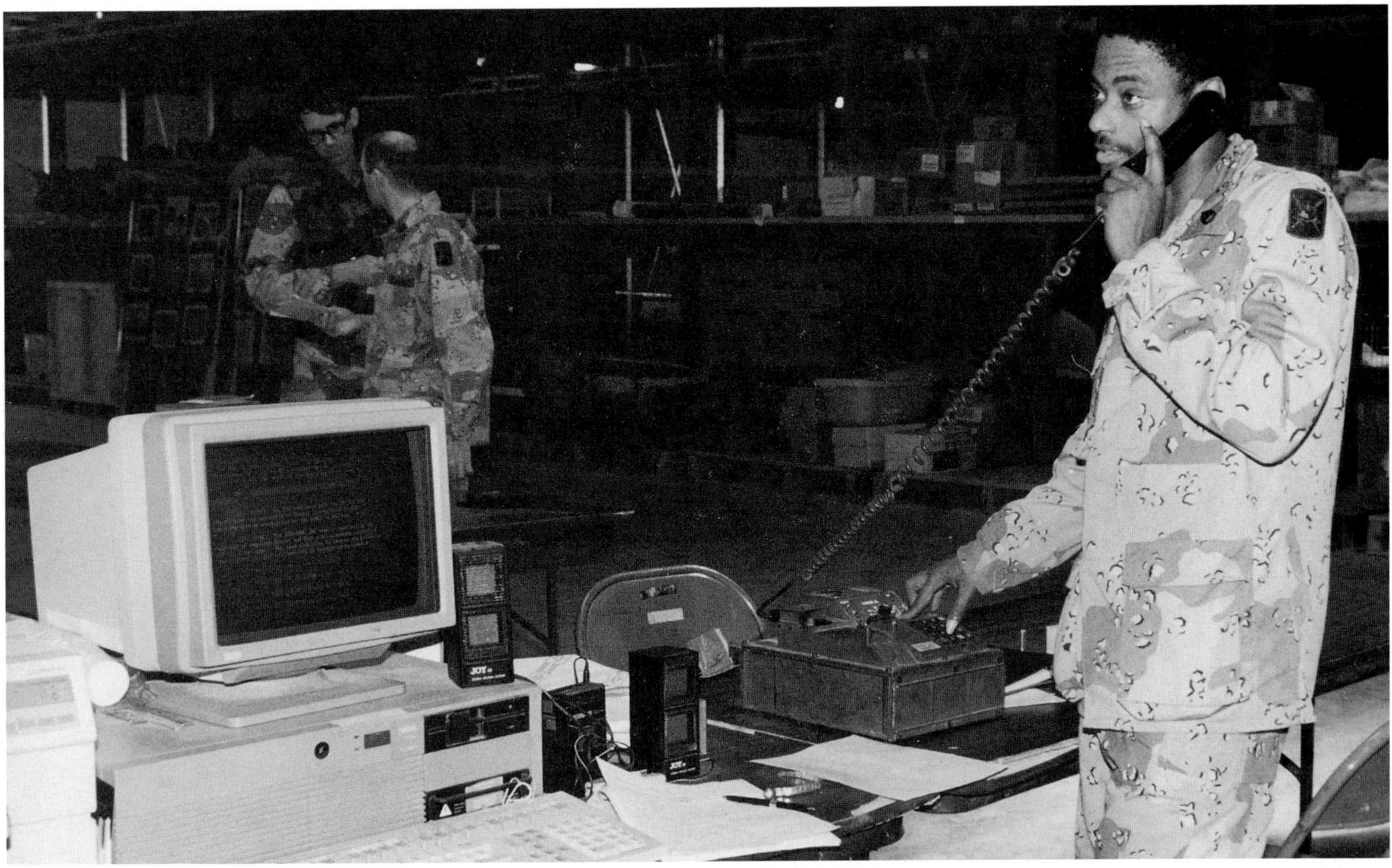

Intelligence Sources

An Unmanned Aerial Vehicle (UAV) blasts off into the sky during Operation DESERT STORM. Employment of UAV's such as the one shown here provided field commanders with a new collection mechanism.

Imagery of the Kuwaiti Theater of Operations (KTO) provided by the developmental Joint Surveillance and Target Attack Radar System (JSTARS). Each blip of light represents the radar track of a moving vehicle.

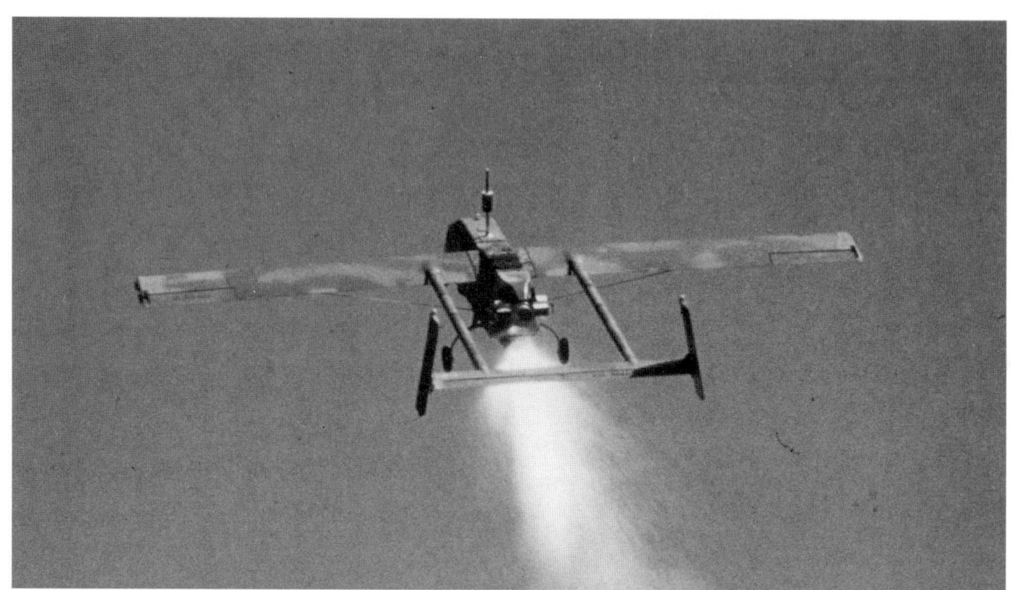

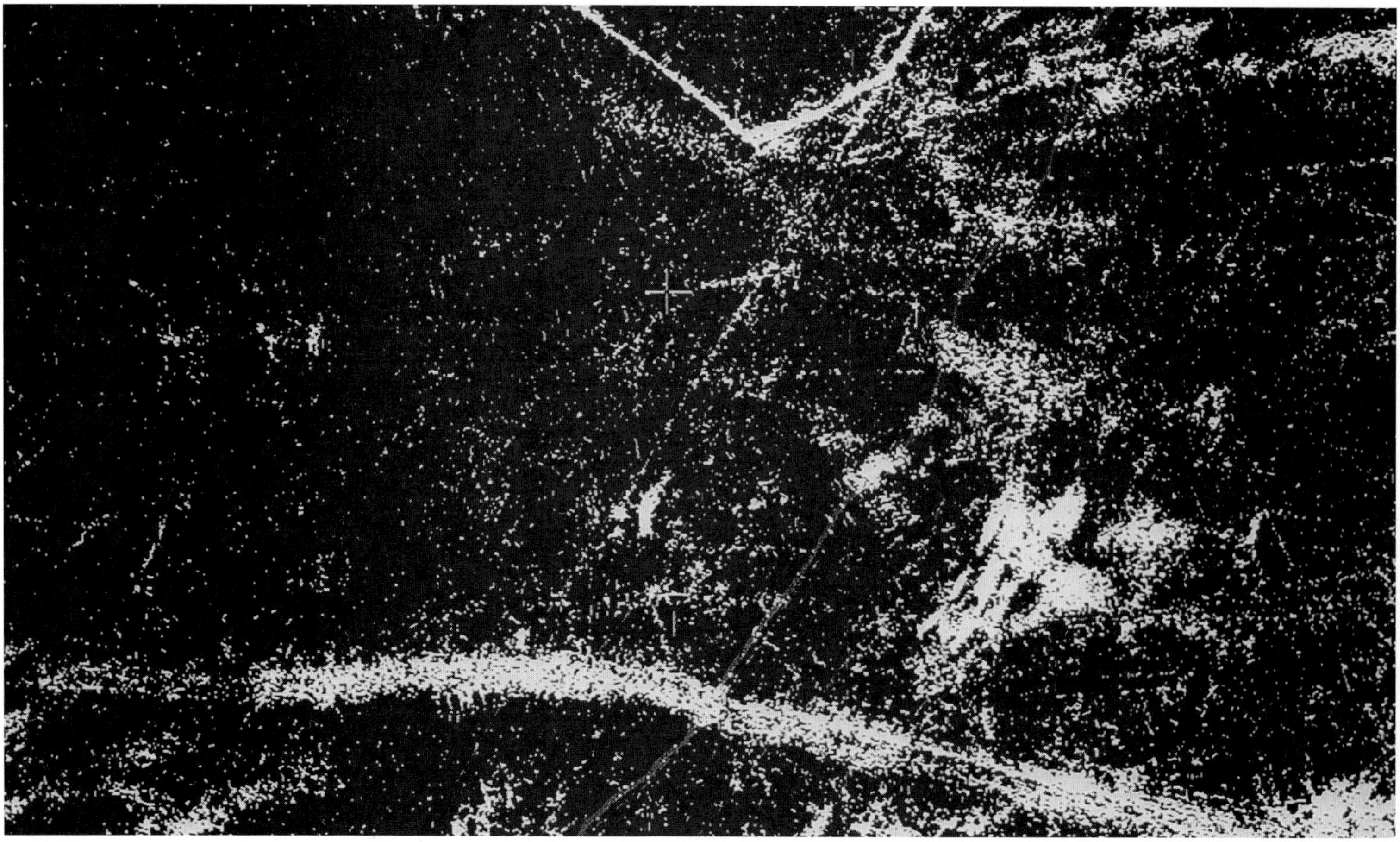

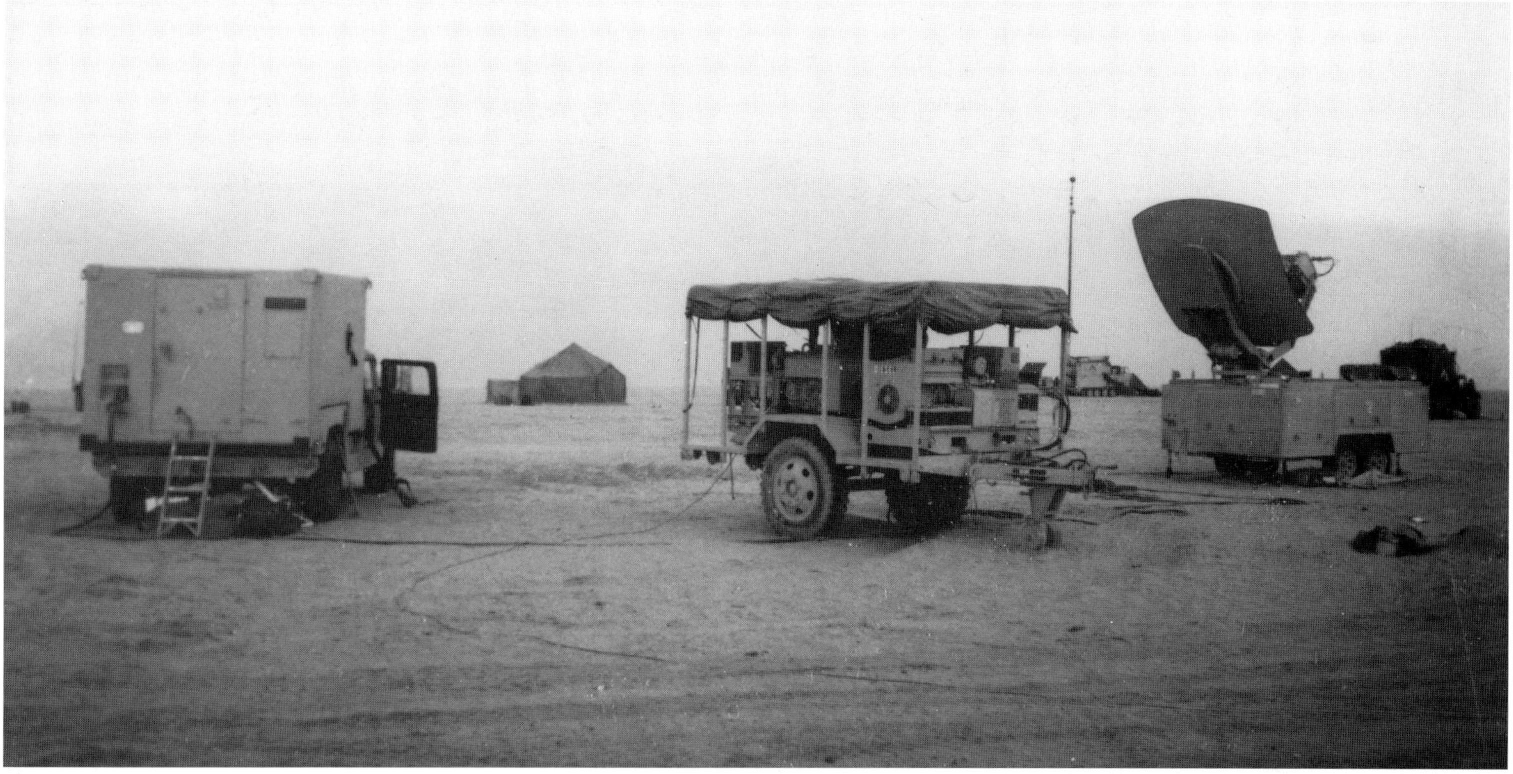

TROJAN Special Purpose Integrated Remote Intelligence Terminals (TROJAN SPIRIT) such as the one shown furnished Army units with dedicated and secure intelligence communication systems, allowing them to access data from national and theater sources.

A prisoner of war compound in the desert. Captured Iraqis provided valuable information, and HUMINT continued to serve as a major intelligence source both on and off the battlefield.

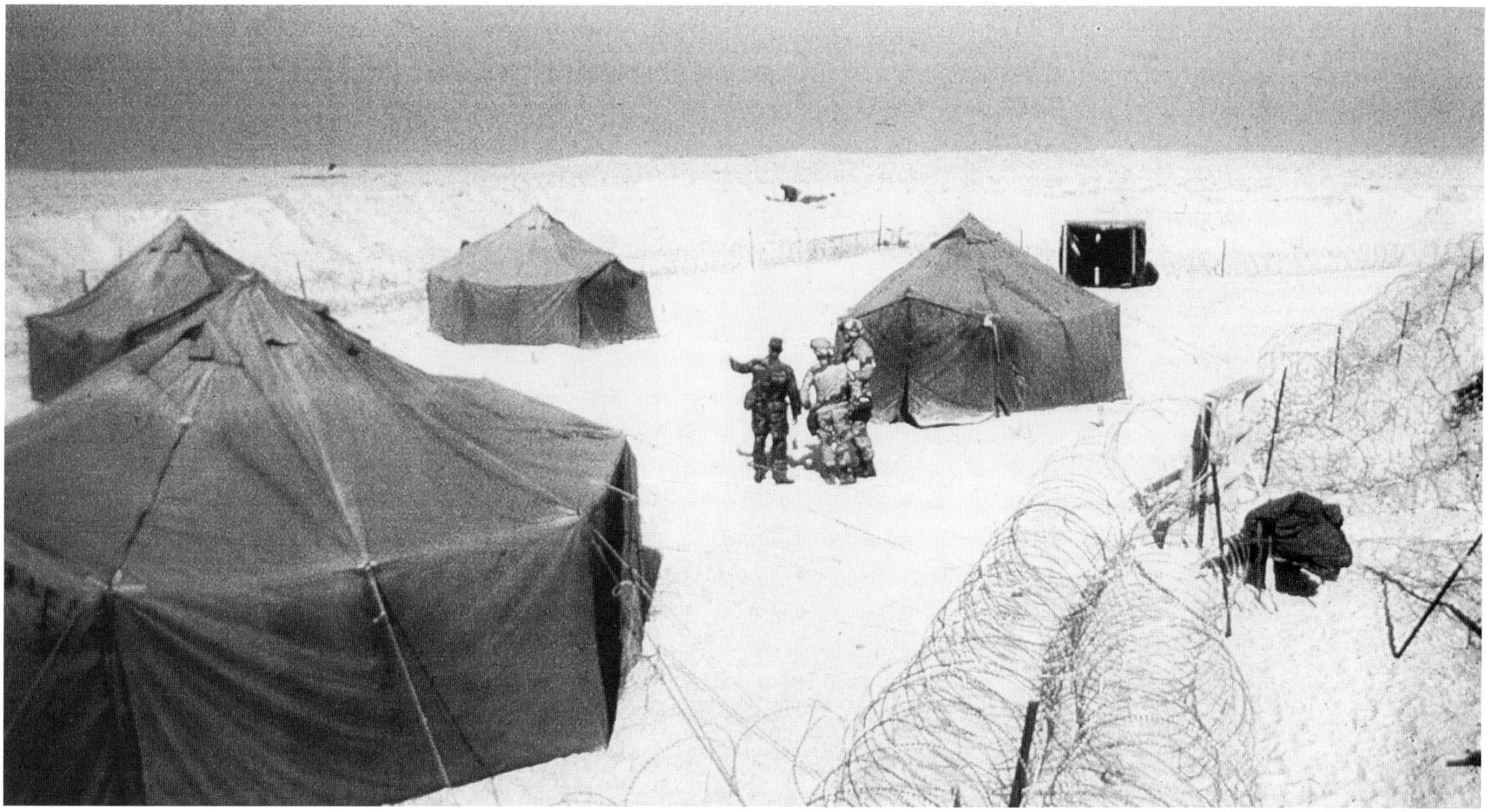

Technical Intelligence

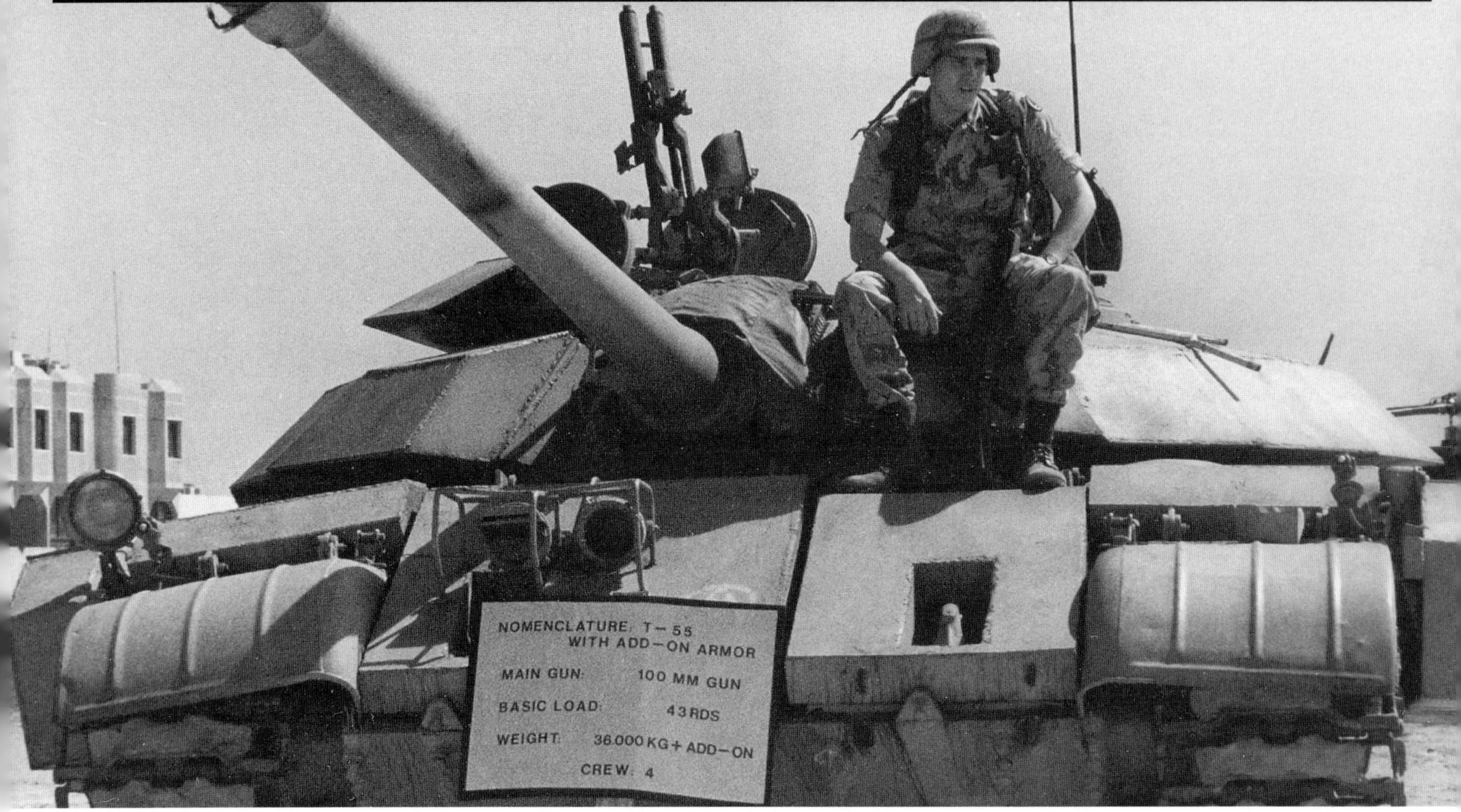

DESERT STORM provided the U.S. Army with a bonanza of captured equipment susceptible to exploitation by technical intelligence. A soldier sits atop an obsolescent Soviet-made T–55 tank that has been upgraded by add-on armor.

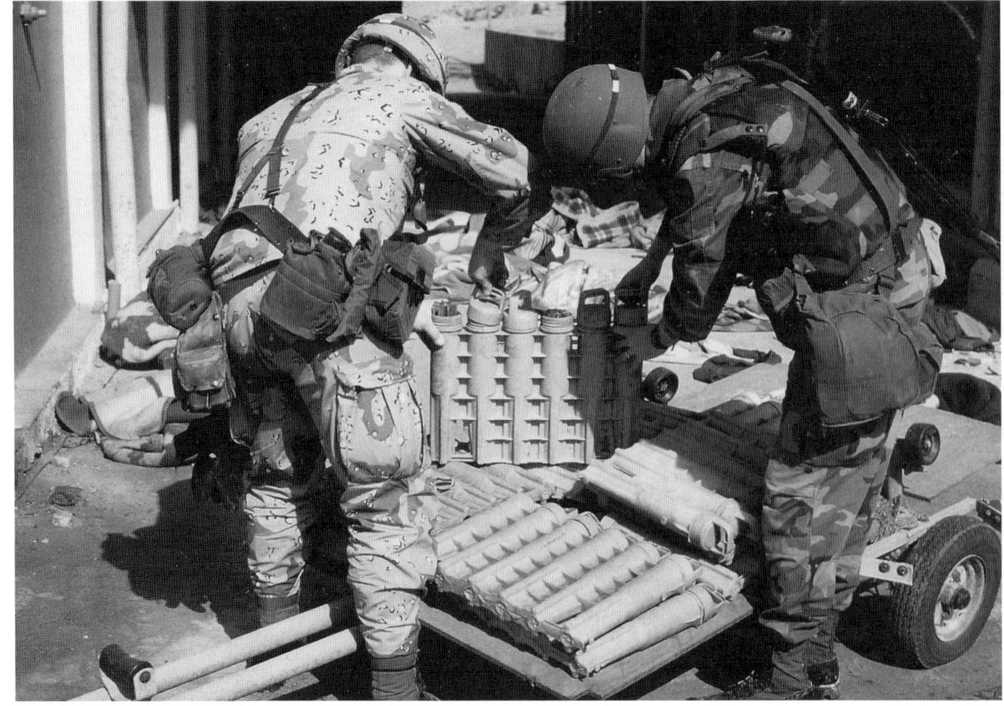

Technical intelligence personnel from the FMIB and the U.S. Army Foreign Science and Technology Center examine Iraqi mortar shells.

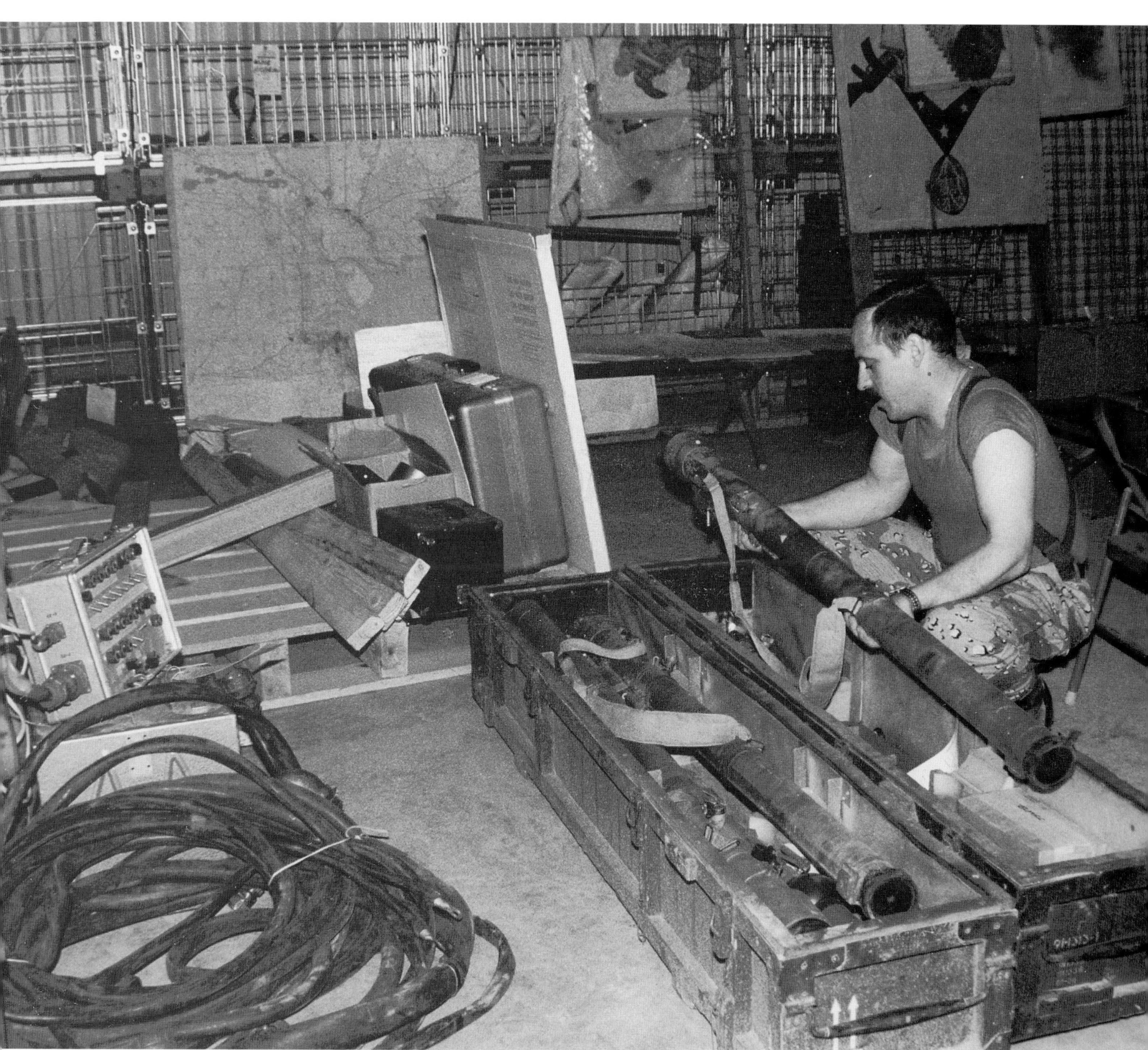

A technical intelligence specialist from the 513th MI Brigade's Foreign Materiel Intelligence Battalion (FMIB) unpacks captured rocket launchers.

Standing Down

THE TRANSFORMATION OF THE WORLD order that followed the fall of the Iron Curtain led to massive structural readjustments within Army intelligence. The rapid downsizing of the U.S. Army as a whole was paralleled by a steady attrition of Army intelligence and security assets. This was particularly noticeable in Europe, where the bulk of the Army's overseas forces had traditionally been deployed. Once the Soviet Union had imploded and the forces designed to stop the Warsaw Pact turned on Saddam Hussein instead, troop units began to stand down. The inactivation of VII Corps in Europe and a number of divisions both in Germany and in the United States led to the corresponding inactivation of their assigned intelligence units. INSCOM closed down three major fixed sites in the European Command's area of responsibility. INSCOM's 66th MI Brigade relocated from its traditional home in Munich to Augsburg and then downsized to provisional group status. The U.S. Army Russian Institute was resubordinated to European Command, redesignated, and given a new mission of fostering East-West relations.

The drawdown of intelligence assets was not restricted to Europe. As the Army grew leaner, a major effort was made to reduce headquarters spaces. The Army Intelligence Agency was discontinued in 1992 and its component elements reassigned to DIA and INSCOM. INSCOM itself reduced the number of its Major Subordinate Command's (MSC's). The Special Security Group was discontinued, and its remaining functions absorbed by the 902d MI Group. In 1995, Army intelligence ceded much of its HUMINT mission and assets to a new Defense HUMINT Service controlled by DIA. As a result of the pending turnover of the Panama Canal to the host government at the end of 1999, INSCOM's 470th MI Brigade was inactivated in 1997. Finally, INSCOM's 500th MI Brigade in Japan was reduced to group status later that same year.

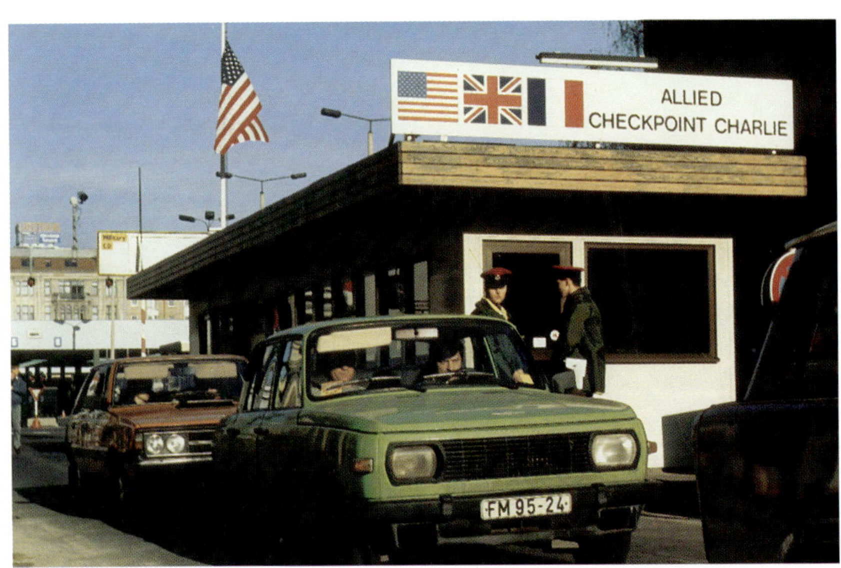

Checkpoint Charlie on the historic dividing line between East and West Berlin. Termination of the Cold War both eliminated the checkpoint and led to a drawdown of the U.S. Army's force structure in Europe that directly affected Army intelligence.

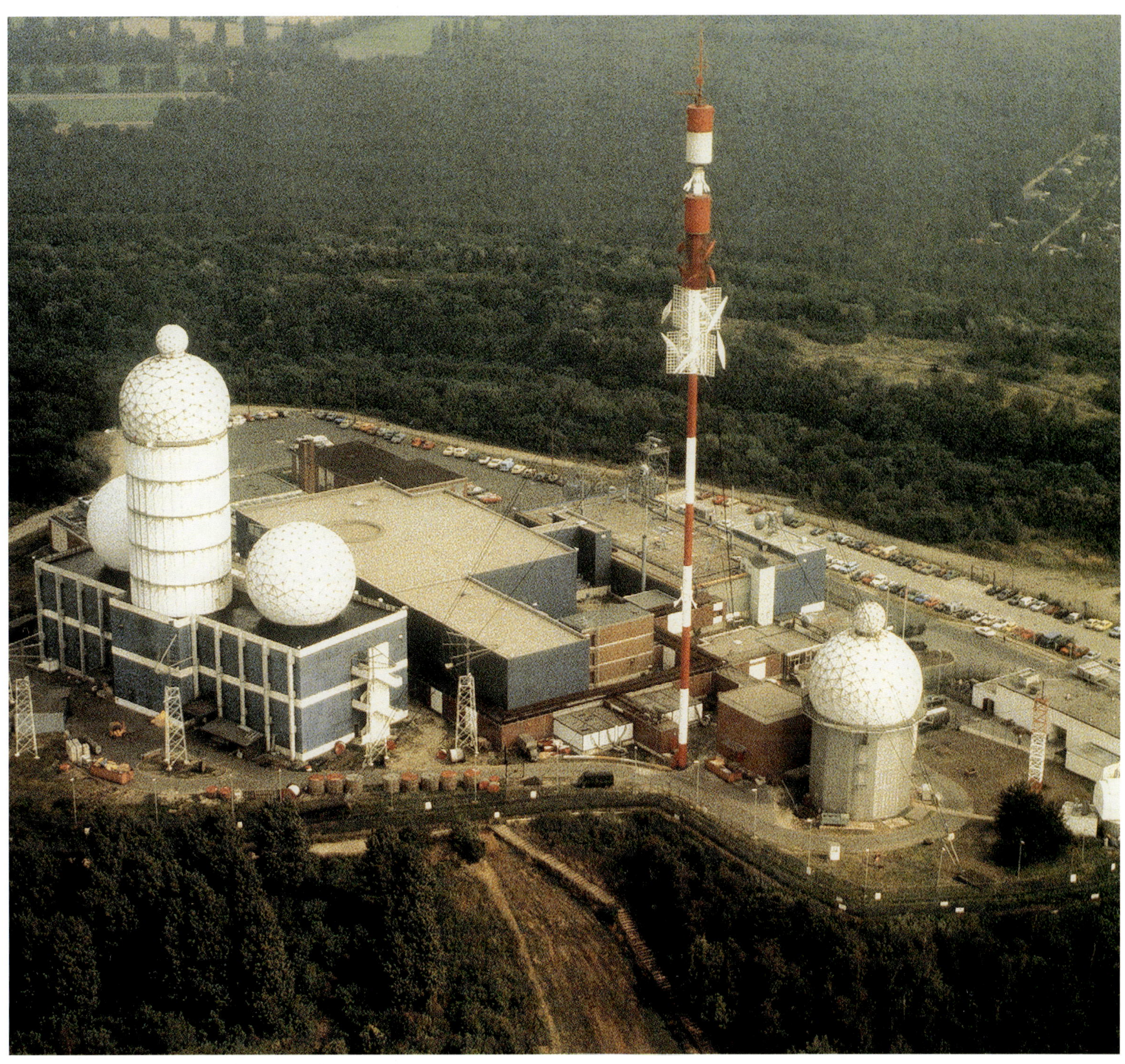

Located 105 miles behind the Iron Curtain, U.S. Army Field Station Berlin stood atop the Teufelsberg—"Devil's Hill"—an artificial mound built out of rubble dragged from the ruins of Berlin after World War II. A major Army outpost during the Cold War, the station was discontinued in 1992.

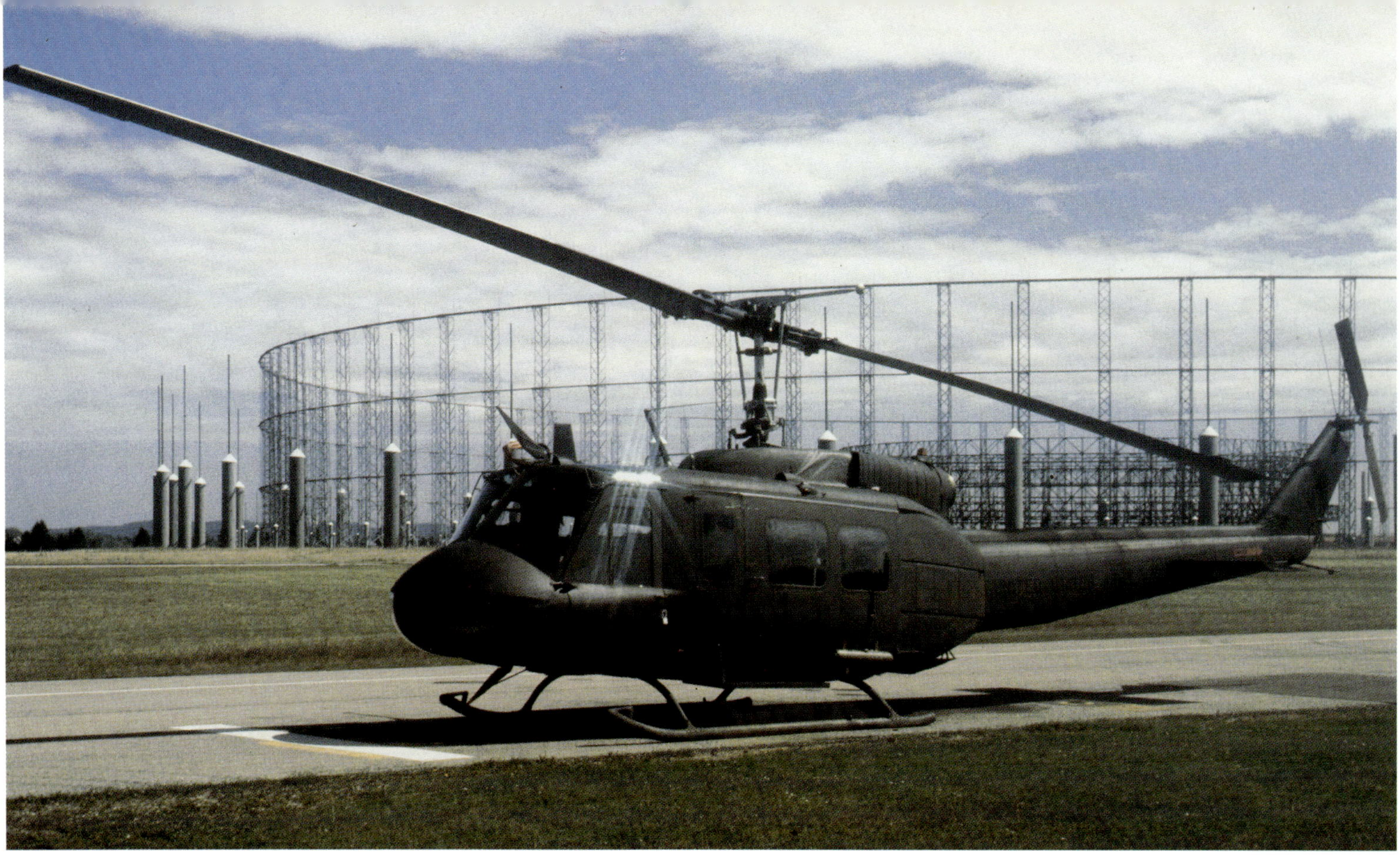

A UH-1 helicopter positioned beside the enormous antenna array of Field Station Augsburg at Gablingen, Germany. At one point, four battalions of soldiers had manned the site. The field station was discontinued in 1993.

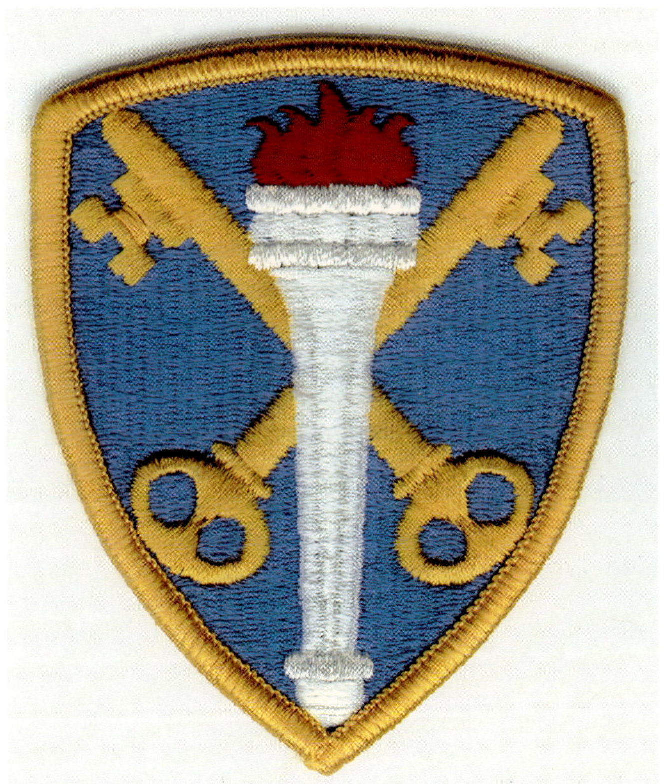

Shoulder Sleeve Insignia of the Army Intelligence Command. The command was set up at Fort George G. Meade, Maryland in the aftermath of the Cold War to better coordinate Army HUMINT and counterintelligence operations. The decision to transfer all Army HUMINT assets funded by the General Defense Intelligence Program to the control of the Defense Intelligence Agency's Defense HUMINT Service (DHS) quickly brought about the unit's discontinuance.

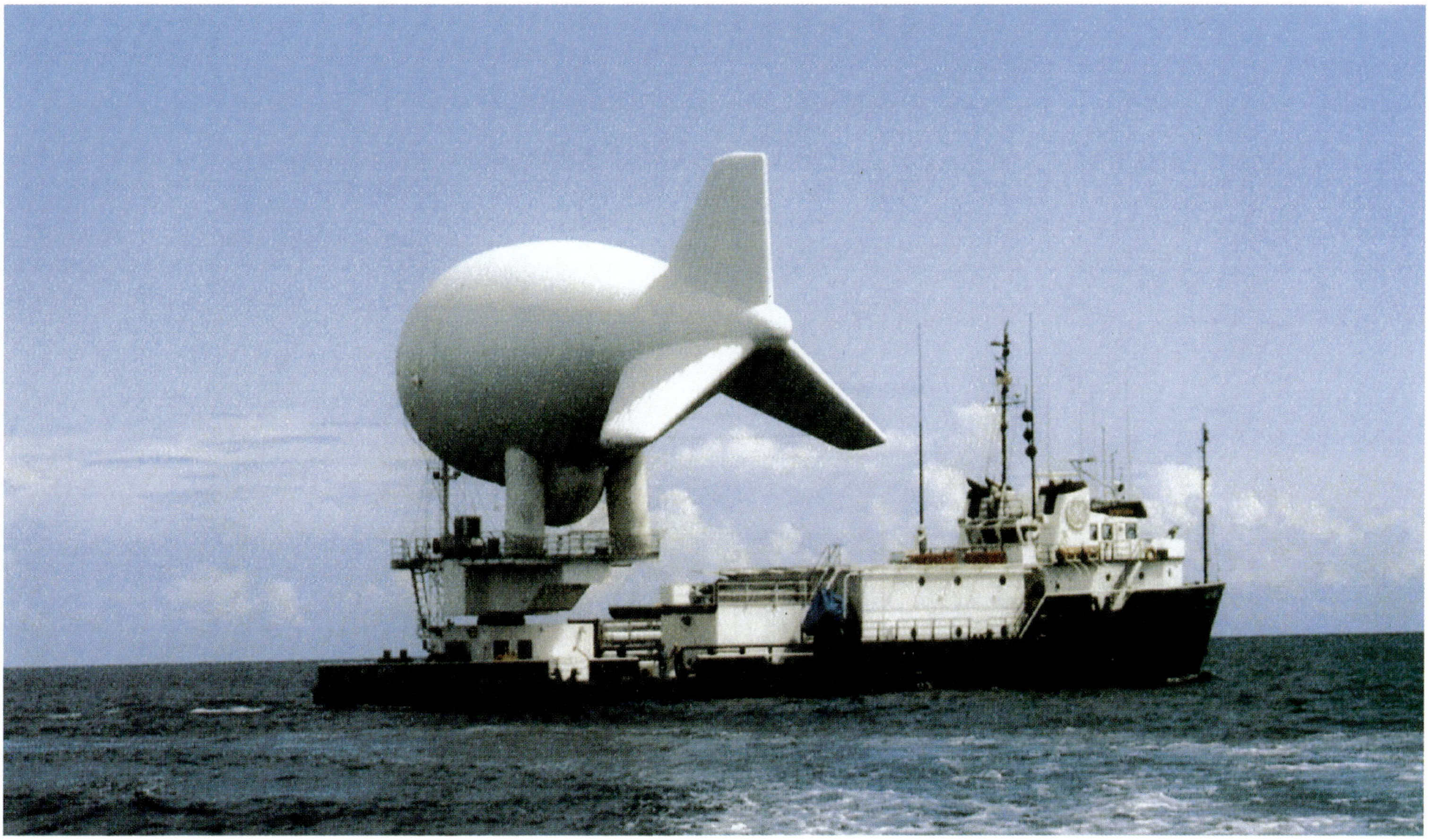

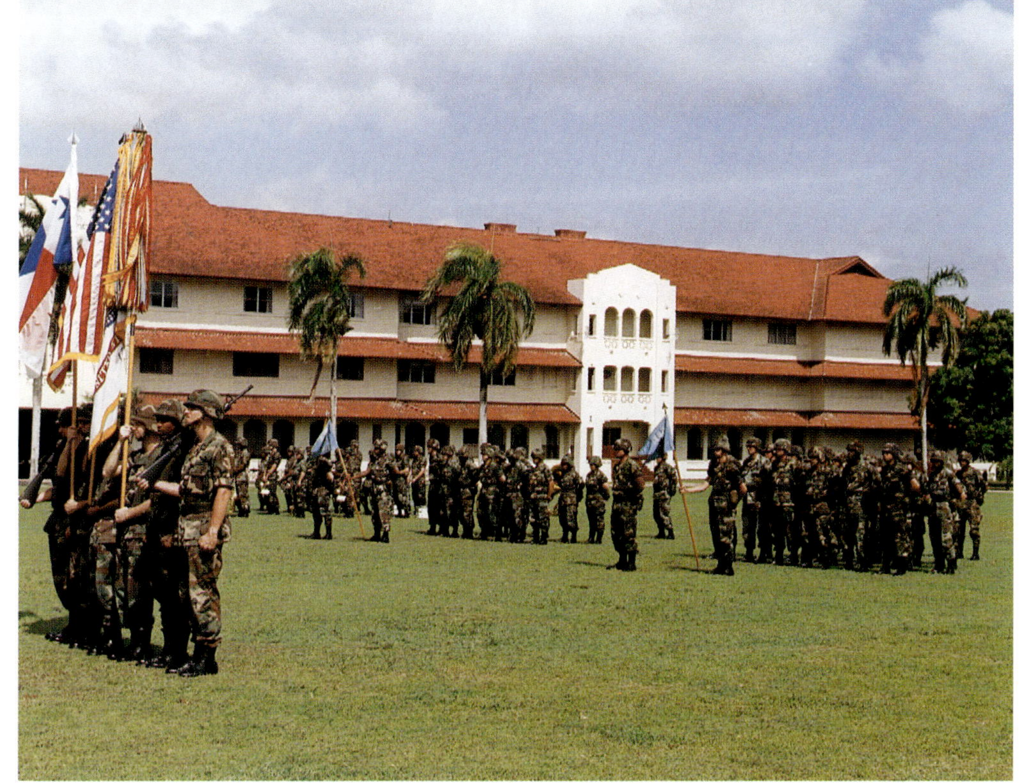

The Army's navy. A shipborne Small Aerostat Surveillance System deployed by the 470th MI Brigade's attached Military Intelligence Battalion (Low Intensity) in the Caribbean during the early 1990's. The program was eventually terminated.

The Last Parade. Inactivation ceremony of the 470th MI Brigade at Fort Clayton, Panama.

Beginning Afresh

THE AFTERMATH OF THE COLD WAR SAW Army intelligence building up as well as drawing down. In 1989, INSCOM moved its headquarters to a brand-new building at Fort Belvoir, Virginia. Subsequently, the command occupied new mission facilities both at home and abroad, including a Regional SIGINT Operations Center at Fort Gordon, Georgia, and sites at Bad Aibling, Germany, and Menwith Hill, United Kingdom. Army intelligence production was centralized under the National Ground Intelligence Center organized at Charlottesville, Virginia. As the need for the Army to fight in a post-industrial environment became apparent, INSCOM set up a Land Information Warfare Activity to achieve information dominance.

To meet the needs of a force-projection Army, INSCOM planned to merge its five theater intelligence brigades into two force-projection intelligence brigades, one oriented towards European, Middle-Eastern, and Southwest Asian contingency operations; the second focused on the Pacific rim. The new units would be built upon the existing 513th and 501st MI Brigade structures and would be able to deploy scalable "packages" of troops and equipment specifically tailored to a given level of threat.

The currents of change within MI extended well beyond INSCOM. In October 1990, the Commander, U.S. Army Intelligence Center became Commander of Fort Huachuca, providing Army intelligence with a home of its own. Additionally, the Army implemented plans to consolidate most intelligence training at a single location at Fort Huachuca. Better links were forged with the Military Intelligence reserve components. Organizational integration was paralleled by technological innovation, as Army intelligence fielded a "system of systems." New collection and communications systems came on line, including the GUARDRAIL Common Sensor and Airborne Reconnaissance Low platforms, the TRACKWOLF mobile intercept and radio direction finding system, and the Mini Deployable Intelligence Support Element (mini-DISE).

As the Twentieth Century drew to a close, the challenge for Army intelligence was to execute a bewildering profusion of new missions in an environment of constrained resources. It was called upon to support peacekeeping, counter-drug, and humanitarian operations that spanned the globe, while at the same time standing ready to deal with the larger threats posed by the activities of rogue states and would-be regional hegemons. In the midst of turbulence and uncertainties, however, the men and women of Army intelligence stood tall, trusting that the traditions and heritage of Military Intelligence would help to guide the way into the future.

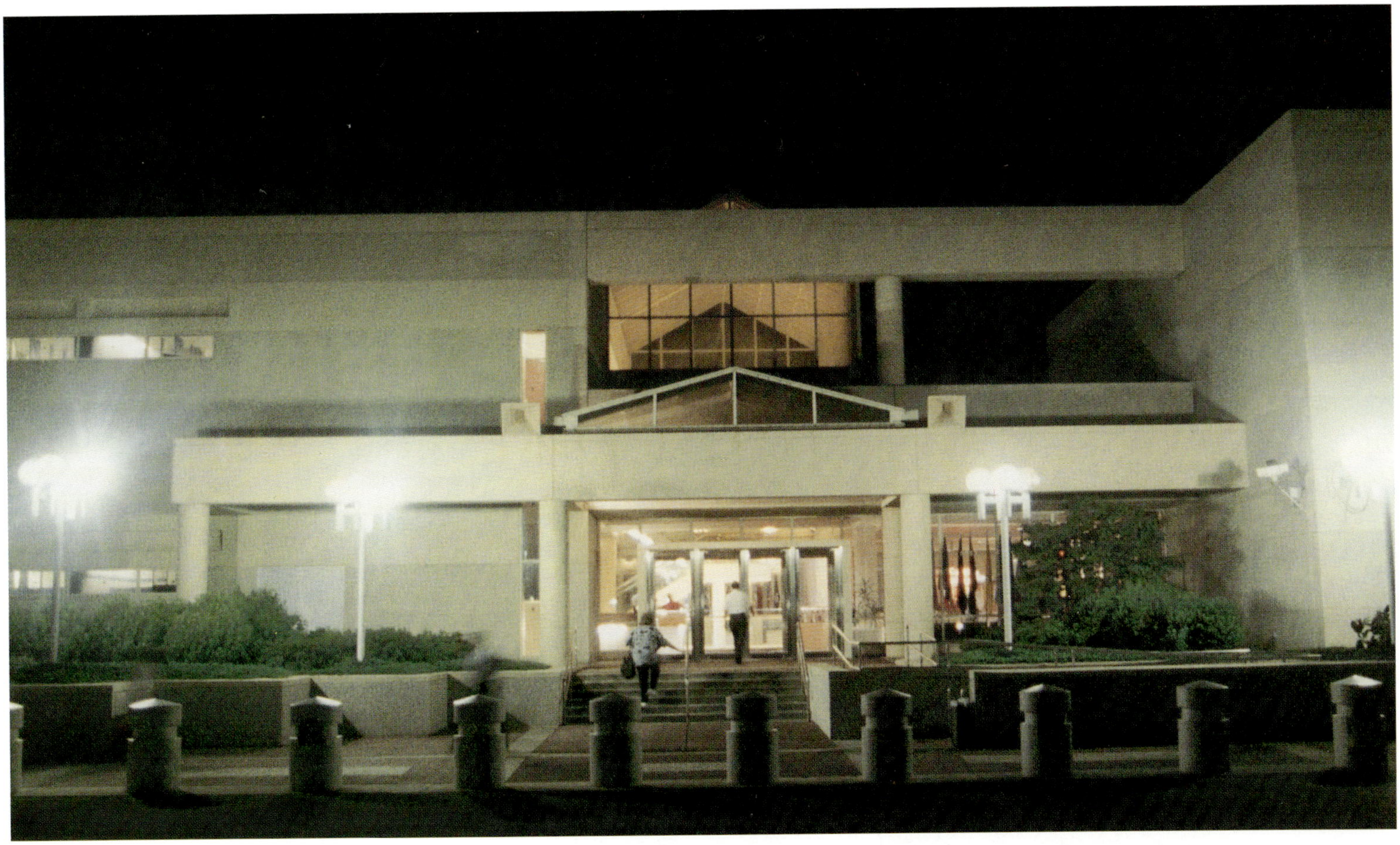

In 1989, INSCOM moved to this new headquarters at Fort Belvoir, Virginia. The Nolan Building was named in honor of MG Dennis E. Nolan, the G-2 for the American Expeditionary Forces in France during World War I. It was the first Army intelligence headquarters ever to be specifically designed for this purpose.

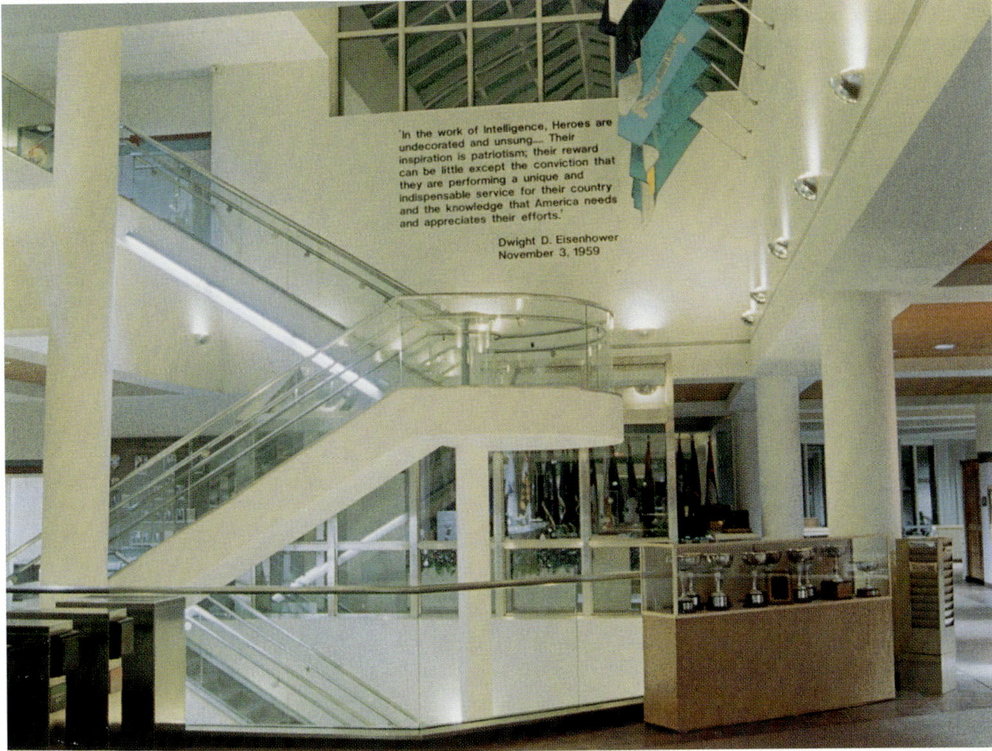

Interior of the Nolan Building.

New Sites

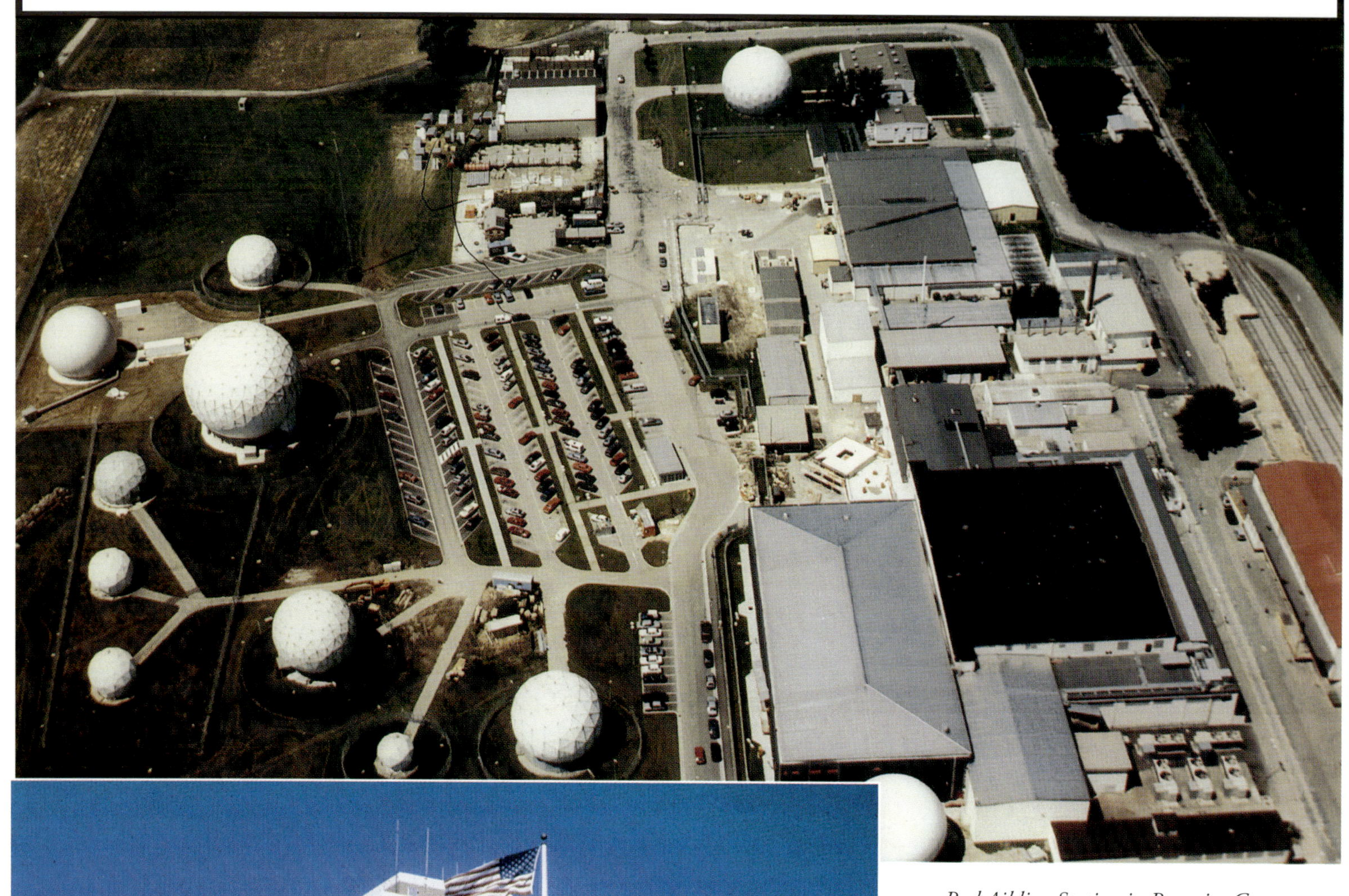

Bad Aibling Station in Bavaria, Germany, became the home of INSCOM's 718th MI Group.

Fort Gordon, Georgia, was selected as the headquarters site for two major INSCOM units, the 513th MI Brigade and the 702d MI Group.

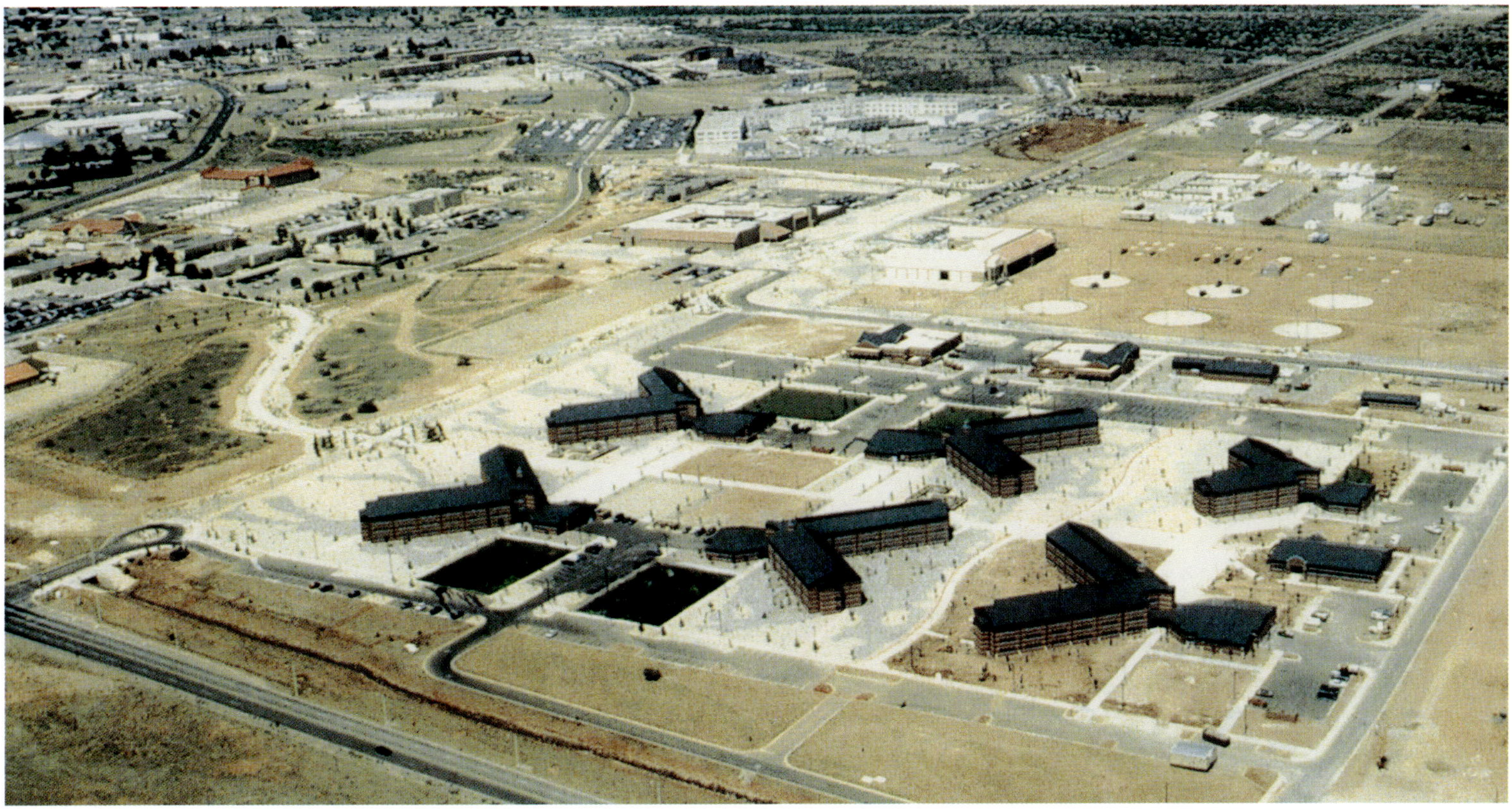

New school buildings at the U.S. Army Intelligence Center and Fort Huachuca. The Fort Huachuca installation was expanded to absorb students from the U.S. Army Intelligence School, Fort Devens, which was discontinued as a result of base closure and realignment actions.

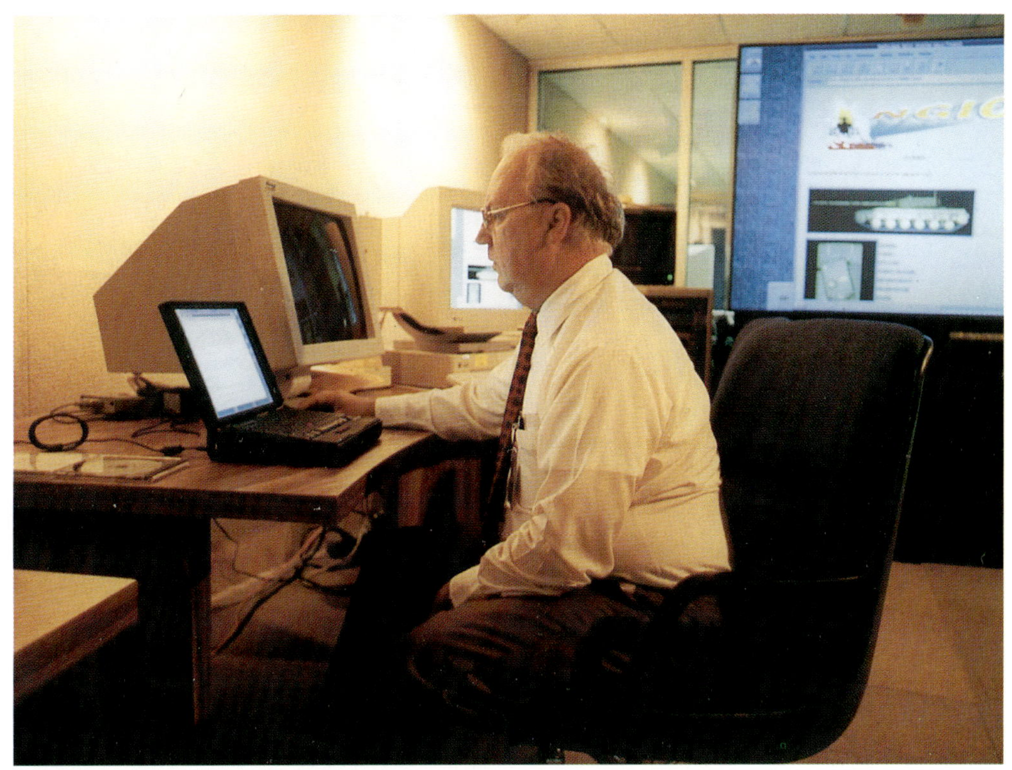

An intelligence analyst at the National Ground Intelligence Center (NGIC) in Charlottesville, Virginia. NGIC brought together Army intelligence production assets formerly controlled by the Intelligence and Threat Analysis Center and the Foreign Science and Technology Center.

New Systems

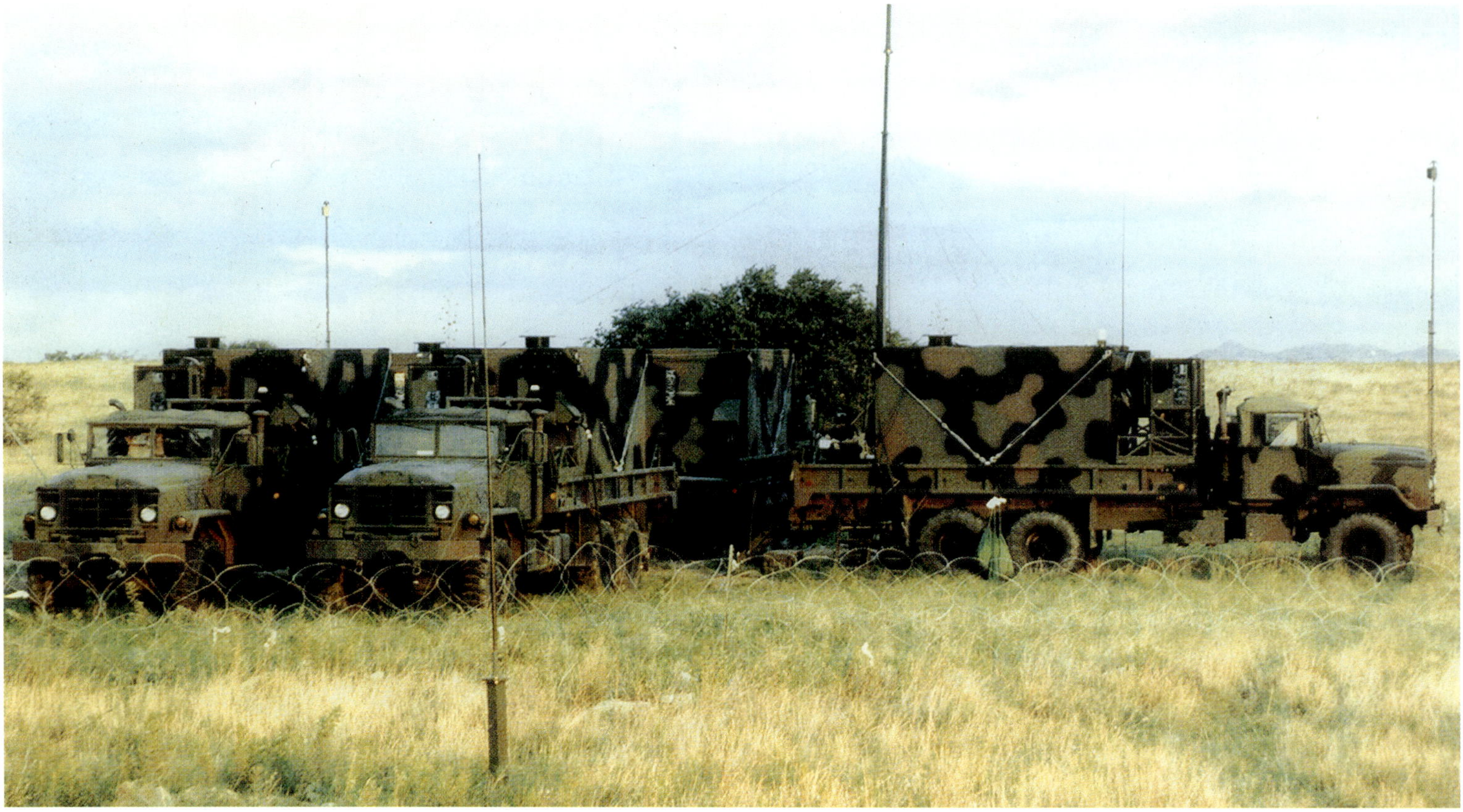

TRACKWOLF, the Army's latest deployable intercept and radio direction-finding system.

An Army RC–12 aircraft equipped with the GUARDRAIL Common Sensor. This represented a significant addition to the Army's aerial intelligence and electronic warfare capabilities.

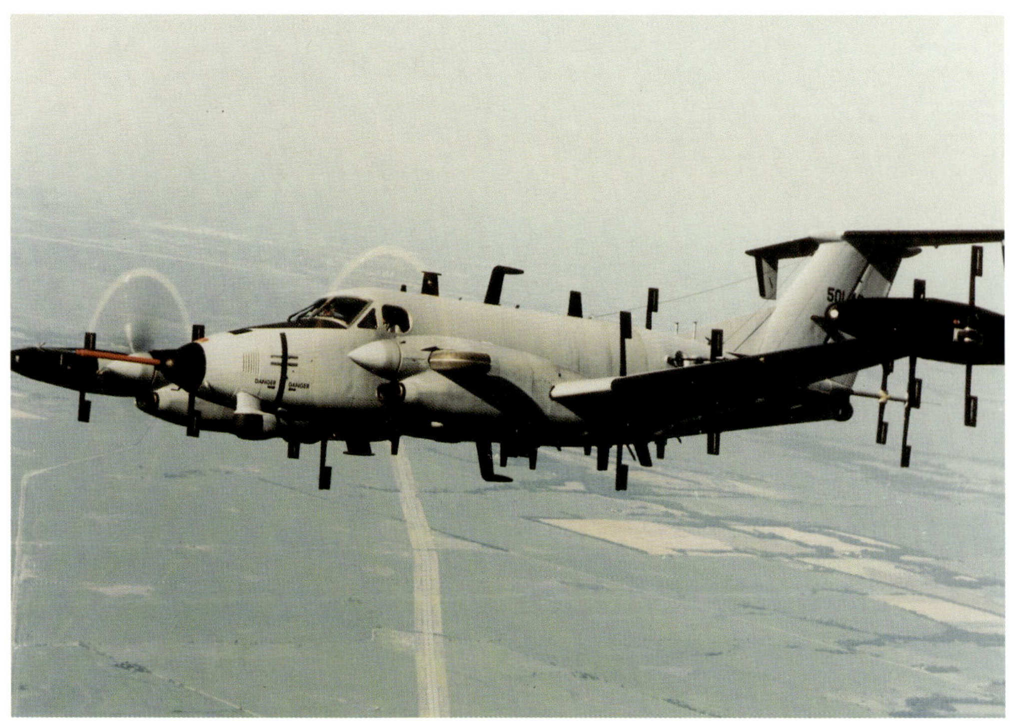

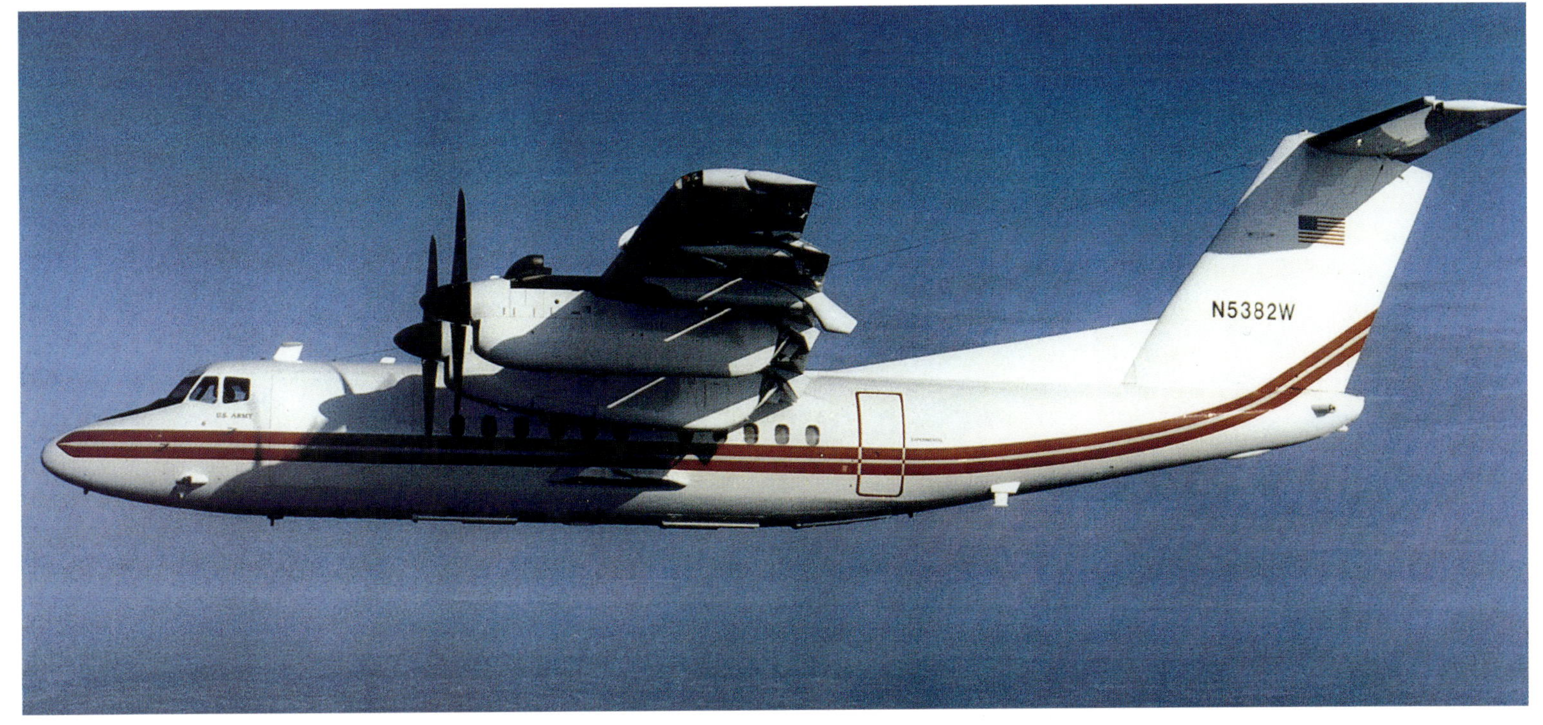

During the course of the 1990's, INSCOM's Airborne Reconnaissance Low (ARL) platform saw service on four continents.

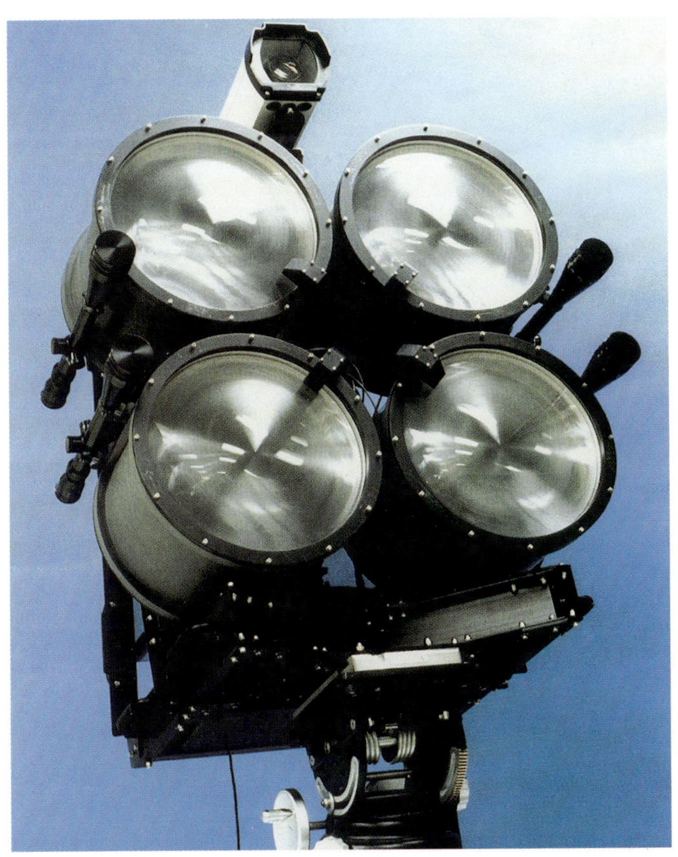

A sophisticated MASINT collection system.

A soldier of a Field Support Team mans an INMARSAT (International Maritime Satellite) communications terminal that links his suitcase-mounted mini-office in the field to INSCOM headquarters.

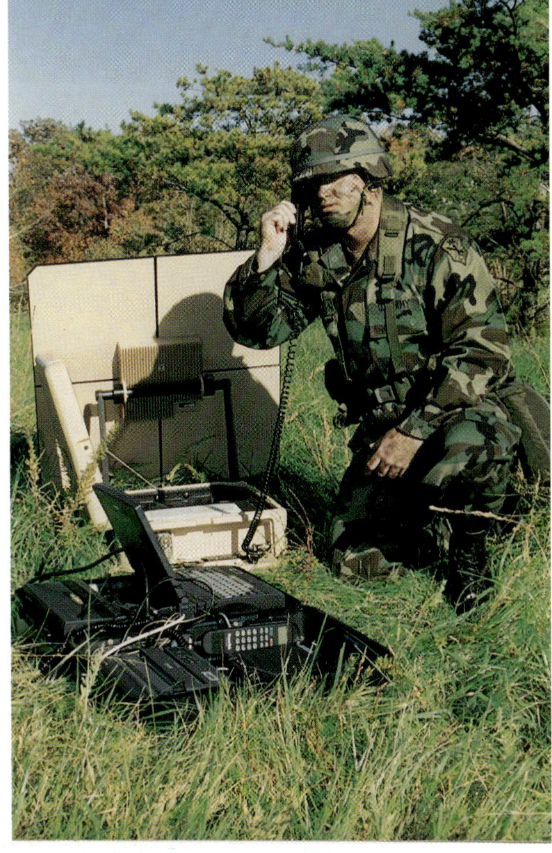

New Missions

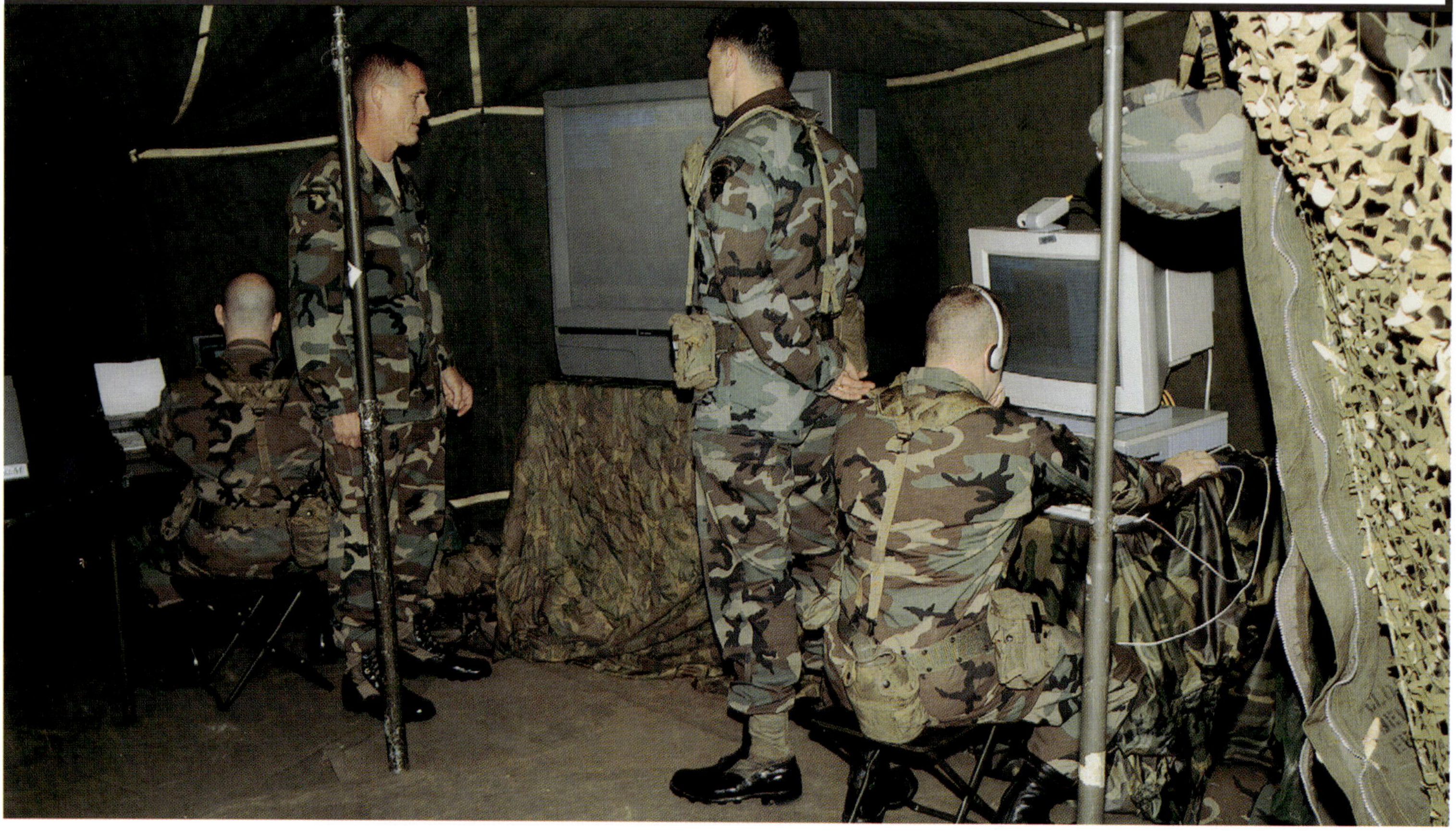

Personnel of INSCOM's Land Information Warfare Activity (LIWA) in the field. To function effectively on the battlefield of the Twenty-first Century, the Army would have to establish information dominance.

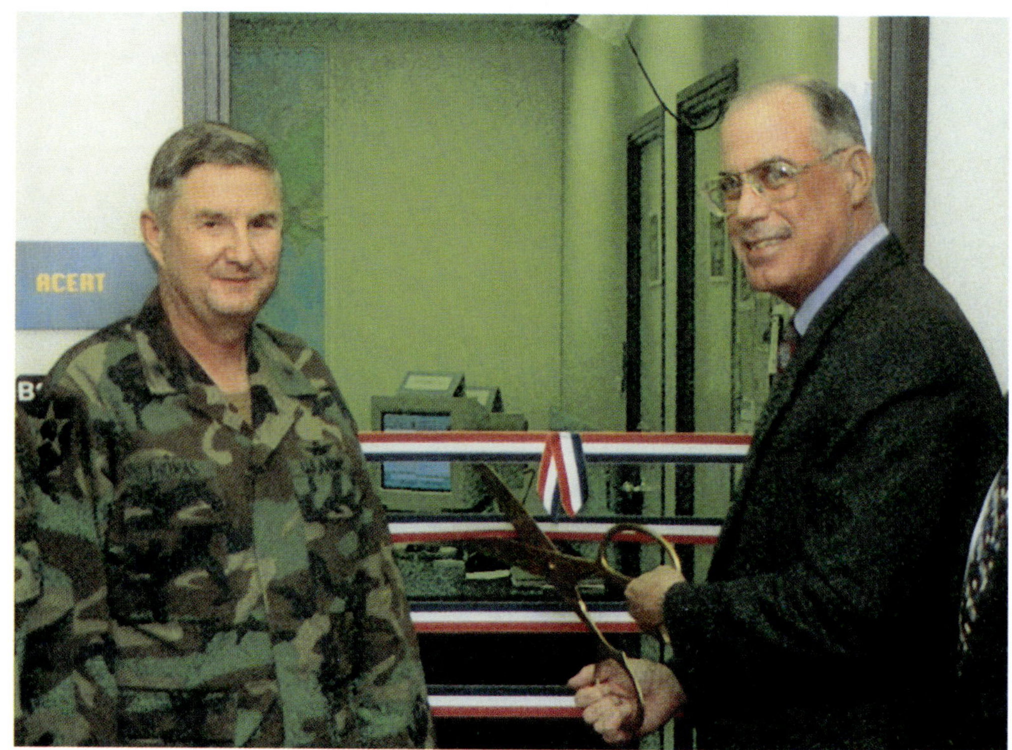

INSCOM Commanding General BG (later MG) John D. Thomas Jr. (left) and former DCSINT LTG Paul E. Menoher, USA (Ret.) (right) take part in a ribbon-cutting ceremony at the Army Computer Emergency Response Team (ACERT) center at Fort Belvoir. The ACERT was designed to provide a rapid reaction capability to deal with intrusions into Army computer networks. An essential part of information operations is protecting increasingly automated military command and control systems.

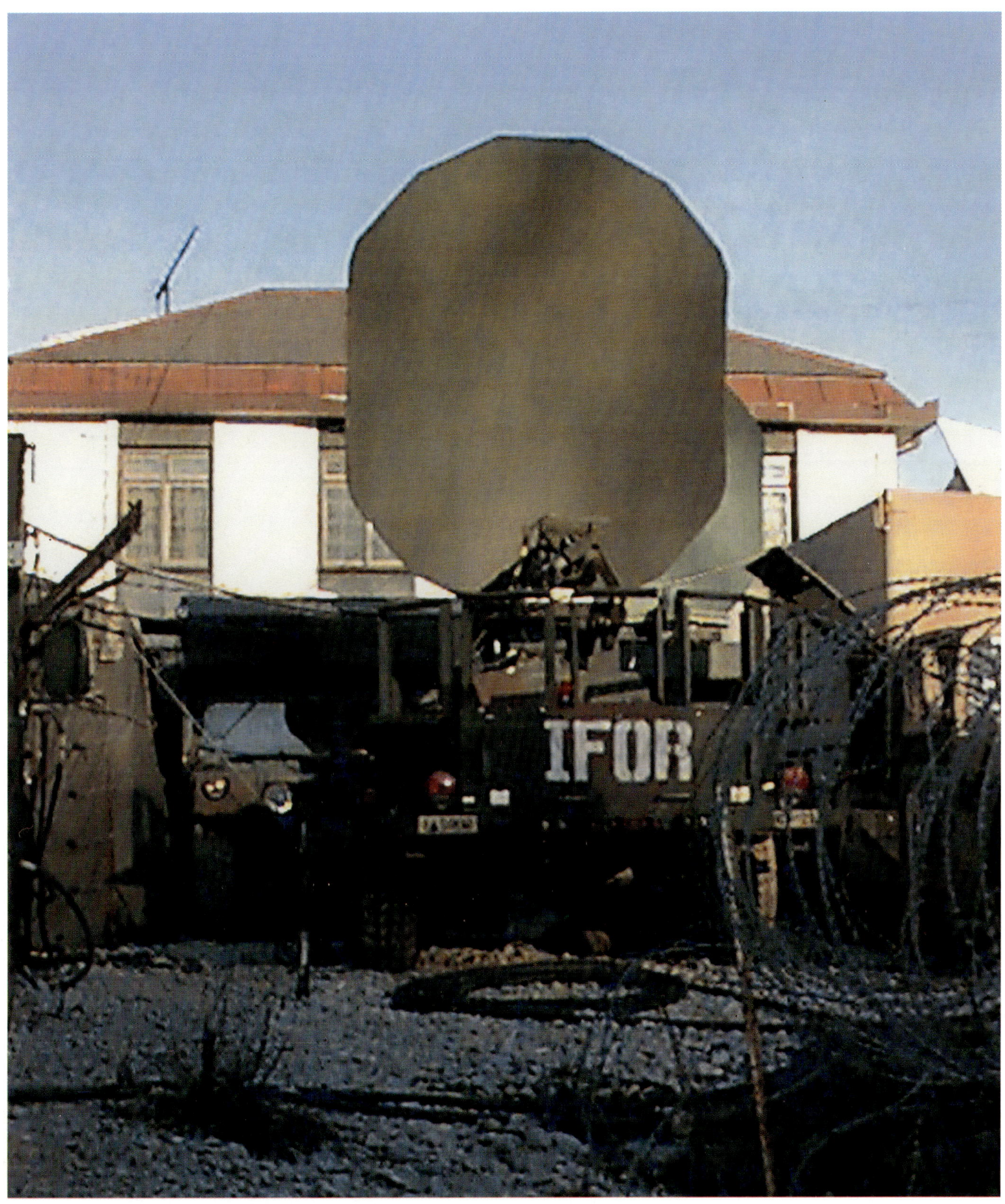

In the aftermath of the Cold War, the Army found itself involved in a variety of humanitarian, counter-drug, and peacekeeping operations, known collectively as Operations Other Than War (OOTW). In Operation JOINT ENDEAVOR, MI units and personnel from around the world were called upon to support NATO's Implementation Force (IFOR) in Bosnia.

MI: Always Out Front

The motto of the MI Corps is "Always Out Front." As the first Chief of MI put it, the formation of the Corps was "a recognition and celebration of our evolution from a plethora of diverse and separate intelligence agencies into the cohesive MI community we enjoy today."

HUMINT/CI: A technician utilizes state-of-the art computerized equipment to conduct a polygraph examination.

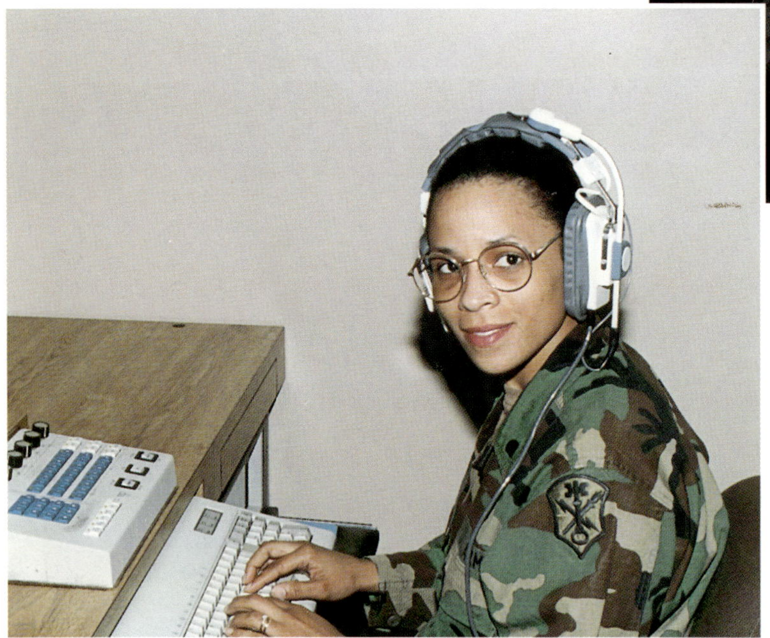

EW: A soldier of the 704th MI Brigade at her automated workstation at Fort George G. Meade, Maryland.

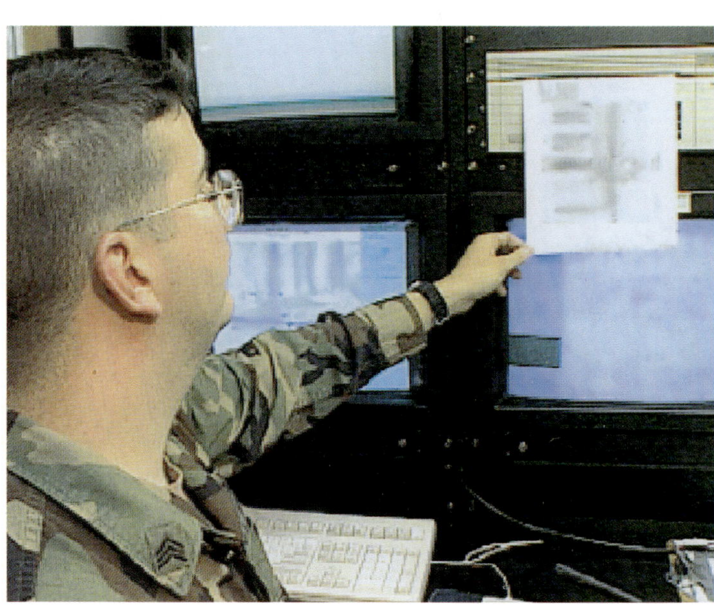

IMINT: An imagery interpreter prepares to scan a display screen at the 513th MI Brigade's Modernized Imagery Exploitation System (MIES).

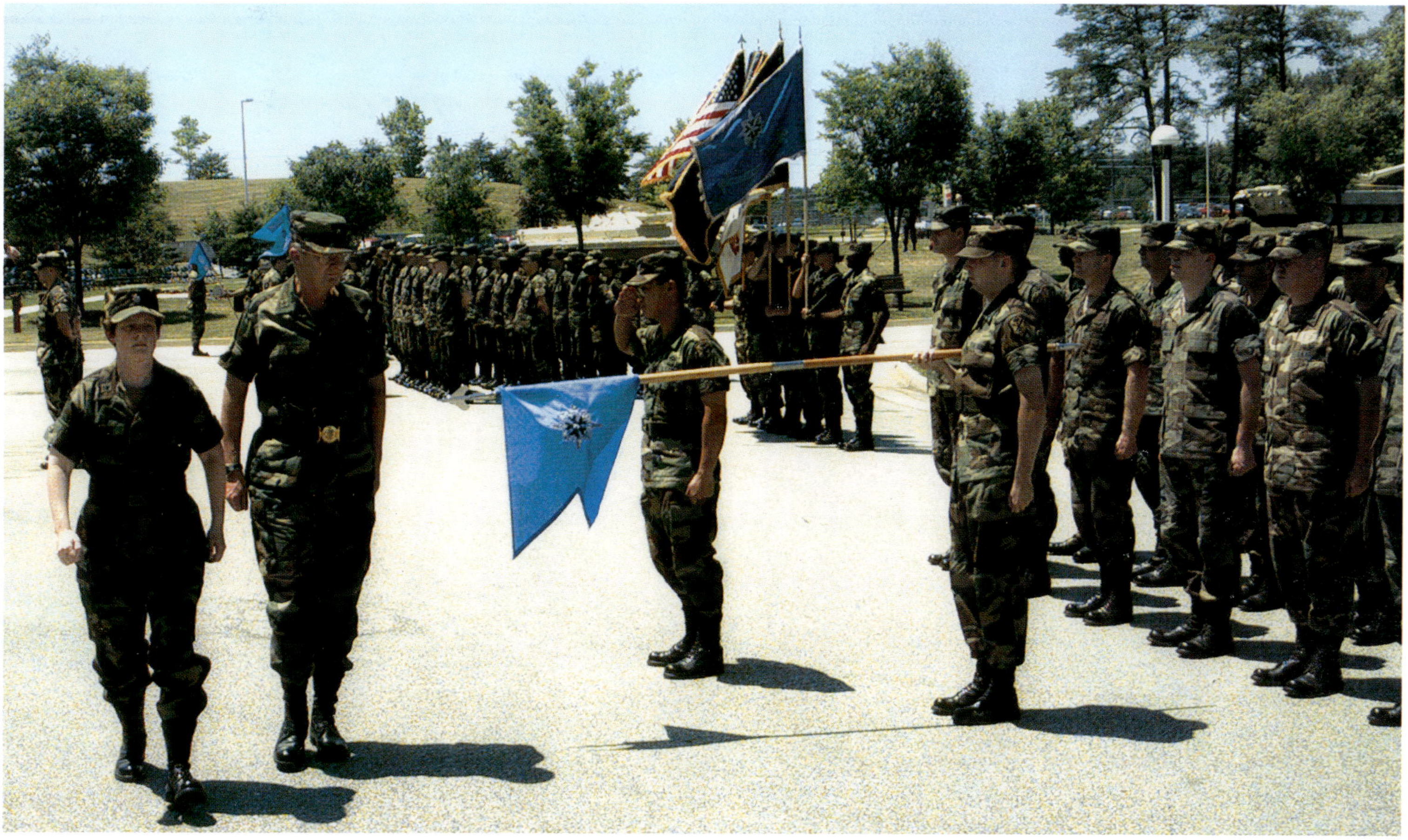

". . . the cohesive MI community we enjoy today." The Commanding General of INSCOM reviews his troops.

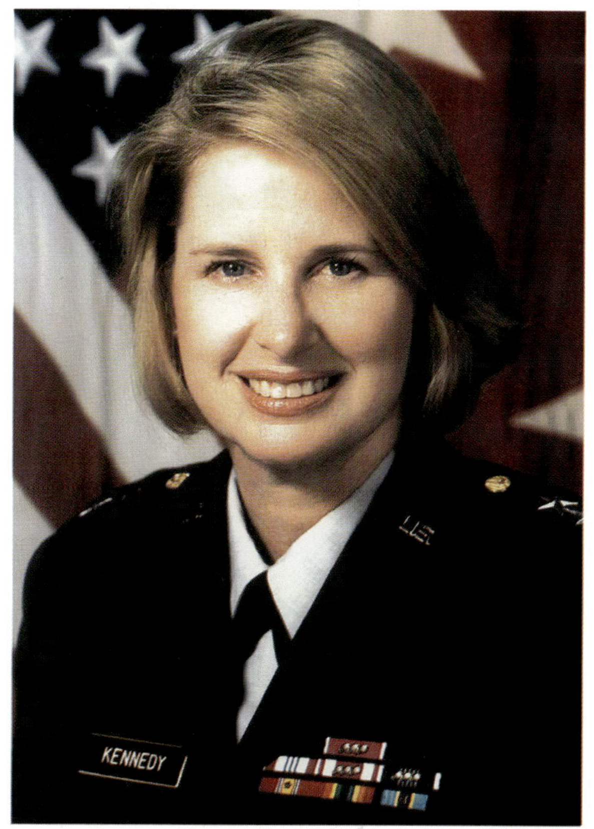

"Always Out Front." MI officer MG Claudia Kennedy was appointed as Department of the Army DCSINT in 1997, becoming the Army's first female lieutenant general.

MI: The Heritage

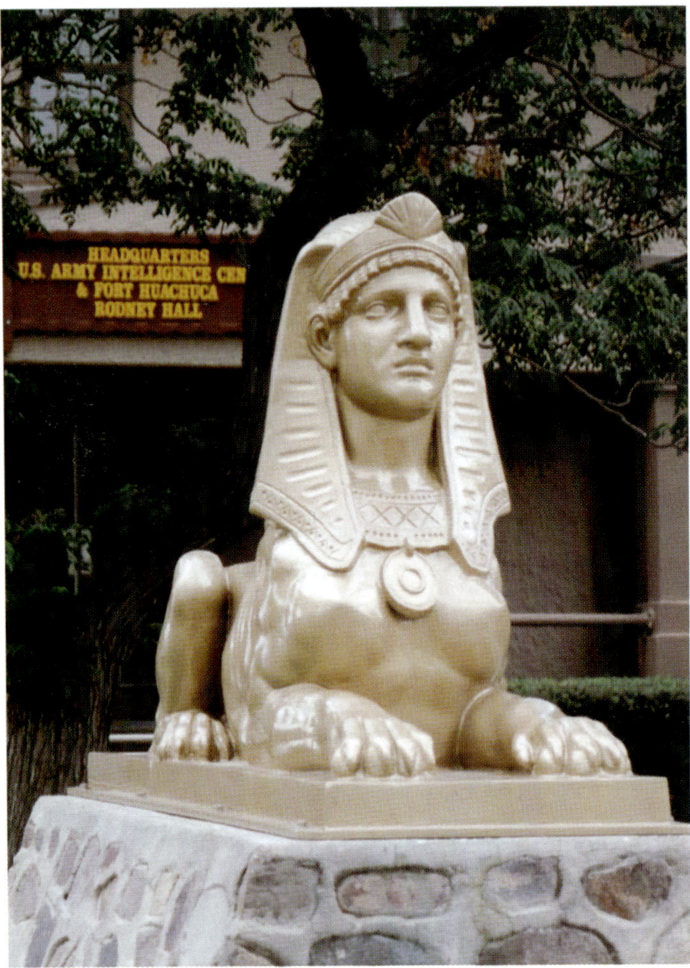

This statue of a sphinx, the traditional heraldic symbol of MI, stands in the courtyard of the headquarters building at the United States Army Intelligence Center and Fort Huachuca.

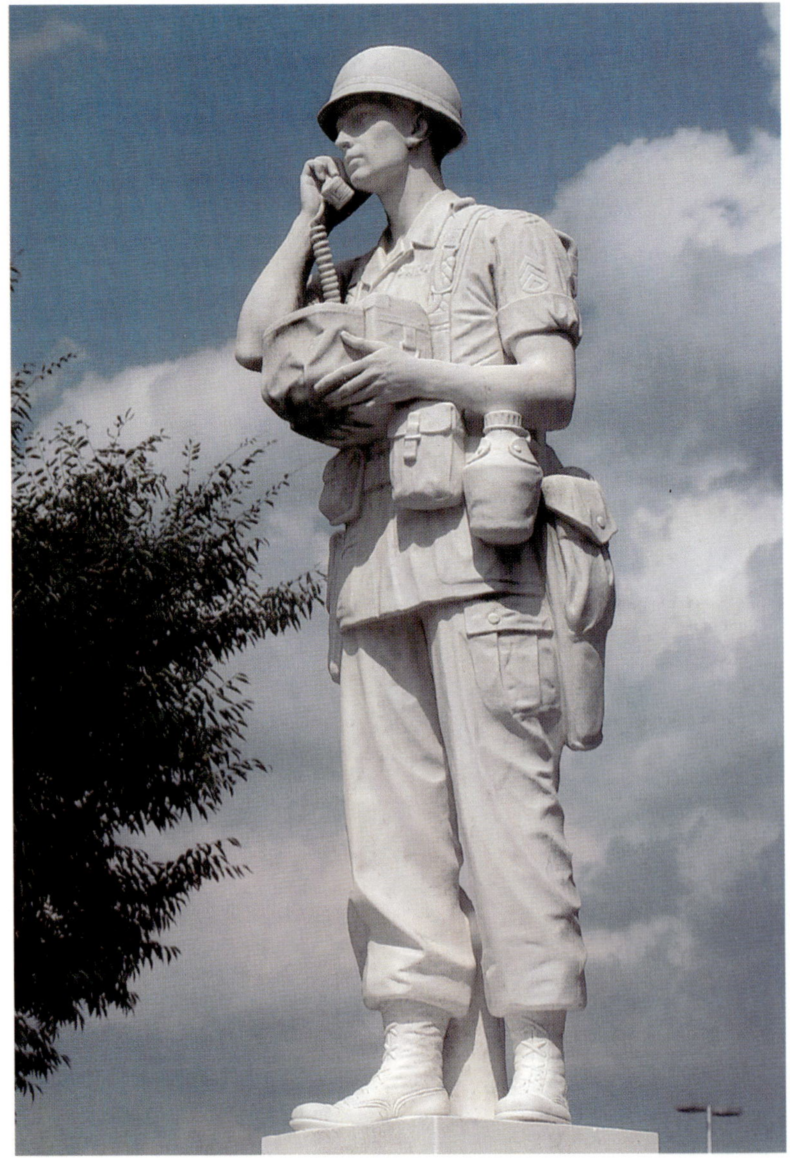

This memorial to the INSCOM soldiers who have fallen in battle from the Korean War to the present is located on the grounds of the Nolan Building.

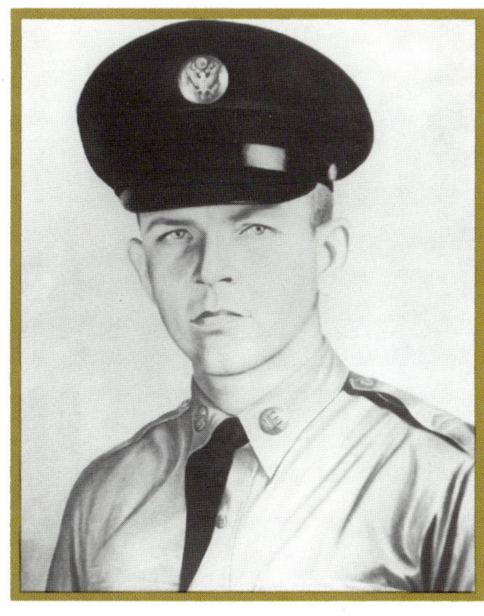

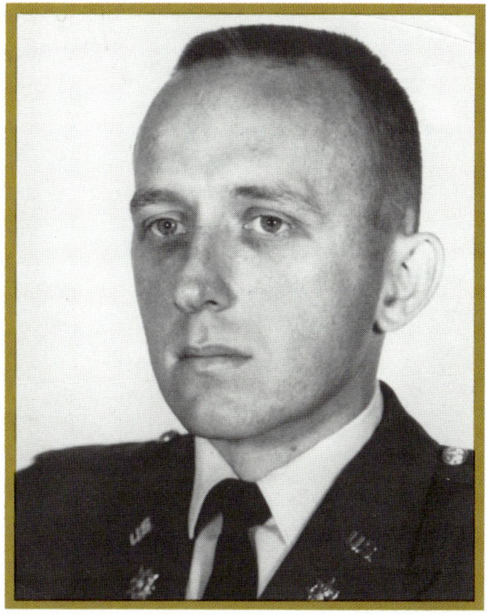

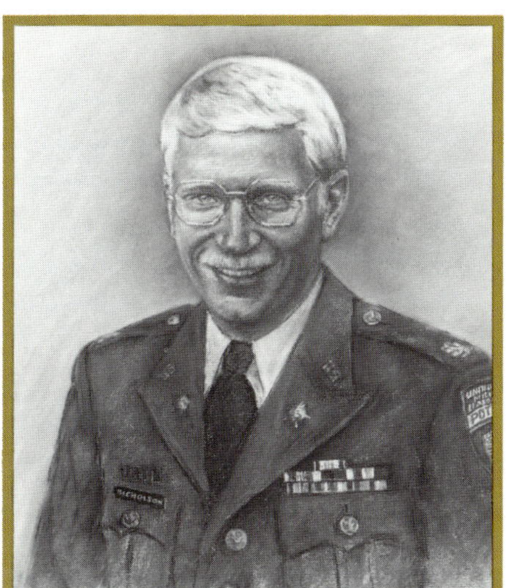

Heroes: MI soldiers who made the supreme sacrifice. Clockwise, SP4 James T. Davis, 3d Radio Research Group; 1LT George K. Sisler, 5th Special Forces Group; LTC Arthur D. Nicholson, U.S. Military Liaison Mission, Potsdam.

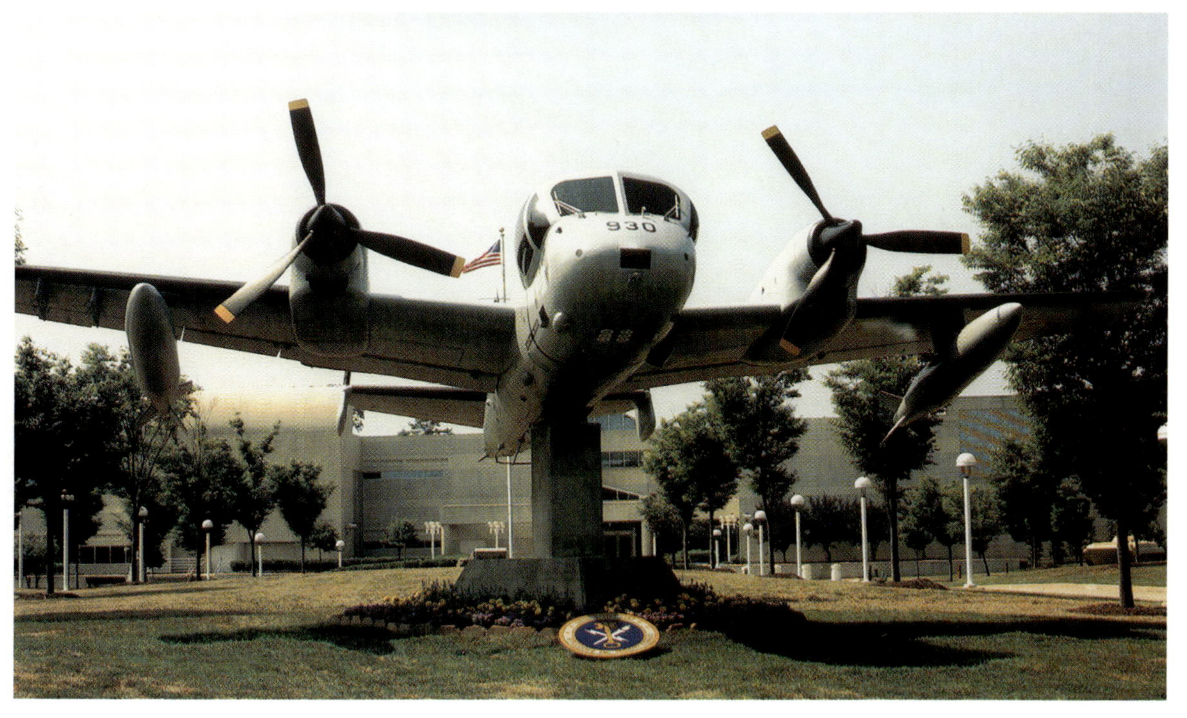

In 1997, to mark INSCOM's 20th anniversary and honor all MI aviators, this OV-1D Mohawk intelligence collection platform was placed on permanent display on the ample grounds of the Nolan Building.

Appendix I

Military Intelligence Milestones

1776—Execution of Nathan Hale

1777—Washington appoints Major Benjamin Tallmadge, 2d Continental Dragoons, as his chief of intelligence.

1802—Foundation of United States Military Academy at West Point, New York.

1804—Captain Merriwether Lewis and Lieutenant William Clark lead expedition to explore the American West.

1833—Congress authorizes Regiment of United States Dragoons, the first Regular Army cavalry unit.

1838—Creation of Corps of Topographic Engineers

1846—Engineer officers perform successful reconnaissance operations in Mexican War.

1861—First use of observation balloons in Civil War.

—Alan Pinkerton conducts intelligence and counterintelligence operations for Union Army.

1862—Control of Government "Secret Service" operation transferred from State to War Department.

1863—Army of the Potomac forms Bureau of Information headed by Colonel George V. Sharpe.

1866—Congress forms Corps of Indian Scouts.

1877—First "military attaché" sent by War Department to Russia to observe Russo-Turkish War.

1885—Division of Military Information created within the Adjutant General's Office.

1889—Congress authorized permanent system of military attachés.

1898—Army sends undercover officers to collect intelligence in Cuba and Puerto Rico at outset of Spanish American War.

—Signal Corps deploys observation balloon with expeditionary force sent to Cuba.

1899—Bureau of Insurgent Records set up in the Philippines to perform counterintelligence operations in support of American expeditionary forces there.

1903—Military Information Division becomes Second Division of War Department General Staff.

1909—Army acquires its first airplane.

1916—Mexican Punitive Expedition makes use of multidiscipline intelligence — aerial observation, communications intercept (COMINT), human informants, and ground reconnaissance— for first time.

1917—Military Intelligence Section of War Department General Staff created after United States enters World War I.

—MI–8 set up as Army's first cryptologic element

—Corps of Intelligence Police organized.

1917—American Expeditionary Forces in France creates G–2 section.

1918—Military Intelligence Division of General Staff organized.

—AEF collects combat intelligence, utilizing multi-source collection, including photographic intelligence (PHOTINT) obtained by the Army Air Service.

1919—Clandestine cryptanalytic bureau under Herbert O. Yardley opens in New York City, jointly funded by War and State Departments.

1929—Yardley's "Black Chamber" discontinued; Army's cryptanalytic functions transferred to Signal Corps' Signal Intelligence Service (SIS), headed by William F. Friedman.

1938—1st Radio Intelligence Company activated—Army's first tactical intelligence unit.

1939—2d Signal Service Company set up as intercept arm of SIS.

1940—SIS breaks Japanese diplomatic machine cipher, known by U.S. as PURPLE. Resulting decrypts are called MAGIC.

1941—First liaison between Army intelligence and British.

—The Army's success against Japanese diplomatic communication fails to provide America with warning of the Pearl Harbor attack. America enters World War II.

1942—Counter Intelligence Corps (CIC) formed.

—Separate Military Intelligence Service (MIS) set up.

—Special Branch, MIS formed to handle COMINT.

—SIS moves to Arlington Hall and is redesignated Signal Security Agency (SSA).

—first large fixed field station set up at Vint Hill Farms Station near Warrenton, Virginia.

1943—Signal Security Agency makes first entry into Japanese military codes.

—Full wartime cryptologic collaboration with the British established; Special Security System implemented to handle dissemination of COMINT.

—Signal Corps forms unit to collect electronic intelligence (ELINT) against enemy radars and "jam" their transmissions through electronic warfare (EW).

1944—Signal Security Agency placed under operational control of Military Intelligence Division.

1945—Army Security Agency is organized.

1946—Separate Military Intelligence Service is abolished.

—"Cold War" against Communist expansionism begins.

1947—Independent Air Force established.

—Central Intelligence Agency created.

1949—Armed Forces Security Agency established.

1950—Outbreak of Korean War leads to organization of large military intelligence units.

1952—National Security Agency replaces Armed Forces Security Agency.

1955—Army Intelligence Center and School established at Fort Holabird, Maryland.

1955—ASA acquires responsibility for conducting ELINT and EW from Signal Corps, becomes Field Operating Agency (FOA) under Army Chief of Staff.

1956—Assistant Chief of Staff, G–2 redesignated as Assistant Chief of Staff for Intelligence (ACSI); intelligence loses position of equality on Army staff as other Assistant Chiefs are upgraded to Deputy Chiefs.

1961—CIC merged into a consolidated Intelligence Corps.

—Defense Intelligence Agency (DIA) organized.

—ASA's 3d Radio Research Unit deploys to Republic of Vietnam.

1964—Photographic intelligence redesignated as Imagery Intelligence (IMINT).

1965—U.S. Army Intelligence Command (USAINTC) organized to conduct all counterintelligence operations in Continental United States (CONUS).

—Ground troops committed to Vietnam.

1966—Intelligence Corps discontinued.

1967-68—Massive civil disturbances lead to demands that Army produce domestic intelligence.

1971—Defense Investigative Service created to conduct personnel security investigations in CONUS.

—Army Intelligence School relocates from Fort Holabird to Fort Huachuca, Arizona.

1973—Last U. S. forces withdraw from Vietnam. Draft terminates, necessitating creation of an All Volunteer Army.

—USAINTC relocates from Fort Holabird to Fort George G. Meade, Maryland.

1974—USAINTC discontinued and replaced by U.S. Army Intelligence Agency (USAINTA), which conducts counterintelligence and human intelligence mission.

1975—Army conducts Intelligence Organization and Stationing Study (IOSS).

1976—First Combat Electronic Warfare and Intelligence (CEWI) units formed.

1977—Organization of INSCOM.

1985—Army Intelligence Agency (AIA) created to consolidate management of Army intelligence production.

1986—INSCOM headquarters consolidated at Arlington Hall Station.

1987—Position of Army's Assistant Chief of Staff for Intelligence (ACSI) upgraded to that of Deputy Chief of Staff for Intelligence (DCSINT).

—Formation of Military Intelligence Corps.

1989—Fall of Berlin Wall marks eclipse of Communism in Eastern Europe and effective end of Cold War.

—Operation JUST CAUSE

1991—Operation DESERT STORM

1992—Intelligence assets draw down in Europe; Army Intelligence Agency discontinued.

1995—Land Information Warfare Activity receives charter.

—Defense HUMINT Service absorbs many Army human intelligence assets.

—Operation JOINT ENDEAVOR.

Appendix II

Chronological List of Senior Army Intelligence Officers

Deputy Chiefs/Assistant Chiefs of Staff for Intelligence

Deputy Chiefs of Staff for Intelligence

LTG Claudia Kennedy—01 Mar 97 to Present
LTG Paul E. Menoher, Jr.—10 Feb 95 to 01 Mar 97
LTG Ira C. Owens—01 Oct 91 to 10 Feb 95
LTG Charles B. Eichelberger—22 Nov 89 to 30 Sep 91
LTG Sidney T. Weinstein—16 Aug 85 to 30 Sep 89

Assistant Chiefs of Staff for Intelligence

LTG William E. Odom—02 Nov 81 to 12 May 85
MG Edmund R. Thompson—29 Aug 77 to 1 Nov 81
MG Harold R. Aaron—05 Nov 73 to 28 Aug 77
MG William E. Potts—08 Sep 72 to 30 Jul 73
MG Phillip B. Davidson, Jr.—03 May 71 to 30 Sep 72
MG Joseph A. McChristian—05 Aug 68 to 30 Apr 71
MG William P. Yarborough—01 Dec 66 to 15 Jul 68
MG John J. Davis—01 Sep 65 to 19 Oct 66
MG Edgar C. Doleman—08 Jan 64 to 8 Feb 65
MG Alva R. Fitch—16 Oct 61 to 5 Jan 64
MG John M. Willems—01 Nov 58 to 15 Oct 61
MG Robert A. Schow—03 Aug 56 to 31 Oct 58
MG Ridgely Gaither—09 Aug 55 to 30 Jul 56

Assistant Chiefs of Staff, G-2

MG Arthur C. Trudeau—16 Nov 53 to 8 Aug 55
MG Richard C. Partridge—11 Aug 52 to 15 Nov 53
MG Alexander R. Bolling—23 Aug 50 to 10 Aug 52
MG Stafford LeRoy Irwin—20 Oct 48 to 22 Aug 50 *
LTG Stephen J. Chamberlin—11 Jun 46 to 19 Oct 48 *
LTG Hoyt S. Vandenberg—26 Jan 46 to 9 Jun 46
MG Clayton Bissell—07 Feb 44 to 25 Jan 46
MG George V. Strong—05 May 42 to 6 Feb 44
BG Raymond E. Lee—01 Feb 42 to 4 May 42
BG Sherman Miles—30 Apr 40 to 31 Jan 42
COL E.R. Warner McCabe—01 Jul 37 to 29 Feb 40
COL Francis H. Lincoln—27 Nov 35 to 29 Jun 37
BG Harry E. Knight—01 Feb 35 to 26 Nov 35
BG Alfred T. Smith—03 Jan 31 to 2 Jan 35
COL Stanley H. Ford—01 May 27 to 1 Sep 30
COL James H. Reeves—01 Jul 24 to 30 Apr 27
COL William K. Naylor—27 Nov 22 to 30 Jun 24
BG Stuart Heintzelman—01 Sep 21 to 10 Nov 22

* Official title of the position was Director of Intelligence.

Chiefs, Military Intelligence Division/Military Intelligence Section

BG Dennis E. Nolan—20 Aug 20 to 31 Aug 21
BG Marlborough Churchill—05 Jun 18 to 19 Aug 20
COL Ralph Van Deman—03 May 17 to 4 Jun 18

Chiefs, Military Intelligence Corps

MG Charles W. Thomas—10 Nov 94 to Present
MG John F. Stewart, Jr.—28 Jul 93 to 10 Nov 94
MG Paul E. Menoher, Jr.—15 Sep 89 to 27 Jul 93
MG Julius Parker, Jr.—01 Jul 87 to 14 Sep 89

Commanding Generals, U.S. Army Intelligence and Security Command

MG John D. Thomas, Jr.—23 Aug 96 to Present
BG Trent Thomas—20 Sep 94 to 23 Aug 96
MG Paul E. Menoher, Jr.—12 Aug 93 to 20 Sep 94
MG Charles F. Scanlon—11 Oct 90 to 11 Aug 93
MG Stanley H. Hyman—21 Nov 88 to 10 Oct 90
MG Harry E. Soyster—27 Jun 84 to 20 Nov 88
MG Albert N. Stubblebine III—07 May 81 to 26 Jun 84
BG John A. Smith (Acting)—17 Mar 81 to 06 May 81
MG William I. Rolya—01 Jan 77 to 16 Mar 81

Commanders of Past Intelligence Organizations

Commanding Generals, U.S. Army Security Agency

MG William I. Rolya—01 Sep 75 to 31 Dec 76
MG George A. Godding—14 Mar 73 to 31 Aug 75
BG George L. McFadden, Jr. (Acting)—05 Feb 73 to 13 Mar 73
MG Charles Denholm—15 Sep 65 to 04 Feb 73
BG Dayton W. Eddy—08 Sep 65 to 14 Sep 65
MG William H. Craig—01 Jul 62 to 07 Sep 65

Chiefs, U.S. Army Security Agency (ASA)

BG Orman G. Charles—01 Jun 62 to 30 Jun 62
MG William M. Breckinridge—01 Apr 60 to 31 May 62
MG Thomas S. Timberman—16 Jul 58 to 31 Mar 60
MG James H. Phillips—16 Aug 56 to 15 Jul 58
BG John C. Monahan—01 Aug 56 to 15 Aug 56
BG Samuel P. Collins—28 Jun 56 to 31 Jul 56
MG Harry Reichelderfer—15 Jan 53 to 27 Jun 56
COL John C. Arrowsmith—19 Dec 52 to 14 Jan 53
MG Robinson E. Duff—01 Aug 51 to 18 Dec 52

COL John C. Arrowsmith—20 Feb 51 to 31 Jul 51
BG William N. Gillmore—10 Aug 50 to 19 Feb 51
COL John C. Arrowsmith—01 Jun 50 to 09 Aug 50
BG Carter W. Clarke—10 Jan 49 to 31 May 50
COL Harold G. Hayes—01 Apr 46 to 09 Jan 49
BG Preston W. Corderman—15 Sep 45 to 31 Mar 46

Commander, Signal Security Agency

BG Preston W. Corderman—01 Jul 43 to 14 Sep 45

Chiefs, Signal Security Service

COL Preston W. Corderman—01 Feb 43 to 30 Jun 43
COL Frank W. Bullock—25 Jul 42 to 31 Jan 43

Chiefs, Signal Intelligence Service/Division

COL Frank W. Bullock—02 May 42 to 24 Jul 42
LTC Rex W. Minckler—07 Jun 41 to 18 Apr 42
COL S.B. Atkin—25 Jul 39 to 02 May 41
MAJ W.O. Reeder—23 Apr 38 to 24 Jul 39
MAJ Haskell Allison—01 Aug 35 to 22 Apr 38
Mr. William F. Friedman—26 Dec 29 to 31 Jul 35

Chief, Code and Cipher Section, OCSigO

Mr. William F. Friedman—01 Jan 21 to 25 Dec 29

Chief, MI–8/"Black Chamber"

MAJ Herbert O. Yardley—10 Jun 17 to 10 May 29

Commanding Generals, U.S. Army Intelligence Agency (USAINTA)

BG James E. Freeze—30 Aug 77 to 01 Oct 77
BG Edmund R. Thompson—01 Jul 75 to 29 Aug 77
COL William S. Wolf—01 Jul 74 to 30 Jun 75

Commanding Generals, U.S. Army Intelligence Command (USAINTC)

COL N. Dean Schanche—01 Oct 72 to 30 Jun 74
COL James R. Waldie—19 Jun 72 to 30 Sep 74
BG Orlando C. Epp—01 Feb 71 to 18 Jun 72
BG Jack C. Matthews—28 Feb 70 to 31 Jan 71
MG William H. Blakefield—05 Jun 67 to 22 Feb 70
MG Elias C. Townsend**—24 Nov 65 to 04 Jun 67
MG Charles F. Leonard, Jr.**—01 Jan 65 to 21 Nov 65

Commanding Generals, U.S. Army Intelligence Corps Agency

MG Charles F. Leonard, Jr.**—01 Dec 64 to 31 Dec 64
MG Richard Collins**—01 Aug 63 to 30 Nov 64
MG Garrison B. Coverdale**—01 Jul 62 to 31 Jul 63

Chiefs, Intelligence Corps

MG Garrison B. Coverdale—03 Aug 61 to 30 Jun 62
MG Richard G. Prather—01 Jan 61 to 02 Aug 61

** Served concurrently as Chief, Intelligence Corps until corps discontinued on 1 March 1966.

Chiefs, Counter Intelligence Corps (CIC)

MG Richard G. Prather—28 Nov 56 to 31 Dec 60
MG Boniface Campbell—22 Oct 53 to 27 Nov 56
MG George B. Barth—21 Aug 53 to 21 Oct 53
MG Philip E. Gallagher—23 Aug 51 to 20 Aug 53
MG John K. Rice—09 Jun 49 to 22 Aug 51
BG Edwin A. Zundel—11 Jan 48 to 08 Jun 49
BG George V. Keyser—26 Apr 47 to 10 Jan 48
COL Meredith C. Noble—15 Jan 46 to 17 Apr 47
COL Harold R. Kibler—13 Jul 45 to 14 Jan 46
—(Office of Chief Abolished)—
COL Harold R. Kibler—10 May 43 to 10 Feb 44
LTC Hugh D. Wise, Jr.—01 Jul 42 to 09 May 43
LTC H.G. Sheen—01 Jan 42 to 30 Jun 42

Chiefs, Corps of Intelligence Police

MAJ H.G. Sheen—07 Oct 41 to 31 Dec 41
CPT Donald B. MacDonald—06 Aug 41 to 06 Oct 41
MAJ Garland Williams—27 Jan 41 to 05 Aug 41

Appendix III

MEMBERS OF THE MILITARY INTELLIGENCE HALL OF FAME

The MI Hall of Fame was established by the Military Intelligence Corps to honor those soldiers and civilians who have made exceptional contributions to the discipline throughout the course of American military history. This list shows those enrolled in the Hall of Fame as of the end of 1997.

LTG Harold R. Aaron
COL John F. Aiso
LT Gardiner P. Allen
MSG Lorenzo Alvarado
COL Alfred W. Bagot
SP5 Gerald R. Beatson
BG Daniel Bissell, Jr.
COL Donald W. Blascak
MAJ John R. Boker, Jr.
MAJ Ann Bray
COL John A. Bross
MSG Travis C. Bunn
COL John M. Carr
LTG Marshall S. Carter
CSM Clifford L. Charron
BG Marlborough Churchill
Dr. Rankin A. Clinton
MG W. Preston Corderman
MG Garrison B. Coverdale
LTC Mercedes Cubria
COL Elvin J. Dalton
LTG Phillip B. Davidson, Jr.
Mr. James D. Davis
LTG John J. Davis
MG Charles J. Denholm
COL Douglas C. Dillard
MG William J. Donovan
MW4 Robert P. Donohue
COL George R. Eckman
Ms. Sarah Emma Edmunds
LTG Charles B. Eichelberger
COL Carl F. Eifler
BG Orlando C. Epp
COL Richard E. Evers
LTG Alva R. Fitch
MG Thomas J. Flynn
MG Benjamin D. Foulois
MG James E. Freeze
Mr. William Friedman
COL Harry K. Fukuhara
COL William H. Gardner
lLT Charles B. Gatewood
LTG Daniel 0. Graham
BG George W. Goddard
MG George A. Godding
Miss Virginia Hall
Senator Chick Hecht
LTC Ethan A. Hitchcock
COL Parker Hitt
SFC Benjamin T. Hodge
COL Leland J. Holland
Mr. Herbert S. Hovey, Jr.
CSM George W. Howell, Jr.
LTC Gordon R. Huff
Mr. John T. Hughes
CSM Clovis D. Ice
LTC Gero Iwai
MAJ William I. Jennings
Mr. Edmund C. Jilli
COL Frederick W. Johnston III
PFC Stanley W. Kapp
Mr. Merrill T. Kelly
COL Robert Kelly
COL James H. P. Kelsey
Mrs. Lillian Klecka
CSM David P. Klehn
BG Oscar W. Koch
Mr. Kenneth T. Koeber
CWO Arthur S. Komori
COL Solomon T. Kullback
Mr. Robert A. Leigh
Mr. Thaddeus S.C. Lowe
COL Duwayne C. Lundgren
Mr. Joseph P. Luongo
COL Paul R. Lutjens
CWO Theodore M. Mack
COL Sidney F. Mashbir
Mr. Hisashi J. Masuda
Mrs. Dorothe K. Matlack
MSG Roy H. Matsumoto
MG Joseph O. Mauborgne
MG Joseph A. McChristian
CWO Ann M. McDonough
COL John I. McFadden
CSM Raymond McKnight
LTG Paul E. Menoher, Jr.
SP5 Edward W. Minnock
lLT Edward R. Moore
LTC Arthur D. Nicholson, Jr.
MG Dennis E. Nolan
COL Seth F. Nottingham
LTG William E. Odom
MG Julius Parker, Jr.
COL Boris T. Pash
SGT Peter de Pasqua
COL John A. Pattison
COL Peter A. Petito
MG Cloyd H. Pfister
Mr. Allan Pinkerton
LTG William E. Potts
CW4 William T. Ragatz
COL Kai E. Rasmussen
LTC Billy C. Rea
CWO Joseph E. Richard
LTG William I. Rolya
Ms. Elaine Griffith Romanones
COL James N. Rowe
Mr. Kurt Rosenow
COL Franz Ross
COL Robert C. Roth
CSM Louis H. Rothenstein
COL Andrew S. Rowan
COL Frank B. Rowlett
Mr. Edward Rybak
LTC Richard M. Sakakida
MG Charles F. Scanlon
COL Harold R. Shaw
COL Joe R. Sherr
Mr. Paul R. Shoemaker
COL Charles S. Simerly
COL Abraham Sinkov
1LT George K. Sisler
LTG Harry E. Soyster
CPL Irving A. Stein
MG John F. Stewart, Jr.
MG Archibald W. Stuart
MG Albert N. Stubblebine III
MAJ Kan Tagami
COL Benjamin Tallmadge
CPT Daniel M. Taylor
Mr. Herbert W. Taylor
MG Edmund R. Thompson
LTG Arthur G. Trudeau
MG Ralph Van Deman
Ms. Elizabeth Van Lew
COL William F. Vernau
COL Eric Vieler
BG George J. Walker
LTG Vernon A. Walters
COL William P. Walters
Mr. Junius A. Watlington
LTG Sidney T. Weinstein
COL Norman S. Wells
COL Jerry G. Wetherill
LTG James A. Williams
MG Charles A. Willoughby
MSG John R. Wilson
LTG Samuel V. Wilson
LTG William P. Yarborough
MAJ Herbert O. Yardley

Picture Credits

The photographs used in this book came from the files of the National Archives and Records Administration (NARA); the Library of Congress (LC); the Central Intelligence Agency (CIA); the National Security Agency (NSA); the Defense Intelligence Agency (DIA); the U.S. Air Force (USAF); the U.S. Navy (USN); the U. S. Army; the National Guard Bureau (NGB); the U.S. Army Intelligence Center and Fort Huachuca (USAIC&FH); the U.S. Army Intelligence School, Fort Devens (USAINTS-Fort Devens); the Office of the Deputy Chief of Staff for Intelligence (DCSINT); and the U.S. Army Intelligence and Security Command, its subordinate units, and its predecessor organizations (INSCOM). Additional contributions were provided by the listed private individuals, corporations, and Military Intelligence units.

ii.–iii. NARA
iv. USAINTS-Fort Devens (left); U.S. Army (right)
viii. INSCOM
x.–xi. NARA
xii. CIA
4. NARA (top); LC (bottom)
5. NARA
6. NARA (top); NSA (bottom)
7. NARA
8. NARA
9. NARA
10. NARA
14. NARA
15. NARA (top), INSCOM (bottom)
16. NARA (top); INSCOM (bottom)
17. INSCOM (top); NARA (bottom)
18. NARA
22. INSCOM
23. NARA
24. INSCOM
25. INSCOM
26. NARA
27. MG Joseph A. McChristian, U.S.A. (Ret.)
28. NARA
29. MG McChristian (top); NARA (bottom)
30. MG McChristian (top); INSCOM (bottom)
31. INSCOM
32–33. U.S. Army
34. U.S. Army
36. NARA
37. INSCOM
38. NARA (top); U.S. Army (bottom)
39. INSCOM
40. U.S.Army
41. U.S. Military Liaison Mission (top), (bottom left); INSCOM (bottom right)
42. INSCOM
43. INSCOM
44. NARA
45. NARA
46. INSCOM (top); USAIC&FH (bottom)
47. INSCOM
48. NARA
49. INSCOM
50–51. INSCOM
52. U.S. Army
54. INSCOM
55. U.S. Army (top); USAF (bottom left); USN (bottom right)
56. NSA
57. INSCOM (top); NSA (bottom)
58. INSCOM
59. DIA
60. INSCOM
61. INSCOM
62. INSCOM
63. INSCOM
64. INSCOM
65. INSCOM
66. INSCOM
67. INSCOM
68. INSCOM (top); U.S. Army (bottom)
69. INSCOM
70. INSCOM
71. INSCOM
72. INSCOM
73. INSCOM
74. INSCOM
75. INSCOM
76. INSCOM
77. INSCOM
78. INSCOM
79. INSCOM
80. 313th MI BN
81. 313th MI BN
82. USAIC&FH (top); 519TH MI BN (bottom)
83. INSCOM
84. USAIC&FH (top); 313th MI BN (bottom)
85. 1ST MI BN (top); 224TH MI BN (bottom)
86. USAIC&FH
87. USAIC&FH (top); USAINTS-Fort Devens (bottom)
88. INSCOM
89. INSCOM
90. INSCOM
91. INSCOM
92. INSCOM
93. INSCOM
94. INSCOM
95. INSCOM
96. INSCOM
97. INSCOM
98. U.S. Army
99. 504TH MI BN (top); INSCOM (bottom)
100. INSCOM
101. INSCOM
102. INSCOM
103. INSCOM
104. U.S. Army
105. USAF
106. NASA
107. NASA (top); INSCOM (bottom)
108. U.S. Army
109. DCSINT
110. USAIC&FH
111. USAIC&FH
112-113. USAIC&FH
114. INSCOM
116. U.S. Army
117. U.S.Army
119. INSCOM
120. INSCOM
121. INSCOM
122. INSCOM
123. INSCOM
124. U.S. Army (top); Grumman Corporation (bottom)
125. INSCOM (top); U.S. Army (bottom)
126. INSCOM
127. INSCOM
128. Department of Defense
129. INSCOM
130. INSCOM
131. INSCOM
132. INSCOM
133. INSCOM
134. INSCOM (top); Fort Gordon PAO (bottom)
135. USAIC & FH (top); INSCOM (bottom)
136. INSCOM (top); U.S. Army (bottom)
137. INSCOM
138. INSCOM
139. INSCOM
140. INSCOM
141. INSCOM (top); U.S. Army (bottom)
142. USAIC&FH (top); INSCOM (bottom)
143. INSCOM (top left, top right); DCSINT (center); INSCOM (bottom)

ISBN 0-16-049335-8